OXFORD MONOGRAPHS ON
CLASSICAL ARCHAEOLOGY
*Edited by*
MARTIN ROBERTSON
JOHN BOARDMAN
JIM COULTON
DONNA KURTZ

# The Treasures of the Parthenon and Erechtheion

DIANE HARRIS

CLARENDON PRESS · OXFORD
1995

Oxford University Press, Walton Street, Oxford OX2 6DP

Oxford    New York
Athens   Auckland   Bangkok   Bombay   Calcutta   Cape Town
Dar es Salaam   Delhi   Florence   Hong Kong   Istanbul   Karachi
Kuala Lumpur   Madras   Madrid   Melbourne   Mexico City   Nairobi
Paris   Singapore   Taipei   Tokyo   Toronto
and associated companies in
Berlin Ibadan

Oxford is a trade mark of Oxford University Press

Published in the United States
by Oxford University Press Inc., New York

British Library Cataloguing in Publication Data
Data available

Library of Congress Cataloging in Publication Data
The Treasures of the Parthenon and Erechtheion / Diane Harris.
(Oxford monographs on classical archaeology)
Includes bibliographical references and indexes.
1. Athens (Greece)—Antiquities—Catalogs.   2. Parthenon (Athens,
Greece)—Antiquities—Catalogs.   3. Erechtheum (Athens, Greece)—
Antiquities—Catalogs.   4. Greece—Religious life and customs—
Catalogs.   I. Title.   II. Series.
DF287.P3H37   1995   938.5—dc20   95-5607
ISBN 0-19-814940-9

Typeset by Regent Typesetting, London
Printed and bound on acid-free paper by
Bookcraft (Bath) Ltd., Midsomer Norton

# Preface

THE aim of this study is to present in the most accessible way the evidence for the treasures kept inside the Parthenon and the Erechtheion between 434 and 295 BC. The largest body of evidence consists of the marble fragments of the annual inventories of the treasurers of Athena. The discussion in Parts I and VII are meant to frame the catalogue, which is subdivided into the Opisthodomos, the Proneos, the Parthenon, the Hekatompedon, and the Erechtheion (Archaios Neos). The catalogue gives the references for each item or object kept inside the temples as treasures, either to the inscription in *IG* or to its first publication elsewhere. Some new readings have been included, but I have tried to avoid lengthy epigraphical discussions: it is the contents of the lists that interest us here. I have had the privilege of studying these inscriptions in the Epigraphical Museum in Athens (1987–90) and the British Museum (1988), and plan to publish the new readings as a separate work.

I must thank Mrs Dina Peppas-Delmouzou for the courtesy of studying these stones in the Epigraphical Museum, and Mr B. F. Cook and Mr Ian Jenkins for the same courtesy in the British Museum. I am happy to acknowledge funding for this work from the United States Fulbright Scholarship Program, the National Endowment for the Humanities, the American School of Classical Studies at Athens, Princeton University, and California State University, Fresno. Several graduate students helped me prepare the manuscript for publication: M. Byers, K. Lawler, D. Ligon, J. Reyes, and D. Richert. My thanks also go to the staff at the Inter-library loan desk of Madden Library, and at the Oxford University Press.

I am grateful to several scholars who have shown their faith in me and interest in my work: Antony E. Raubitschek, Jody Maxmin, T. Leslie Shear, Jr., the late David M. Lewis, and John Boardman, who persuaded me to write this book and knew I could do it. To my husband, Eric H. Cline, I give thanks for proofreading, moral support, and encouragement in all that I do.

D.H.
*University of Cincinnati*
*May 1995*

*For Hannah*

# Contents

LIST OF FIGURES     ix

ABBREVIATIONS     x

NOTE ON CONVENTIONS     xii

I. The Historical Context of the Treasures     1

  Introduction     1
  The Panathenaic Festival and the Treasures inside
    the Parthenon     8
  The Role of the Treasurers in Athenian Civic and
    Religious Life     9
  A History of the Treasures on the Akropolis     11
  The Function of the Inventories in the Administration
    of the Cult of Athena     20
  The Method of Taking the Inventory     22
  Historical Overview of the Inventories     25

II. The Treasures of the Opisthodomos     40

  The Inventory Lists     40
  The Treasures     44
  Observations     61

III. The Treasures of the Proneos     64

  The Function of the Proneos     64
  The Treasures     65
  Observations     77

IV. The Treasures of the Parthenon     81

  The Treasures     81

V. The Treasures of the Hekatompedon     104

  Observations     104
  The Treasures     115

VI. The Treasures of the Erechtheion   201

    The Treasures   206
    Observations   217

VII. The Treasures and the Worshippers   223

    Private Dedications   223
    Dedicants of Objects in the Parthenon   225
    Dedicants of Objects in the Erechtheion   227
    Famous Dedicants   228
    Gender Patterns of Votive Offerings   236
    State Dedications   238
    The Akropolis: Panhellenic, International,
      or Local Sanctuary?   241
    Piety and the Parthenon   242

APPENDICES   245

    I. Personal Names Associated with Objects in the
      Inventories   245
   II. Civic Dedications in the Inventories   250
  III. The Inventories in Chronological Order   253
  IV. Primary Sources for the Opisthodomos   258
   V. Primary Sources for the Erechtheion   259
  VI. Primary Sources for the Parthenon   260
 VII. Primary Sources for the Panathenaic Festival   261
VIII. References to the Chryselephantine Statue in
      the Inventories   263
  IX. The Doors and Keys to the Temples on
      the Akropolis   266
   X. Broken or Damaged Items in the Parthenon
      and Erechtheion   268
  XI. The Standard Weight Used in Making Gold
      and Silver Vases   269
 XII. The Golden Nikai Revisited   272
XIII. Persian Objects in the Inventory Lists   276

GLOSSARY   Greek   279
           English   284

BIBLIOGRAPHY   287
INDEX OF OBJECTS   300
GENERAL INDEX   304

# List of Figures

1. The Room called the Parthenon                                3
2. Plan of the Parthenon                                        5
3. Ground-plan of the Akropolis of Athens                     6–7
4. Scatter-chart of gold–silver ratio over time               271

# Abbreviations

Works from the bibliography are cited by author's name and date. The following abbreviations are mainly for periodicals and reference works.

## A. PERIODICALS AND SERIALS

| | |
|---|---|
| *AJA* | *American Journal of Archaeology* |
| *AJAH* | *American Journal of Ancient History* |
| *AJP* | *American Journal of Philology* |
| *AM* | *Mitteilungen des Deutschen Archäologischen Instituts, Athenische Abteilung* |
| *Ant. K.* | *Antike Kunst* |
| *BCH* | *Bulletin de correspondence hellénique* |
| *BICS* | *Bulletin of the Institute of Classical Studies* |
| *BSA* | *Annual of the British School at Athens* |
| *CQ* | *Classical Quarterly* |
| *CR* | *Classical Review* |
| *CSCA* | *California Studies in Classical Antiquity* |
| *Delt.* | *Archaiologikon Deltion (Meletai, Chronika)* |
| *ÉAC* | *Études d'archéologie classique* |
| *Eph.* | *Archaiologike Ephemeris* |
| GRB Mon. | Greek, Roman and Byzantine Monographs |
| *GRBS* | *Greek, Roman and Byzantine Studies* |
| *HSCP* | *Harvard Studies in Classical Philology* |
| *JHS* | *Journal of Hellenic Studies* |
| *JDAI* | *Jahrbuch des Deutschen Archäologischen Instituts* |
| *LIMC* | *Lexicon Iconographicum Mythologiae Classicae* (1981– ) |
| *NC* | *Numismatic Chronicle* |
| *RA* | *Revue archéologique* |
| *RE* | *Real-Encyclopädie der classischen Altertumswissenschaft*, ed. A. Fr. von Pauly, rev. G. Wissowa *et al.* (Stuttgart, 1894–1980) |
| *RÉG* | *Revue des études grecques* |
| *SEG* | *Supplementum Epigraphicum Graecum* |
| *TAPA* | *Transactions of the American Philological Association* |
| *ZPE* | *Zeitschrift für Papyrologie und Epigraphik* |

B. BOOKS AND ARTICLES

*Agora* iii        R. E. Wycherly, *Literary and Epigraphical Testimonia*
                   (The Athenian Agora, 3; Princeton, 1957)

*ATL*              B. D. Meritt, M. F. McGregor, and H. T. Wade-Gery,
                   *The Athenian Tribute Lists* (4 vols.; Cambridge, Mass.,
                   and Princeton, 1939–53)

*APF*              J. K. Davies, *Athenian Propertied Families, 600–300 B.C.*
                   (Oxford, 1971)

Berve              H. Berve, *Das Alexanderreich auf prosopographischer
                   Grundlage* (2 vols.; 1926, repr. New York, 1973)

*CAF*              T. Kock, *Comicorum Atticorum Fragmenta* (3 vols.; Leipzig,
                   1880–8)

*DAA*              A. E. Raubitschek, with L. H. Jeffery, *Dedications from the
                   Athenian Akropolis: A Catalogue of the Inscriptions of the
                   Sixth and Fifth Centuries B.C.* (Princeton, 1949)

*FGrH*             F. Jacoby, *Fragmente der griechischen Historiker* (15 vols.;
                   Leiden, 1923–62)

*ID*               *Inscriptions de Délos*

*IG*               *Inscriptiones Graecae* (i–iii$^1$, 1877–1903; i–ii$^2$, 1924–40; i$^3$,
                   1981)

*LSAG*             L. H. Jeffery, *The Local Scripts of Archaic Greece: A
                   Development from the Eighth to the Fifth Centuries*
                   (Oxford, 1961); rev. A. W. Johnstone, Oxford, 1990)

*ML*               R. Meiggs and D. M. Lewis, *A Selection of Greek Historical
                   Inscriptions to the End of the Fifth Century B.C.*$^2$ (Oxford,
                   1988)

*PA*               J. Kirchner, *Prosopographia Attica* (2 vols.; Berlin, 1901–3)

*SIG*              W. Dittenberger, *Sylloge Inscriptionum Gracecarum*$^3$ (4
                   vols.; Leipzig, 1915–24)

Tod *GHI*          M. N. Tod (ed.), *A Selection of Greek Historical Inscriptions,*
                   ii. *From 403 to 323 B.C.* (Oxford, 1948)


C. VARIA

Ag.                Agora, Stoa of Attalos, Athens
BM                 British Museum, London
EM                 Epigraphical Museum, Athens
NM                 National Museum, Athens
dr.                drachma(i)
ob.                obol(s)

# Note on Conventions

For convenience the texts are given throughout in the familiar Ionic alphabet and dialect, even where the inscription transcribed employs the older Attic forms. In most cases, the Greek is taken from the best preserved inscription and modified only by conversion to the Ionic forms. Where an item appears in more than one inventory, the text given in its catalogue-entry is not necessarily that of the earliest occurrence, but rather the most informative and/or best-preserved version. The *IG* number of the version chosen is given in italic type in the list of citations. Sometimes it has seemed best to conflate several texts in order to give the fullest information possible: these artificially generated entries may be identified by the bold facing of two or more references. Note that the editorial punctuations and brackets signalling restoration have been omitted here; one must confer with *IG* or the original publications to investigate the extent of the preservation of any given inscription.

Ordering within each catalogue section is by shape or type: thus, *auloi* and lyres appear under 'M' for musical instruments. In Part V the wreaths are organized first by those bearing letter-labels and archon-names, then by donor: the *demos* or parts thereof, followed by foreign cities.

Cross-references are given in bold type and refer to Part and catalogue-entry within the part: **V.237** etc.

Items which changed location over time are given separate catalogue entries in the relevant Parts, but the text, translation, and references are given only at the first occurrence; subsequent entries recording the same item are reduced to cross-references.

*Numerals*

The Greek acrophonic numeral system was employed by the treasurers in the inventories. Six obols equals one drachma; 6000 drachmas equals one Talent.

ꓐ = ¼ obol  
Ⱶ = ½ obol  
| = 1 obol  
Ⱶ = 1 drachma  
Γ = 5  
Δ = 10  
Ͷ = 50  
H = 100  
Ͷ = 500

X = 1000
Γ = 5000
T = 1 Talent or 6000 dr.
M = 10,000
Σ = 1 Persian stater
Ϟ = 10 Persian staters

*Symbols*

.... represent lost or illegible letters, each dot representing one letter
--- represent an uncertain number of lost or illegible letters
[ ] enclose words or letters supplied where there is a gap in the text
( ) information supplied by the author (dates for archons) or restoration of abbreviations e.g. στα(θμὸν)

# PART I

# The Historical Context of the Treasures

## INTRODUCTION

'Our knowledge of the architecture of the Parthenon only really falters when we try to envisage details of its interior. Much of the outer colonnades and walls still stand and the rest can be confidently restored, but the requirements of its Orthodox, Catholic and Moslem occupiers have stripped its interior of all but pavement traces of what once stood there.'[1] To reconstruct the appearance of the interior of the Parthenon architecturally is still a challenge, but to restore what was kept inside the temple is now possible, thanks to the preservation of some 200 marble inscriptions which record the inventories of the Parthenon in the classical period. A variety of types of furniture, vases, musical instruments, armour, and jewellery were kept in all the rooms of the Parthenon, as well as the Erechtheion, Chalkotheke, Stoa of Artemis Brauronia, and the Opisthodomos. The inventories allow a reconstruction of the interior arrangement of the Chalkotheke, and to a lesser extent shed light on the murky interiors of the Erechtheion and Parthenon.[2] The inventory lists indicate that shelves and storage boxes, labelled alphabetically for keeping gold wreaths and other small valuable objects, were used inside the Parthenon.

The shelves were probably in the form of open cases or cupboards, placed against the cella walls. From representations on vase paintings, we know that shelving was used in cobblers' shops, in armouries, and in the kitchens of Greek homes, where shelves held an array of vases, just as they would have done inside the Parthenon.[3] Shelving is mentioned specifically in the inventories of the Erechtheion: 'On the cupboard, 1 + silver phialai, other silver phialai right, opposite the sacred objects . . . A small silver phiale against the lintel; another small phiale is against the door-jamb on the left as you

---

[1] Boardman (1985) 225.
[2] For the Chalkotheke see Tréheux (1955–6) 133–46; (1965) 3–85; Travlos (1971a) 196; La Follette (1986).
[3] Cf. Richter (1987) 379.

enter. Against the door-jamb on the right as you enter is another silver phiale with gold overlay, which the judges dedicated.'[4] At least thirty bronze boxes are listed in the Parthenon inventories (v. 36). Baskets were also used for storing items, and many were decorated with silver or gold leaf. Two such baskets bore images of Apollo and Zeus (ii. 3–4), made of bronze with gold decoration. The Athenian *boulē* dedicated a silver basket in 318/7 (v. 44). Detailed descriptions such as these help to restore the interior appearance of the Parthenon.

The inventory lists of the Treasurers of Athena describe the contents of the Parthenon, the Erechtheion, the Opisthodomos, and the Chalkotheke.[5] They are not exhaustive; rather, they list permanent objects of value to the goddess and society for which the treasurers were held responsible. This study attempts to place the inscriptions in their historical context, to describe the treasures kept in the Parthenon and Erechtheion, and to analyse the types of treasure and the worshippers who dedicated valuable gifts to Athena on the Akropolis.

The first matter that needs to be addressed is the nomenclature of the buildings on the Akropolis. The inventory lists of the fifth century clearly indicate that there were four separate areas or rooms that contained the treasures of Athena: the Proneos, the Hekatompedos Neos, the Parthenon, and the Opisthodomos.[6] The location of these rooms or buildings has been the subject of debate for over a century, since the days of Dörpfeld.[7] On the face of it, these terms would seem to refer to the four rooms of the temple we call the Parthenon in order from east to west: the Proneos was the east-end portico, the Hekatompedos Neos was the eastern cella with the chryselephantine statue; the Parthenon was the western room with the four Ionic columns, and the Opisthodomos was the western portico. This would satisfy Occam's razor, that the simplest explanation is usually correct. The literary and epigraphical evidence does not support this reconstruction. Only the identification of the location of the Proneos is secure: it must be the eastern portico of the building which we call the Parthenon.

Definitive evidence that the Hekatompedos Neos and the Parthenon refer to two different places is provided by the inventory

---

[4] *IG* II², 1489 lines 1–14.
[5] The Chalkotheke inventories are not included in the present study.
[6] By the 4th cent. the Chalkotheke and the Archaios Neos had been added to the list.
[7] Dörpfeld (1881) revised in (1886–97; 1911); followed by Dinsmoor (1947) 128 n. 93. Cf. Milchhöfer (1894); White (1895).

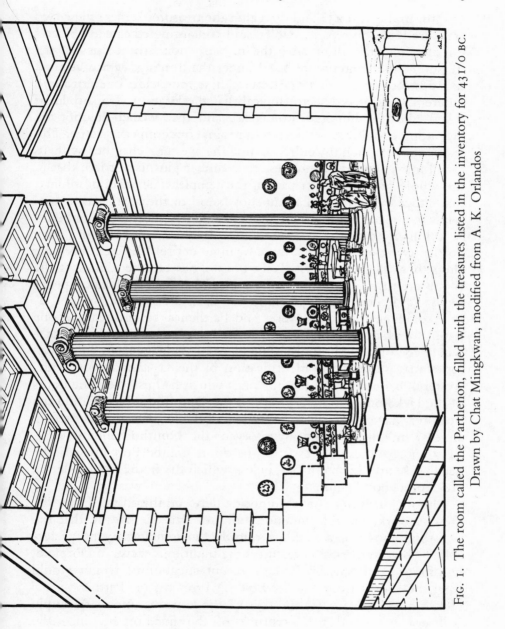

Fig. 1. The room called the Parthenon, filled with the treasures listed in the inventory for 431/0 BC. Drawn by Chat Mingkwan, modified from A. K. Orlandos

lists, for in the year 434 and thereafter the treasures kept in these two areas are listed on separate tablets and contain no duplicate objects.[8] On the inventory lists, after the prescript with the names of the treasurers, the contents are listed under the headings ἐν τῷ νεῷ τῷ ἑκατομπέδῳ or ἐν τῷ παρθενῶνι. These must clearly refer to two different locations. It seems logical that the largest room should be called 'the one-hundred-foot cella', and that would identify the Hekatompedos Neos as the eastern room, containing the statue. This leaves the 'Parthenon' either as just the western chamber with its four Ionic columns or the western chamber plus its portico, that is, the whole of the western part of the temple. The third possibility, that either the term 'Hekatompedos Neos' or the term 'Parthenon' refers to a place outside the temple, is unlikely, not to say heretical.

It follows that the Opisthodomos is either the extreme back portico (west end) of the temple or in an entirely different building altogether. The two most likely possibilities for the names of the rooms are therefore, from east to west: (1) Proneos, Hekatompedos Neos, Parthenon, and Opisthodomos all in the same temple; or (2) Proneos, Hekatompedos Neos, and Parthenon (entire rear) in one temple, with the Opisthodomos located in a separate building somewhere else on the Akropolis. One piece of evidence from the inventories may support the identification of the Opisthodomos as the western chamber of the temple: parts which had fallen off the doors of the Hekatompedon were kept in the Opisthodomos.[9] Would the treasurers have taken these pieces out of the temple, to be stored in another building? In the inventory of the Opisthodomos (*IG* II², 1457 line 20) these pieces from the doors immediately precede the heading ἐν τῶι ἑκατομπέδοι, below which the inventory inside the Hekatompedon begins.

Although it is not crucial to decide between these options for the present work, textual evidence indicates that the theory that the Opisthodomos was a building outside the temple may be preferable.[10] This interpretation reaffirms the traditional views of Dörpfeld, Dinsmoor, and Shear.[11] Roux's recent suggestion, which would label the rooms from east to west (1) Proneos, (2) Parthenon *and* Hekatompedos Neos, (3) and (4) Opisthodomos (entire rear), simply will not withstand the evidence of the inventories, since the

    [8] *IG* I³, 317, 343.

    [9] See II.60 = V.203 below.

    [10] Hdt. 8. 53; Pollux 9. 40; Dem. 24. 136 and Σ; Σ Ar. *Plut.* 1193; *Suda*; Photios; Harpokration; Hesychios; Σ [Dem.] 13.14; Luc. *Tim.* 53; cf. Jahn and Michaelis (1901) 55–6.

    [11] Dörpfeld (1890, 1897; 1911); Dinsmoor (1947) 128 n. 93; Shear (1966) 56–8.

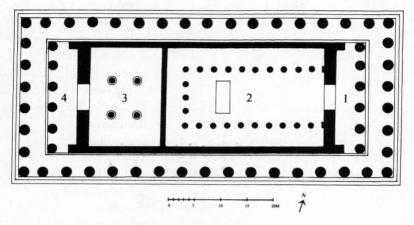

FIG. 2. Plan of the Parthenon. Drawn by Robert S. Harris, modified
from W. B. Dinsmoor

1. Proneos    2. Hekatompedon    3. Parthenon    4. Opisthodomos? *(but see p. 4)*

Parthenon and the Hekatompedos Neos have separate lists of inventoried treasures between 434 and 408 BC, nor does it agree with the
literary sources which place the Opisthodomos behind the temple of
Athena Polias.[12]

The terms 'Hekatompedon' (or 'Hekatompedos Neos') and
'Parthenon' were also used for the building as a whole.[13] Several
ancient writers use them interchangeably. For example, Hesychios
writes, Ἑκατόμπεδος Νεώς· ἐν τῇ Ἀκροπόλει, ὁ Παρθενών ('The
Hekatompedos Neos: on the Akropolis, the Parthenon'). Likewise
the *Suda*: Ἑκατόμπεδος Νεώς· ὁ Ἀθήνησιν Παρθενών ('the
Hekatompedos Neos: to the Athenians, the Parthenon').[14] Plutarch,
*Perikles* 13. 4, conflates the two terms and calls the temple ἑκατόμπεδον Παρθενῶνα: 'For the Hekatompedon Parthenon, Kallikrates
and Iktinos were the architects . . .' Few ancient authors had reason
to label the individual rooms within the temple. When referring to
the building as a whole they used 'Hekatompedon', 'Hekatompedos
Neos', and 'Parthenon' interchangeably.

The Treasurers of Athena also had occasion to refer to the whole
temple, and when they did they used the term 'Hekatompedon'.
The inventories describe pieces of the doors of the temple which

[12] Roux (1984), esp. 305 fig. 3.

[13] See Shear (1966) 245–6; Dinsmoor (1947) 123–4.

[14] Other ancient references which are directly comparable are Harpokration. the *Etymologicum
Magnum*, and the *Glossa Patmia* (*BCH* 1 (1877) 149) s.v. Ἑκατόμπεδον. See also Aristides 51. 61; Plut.
*De soll. anim.* 13; *Cato* 5; *De glor. Ath.* 8.

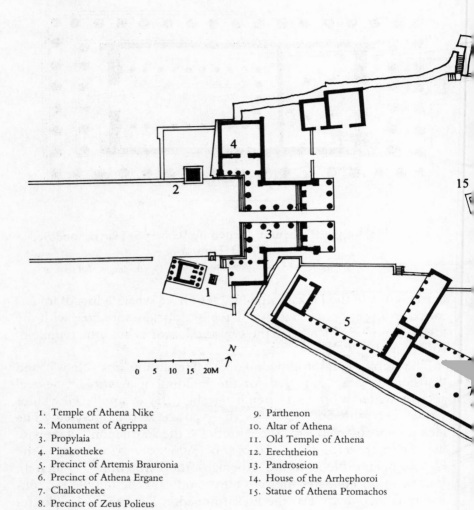

FIG. 3. Ground-plan of the Akropolis of Athens. Drawn by
Robert S. Harris

1. Temple of Athena Nike
2. Monument of Agrippa
3. Propylaia
4. Pinakotheke
5. Precinct of Artemis Brauronia
6. Precinct of Athena Ergane
7. Chalkotheke
8. Precinct of Zeus Polieus

9. Parthenon
10. Altar of Athena
11. Old Temple of Athena
12. Erechtheion
13. Pandroseion
14. House of the Arrhephoroi
15. Statue of Athena Promachos

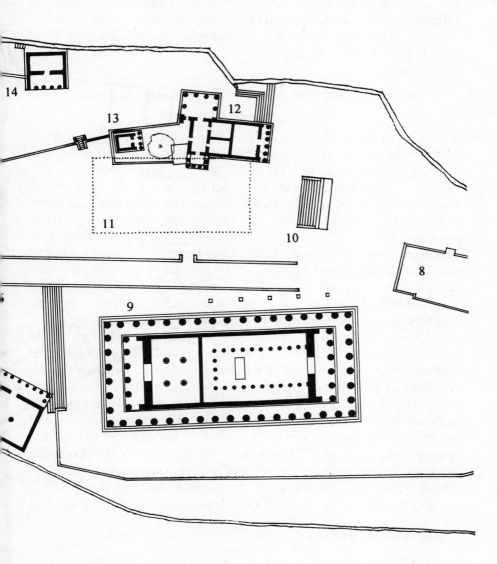

had fallen off by the fourth century: αἱ θύραι αἱ ἐν τῷ Ἑκατομπέδῳ ('the doors in the Hekatompedon').[15] Likewise, the keys to the doors or grills were kept in the Chalkotheke: κλεὶς τοῦ Ἑκατομπέδου ('the key to the Hekatompedon').[16]

## THE PANATHENAIC FESTIVAL AND THE TREASURES INSIDE THE PARTHENON

The Panathenaia, the festival of Athena celebrated around 28 Hekatombaion in late July or early August, is one of the best-attested festivals of ancient Greece.[17] It was an early Athenian celebration, reorganized in the 560s, perhaps under the eye of the tyrant Peisistratos, and embellished with a Great Panathenaia every fourth year.[18] We know that elaborate Greek rituals such as those associated with the Panathenaia evolved over the course of the sixth century BC, and as late as the time of Perikles new rites and traditions were still being introduced (e.g. the addition of musical competitions).[19] The elements of the festival included songs and dances on the Akropolis by young men and women, the procession, athletic contests, musical contests, the *euandria*, equestrian contests including the *apobatēs* and chariot-racing, and recitations of Homer. The competitions were arranged by age-group, and the prizes awarded included Athena's sacred olive oil and gold, silver, or olive-branch wreaths.[20] A highlight of the ceremony was the presentation of a new robe to Athena, the Peplos, made by two *arrhēphoroi*, girls of between 8 and 11 years of age, who lived on the Akropolis and performed various cult functions, including the carrying of the 'unspoken things' (*arrheta*).[21] The peplos was brought to the Akropolis in a spectacular way, as a sail on a float representing a ship.[22] The representatives of the allied cities sent a cow and panoply (full set of armour) for the festival. One hundred cows were alleged to

---

[15] See II.60 = V.203, V.202 below.

[16] *IG* II², 1424A lines 386–7; 1425 line 389; cf. app. IX below.

[17] See Neils (1992); Boardman (1985) 222–5; Burkert (1985) 232–4; Simon (1983) 55–72; Parke (1977) 29–50; Deubner (1966) 22–35; Michaelis (1871) 318–33; Mommsen (1864) 116–205; Ziehen in *RE* 457–89. See app. VII for primary sources for this festival.

[18] Paus. 1. 26. 6; cf. Plut. *Theseus* 24, 'and he [Theseus] named the city Athens and created a Panathenaic festival as a ceremony for the whole of Attica.'

[19] Plut. *Per.* 13. Recitations of Homer may have preceded the Periklean musical contests; cf. Plato *Ion* 530B; [Plato] *Hipparchus* 228B; Isoc. 4. 159; Lycurgus *In Leocratem* 102; Plut. *Per.* 13. 6; Diog. Laert. 1. 57; cf. Davison (1955) 7–15.

[20] A few prize-lists have been discovered on marble stelai; see *IG* II², 2311–17.

[21] Paus. 1. 27. 4; cf. Boardman (1985) 222.

[22] Philostr. *VS* 2. 550; cf. Tobin (1993) 81–9; Norman (1983) 41–6.

have been slaughtered for the rites of Athena. Some of the sacred knives and basins for catching the blood may in fact appear in the inventory lists of the temples on the Akropolis. The musical contests involving kithara and aulos known to have taken place during the festival also appear in the inventories and on the Ionic frieze. Sacred instruments, belonging to Athena and kept in the Parthenon, accompanied the procession and were played at the festival competitions.[23]

## THE ROLE OF THE TREASURERS IN ATHENIAN CIVIC AND RELIGIOUS LIFE

From the moment when groups of Attic villagers first began to meet in the Athenian Agora, there was a need for treasurers. People gathered to worship together and make joint decisions affecting their community. Someone had to take responsibility for overseeing the sacrifices that had to be made, constructing the buildings to house developing political institutions, supervising their construction, and disbursing pay to the workmen. Treasures accumulated in the worship of the city goddess, and these required protection and safe-keeping. These societal needs shaped the institution of the Treasurers of Athena and the other financial institutions of Athens.

It is impossible to say where civic needs ended and religious needs began for archaic Athens. The earliest physical evidence of the for-mation of the city are religious structures and common burials. The *synoikismos* or unification of Attica was a political concept but was commemorated in the city with a religious festival in honour of Athena. From the beginning, the idea of one state composed of many villages included taxation for common festivals and buildings. Thucydides attributed the *synoikismos* to Theseus, which only means that by classical times the event seemed to be of great antiquity. 'This became a great city, since all were now paying taxes to it, and was such when Theseus handed it down to his successors. And from his time even to this day the Athenians have celebrated at the public expense a festival called the Synoikia, in honour of the goddess.'[24] Public expenses covered sacred ceremonies, and the Treasurers of Athena performed both civic and sacred duties.

Homer refers to a temple of Athena on the Akropolis, and there

---

[23] Perikles is said to have instituted the musical competitions and to have built the Odeion for this purpose: Plut. *Per.* 13.

[24] Thuc. 2. 15. 2.

are architectural remains of a temple dating back to the seventh century BC.[25] Treasures accumulated within the sanctuary. Dedicatory statue-bases and monuments in marble preserve inscriptions as witness to the growth of cult practice in honour of the city's eponymous deity over the course of the centuries. Tithes, dedications, and first-fruit offerings are all attested. Doubtless there were many more inscriptions and dedications in perishable materials and precious metals. Management of the sanctuary rested on the shoulders of the treasurers and priests.

Xenophon describes the organization of an Athenian household in these terms:

the things that we use only for festivals or entertainments, or on rare occasions, we handed over to the housekeeper (ταμία), and after showing her their places and counting and making a written list of all the items, we told her to give them out to the right servants, to remember what she gave to each of them, and when receiving them back to put everything in the place from which she took it.[26]

The Parthenon was the house of the goddess Athena, rather than a place for congregational worship. In her home she kept her possessions, her *chrēmata*. The Treasurers of Athena were her housekeepers, hired to help Athena keep track of her belongings. The inventories took place during the annual Panathenaic festival, perhaps just after the procession, when the gold and silver trays and hydriai (water-jars), the furniture and cult items were distributed to worshippers for the Panathenaic procession.[27] The 'things that we use only for festivals' were received back and checked against the 'written list of all the items', and when the treasures were back in 'their places' the treasurers presented their results to the *boulē* and handed over their responsibility to the next board.

Aristotle describes the principal responsibility of the Treasurers of Athena in this way: 'These Treasurers take over, in the presence of the Council [*boulē*], the statue of Athena, the [golden] figures of Nike, the other precious articles of the sacred treasure, and the money.'[28] The inventory lists of the Treasurers of Athena document the contents of the Parthenon (with its rooms the Proneos, Hekatompedon, and the Parthenon proper and Opisthodomos), the Erechtheion, and at times the Chalkotheke.

After 434 BC the Athenians produced three types of temple inven-

---

[25] *Il.* 3. 546–51; *Od.* 7. 80–1.               [26] Xen. *Oec.* 9. 10 (trans. E. C. Marchant).
[27] See Develin (1984); Rhodes (1972) 236.        [28] *Ath. Pol.* 47. 1 (trans. K. von Fritz).

tories, all published on marble stelai: *paradosis, exetasmos,* and *kathairesis.*[29] The first type is standard: the *paradosis* was produced after the annual *euthynai* to record the proper transfer of responsibility from one year's board of treasurers to the next. In cases where there were discrepancies, an additional inventory was conducted and published as an *exetasmos.* These occur relatively rarely. Still more rare are the inventories which record the melt down of older metal dedications in order to manufacture new cult objects: the *kathairesis.*[30] All of these inventories are concerned with the 'house-keeping' of Athena's treasures. Their publication on stone was a guarantee to the public that the activities of the treasurers were accounted for and became part of the public record.

## A HISTORY OF THE TREASURES ON THE AKROPOLIS

To trace the duties of the Treasurers of Athena prior to 434 BC is to see the development of their powerful role in Athenian civic life. It is evident that there was originally one financial body in archaic Athens, which became subdivided in the fifth century. The Treasurers of Athena were the core institution from which other financial units split. By the time of the construction of the Parthenon they were the supreme financial board on the Akropolis. Other financial boards were created and dissolved, but the Treasurers of Athena were the constant financial overseers. The bureaucratic system for the flow of money through taxation, rents, and fines can be shown to pass through the hands of the Treasurers of Athena and the Treasurers of the Other Gods (οἱ ταμίαι τῶν ἄλλων θεῶν).

The Treasurers of the Athenian state and of Athena were one board in archaic Athens. Their earliest name may have been *naukraroi,* rather than *tamiai* as they later came to be called.[31] Another early financial board was the *kolākretai,* who occur in *Ath. Pol.* and in inscriptions until the end of the fifth century, when their functions were absorbed into those of the *pōlētai,* the Treasurers of Athena, or some other financial board.[32] The responsibilities of the Treasurers of Athena included the collection of taxes and disbursement of revenue for civic functions.[33] In archaic Athens these taxes

[29] On the three types of inventories see Aleshire (1989) 107–8; Harris (1992) 637–9.
[30] See e.g. Harris (1992).
[31] Jordan (1970) 173. The stem ναυ- may derive from ναός (temple) rather than ναῦς (ship); see Jordan (1979) 58.
[32] Cf. *Ath. Pol.* 7. 3.
[33] Jordan (1970) 159–62. Harpokration and *Suda* s.v. ναυκραρικά; *Ath. Pol.* 8. 3; Pollux 8. 108; Androtion *FGrH* 324. 36.

would have been tithes of farm properties or harvests presented in kind or as gold and silver objects, since coins were not yet employed. *Eisphora* was a concept introduced later, perhaps under Peisistratos, but must have been a reorganization of a pre-existing system, since there were public expenses which had to be met in the earlier period.[34] Originally the term referred to one's contribution or share of expenses, and later became a tax. The expenses mentioned in ancient sources included paying for public sacrifices and funding sacred embassies to Delphi.[35] The treasury containing the collected taxes would have been kept on the Akropolis, under Athena's protection.

The literary accounts of the Kylon affair of *c*.632/1 confirm that officials called the *naukraroi* were in existence and that the seat of government, or at least the stronghold of the government, was on the Akropolis.[36] Herodotos refers to a board of *naukraroi* who protected the sanctuary in the Kylon affair, and they were in charge of the Akropolis when Kylon and his associates attempted their coup.[37] Herodotos and Thucydides differ concerning the role of the *naukraroi*.[38] The former suggests that they ruled Athens at the time, while Thucydides seems to correct him by asserting that the archons held power at this point. The *naukraroi* were responsible for collecting the *eisphora,* the contribution of each citizen in return for the benefits of city life.

The literary accounts suggest that there was a statue of Athena, probably the ancient wooden image, and an altar on the Akropolis. Scholiasts on the passage describing the Kylon affair in Thucydides suggested that Kylon deserved to be cursed since he had looted the temple of Athena during his attempted coup.[39] A temple as early as the second half of the seventh century is not an impossibility, but there is virtually no physical evidence. That it would have been filled with treasures that could be looted is also possible, and parallels can be found at other sanctuaries such as the early Artemision at Ephesos, the Heraion at Samos, and the temple of Apollo at Delphi, where all have revealed riches of ivory and gold dating to the seventh century. The *naukraroi* had to have a repository for their treasures.

Another possibility is that the treasures were kept in the vicinity

[34] Hignett (1952) 70–1.

[35] *FGrH* 324. 36.

[36] For a review of the literary evidence for the Kylon affair, with commentary, see Rhodes (1981) 79–84.

[37] Hdt. 5. 71. 2; Jordan (1970) 153–75; (1979) 56.

[38] Hdt. 5. 71; Thuc. 1. 126. 3. See also Jordan (1979) 56–62.

[39] Rhodes (1981) 82; Stroud (1968) 71 n. 28; Jones and Wilson (1969), 114–15.

of the Athena Nike *pyrgos*. The archaic altar of the shrine is still *in situ*, and dates from the seventh century BC. Raubitschek suggested that a statue of Athena stood at this spot, perhaps the cult statue later housed in the Erechtheion.[40] The depiction of the figure of Athena in archaic Athenian vase-paintings, and particularly on the prize amphoras, is generally consistent, including shield and helmet and the goddess standing with spear, perhaps because these representations take after one common statue of her on the Akropolis.

The *naukraroi*, who became the *tamiai*, were the earliest magistrates specifically charged with financial matters.[41] The first communal activities were religious in nature, and paid for by the community. The mix of sacred and secular was complete, and at this early period the two concepts were inseparable. The profound link between civic office and sacred rites is shown by the fact that all magistrates swore an oath upon taking office, the beginnings of wars were marked by sacrifice and offerings, and the Agora, the heart of the 'secular' city, had *perirrhantēria* (lustral basins) and altars. These are old traditions which reach back to the archaic period; the classical concept of the *polis* saw the secular and sacred as parallel yet distinct, equivalent to the body and the mind.[42]

The Treasurers of Athena are first mentioned in the Aristotelian *Ath. Pol.* (4. 2) in the context of the laws of Drakon (621/0).[43] These treasurers were in charge of public funds, principally the income from fines, and sacred dedications to Athena, whatever their nature may have been at this early date. Their principal expenses were the common ceremonies. There is now some doubt whether any constitutional features can be positively assigned to Drakon beyond the death penalty for murder.[44] Yet the inspiration for the law-code of Drakon has been attributed to the need for laws governing such offences as occurred during and after the attempted coup of Kylon.[45] The laws would have pertained not only to murder but also to questions of the proper conduct in sanctuaries and division of jurisdiction among the magistracies, to answer questions raised by the coup attempt.

After Solon's legislation (*c.*594/3 BC) the treasurers were selected

[40] Raubitschek, *DAA* commentary on no. 329; cf. Herington (1955) 41–2 n. 2.
[41] *Ath. Pol.* 21. 5; Hignett (1952) 68.
[42] Connor (1987); (1988) 171–7.
[43] Von Fritz (1950) 71; Rhodes (1981) 84–8, 108–12.
[44] See Rhodes (1981) 110–12 on the arguments concerning Drakon's laws. For discussions of the homicide laws see Stroud (1968); Gagarin (1981). For the text of the revision of Drakon's law-code and additional bibliography see *IG* I³, 104.
[45] Stroud (1968) 72.

from the first economic class, the *pentakosiomedimnoi*. 'A con-
firmation of the fact that the magistrates were to be selected by lot
from the respective property classes mentioned is the law concerning the Treasurers, which is still in use down to the present day. This
law orders that the Treasurers are to be chosen by lot from among
the *pentakosiomedimnoi*.'[46] Aristotle mentions that the court of the
Areopagos 'deposited the money exacted through fines in the
Akropolis without having to indicate the reasons for the imposition
of the fine'.[47] Some early temple or *oikos* must have served as the
treasury for these deposits. Once the money had been deposited on
the Akropolis, the treasurers would have taken over responsibility.

The cults of Attica were established by the sixth century, and the
calendar of festivals of the various gods which was firmly established
by the fifth century must have been worked out in the sixth. It is in
the sixth century that the various cults grew and co-ordination
between their activities became necessary. Peisistratos may have
cultivated and organized the local sanctuaries of Attica, to bring
them into a unified system through the Attic calendar of festivals and
to establish formal priesthoods and treasurers.[48]

One of the earliest inscriptions to have survived from the
Athenian Akropolis is dated to *c*.550 BC.[49] It reads, 'The treasurers
[dedicated] these metals [on behalf of the city], having collected
them; to [the daughter] of mighty-[minded] Zeus; [The treasurers
were] Anaxion and Eudikos and S[--- and ---] and Andokides and
Lysimach[os and --- and ---].' The treasurers are shown in their role
as successors to the *naukraroi*, in collecting the *eisphora* or contributions of citizens to pay for their festivals and civic events. The
metals they collected were called *chalkia* (χαλκία), a term which was
not exclusive to bronze or copper until relatively late (first century
BC) but was a generic term.[50] Strictly speaking, the inscription is a
dedicatory plaque, not an inventory list. Here eight treasurers are
listed. Ferguson assumed that two were chosen from each tribe. If
so, this inscription confirms the existence of a unified, organized
body of treasurers, known as the *tamiai*, elected as outlined in the
*Ath. Pol.* under the laws of Drakon and Solon.

The Chalkeia was a festival held on the last day of the month of

[46] Arist. *Ath. Pol.* 8. 1 (trans. Kurt von Fritz); cf. 7. 3.

[47] Ibid. 8. 4–5.

[48] Shapiro (1989) 12–15.

[49] *IG* I³, 510 (EM 6975); cf. *LSAG* 77, no. 21; Kirchner (1935) 9, no. 6, pl. 3; Ferguson (1932) 6
n.1; Cavaignac (1908) 30; Threatte (1980) 2.

[50] Muhly (1973) 174–6, cf. D. Clay (1977) 265 for a Delian inventory with metal dedications listed
as χαλκᾶ.

Pyanopsion in late October or early November.[51] The festival, cele-brated every fourth year, marked the setting up of the loom to make Athena's new Peplos, to be presented at the Panathenaia. But the name 'Chalkeia' refers to the early craftsmen in bronze, who honoured Athena Ergane. It may be one of the oldest festivals in Athens, and the making of the peplos would have been an addition to the festival in the sixth or even fifth century BC. The *Suda*, following Harpocration, refers to the Chalkeia as an 'ancient festival and popular from early times' (ἑορτὴ ἀρχαία καὶ δημώδης πάλαι).[52] In an inscription of 277/6 BC recording the expenses for the festival the people of Athens call the goddess of the Chalkeia 'Athena Archegetis', which may be translated 'Athena the founding goddess'.[53] In what sense is the founding of the city related to the festival of the Chalkeia? The first real mark of the community's coalescence is in the shared expenses for sacrifice and worship. In the Dark Ages, as the Athenians began to join with each other in a com-munity, they contributed *chalkia* (χάλκεια), metal objects or dedica-tions, which paid for their communal needs. Sophokles preserves some symbols of the festival in fragment 844R of a lost play: 'Step into the road, then, all you host of handicraftsmen who in honour of the grim-eyed daughter of Zeus, the goddess of Labour [Ergane], attend with standing wheat-baskets and by the anvil with weighty hammer . . .'[54] Is it a coincidence that from the very first year, and all the way through the history of the inventory lists, one entry reads 'twelve golden wheat-stalks'?[55] The treasures were still stored in the old temple of Athena, until the Persian sack of the Akropolis.

Kleisthenes reorganized the tribal system in the last decade of the sixth century BC.[56] The board of treasurers was expanded from eight to ten members, one from each tribe, and was still composed of men selected from the first economic class. It was surely an honour to be a treasurer of Athena, but also a risk: the treasurers were subject to both the *dokimasia* and *euthynai,* and any discrepancy could result in a fine, exile, or even the death penalty. There is epigraphical evidence which suggests that in some years

[51] Deubner (1966) 35–6; Simon (1983) 38–9; Parke (1977) 38, 92.

[52] *Etym. Magn.* 805. 43; Deubner (1966) 35.

[53] *IG* II², 674 lines 16–17 ὅπως ἂν δὲ καὶ τὰ Χαλκεῖα θύσωσιν τῇ Ἀθηνᾷ τῇ ἀρχηγέτιδι τῆς πόλεως.

[54] Parke (1977) 93.

[55] See **IV.23** = **V.109**.

[56] According to Aristotle (*Ath. Pol.* 21. 1), 509/8 BC; see Sealey (1976) 144–64 for the dating of Kleisthenes' reforms.

there were vacancies on the board; several inventories and accounts are preserved with fewer than ten names. Between 403/2 and 344/3 there were twenty-three boards of treasurers, and only nine had all ten; the other fourteen boards had between six and nine members each.[57] Hansen notes that two conclusions can be drawn: 'that not enough volunteers came forward for the selection process, but that the Athenians did not resort to compulsion to fill the lists.'[58]

The period between the ousting of the Peisistratids and the end of the Persian war was one of growth and change. The increase in wealth and power is visible in the literary and archaeological testimony. With the growth in wealth, the management of the treasury had to adjust, and the physical needs for security required the construction of new buildings and fortifications.

Record-keeping was a vital function of the treasurers. They played an important role in monitoring conduct in the sanctuary, collecting fines, and opening the *oikēmata* three times each month for inspection and inventory.[59] There is a ritualistic aspect to these orders. The sacred calendar which included festivals and ceremonies was now to include inventory days. At the conclusion of the festivals the treasures were inventoried and returned to their proper storage places, and the treasurers' accounts were audited.[60] The ten treasurers sent their records to a board of ten accountants (*logistai*) and ten advocates (*synēgoroi*), both groups selected by lot, for review.[61] A finding of maladministration would result in a trial before a jury for theft. If the financial records proved accurate, the treasurers then appeared before the *boulē*. Apparently they conducted themselves honourably, for the most part, since very few of the annual audits demanded an *exetasmos*, or second inventory, to check against the first; usually the treasurers passed their tests. The publication of the lists represents the final act of the treasurers as they confronted their successors before the *boulē* on the Akropolis; publication on stone stelai served to certify the transaction for the public's interest.[62]

Some scholars have suggested that the stone stelai are copies of the papyrus documents or wooden boards which were filed in the

[57] Hansen (1991) 232–3; for examples see Develin (1989) 237, 292, 312, 325.
[58] Hansen (1991) 233.
[59] The Treasurers of Athena are mentioned in the following lines: *IG* I³, 4A lines 11 and 16; 4B lines 3–4, 8, 13–14, 16–17, 18–19.
[60] Harris (1991) 1–2.
[61] *Ath. Pol.* 54. 2; 48. 3–5; cf. Hansen (1991) 218–24; Sinclair (1988) 79; Hignett (1952) 203–5.
[62] Linders (1988*b*).

Metroon.[63] Rosalind Thomas has shown that our terms 'original' and 'copy' are anachronistic and inappropriate for such cases.[64] The inventories are not comprehensive in recording all items kept in the temples, and appear to be representative selections rather than actual lists of the contents of the temples.[65] 'Texts of inscriptions on stone generally do not faithfully render the texts of the original documents.'[66] The records, published on perishable material, would have been filed in the Metroon (after *c.*408 BC) along with the other financial records directly related to the supervision of state officials by the *boulē*.[67] Alternatively, there is one reference to an archive of wooden tablets inside the temple of Athena (it is not clear whether the Parthenon or the Erechtheion is meant): 'Well, of Aristogeiton's debt to the State the terms still exist, namely the laws under which all defaulters are registered; and the pillar [i.e. the pledge] is the wooden tablet of the law deposited in the temple of the Goddess (ὅρος δ' ἡ σανὶς ἡ παρὰ τῇ θεῷ κειμένη).'[68] Other records were kept by the Treasurers of Athena, including the list of state debtors, on which additions and deletions were made.[69]

The Hekatompedon decrees (485/4 BC) outlined the rules concerning the use of and access to the Akropolis.[70] Several phrases are of particular interest for the Treasurers of Athena. First, at lines 1–4 the inscription reads: 'The bronze vessels on the Akropolis—all the vessels that they use, except those in the sealed houses. If the vessels remain with each one [sc. of the users?] upon the Akropolis, the treasurers are to make a record of them.'[71] In this early period χαλκία need not be specifically bronze but can refer to any metal.

The *oikēmata* mentioned in the Hekatompedon decree may have been either rooms or treasury buildings, which the treasurers were required to open and seal. No traces of foundations have survived which might correspond to the *oikēmata*; but some fragments of superstructure have been identified as belonging to small treasury buildings, dating to the second half of the sixth century and the early part of the fifth. Architectural sculpture, such as the so-called 'Olive-

[63] Posner (1972) 100; cf. Boegehold (1972) 24; Klaffenbach (1960) 21 ff., no. 6.

[64] Thomas (1989) 47.

[65] Posner (1972) 41; Tréheux (1959), 266–71.

[66] Posner (1972) 100. Cf. Boegehold (1972) 24: 'The document itself or a copy or abstract of the document is official and valid in whatever disposition it exists, no matter if form and phraseology in the original vary somewhat from that in copy or abstract.'

[67] Posner (1972) 108–9, 115–16; cf. Boegehold (1972) 24.

[68] [Dem.] 25. 69–70; tr. J. H. Vine; cf. Boegehold (1972) 26.

[69] Boegehold (1990) 154; Rhodes (1972) 148–51.

[70] *IG* I³, 4; cf. Bancroft (1979) 12–25.

[71] Trans. Jordan (1979) 21.

tree' pediment and the 'Introduction of Herakles' pediment, may be
as early as 566, and probably decorated early treasury buildings constructed to house ceremonial vases and equipment associated with
the Panathenaia.[72]

The *oikēmata* may be the predecessors of the classical
Chalkotheke, since it is the only building to be referred to as an
*oikēma* in later literature.[73] Both served similar functions: the archaic
*oikēmata* housed the metal vessels mentioned in the Hekatompedon
decrees, and the very name Chalkotheke reflects the metal items
stored there in the classical period.

When the Persians came to attack Athens in 480 BC, the
treasurers and priests were charged with the protection of the
Akropolis while the rest of the Athenians evacuated to Troizen and
Salamis. Two versions of the preparations for evacuation have
survived in the ancient sources. The first is a passage in Herodotos
(8. 51): 'And they took the abandoned city; but when they went
into the sanctuary they found a certain number of Athenians, the
treasurers of the sanctuary (ταμίαι τοῦ ἱεροῦ) and needy men, who
warded off the attackers by barricading themselves in the Akropolis
with doors and wooden beams.' Herodotos then records the state of
the Akropolis at the time of the arrival of the Persians:

When the Athenians saw that they had broken into the Akropolis, some
of them threw themselves down off the walls and were killed; but
others sought refuge in the cella (μέγαρον). The first of the Persians
to break in assaulted the gates (τὰς πύλας), and when they opened
them, they slew the suppliants. When they (the Persians) had killed them
all, they plundered the temple and then burnt the whole Acropolis.'[74]

Herodotos is in places confirmed and elsewhere contradicted in
the so-called 'Themistokles decree'.[75] In line 11 the decree says 'and
that the treasurers and priests should remain on the Akropolis guard-
ing the belongings of the gods.' The treasurers stayed behind in
order to defend the sanctuary as a whole; it is not likely that the contents of the treasury of Athena remained behind as well. The authors
of *ATL* believed that the Persians found the treasury on the
Akropolis intact and confiscated it, so that when the Athenians
returned the treasury was empty.[76] Evidence for the treasures being

---

[72] Shapiro (1989) 21; Ridgway (1977) 201.
[73] Dinsmoor (1947) 122, fig. 3; I. T. Hill (1969) 239 n. 12; Jordan (1979) 48. See La Follette (1986)
75–87 for the physical evidence for the Chalkotheke.
[74] Hdt. 8. 53 (trans. A. D. Godley).
[75] ML 23.
[76] *ATL* iii. 337–8.

taken away to Persia where they were distributed as booty to the soldiers or kept by the Great King includes the fact that Themistokles claimed actually to have seen, in Sardis, a statue he himself had dedicated on the Akropolis before the war.[77] Yet the statue was perhaps too large for the Athenians in their panic and haste to move easily, unlike metal bowls and vases, knives and coins, jewels and other precious items that could be easily transported. More likely, the majority of items kept in the treasury were removed during the preparation for war. A parallel may be seen in the preparations against the Persians at Delphi, where the first act of the local population was to secure the treasures.[78]

The responsibilities of the Treasurers of Athena included keeping the oil which the archons collected from the sacred groves (*Ath. Pol.* 60. 3). At the next Panathenaic festival they handed the amphoras of oil over to the Commissioners of Games (*athlothetai*) as prizes. The oil is never mentioned in the inventories. The quantity was quite considerable: one Panathenaic prize amphora held 12 choes of oil, and at least 700 of them were awarded at the games.[79] The oil may have been kept near the olive groves, or somewhere on the Akropolis, although it is difficult to imagine a place on the Akropolis where 700 amphorae could be stored.

The Treasurers of Athena had duties beyond maintaining the treasures of Athena and disbursing sums. They may have been responsible for erection of all stelai and monuments on the Akropolis. *IG* I³, 106 lines 21–3 (dated about 411–408 BC) directs the treasurers of the goddess to delete certain words on a stele set up on the Akropolis.[80] The treasurers may have owned the equipment required for setting up monuments and stelai, and for maintenance of the grounds. The role which they played in erecting and maintaining the monuments and stelai on the Akropolis appears to have ceased by 377/6 BC.[81] Their powers may have been taken over by the treasurer of the *dēmos* by or at this time.

---

[77] Plut. *Them.* 31.

[78] Hdt. 8. 38; cf. Jordan (1979) 81–4; Ehrhardt (1966).

[79] For the amount of oil that a Panathenaic amphora could have held see Boardman (1988) 29 and Lang and Crosby (1964) 59. Pritchett and Amyx (1958) 182 calculated on the basis of *IG* II², 2311 that at least 700 amphoras were awarded every four years, and possibly as many as 1300. Over the course of the century the treasurers (or the ἀθλοθέται) would have had to commission potters for 32,500 amphoras. Johnston (1987) 129 has recently argued that at least 1423 were awarded per festival; cf. Immerwahr (1990) 183–5; Hamilton (1992) 231–40. On the workshops commissioned to make Panathenaic amphoras see Shapiro (1989) 18; Scheibler (1983) 141–4.

[80] Cf. Lalonde (1971) 44–5; Tod *GHI* ii. 147. 39–40.

[81] Dinsmoor (1932) 165–6.

### THE FUNCTION OF THE INVENTORIES IN THE
### ADMINISTRATION OF THE CULT OF ATHENA

The *Ath. Pol.* attests that the treasurers presented their inventories to the *boulē*, as specified in the Kallias decrees.[82] The ceremony in which the treasurers took over the treasure in the presence of the council may have taken place on the Akropolis: ἐναντίον τῆς βουλῆς ἐν πόλει.[83] It may also have been closely associated with the Panathenaia, since the inscriptions record that their term of office extended from one Panathenaia to the next.[84] Linders described it as, 'a handing-over, i.e. from one board of administrators to the following, like the torch in a relay race'.[85]

Most office-holders in Athens were required to undergo an audit and examination, *euthynai* (εὔθυναι) after the year of their office. The idea of accountability underlies the need for making inventories, accounts, and other financial inscriptions. In the case of the treasurers, their audit was conducted before the *boulē*, perhaps on the Akropolis inside the temples with lists in hand, visually inspecting the treasures to verify that their duties had been fulfilled. In addition to taking the inventories, the treasurers published accounts of receipts and expenditures during the fifth century (*IG* I³, 363–82).

Like the Treasurers of Athena, the Treasurers of the Other Gods loaned money to the state for the Peloponnesian war. The accounts of loans from the Treasurers of the Other Gods were recorded by the *logistai* who published them on stone stelai.[86] The treasurers would turn over the loans to the *Hellēnotamiai*, to disburse to the generals. The accounts are quite detailed in order to hold all to strict accountability for the *euthynai*.

In 438/7 the Parthenon was dedicated, and the treasurers began to make yearly inventories in 434/3. The date of dedication is based on the fragment of Philochoros found in the scholiast on Aristophanes' *Peace*, *FGrH* 328 F 121: 'Philochoros says that in the archonship of Theodoros [438/7] also the gold statue of Athena was set up in the great temple, having a weight in gold of 40 talents; Perikles was the overseer, Phidias the creator.'[87] That the statue was complete by

---

[82] *Ath. Pol.* 47. 1; *IG* I³, 52 lines 18–24. Cf. Rhodes (1972) 91–2; (1981) 551; Linders (1987) 117 for παράδοσις.

[83] *IG* I³, 52 lines 20–1.

[84] Rhodes (1972) 236.

[85] Linders (1987) 117.

[86] e.g. ML 72 (*IG* I³, 369).

[87] See Jacoby's commentary on 328 F 121 in *FGrH* 3b suppl. i. 485–96.

439/8 is confirmed by the dates given in Eusebius (440/39) and Jerome (439/8). Dinsmoor concluded that the official dedication must have occurred in the Panathenaic year 438/7.[88] The building accounts of the Parthenon show that extra gold and ivory was being sold off in the ninth year of construction, pointing to 439/8 again as the year of the statue's completion.[89]

By this time a unified board of Treasurers of the Other Gods was deemed necessary, and the decrees of Kallias (*IG* I³, 52A and B) ordered the foundation of a separate board with that title:[90]

Resolved to pay back to the Gods the money that is owed them, since the 3,000 Talents for Athena, of our own currency, which were voted on, have been brought up to the Acropolis . . . (Resolved) to elect treasurers for this money by lot, when the other magistracies are filled, just as the Treasurers of Athena. And let these fulfill their office as treasurers of the monies of the Gods on the Acropolis in the Opisthodomos as divine law sanctions, and let them join in opening, closing, and sealing the doors of the Opisthodomos with the Treasurers of Athena. Let them take the treasure from the present treasurers and the superintendents and the over-seers of the shrines, who now have the management of it, and count it up and weigh it in the presence of the Boule.'[91]

The city-state of Athens voted to create a new board of treasurers, with responsibilities comparable to those of the treasurers of Athena, to control the treasures of the other gods. The Treasurers of the Other Gods and the Treasurers of Athena were amalgamated into one board of ten members in the period between 406/5 and 386/5, then separated, and then again amalgamated from 346/5 onwards.[92] In the intervals when the boards were not amalgamated the Treasurers of the Other Gods issued separate inventories from those of the Treasurers of Athena.[93]

The Treasurers of Athena were a religious institution, yet from the beginning they formed an integral part of the city-state, bound to its constitution with economic and legal checks and balances. Their place in the bureaucracy of Athens was a vital one, especially in the fifth century, when money was loaned by them to the

[88] Dinsmoor (1913) 70.

[89] *IG* I³, 443–4.

[90] The bibliography on the decrees of Kallias is extensive. For the most recent thorough treatment, see Kallet-Marx (1989*a*), who dates the inscription to 431/0. I prefer 434/3, the date assigned by Meiggs and Lewis (1988) 58, following Wade-Gery (1933) 135.

[91] *IG* I³, 52, ML 58; in the Louvre Museum, Paris (inv. no. MA 856). Translation by C. Fornara, (1970: 192).

[92] Develin (1989) 8; Rhodes (1981) 549–50; Ferguson (1932) 104–9.

[93] Cf. Linders (1975).

*hellēnotamiai* for the Peloponnesian war, but also in the fourth, when the treasures on the Akropolis were inventoried annually and items continually dedicated. Throughout all of the constitutional changes and transfers of power from the time of Solon until the end of the fourth century, the worship of Athena on the Akropolis was a source of continuity and immutability for the community of Athens.[94]

### THE METHOD OF TAKING THE INVENTORY

Every year the treasurers inscribed their inventories on stelai which have survived in over 200 fragments. They probably also sent a copy to the Metroon, or kept a papyrus copy on the Akropolis as a convenient check-list. An *antigrapheus* or copy-clerk assisted the stone-cutter by providing a manuscript from which he would carve the stele, whenever an inventory or decree or any other official document was commissioned by the state to be inscribed on stone.[95] These documents need not have matched word for word, and the stone version was just as authoritative as the document filed in the Metroon.[96]

Most of these inscriptions have been published in *IG* by Köhler and *IG* II² by Kirchner. More fragments have come to light in the excavations of the Athenian Agora and North Slope; a few others have been discovered in Athenian marble dumps, modern house demolitions, and in private collections. These were published in a variety of periodicals, principally by Meritt, Schweigert, Stroud, W. E. Thompson, and Woodward. The fifth-century fragments have recently been re-edited by W. E. Thompson and D. M. Lewis in *IG* I³; they are reorganized incorporating new fragments and dates and are in satisfactory condition. The fourth-century remains have not had such good fortune, and publication of revised texts is still awaited.

The inscriptions which list the inventories of the Parthenon are generally formulaic and predictable. Over time the format of the stelai and the organization of the objects under rubrics changed, and these changes permit the identification and dating of fragments which do not themselves preserve dates. The importance of these changes cannot be underestimated in the process of assigning the fragments to their correct chronological order.

[94] Cf. Herington (1963) 65–6.
[95] Wycherley, *Agora* iii, p. 160 n. 519; cf. Posner (1972) 111–12.
[96] Thomas (1989) 47; Boegehold (1972).

Most objects made with precious metals were recorded in the inventories with their weight. Two words were used for those which could not be weighed in order to assess their value, *astathmos* and *astatos*. The first is related to the verb σταθμάω—to measure, attach weight, estimate the value of a thing. The second derived from ἵστημι means 'unweighed' or 'unweighable'. In one of the most complete lists, *IG* II², 1424a (371/0), one of the headings for items in the Hekatompedon (lines 70–71) is τάδε χρυσᾶ καὶ ἐπίτηκτα καὶ ὑπόχαλκα ἄστατα ('these are the gold objects, consisting of a gilt layer over bronze, unable to be weighed'). The heading is followed by items including two krateres, four miniature shields and three large ones, a gorgoneion (an apotropaic device featuring the grotesque face of the mythical gorgon) from a shield blazon, an ἀκινάκης (Persian dagger), an anthemion (a gilded bronze flower), and a basket (*IG* II², 1424A lines 72–86). The materials used in each item are further elaborated, so that it is very clear that the variety of materials prevents the item from being given a value by weight.

Identical objects were distinguished from each other in many ways. The materials were described in detail to distinguish objects with similar shapes.[97] If they were both of the same shape and material, the name of the dedicant was occasionally used to distinguish them.[98] The place of manufacture was sometimes used to single out specific items, since their place of origin determined their unique shape or appearance, as, for example, the Illyrian helmets[99] or Milesian couches.[100] Place names were also used when the object was captured in war or dedicated as war booty, as for example the shield 'from Lesbos' dedicated in 427/6.[101]

Another way for the treasurers to identify objects was by the name of the god to whom the item belonged.[102] The year in which an item was dedicated was an alternative way to describe objects, using the name of the archon.[103] These methods all required a tag or inscription on the vessel or shelf which stated the name of the archon or dedicant or god to whom the item belonged.

Sometimes the inventory lists state that an item was inscribed or had a tag attached. The word *epigegraptai* indicates that the object was inscribed, for example: 'a silver basket, on which is inscribed "Sacred

---

[97] e.g. *IG* II², 1433 lines 10–13, where two ἀλαβαστοθῆκαι are differentiated by material: 'the ἀλαβαστοθήκη which has a silver chain . . . the ἀλαβαστοθήκη of wood.'

[98] e.g. V.273–4.     [99] V.5 = V.10.     [100] IV.26 = V.115.

[101] IV.10 = V.20.     [102] e.g. V.211–27.     [103] e.g. V.389–412.

to Asklepios"; weight: 2906 dr. 4 ob.' (V.214).[104] Letter-labels were mentioned in the stelai, indicating that the object was tagged, inscribed, or else placed on a shelf bearing a letter designating its identity.[105] The combination of letter-labels and inscriptions may suggest that the letter-label was in fact a sign on the shelf: see, for example, V.217: 'A silver hydria, which is marked "E" inscribed "Sacred to Asklepios; Nikokrates of Kolonos made me in the archonship of Simonides [311/10]"; weight: 1050 dr.'[106] Sometimes items are remarked upon for their lack of identifying inscription, as, for example, a wreath (V.425): 'A wreath dedicated by Aristophon; weight of this: 83 dr.; the archon was not inscribed.[107]

From 434/3 to about 300/299 BC annual inventories were kept of the temple treasures on the Akropolis. The format of the published stelai changed over time. Ferguson observed the change in *The Treasurers of Athena*. The format and grouping of the objects indicate the way the Athenians thought about the treasures, and the relative values and esteem of art objects, booty, and functional religious vessels can be distinguished by paying close attention to the order in which they appear on the stelai.

The inscriptions always begin with a prescript which lists the names of the treasurers. Their title is modified to include or exclude the Treasurers of the Other Gods, depending on whether they are jointly publishing the stelai or not.[108] Beneath the names of the treasurers is a rubric for the location of the treasures. Underneath headings such as 'in the Proneos', 'in the Hekatompedon', 'from the Parthenon' are the lists of objects. Metal objects were usually weighed; ivory, wooden, silver, or gold objects were unweighed, presumably because filing or pinching off material would not devalue the object or profit the thief, whereas the metal objects were vulnerable in this way. Weighing the metal ensured that no tampering had occurred since the last inventory. Acrophonic numerals follow the word *stathmon* (weight) if the object was weighed.

Each year certain items were added to the inventory, and were

---

[104] Objects which were inventoried with the term ἐπιγέγραπται or variant, indicating that they were inscribed, include 44, 168, 212, 214–21, 223–5, 227, 251, 309–10, 327, 330, 331, 422, 425, and 469.

[105] On letter-labels see Tod (1954).

[106] Cf. Harris (1988), pl. 88.

[107] See also V.422. Aleshire describes the uninscribed objects in the Asklepieion inventories: Aleshire (1985) 157, 232–3; (1992) 87.

[108] The two boards were separated from 434 to 406/5, when they amalgamated. They published their lists jointly until 385/4, when they again separated. They joined again in 346/5 as the ταμίαι τῆς θεοῦ; see Linders (1972) 74 n. 57 with bibliography; Woodward (1940) 404ff.; Tréheux (1965) 71 n. 1. Kirchner and Ferguson had proposed 342/1 or 341/0 as the date of reconciliation.

labelled *epeteia*, 'the items in this year'. Originally, the new additions would be entered under the heading *epeteia*, and the following year they would be absorbed into the main body of text so that the additions in the following year could be labelled *epeteia*. Later, to make the task easier, the new items remained under the rubric *epeteia* for years, and were incorporated into the main text only when there was a major reorganization of the inventory. Every so often a board of treasurers would reorganize the inventory lists and change the format of the stelai. The changes were then passed down to the next board and maintained until a similar reorganization occurred.

### HISTORICAL OVERVIEW OF THE INVENTORIES

From 434/3 to 405/4 the treasurers inscribed separate stelai for the Proneos, Hekatompedon, Parthenon, and Opisthodomos.[109] After 405/4 the Proneos was no longer inventoried, and the contents of the Opisthodomos were only irregularly published. In the fifth century the entries for four years were usually inscribed on one large stele.[110] Each year was inscribed as a single paragraph, with consecutive entries within the lines. According to the tastes of the masons, the entries were separated by punctuation, numerals, or *vacats*, or often nothing at all.

In 403/2 the Ionic alphabet was formally adopted for the publication of public documents in Athens, and the inventory lists reflect this change. Threatte suggested that this alphabet may have been introduced by the Four Hundred in 411, since the account of the Treasurers of Athena (*IG* I³, 373) uses it in that year, but reverts to Attic in the following year (*IG* I³, 375).[111]

At the time of dedication, the treasury in the Parthenon was already substantial. The following lists show clearly that when the first inventory was taken the majority of objects resided in the chamber called the Parthenon, while the Proneos and Hekatompedon remained relatively clear of treasures except for some vessels in precious metals.

*In the Proneos in 434/3:*

**III.6.** A gold phiale, from which lustrations are made; unweighed
**III.7.** 104 silver phialai; weight of these 10,500+ dr.

---

[109] The inscribed inventory lists for the period from 434/3 to 405/4 include *IG* I³, 292–362 and *IG* II², 1382 and 1383.
[110] The exception is the first stele of the Hekatompedon, where eight years are inscribed on one stone (*IG* I³, 317–24).    [111] Threatte (1980) 29.

**III.2.** 3 silver drinking-horns; weight of these 528 dr.
**III.33.** 3 silver drinking-cups; weight of these: ---
**III.4.** A silver lamp; weight of this: 38 dr.
**III.8.** 9 silver phialai; weight of these: 970+ dr.
**III.1.** A small goblet in a small box, gilt wood

*In the Hekatompedon in 434/3*

**V.334.** 2 gold phialai; weight of these: 1344 dr.
**V.90.** A gold kore on a base; unweighed
**V.204.** A silver lustral basin; unweighed
**V.335.** A gold phiale; weight of this: 1200 dr.

*In the Parthenon in 434/3*

**IV.57.** A gold wreath; weight of this: 60 dr.
**IV.50.** 5 gold phialai; weight of these: 782 dr.
**IV.17.** Unmarked gold; weight of this: 1 dr. 4 ob.
**IV.53.** A gold goblet having a silver base, sacred to Herakles in Elaious; weight of this: 138 dr.
**IV.47.** Two nails, silver gilt; weight of these: 184 dr.
**IV.24.** A mask, silver-gilt; weight of this: 116 dr.
**IV.48a.** --- silver phialai; weight of these: 723+ dr.
**IV.1.** 6 Persian daggers overlaid with gold
**IV.23; V.109.** Golden wheat: 12 stalks
**IV.13.** 2 gilt-wood baskets
**IV.54; V.265.** An incense-burner, gilt wood
**IV.20.** A gilt kore on a base
**IV.14; V.35.** A gilt-wood box
**IV.21; V.102.** A gorgoneion, gilt monster-figures
**IV.22.; V.103.** Horse, griffin, griffin's protome, large griffin, lion's head, flowery wreath, snake, all these gilt
**IV.3.** A gold-plated helmet
**IV.7; V.28.** 31 brazen shields
**IV.25; V.113.** 7 Chian couches
**IV.26; V.115.** 10 Milesian couches
**IV.45; V.208.** 9 sabres
**IV.46A.** 4 swords
**IV.6A; V.5.** 14 breast-plates
**IV.8A.** Six shields with blazons
**IV.7; V.28.** 31 brazen shields
**IV.31.** 6 thrones
**IV.27.** 4 stools
**IV.29A; V.119.** 9 campstools
**IV.42; V.192.** A gilt lyre
**IV.43A; V.195.** 3 ivory lyres

IV.44A; V.197. 4 wooden lyres
IV.30; V.121. An ivory-inlaid table
IV.4; V.14. 3 bronze helmets
IV.28. 13 feet for couches, overlaid with silver

Many of the items listed above were probably commissioned for the temple, such as the furniture and ritual vessels necessary for religious purposes. Others may have already been in the possession of the goddess, but stored elsewhere until the Parthenon was ready.

The furniture included chairs, thrones, footstools, couches, an ivory table, amounting to 57 items of furniture in one room alone. These were the furnishings of Athena's temple; never again would so much be added in one year. In addition, 14 knives and 13 lyres were dedicated that year, articles probably to be used in her rites. The shields may have been war booty from the Delian League campaigns, or possibly left over from the Persian wars. The room was thus completely filled with treasures, from the first year of its opening.

Certain items indicate what suppliants or priests might have done in the temple; the gold phiale, kept in the Proneos, listed first, was for the purpose of making lustrations. It may have been used in conjunction with the *aporrhantērion* kept in the Hekatompedon. The 104 silver phialai may have also been for the same purpose, especially since they were kept in the first room inside the temple and lustrations may have been the first function performed. The phialai may also have been used for making libations with wine. The lyres may indicate that the rituals for the worship of Athena were performed to music. *Diphrophoroi* carried stools in the Panathenaic procession, and the *diphroi* dedicated in the Parthenon may have been the ones carried by them.

Curiously, not all items seem to be functional or of use in cultic rituals. What exactly were the silvergilt nails, weighing 184 drachmas—extraordinarily large? Why store armour in the temple? Some items may have been relics or heirlooms, survivals from the archaic period before the Parthenon was built. These might include the griffins, the Persian daggers which may have been war booty, and the two gold korai, which may have been statues of á woman on a column such as the marble ones which were common dedications on the Akropolis in the archaic period.[112] Another possible set of heirlooms is the group of gold-leaf objects which entered the

---

[112] See IV.19; V.90; one was kept in the Parthenon chamber, the other in the Hekatompedon.

Parthenon in 434 and were never separated in the inventory lists or melted down, namely 'the gorgoneion, gilt monster figures; a horse, griffin, griffin's protome, large griffin, lion's head, flowery wreath, snake, all these gilt'.[113] These may all have been parts of bronze cauldrons, perhaps of the orientalizing period, which survived into the classical treasury as fragments. They were not thrown into the melting-pot during the last decade of the fifth century, as if they were somehow more venerated than other dedications.

Again, why were these particular items inventoried, and not others? Possibly the inventories were meant to be a register of the sacred objects belonging to Athena and required by cultic needs. They did not include private dedications, at least in the fifth century BC. At the beginning of the fourth century the names of individual donors appear more frequently in the inventories. The exclusion of expensive gifts no longer made sense: many of the private dedications had become more valuable than the state-provided cultic equipment. The treasurers therefore began to include these items in their lists.

Alternatively, the criterion for inclusion in the inventories may have been whether or not an item ever left the temple, either for use on the Akropolis in ceremonies or in the Panathenaic procession. If items were removed, the treasurers had to ensure that they had been returned. Objects which always remained locked in the temple would not require such careful checking.

Major reorganizations of the treasury appear to have taken place in the following years: at some time between 410 and 403, 378/7, 368/7, 355, and between 334 and 331. In at least two cases changes in the format of the stelai also show the disappearance of some objects and the addition of some new ones, an indication that older offerings had been melted down to make new *pompeia* (processional objects). The Athenians included the gold and silver kept on the Akropolis as an important financial resource of their empire. The treasures were actually used for minting coins at the end of the Peloponnesian war. Thucydides says that Perikles believed that the dedications, war booty, and processional vases were available on the Akropolis as cash on hand for the Peloponnesian war. At 2. 13. 4 he lists the following categories of objects available for wartime use: uncoined gold and silver in public and private dedications, sacred vessels, and Persian spoils. It is evident from the inventories that the

[113] See V.102–3.

treasurers did allow objects to be melted down at the end of the Peloponnesian war, but many survived that event.

The earliest example of a melt down may be seen in the inventories between 410/9 and 403/2 BC.[114] The literary source for the manufacture of gold coinage in 407/6 attests only to the use of golden Nikai, or statues of Victory, for minting the coins. Philochoros said that the gold for the coins came from the statues of Nike (*FGrH* 328 F 141). The gold from these Nikai came to sixteen talents.[115] By 403/2 at least twenty new silver hydriai as well as an assortment of other new votive offerings were inventoried.[116] If the Athenians borrowed from the treasury for the mint, they replenished the treasury almost immediately. To accomplish that just after the war must have meant sacrifice and hardship for the Athenians. They were assisted in the task by the confiscation of the property of the Thirty.[117] A fragment of Philochoros attests that the first ceremonial objects (*pompeia*) after the Peloponnesian war were purchased with the property of the Thirty, probably in 402/1.[118]

Twenty-seven new silver hydriai, or water-jars, appear in the temple inventories by 401/0. These each weighed about 1000 drachmai, amounting to some four and a half talents. The property of the Thirty may have been used to purchase these vessels, as suggested in the sources, and possibly also the washbasin, *pinax,* (platter), and three wine-jugs listed at the beginning of the inventory of 402/1 (V. 260, 230, 354, 297). But this was not enough. Clearly the public were making personal sacrifices of valuables in order to pay Athena back for all that the war effort had taken. Even Lysander of Sparta dedicated a gold wreath, which first appears in the inventory lists in 401/0 (V.428). Names of Athenians on the lists now include metics, male citizens, their wives, daughters, and mothers, from the aristocracy downwards. Apparently, all of the Athenians felt a genuine need to refurbish their temple to Athena as grandly and as quickly as possible: the debt owed to the goddess had to be repaid. This they did many times over with splendid new dedications which flowed into the temple at an increased pace, especially in the first decade of the fourth century. Whether this was due to guilt, piety, or a combination of motives is difficult to assess.

---

[114] *IG* I³, 314–16, 339–42. 359–62.
[115] Cf. Schweigert (1940) nos. 27, 28, 32; D. B. Thompson (1944); W. E. Thompson (1964a) 115–20; (1965d); (1970a); Krentz (1979) 62–3; Samons (1993) 133.
[116] *IG* II², 1370+1371+1384 (403/2) and 1372+1402+EM 13409 (402/1).
[117] Walbank (1982), esp. 97–8.
[118] *FGrH* 328 F 181, cf. Arist. *Ath. Pol.* 39. 6; Philochoros *FGrH* 328 fr. 181.

At the end of the Peloponnesian war the treasures were listed under a single heading, 'in the Hekatompedon'. No more inventories of the Proneos were made after *IG* I³, 316 (*c.*407/6 BC), and after 399/8 objects which were formerly in the western chamber (*IG* II², 1374, of 400/399) began to be listed on the stelai for the treasures of the Hekatompedon under the heading 'from the Parthenon' (ἐκ τοῦ Παρθενῶνος).¹¹⁹ The term 'Parthenon' here must be interpreted in the narrow sense of the room within the temple called the Parthenon, presumed to be the rear chamber with the four interior Ionic columns.

After the reorganization the Proneos was no longer used for storing treasures, and there are thus no more inventory lists. The Parthenon proper may have been emptied and the items transferred to the Hekatompedon, where they were kept together and inventoried separately under the rubric 'from the Parthenon'.¹²⁰ Either these items were shelved or stored together with a tag, or else each object had a tag which specified that it had originally been in the Parthenon, so that the treasurers could identify them when they made the inventory each year.

Beginning in the year 405/4, the Treasurers of Athena became responsible for the treasures of the other gods, and began to publish combined inventory lists. W. E. Thompson suggested that 28 Hekatombaion 406/5 was 'the most likely date for the merger, for this was the end of a Panathenaic penteteris'.¹²¹ The joint board issued three stelai annually: the contents of the Hekatompedon, the items 'from the Parthenon', and some items 'from the Opisthodomos'. The prescripts of each stele begins with the phrase 'These are the Treasurers of Athena and the Other Gods, in the archonship of X.' The names of the treasurers plus the secretary follow. The next clause states that they handed over their responsibilities to the treasurers in the next year's archonship, listing the names of the new board of treasurers and their secretary. A final clause states that they received all this from the first board, naming the chairman and the secretary.¹²² The last phrase of the prescript was either 'in the Hekatompedon cella counted and weighed' or 'from the Opisthodomos' or 'from the Parthenon'. The few objects which

---

¹¹⁹ e.g. *IG* II², 1377 line 9 (399/8 BC).

¹²⁰ The first example is found in *IG* II², 1377 lines 9–10.

¹²¹ W. E. Thompson (1970*c*) 63.

¹²² For examples see *IG* II², 1378, 1388, 1392. The phrase 'from Panathenaia to Panathenaia' has been interpreted as either the one-year or the four-year cycle; Develin (1984) discusses the subject with bibliography.

were still kept in the Opisthodomos were inventoried on the stelai of the Hekatompedon under the rubric 'These are in the Opisthodomos' (τάδε ἐν τῷ Ὀπισθοδόμῳ).[123] In these headings we read the nomenclature understood by Athenians of the fifth and fourth centuries BC; yet the business of assigning buildings to these names (Hekatompedon, Opisthodomos, Proneos, Parthenon) is still problematic for us today.

After 385 BC the inventory for each year continued to be inscribed, with all rooms inventoried on one stele. The Treasurers of Athena issued one inventory stele per year, which included the Hekatompedon and the Archaios Neos (Erechtheion). Objects were listed irrespective of their place of origin or of deposit. The confusion of the treasurers is apparent in the fact that the scribes did not record the items in the same order year after year, as they had in the previous period. As a result, the arrangement of the fragments into a coherent order is difficult unless the names of the archon or treasurers are preserved. A group of inscriptions which are related but belong to separate years has to be dated as 'after 385, prior to 374': *IG* II², 1416, 1418+1419, 1420, 1452, and 1433; with further refinement impossible.

The Treasurers of Athena reorganized the inventories again in 378/7. The lists for 377/6 (*IG* II², 1410) and 376/5 (*IG* II², 1411) contain no more than their prescripts, and do not help to determine whether or not a melting down of gold and silver treasures had occurred. Dinsmoor argued that the aberration in the lists was due to the burning of the Opisthodomos in 377/6, but Lewis demonstrated that the date of the burning must be pushed back to 406/5.[124] The evidence for a reorganization of the treasures in 378/7 by melting down objects is presented by Ferguson in *The Treasurers of Athena*, where he shows that many of the objects dedicated prior to 378/7 disappeared from the inscriptions after that date.[125] The chryselephantine statue of Athena is recorded as having been checked in *IG* II², 1410 (377/6), which may indicate some concern for the completeness of the inventory for that particular year.[126]

In 377 some of the Greek city-states joined Athens in a maritime league. *IG* II², 1410 is capped by a relief, which may be a further

[123] Cf. *IG* II², 1388B line 73.

[124] Lewis (1954) 47–8; Dinsmoor (1932).

[125] See Ferguson (1932) 118–21.

[126] *IG* II², 1410 line 7 has been restored as [ἄγαλμα χρυσοῦν τὸ ἐν τῳ Ἑκατομπ]έδῳ ἐντελὲς [κα]τὰ τὴν στή[λην τὴν χαλκῆν] ('[The gold statue in the Hekatom]pedon complete according to the [bronze] stele').

indication that it received special attention. The sculpture depicts a seated, bearded male, identified as Erechtheus, facing left, with a woman walking leftwards away from him. A few of the allies presented Athena with gold wreaths which were then dedicated between 377/6 and 368/7.[127]

The year 374/3 marks a milestone in the sequence of inventory lists, for it was then that the Treasurers of Athena first issued their inventory in a columnar format.[128] The stelai of this period have three columns, with only one or a few entries per line. The objects are arranged within the columns under rubrics by material, except for the group of objects labeled 'from the Parthenon'. The Opisthodomos, Archaios Neos (Erectheion), and occasionally the Chalkotheke all appear on the same stelai, which are larger in size than the earlier ones.[129] The prescript runs along the top in continuous lines, unbroken by columns. A decree authorizing the commission of new votive offerings in 375/4 or 374/3 has been restored with the heading 'These things the priests handed over in the archonship of Hippodamas for the golden procession vases (πομπεῖα), the golden Nikai, and the oinochoai, and the other decorations.'[130]

Another melting down of metal dedications and reorganization of the inventory lists occurred in either 367/6 or 365/4, as shown by *IG* II², 216+261, and *IG* II², 217. Lewis suggested that Androtion may have been responsible for this, and Demosthenes refers back to the event of the mid-360s in his speech *Against Androtion*.[131] Some scholars, however, believe that the melting instigated by Androtion took place in 355/4. Jacoby argued that Androtion was responsible for two meltings of the treasures:

Probably in 377/6 B.C. A. was (as ταμίας or rather as a member of a special board) engaged with an inventory of the stores of Athena (cult-statue, objects used in processions, votive gifts). On this occasion he brought about the making of new πομπεῖα and carried a decree about the administration of the holy treasure, a decree re-iterated in 346/5 BC.[132]

---

[127] e.g. *IG* II², 1425, 1438; cf. Lewis (1954) 44–5; Schweigert (1938) 281–2 no. 16.

[128] Inscriptions with columnar format include *IG* II², 1421+1423+1424+Ag. I 4527; *IG* II², 1422, 1424a, 1425, 1427, 1428, 1429, 1430, 1431, 1432, 1433, 1434, 1435.

[129] For example, *IG* II², 1428 has a thickness of 0.25 m. and *IG* II², 1424a 0.24 m.

[130] Broneer (1935) 167, no. 28; cf. Ferguson (1932) 118–22, Lewis in Develin (1989) 241.

[131] Dem. 22, 26; Lys. *Against Androtion*; see Lewis (1954) 39–49. For Androtion see *APF* 913 (pp. 33–4); Jacoby *FGrH* 324 and IIIb (suppl.), Text (1954) 87ff.

[132] *FGrH* IIIb (suppl.), Text (1954) 88. Jacoby was following the old dating of *IG* II², 216 to 346/5, prior to the join with *IG* II², 261 made by Lewis (1954: 39–49), which moved the date of the proposal to 365/4.

The speeches by Demosthenes *Against Androtion* and *Against Timocrates* both refer to a melting down of temple treasures. These texts are traditionally dated to 355 and 352 respectively, on the basis of the chronology of the speeches established by Dionysios of Halikarnassos.[133] Major reorganizations appear to have occurred in 377/6, 368/7, and 355/4. All three have been attributed to Androtion, whose name may be restored in *IG* II², 216 as the mover of a *psēphisma* to make *pompeia*, and was accused in Demosthenes' speech.[134]

Androtion's melting down and the consolidation of the treasures were thought by Ferguson to have taken place between 358 and 355.[135] The epigraphical evidence for these events supports this dating, although whether they may be associated with Androtion is still debated. In *IG* II², 1436 (350/49) the list of gold wreaths includes a yearly donation down to 354/3, when the practice abruptly stops. Shortly after 350 BC, new hydriai for the other gods, perhaps created by the melting, appear.

The motivation for melting down old votive offerings was probably to simplify housekeeping inside the temples, and to make new cult equipment. Demosthenes describes Androtion's argument before the people, which was evidently convincing enough for them to vote for it:

The greater part of the speech by which he threw dust in your eyes I will leave unnoticed; but, by alleging that the leaves of the crowns were rotten with age and falling off—as though they were violet-leaves or rose-leaves, not leaves made of gold—he persuaded you to melt them down.[136]

Demosthenes makes the claim sound ridiculous; but there is one entry in the inventories which shows that wreaths did lose leaves from time to time: 'Four gold petals from the wreath which the Nike holds, the Nike in the hand of the statue; weight of these: 6 dr. 2 obols.'[137]

The decade between 340 and 330 is poorly represented in the surviving inventories. This is unfortunate, since it was an interesting time for the treasurers and for Athens. The most significant event for the treasury in this period was the reform programme of Lykourgos,

[133] *Pros Ammaion* 4, p. 724; cf. Ferguson (1932) 121–2; Bloch (1940) 341–55, esp. 342; Jaeger (1938) 220 n. 21; Lewis (1954) 43 n. 18. Lewis places Androtion's Council in 359/8 and argues, on the basis of historical problems during the Social War and on the naval lists, that Dem. 22 must date to 357, *contra* Cawkwell (1962) 40–5.

[134] A. C. Johnson (1914*a*) 16 stated the case for 377–373 as the period of the melting moved by Androtion.

[135] Ferguson (1932) 121.        [136] Dem. 22. 70.        [137] See **V.95** for references.

the orator and epimelete for the Akropolis from 338/7 to 326/5.[138] The melting down of treasures which occurred between 334/3 and 331/0 is asserted by information from sources outside of the inventory lists. Lykourgos is mentioned in many ancient sources as the originator of a proposal to make new ceremonial vases for the temples of Attica.[139] Extensive epigraphical evidence shows that he proposed legislation and had to have it approved before the necessary melting could take place. The *nomothetai*, on the motion of Lykourgos, voted to reorganize the financial resources of the religious cults.[140] The economy of Athens had improved to such an extent that there were annual surpluses in the city's income for several years consecutively, and the sanctuaries became the beneficiaries of that affluence.[141] The resolution shows that the Athenians proposed to make new golden Nikai and *pompeia* for the festivals, and refurbish the major sanctuaries of Attica. Lykourgos received honours for his work in the decree of Stratokles, *IG* II², 457. He ordered new golden Nikai to be made in the 330s, according to ancient literary sources.[142] Unfortunately, no inventories have survived from between 334/3 and 331/0 to supplement the other epigraphical and literary evidence. Later inventories, however, do reflect a substantial reorganization during the 330s in that new items came in at the same time that many smaller, older dedications disappeared, which indicates that a melting had occurred. Lykourgos undertook a major reorganization of the system of drawing up inventories of the treasures, and he improved the labelling system. As a former student of Plato and Isocrates, he may have been trying to apply principles of systematic organization and categorization in his reforms of temple-management.[143]

The procedure for melting down old dedications for new *pompeia* was regulated at every stage, and the epigraphical record preserves the procedure for the melting under Lykourgos.[144] The first step is

---

[138] See Berve ii. 238–9, no. 477; Lewis (1988) 297–8; Burke (1985) 251–64; Schwenk (1985) 108–26, no. 21; Mitchel (1970) 163–214; Linders (1972) 74–5; Mitchel (1962); Woodward (1956) 102; Tod (1954) 2–5; Woodward (1951); Ferguson (1932) 122–6.

[139] For the ancient sources see *IG* II², 333, 457, 1493–96; [Plut.] *Vit. X orat.* 841 B, 852 B; Dem. 22, 24; Diod. 16. 88. 1.

[140] *IG* II², 333. See also Mitchel (1962), esp. 215.

[141] Burke (1985) 251, 256; cf. [Plut.] *Vit. X orat.* 852.

[142] Diod. 15. 88. 1; [Plut.] *Vit. X orat.* 841 D, 852 B; Paus. 1. 29. 16; *IG* II², 1493–97 and *Ath. Pol.* 49. 3. Modern commentaries include Ferguson (1932) 89–95, 118 n. 1, 122 n. 2; D. B. Thompson (1944); Mattingly (1974) 94–7; Krentz (1979) 61–3; Rhodes (1981) 551.

[143] Diog. Laert. 3. 46; [Plut.]. *Vit. X orat.* 841 B; Zosim. *Vit. Isoc.*

[144] *IG* II², 333, 1493+1494+1495, 1496. Aleshire (1989) 146–7 discusses the reorganization of the Attic sanctuaries under Lykourgos.

the collection of the objects in precious metal to be melted down. 'When chosen by the *dēmos*, Lykourgos brought together large sums of money on the Akropolis, providing adornment for the goddess, solid gold Nikai, processional vessels of gold and silver, and gold ornaments for 100 *kanēphoroi*.'[145] Once he had accomplished the collection, Lykourgos was then in a position to assess the materials and decide upon the amount to be devoted to the melting-pot. He was then able to formulate a proposal to put before the *nomothetai*. *IG* II², 333 records the resolution of the *nomothetai* to melt down some votive offerings and wreaths and to make new ceremonial vessels from the metal.[146] Λυκοῦργος Λυκόφρονος Βουτάδης is preserved as the proposer of the law in line 13. New ornaments (*pompeia*) were ordered for a number of the other gods. The act was calculated to rejuvenate the Athenian festivals, provide a sounder basis for the sanctuaries, restore morale and faith in the state, and provide an opportunity to assess and catalogue all the religious holdings of Attica.

The next step was to farm out to smiths the contracts for the new vessels. These are preserved as *IG* II², 1496 lines 213–30. The names of the smiths were Nikokrates of Kolonos, Mus Hermos, Kratippos of Olynthos, [---]machos, a metic living in Kydathenaion, and Ephialtes of Angkyle.[147] Once the contracts were let out, the Treasurers of Athena handed over to the commissioned craftsmen the old objects to be melted and crafted into new ones. *IG* II², 1469A lines 3–7 shows that some phialai dedicated by freedmen were used by a smith named Diomedon to create his three silver hydriai, and the same can be seen for several other craftsmen in lines 12–26.

The craftsmen who made the vessels were not included by name in earlier inventory lists. Only after the melting under Lykourgos are the names of craftsmen given.[148] This may be due to a desire to give recognition to these workers, or perhaps it was simply a convenient way of labelling the items in question for the purpose of the inventories. During the process, the craftsmen were required to undergo *euthynai* or examination and audit for the quantity of metal for which they were held responsible. The method is not yet fully understood, but somehow *dokimeia* (testers) were used and kept by the Treasurers of Athena in the Erechtheion.[149] The inscription in which these are

---

[145] [Plut.] *Vit. X orat.* 852 B.
[146] For commentary and recent bibliography on *IG* II², 333 see Schwenk (1985) 108–26.
[147] See Harris (1988) 329–37.
[148] See in particular *IG* II², 1469A, 1470, 1471+1462A, 1474B, 1479A, 1480, 1492, 1496.
[149] *IG* II², 1428, add. lines 152–9. For the testers see Giovannini (1975) 191–5.

mentioned dates from 367/6, but the testers were created for a different, earlier melting and preserved, perhaps being reused by the Lykourgan craftsmen.

The accounts of the Treasurers of Athena and of the board created by Lykourgos to supervise the creation of new Nikai, processional vessels, and kanephoric ornament are preserved as *IG* II², 1493–97. *IG* II², 1495 records the formulae used for the *euthynai* of the craftsmen. Certain goldsmiths received a sum of drachmas in gold (in the form of old dedications) to be melted down. In the process a certain number of drachmas were lost, a certain quantity of pure gold was refined, and a certain amount was recovered from the ashes, resulting in a total of pure gold returned by the goldsmith.[150]

Once the new vessel was finished, it was dedicated to a particular god or to Athena, and entered the treasury. Many of the new vases created under the Lykourgan programme have complicated, unusual labels. Vases were grouped together by the name of their craftsman, and given distinctive letter-labels. Some were labelled with the names of the gods to whom they were dedicated. Once the identification of the vessel was established, a tag must have been made and affixed to the object. Or, if there was shelving, the identification mark may have been affixed to the position on the shelf.

After all the vases had been made, there would have been some loss of metal resulting from the process of melting. Remarkable as it may seem, the Treasurers of Athena purchased additional gold to make up to the goddess the quantity lost in the making, as can be seen in *IG* II², 1496B lines 197–204: 'The total sum of the weight of the necklaces and bracelets and wreaths: 3 talents 3220 dr. We received from the gold from the Akropolis, remaining after the process of refining, 2 talents 1580 dr. 5¾ ob. Gold which we purchased [to make up the difference]: 1 talent 1639 dr. ¼ ob.' As A. M. Woodward noted, this amounted to an extraordinarily high loss of 35.5 per cent of the gold in the process of refining and manufacturing new items from old.[151]

The inscriptions continued to be produced in the three-column format introduced in 374/3. Almost all of these stelai were inscribed on both sides. Inscriptions on the reverses are often inventories of

---

[150] The process of ἀπόκαυσις (called ἀπουσία when referring to a melting for the purpose of minting) is explained more fully in Woodward (1951) and Mitchel (1962; 1966). See also Linders (1987) 116–17. The recovery of gold from the ashes is recorded in *IG* II², 1388B line 66 (probably from the creation of the golden Nike in 403/2–402/1) and 1495 lines 7–8, 16.

[151] Woodward (1951).

the Chalkotheke.[152] Objects which were labelled with the date of their dedication serve as the *terminus post quem* for dating most of these stelai. Very few prescripts are preserved with archon names.[153] Between the Lykourgan reforms and 304/3 there were no meltings, as far as we know.

Between 307 and 304 a brutal war was waged between Kassandros and Demetrios Poliorketes, the Four Years war. The walls of Athens were repaired and refortified, an operation paid for by personal contributions from citizens and foreigners, and through increased taxes.[154] Demetrios proved successful, and took as his reward a place of residence in the back of the Parthenon.[155] His justification for this act was his status as a deity: he claimed to be a younger brother of Athena. In this vein he had gold coinage minted bearing a portrait in which his own physiognomy was superimposed on the head of Athena.[156] Greek custom respected the sanctity of the temple as the house of the deity, not a place for mortals to live in. 'Even to reside in the back hall was *hubris* characteristic of a Hellenistic king.'[157] His occupation of the temple and residence in the Parthenon must have disturbed the treasury greatly. Dinsmoor (1931) 37 noted that *IG* II², 482, a decree of 304, shows that the chryselephantine statue in the Hekatompedon may have been in need of repair. The occupation of the temple by Demetrios may have resulted in damage to and/or loss of some of the treasures.[158] In any event, the usurper would not want to make his crimes known by publishing inventories which revealed the damage he had caused.[159]

Lachares, friend of Kassandros and rival of Demetrios Poliorketes, brought an end to the publication of treasury inventories.[160] In 295

---

[152] The reverses of *IG* II², 1479, 1480+1509, and 1491+1492+1486 are accounts of the Treasurers of Athena rather than inventories of the Chalkotheke.

[153] Only *IG* II², 1459 (321/0) and 1456+1483 (307/6) are dated on the basis of the name of the archon in the prescript, and in the latter case the archon's name is restored.

[154] *IG* II², 463; Plut. *Demetr*. Cf. Ferguson (1911) 112–14.

[155] Diod. 20. 110; Plut. *Demetr*. 23–4, 26–7. Cf. Ferguson (1911) 118–19; Dinsmoor (1931) 37, 64, 383; (1934) 96; Burkert (1988) 37 n. 28.

[156] Seltman (1909) 267, no. 3, 268–9; Ferguson (1911) 118.

[157] Burkert (1988) 37.

[158] On Demetrios in the Parthenon: Plut. *Demetr*. 26; Demochares *FGrH* II 449. See Dinsmoor (1931) 37; Burstein (1978); Lewis (1988) 304–5. Demetrios also stayed in a temple in Delos in the summer of 304: *IG* XI/2, 146 lines 76–7; cf. Ferguson (1910) 193; Homolle (1887) 67–8, 115.

[159] See Lewis (1988).

[160] The chronology of his tyranny is based on *Pap. Oxy*. 17. 2082, identified as a fragment of Phlegon of Tralles (Phlegon (?) *FGrH* IIB 257a F 3). Cf. A. C. Johnson (1915) 433–6; Ferguson (1929) 1–20; Dinsmoor (1934) 96; Habicht (1979) 1–21; Shear (1978) 52–3 n. 144; Mansfield (1985) 160–1 n. 29; Linders (1987) 117. Ancient sources: Paus. 1. 25. 7, 1. 29. 16; Phlegon (?) *FGrH* IIB 257a F 3; Demetrios Areiopagites fr. 1, III, p. 357 Kock; Athen. 9. 70, 405 F; Polyainos 3. 7. 1, 4. 7. 5; Plut. *Demetr*. 33; *Isis and Osiris* 71.

BC he staged a *coup d'état*. This was dated by Ferguson to 300 BC, its eventual failure taking place in 295; Ferguson was followed by Dinsmoor and Meritt, among others. G. De Sanctis revised the chronology, placing Lachares' coup in 295 and his fall in 294.[161] Having seized the Akropolis, in the course of his tyranny he melted down the gold shields on the epistyle of the Parthenon, the golden Nikai, and possibly even the gold plates on the statue of Athena Parthenos. The gold shields may have been those sent to Athens by Alexander the Great: after the battle of Granikos Alexander had sent 300 full sets of armour (panoplies) to Athens, and some of the shields were placed on the epistyle of the temple.[162] Lachares' tyranny was ended by Demetrios Poliorketes in 294, but not before the damage to the treasuries had been done.

There is some doubt over whether the gold was actually stripped from the Phidian cult statue. The evidence for damage to the treasury by Lachares rests principally on Pausanias 1. 25. 6, where Pausanias states that Lachares 'stripped Athena naked'. There is in fact evidence to suggest that Lachares did not remove the goddess's gold. The cult statue continued to stand in the temple and was copied in marble repeatedly in the period following Lachares, as in, for example, the marble copy which stood in the library at Pergamon. Copies would probably not have been so popular if the statue was no longer whole. There is no obvious time at which the Athenians could have replaced that much gold in the years following Lachares. Linders has proposed that Pausanias is referring to Lachares' robbery of the gold and silver treasures which belonged to Athena: 'stripping her naked' means stripping her storerooms in the temple.[163]

No inventories have been identified with certainty from the third century BC, and it is doubtful whether the Treasurers of Athena were still intact as a board. They may have been replaced at the beginning of the third century by a new office, the στρατηγὸς ἐπὶ τὴν παρασκευήν, mentioned in an inscription of 296/5.[164] Without a democratic government, there was little need to keep the people informed of the public accounts, and by this time the treasury of Athena was surely counted among the resources available to the ruler. The damage to the treasures was perpetrated by Demetrios and

[161] See Ferguson (1929). Jacoby followed the dating of De Sanctis in his discussion of *FGrH* IIB 257a F 1–3 (in *FGrH* IID 849); cf. Shear (1978) 52–3 n. 144.

[162] Arr. *Anab*. 1. 16. 7.

[163] Linders (1987), esp. 117 nn. 18–20.

[164] *IG* II², 682 lines 21–4. Cf. Ferguson (1932) 126; Rhodes (1972) 126 n. 3.

possibly by Lachares; the shame of such indignities prevented the treasurers from publishing their inventories on stone for all to view.

When exactly did the religious fervour which created so strong a treasury die? When did the treasury of Athena become the property of the state rather than the goddess? Although some studies of Greek religion ascribe the beginning of cynical doubts about the reality of the gods to Socrates, it is clear from the Akropolis inventories that private dedications continued throughout the fourth century and that the treasury grew steadily. Lykourgos used the addition of precious objects to the treasury of Athena in order to gain prestige and please the populace as late as the 330s; gifts to the gods and processions in religious festivals were still central components of Athenian life. For as long as the inventory lists were inscribed on stone, it is safe to assume that the worship of Athena was strong, steady, and genuine.

# PART II

# The Treasures of the Opisthodomos

## THE INVENTORY LISTS

The location of the so-called Opisthodomos has been the subject of controversy and speculation for well over a century.[1] The term itself is usually used to mean the rear chamber of a temple. The most obvious assumption would be to identify the Opisthodomos as the western portico of the temple of Athena Parthenos; but it has been conjectured that the name belongs to the back (western) room of the Old Temple to Athena which was rebuilt as a temporary shelter to house the cult statue and serve as the repository for treasures after the Persian sack of the Akropolis.[2] This room in the western half of the so-called Dörpfeld foundations has been variously identified as the Opisthodomos, the Hekatompedon, and the Archaios Neos. For the purposes of the following catalogue of objects, it is not essential to decide where exactly the collection of treasures resided, whether in the west porch of the Parthenon or in the temporary shelter of the Dörpfeld foundations. I prefer to place these objects in the latter location because of the literary references, which agree in referring to the Opisthodomos as a separate building behind the temple of Athena Polias (the Erechtheion).

The preserved foundations of the Old Temple to Athena indicate a split cella, which would match the description given in the Kallias decrees (*IG* I³, 52), the earliest literary reference to the Opisthodomos as a building: 'They [the Treasurers of the Other Gods] are to be stewards, on the Akropolis in the Opisthodomos, of the money of the gods . . . to join both in locking the doors of the Opisthodomos and in sealing them together with the Treasurers of Athena.' On side B of the stele the inscription reads: 'When the amount which is owed for the 200 talents which the *dēmos* voted as

---

[1] Cf. Michaelis (1871) 293-5; Milchhöfer (1894); White (1895); Jahn and Michaelis (1901); Paton (1927) 462-3, 470-3; Wade-Gery (1931) 76-81; Dinsmoor (1932); Hess (1935); Stevens (1942); Shear (1966) 56-8; I. T. Hill (1969) 137-8, 158, 239 n. 12; Travlos (1971b); Roux (1984). For the primary sources see App. IV.

[2] Cf. Dinsmoor (1947) 140.

repayment to the other gods has been paid, let them steward the money of Athena in the right-hand side of the Opisthodomos, and that of the other gods on the left.' Two distinct sides are mentioned, which correspond to the split cella of the Dörpfeld foundations.[3]

Harpokration defines an Opisthodomos as a rear porch or rear part of a temple, yet goes on to use the example on the Akropolis: 'the building behind the temple of Athena in which are deposited the monies.' That the room held money seems to be true enough: in an account of the *logistai* for the years 426–422 the treasurers refer to the Opisthodomos as a place where money was kept (*IG* I³, 369). The 'temple of Athena' mentioned in the inscription must be the Erechtheion. In *IG* I³, 386 (408/7), Eleusinian money was stored in the Opisthodomos 'in a bronze box on the fourth shelf'.

In the 420s an inscription refers to setting up a stele 'behind the Opisthodomos' (*IG* I³, 207): 'Let the column be erected behind the Opisthodomos in the prytany of Hippothontis'. 'Behind the Opisthodomos' again indicates that it existed somewhere outside of the temple; otherwise, the text should have said 'behind the Hekatompedos Neos'. The last reference to the Opisthodomos in the literary sources is in a speech of Demosthenes in 353/2 (Dem. 24. 136).

Below are listed all of the inventories in which the treasures of the other gods kept in the Opisthodomos were listed. There are no inventories of treasures in the Opisthodomos for the fifth century BC.

*Lists of Objects Labelled 'from the Opisthodomos' and transferred to the Hekatompedon*

1. 399/8: *IG* II², 1378+1398, add. 797–8, lines 12–25
2. Beg. 4th cent.: *IG* II², 1396 lines 1–34
3. Beg. 4th cent.: *IG* II², 1397 lines 1–5
4. 398/7: *IG* II², 1392 lines 1–23
5. Before 385/4: Ag. I 5363 [*Hesperia*, 32 (1963) 165–8] line 1
6. 382/1: *IG* II², 1412 line 26
7. 385/4 (?): *IG* II², 1405
8. 315/4: *IG* II², 1415 lines 3–6

*Lists of Objects inside the Opisthodomos*

9. 403/2: *IG* II², 1399
10. 402/1 or 401/0: EM 12392 [*Hesperia*, 7 (1938) 272, no. 7] lines 1–7

---

[3] Cf. I. T. Hill (1969) 137–8, 158.

11. 400/399: EM 12916 [*Hesperia,* 7 (1938) 277, no. 11; *BSA* 70 (1975) 184] lines 1–5
12. 398/7: *IG* II², 1388 lines 73–93+1403 lines 3–4+1408 lines 15–16
13. 397/6: *IG* II², 1448 lines 1–12+1449 lines 3–4, 9
14. 390/89: *IG* II², 1400 lines 61–72
15. After 385/4: *IG* II², 1417 line 9
16. After 385/4: *IG* II², 1418 lines 18–19
17. 371/0: *IG* II², 1424a lines 115–22

*Lists of Objects (in the Opisthodomos?) Inventoried by the Treasurers of the Other Gods*

18. 376/5: *IG* II², 1445 lines 9–42
19. 375/4: *IG* II², 1446
20. Before 371/0: *IG* II², 1447
21. After 366/5: *IG* II², 1450
22. After 365/4: *IG* II², 1451
23. After 360/59, before 358/7 (?): Akropolis 18/5/89 line 5
24. After 352/1: Robinson Collection [*AJP* 58 (1937) 43]
25. Before 350: *IG* II², 1452 lines 1–12
26. Before 350: *IG* II², 1453 lines 1–11

*(In the Opisthodomos?), Inventoried by the Treasurers of Athena and the Other Gods*

27. 341/0: *IG* II², 1455 lines 23–52
28. After 340/39: *IG* II², 1459 col. II lines 1–10
29. After 316/5: *IG* II², 1457 lines 1–11
30. After 318/7: *IG* II², 1471 B line 60
31. After 316/5: *IG* II², 1478 lines 26–30

The Opisthodomos was the domain of the Treasurers of the Other Gods, as authorized by the Kallias decrees.[4] The items listed below in Section I were all kept in the Hekatompedon within the temple, but were grouped together as having been formerly in a place called the Opisthodomos. The Opisthodomos housed money as well as treasure, but the inscribed inventories recorded only the precious objects other than coins. The items were meticulously segregated until 385, when the Treasurers of Athena and the Treasurers of the Other Gods stopped publishing their inscriptions together. Items which were formerly under the rubric 'from the Opisthodomos' were carelessly lumped together with items from the Parthenon and Hekatompedon in the inventories after 385.[5] By

---

[4] On the Treasurers of the Other Gods see Linders (1975).
[5] e.g. *IG* II², 1417, 1418.

376/5 the inscriptions were more orderly, and thoroughly amalgam-ated items formerly from the Opisthodomos into the inventories of the Hekatompedon. These stelai were organized in three columns, sorting objects by their materials.

Items still actually in the Opisthodomos were occasionally added to the Hekatompedon inventories as a subgroup, as in the most complete list preserved, *IG* II², 1424a (371/0). More often they were inventoried on their own. Unfortunately, no rubric has survived on the stelai listed as 18–26 which would place the items securely in the Opisthodomos. The contents of these lists are similar to the contents inventoried in 12–16, so it may be presumed that the stelai refer to items kept in the Opisthodomos. Yet the only inscription of the period between 375 and the end of the century to have a pre-served heading 'in the Opisthodomos' is *IG* II², 1424a, in which the inventory of the Opisthodomos is completely preserved and lists relatively few items, namely 'ivory figures from the thrones, two ivory hands, half of a silver snake, four iron anvils, two hammers, twenty-two dies, a box, two-hundred and ninety-nine cases of arrows, and twenty more of this year'.[6] The anvils and dies had formerly been housed in the Hekatompedon (*IG* II², 1408 lines 11–13, 398/7). Eight and a half cases of arrowheads were kept in the Hekatompedon from at least 371/0.

Because so many more items appear in the other inventories of the Treasurers of the Other Gods for the years 376/5 and following, Dinsmoor suggested that the lists published by them were not of the building called the Opisthodomos, but rather catalogued items separately housed in the Erechtheion and the Hekatompedon and which came under their authority.[7] The anvils and dies, and the few odd remaining items left in the Opisthodomos after *c*.376/5, were kept with all of the stored coinage, and anything other than coinage was transferred to one of the two temples. And even the anvils and dies were recorded on inventories of the Chalkotheke by *c*.350 (*IG* II², 1469 lines 106–9, 1471 lines 55–7), implying that the Opisthodomos was completely cleared of treasures by then and may have been taken out of use, at least as a repository for treasure if not for coinage.[8] Again, after 341 the Treasurers of the Other Gods were merged with the Treasurers of Athena, so that composite stelai were then produced, listing the items kept in all of the buildings on the Akropolis.

---

[6] Trans. Dinsmoor (1932) 168-9.     [7] Dinsmoor (1932) 168.     [8] Dinsmoor (1932) 169.

THE TREASURES

Section I below describes the items that, at some point before the inventories were taken, were housed in the Opisthodomos, but by the time of the inventory were transferred to the Hekatompedon. The heading in the inscriptions usually reads 'From the Opisthodomos' for this group. Section II describes items inventoried in the Opisthodomos at the time of the inventory. Cross-references to Part V indicate that the item was transferred from the Opisthodomos to the Hekatompedon. Bold type indicates the source(s) of the cited Greek.

I. The Objects labelled 'from the Opisthodomos' kept in or transferred to the Hekatompedon:

CONTAINERS OTHER THAN VASES

1. (V.40)   A gilt wood basket, where the ivories are; weight of this: 2406 dr.

κανοῦν χρυσοῦν ὑπόξυλον ἵνα τὰ ἐλεφάντινα σταθμὸν τούτου ΧΧΗΗΗΗΓӀ-

IG II², 1378, add. p. 797 line 13 (399/8)
[Hekatompedon]
1392 lines 16–17 (398/7)
1396 lines 2–4 (beg. 4th cent.)

2. (V.41)   A gilt wood basket, where the ivory figurines are; unweighed

κανοῦν ὑπόξυλον κατάχρυσον ἵνα τὰ ἐλεφάντινα ζῷα ἄστατον

IG II², 1414 **line 20 (385/4)** [Hekatompedon]
1421 lines 128–9 (374/3)
1424a lines 190–1 (371/0)
1425 line 136 (368/7)
Ag. I 2260 [*Hesperia* 25 (1956)103] line 7 (after 346/5)
IG II², 1443 **line 161 (344/3)**

3. (V.42)   A basket, gold over bronze, the one with an Apollo; weight: 3596 dr.

κανοῦν χρυσοῦν ὑπόχαλκον ἵνα ὁ Ἀπόλλων
σταθμὸν ΧΧΧΓӺΔΔΔΔΓӀ-

IG II², 1399 **lines 5–6 (403/2)** [Opisthodomos]

1378+1398, add. p. 798 lines 21–2 (399/8)
[Hekatompedon]
1392 lines 19–20 (398/7)
1396 lines 10–12 (beg. 4th cent.)
1421 lines 42–4 (374/3)
1424a lines 91–2 (371/0)
**1425 lines 87–8 (368/7)**
1429 lines 25–6 (367/6)
1436 lines 49–50 (350/49)
1443 lines 157–8 (344/3)

Ag. I 2260 [*Hesperia* 25 (1956) 103] lines 20–1 (after 346/5)

4. (V.43)    A basket, gold over bronze, the one with a Zeus, weight: 3690 dr.

κανοῦν χρυσοῦν ὑπόχαλκον ἵνα ὁ Ζεύς σταθμὸν ΧΧΧΓΗΕ𐅄ΔΔΔ

*IG* II², 1399 lines 6–7 (403/2) [Opisthodomos]
1378+1398, add. p. 798 lines 23–4 (399/8)
[Hekatompedon]
1392 lines 20–1 (398/7)
**1396 lines 12–14 (beg. 4th cent.)**
1407 lines 20–1 (385/4)
1421 lines 44–5 (374/3)
1424a lines 93–4 (371/0)
1425 lines 89–90 (368/7)
1429 line 27 (367/6)
1436 lines 51–2 (350/49)
1443 lines 158–60 (344/3)

Ag. I 2260 [*Hesperia* 25 (1956) 103] lines 10–11 (after 346/5)

JEWELLERY

5. (V.128)    Two stone (bead) bracelets; weight of both: 108 dr. 5 ob.

ἀμφιδέα διαλίθω σταθμὸν τούτοιν ΗΓΗΗΙΙΙΙΙ

*IG* II², **1378+1398, add. p. 798 lines 17–18 (399/8)**
[Hekatompedon]
1396 lines 8–9 (beg. 4th cent.)
1392, add. p. 798 line 18 (398/7)

6. (V.166)    These things unweighed: 11 bare stone seals; a stone seal having a gold ring; seven stone seals having gold rings; two gold seals without rings

ἄσταθμα τάδε· σφραγῖδες λίθιναι ψιλαί ΔΙ· σφραγὶς λιθίνη χρυσοῦν δακτύλιον ἔχουσα· σφραγῖδες

λίθιναι χρυσοῦς δακτυλίους ἔχουσαι ἑπτά· ἄνευ
δακτύλιων περιχρύσω σφραγῖδε δύο

EM 12392 lines 1–3 [*Hesperia* 7 (1938) 272–4] (402/1 or
401/0) [Opisthodomos]
*IG* II², 1396 lines 21–6 (beg. 4th cent.)
[Hekatompedon]
1398 lines 9–10 (399/8)

MISCELLANEOUS SILVER AND GOLD

7. (V.48)     In a small box, gold from the basket where the ivory
figurines are; weight: 43 dr.

ἐγ κιβωτίω χρυσίον ἀπὸ τοῦ κανοῦ ἵνα τὰ
ἐλεφάντινα ζώδια σταθμὸν ΔΔΔΔΗΗ

*IG* II², 1412 line 26 (382/1) [Opisthodomos]
**1415 line 5 (375/4) [Hekatompedon]**
1424a lines 38–9 (371/0)
1425 line 33–5 (368/7)

8.          Two gold pieces, unfired; weight of both: 21 dr. 5 ob.

χρυσίω ἀπύρω δύο σταθμὸν τούτοιν ΔΔΗΙΙΙΙΙ

*IG* II², 1378, add. p. 798 lines 16–17 (399/8)
[Hekatompedon]
**1396 lines 33–4 (beg. 4th cent.)**

VESSELS

9. (V.268)    An incense-burner, gold over bronze decorated with
curvy petals; weight: 2960 dr.

θυμιατήριον χρυσοῦν ὑπόχαλκον ἵνα τὰ καμπύλα
πέταλα σταθμὸν ΧΧΓΗΗΗΗϜΔ

IG II2, 1399 lines 7–8 (403/2) [Opisthodomos]
1378+1398, add. p. 797, lines 24–5 (399/8)
[Hekatompedon]
1392 lines 22–3 (398/7)
**1396 lines 14–16 (beg. 4th cent.)**
1405 lines 13–14 (385/4?)

10. (V.269)   An incense-burner, gold over bronze decorated with
straight petals; weight: 2940 dr.

θυμιατήριον χρυσοῦν ὑπόχαλκον ἵνα τὰ ὀρθὰ πέταλα
σταθμὸν ΧΧΓΗΗΗΗΔΔΔΔ

*IG* II², 1399 lines 8–9 (403/2) [Opisthodomos]

1396 lines 16–19 (beg. 4th cent.)
[Hekatompedon]

11.   An incense-burner, silver on a wooden mount; weight:
1357 dr. 2 ob.

θυμιατήριον ἀργυροῦν ὑπόξυλον σταθμὸν
ΧΗΗΗϜΓΗΙΙ

> *IG* II², 1378+1398, add. pp. 797–8, lines 14–15
> (399/8) [Hekatompedon]
> 1396 lines 4–6 (beg. 4th cent.)
> 1392 lines 17–18 (398/7)

12. (V.270)   An incense-burner, silver on a wooden mount, decorated
with a Nike; weight: 1448 dr. From this incense-
burner with the Nike, a silver cover, weight: 68 dr.

θυμιατήριον ἀργυροῦν ὑπόξυλον ἵνα ἡ Νίκη σταθμὸν
ΧΗΗΗΗΔΔΔΔΓΗΗ· τοῦ θυμιατηρίου τούτου ἵνα ἡ
Νίκη καλύπτρα ἀργυρᾶ σταθμὸν ἄγει ϜΔΓΗΗ

> EM 12392 [*Hesperia* 7 (1938) 272–4] lines 6–7 (402/1 or
> 401/0) [Opisthodomos]
> *IG* II², 1378+1398, add. p. 798 lines 19–20 (399/8)
> [Hekatompedon]
> **1396 lines 28–33 (beg. 4th cent.)**
> 1397 lines 1–5 (beg. 4th cent.)
> Ag. I 5363 [*Hesperia* 32 (1963) 165–8] line 1 (before
> 385/4)
> *IG* II², 1407 lines 12–13 (385/4)

13. (V.294)   A silver wine-jug; weight of this: 652 dr.

οἰνοχόη ἀργυρᾶ σταθμὸν ταύτης ΓΗϜΗ

> EM 12392 [*Hesperia* 7 (1938) 272–4] line 5 (402/1 or
> 401/0) [Opisthodomos]
> *IG* II², 1378+1398, add. p. 798 lines 18–19 (399/8)
> [Hekatompedon]
> **1392 line 19 (398/7)**
> **1396 lines 9–10 (beg. 4th cent.)**
> 1415 line 3 (375/4)

14.   Silver wine-jugs; weight of these: 1405 dr.

οἰνοχόαι ἀργυραῖ σταθμὸν τούτων ΧΗΗΗΗΓ

> *IG* II², 1392 line 18 (398/7) [Hekatompedon]

15.   A gold krater, the small one; weight of this: 2569 dr. 3 ob.

κρατὴρ χρυσοῦς ὁ μικρὸς σταθμὸν τούτου
ΧΧΡϜΔΓΗΗΗΙΙΙ

> *IG* II², 1396 lines 19–29 (beg. 4th cent.)

1398 lines 7–9 (399/8)
1415 line 6 (375/4)

16.
Gold phialai of the goddess: first shelf, 8 phialai; weight: 1405 dr. 3 ob.

χρυσίδες φιάλαι τῆς θεοῦ πρῶτος ῥυμὸς φιάλαι ὀκτώ σταθμὸν ΧΗΗΗΗΓΙΙΙ

IG II², 1378, add. p. 798 lines 15–16 (399/8)
**1396 lines 26–28 (beg. 4th cent.)**

## II. The Contents of the Opisthodomos

COINS

17.
Attic drachmai

δραχμαὶ Ἀττικαί

IG II², 1453 line 7 (before 350)

18.
A half-drachma piece set in a silver mount

τριώβολον ἀργυρίῳ δεδεμένον

IG II², 1414 line 20 (385/4)
1428 line 145 (367/6)
1455 line 36 (341/0)
**1453 lines 8–9 (after 316/5)**
1459 lines 9–10 (after 340/39)

19.
15 silver ---

---ἀργυρᾶ ΔΓ

IG II², 1447 line 22 (before 371/0)
**1451 line 21 (after 365/4)**

20.
A gold Phokaian coin

χρυσίον Φωκαϊκόν

IG II², 1455 lines 32–3 (341/0)
**1457 line 5 (after 316/5)**
1459 line 6 (after 340/39)

21.
Silver pieces overlaid with gold

ὑπάργυρα χρυσία ἐπίτηκτα

IG II², 1445 line 15 (before 376/5)
**1453 line 2 (before 350)**
1457 line 3 (after 316/5)
1459 lines 3–4 (after 340/39)

22. (V.71)   Of the cursed mixed gold, unmarked --- ; weight: 614 dr. 3 ob.

ἐξαγίστου χρυσίου συμμείκτου ἀσήμου --- σταθμὸν ΓΗΔΗΗΗΙΙΙ

> IG II², 1408 lines 7–8 (398/7)
> **1401 lines 26–7 (394/3)** [Hekatompedon]
> **1400 lines 42–3 (390/89)**
> 1453 lines 2–3 (before 350) [Opisthodomos]

23.   Gold pieces to the Two Goddesses [Demeter and Kore]; weight: 300+ dr.

χρυσῆ τοῖν θεοῖν σταθμὸν Η[Η]Η---

> IG II², **1445 line 34 (376/5)**

24.   [Something made of] overlaid gold; weight: 3 dr.

ἐπίχρυσα ἐπίτηκτα σταθμὸν ΗΗ

> IG II², **1445 line 18 (376/5)**

25.   Uncoined silver, for this year, 20 pieces

ἀργύριον ἄσημον ἐπέτειον ΔΔ

> IG II², **1445 line 36 (376/5)**
> 1453 line 8? (before 350)

26. (V.58)   25 counterfeit silver pieces from Eleusis

ἀργύριον κίβδηλον τὸ Ἐλευσινόθεν ΔΔΓ

> IG II², **1338 line 53–4 (378/7)** [Hekatompedon]
> 1393 lines 33–4 (397/6)
> 1401 line 39 (394/3)
> 1400 line 53 (390/89)
> 1445 line 17 (376/5) [Opisthodomos]

27. (V.78)   Gold plate, weight of this: 15 dr. 4 ob.

χρυσίον ἐπίτηκτον σταθμὸν τούτου ΔΓΙΙΙΙ.

> IG II², 1377 lines 20–1 (399/8) [Hekatompedon]
> **1394 lines 3–4 (397/6)**
> 1395+Ag. I 1182 [*Hesperia* 5 (1936) 390] line 21 (395/4)
> 1447 lines 23–4 (before 371/0) [Opisthodomos]
> 1451 lines 22–3 (after 365/4)
> 1452 line 2 (before 350)

28.   Items taken from the Metroon: A washbasin; weight: 16+ dr. This is not in good condition: [some things] cursed --- sealed with the public seal. To the Two Goddesses [Demeter and Kore], [some things] not in good condition; weight of the first: 700+ dr.; [the second,

--- the third,] weight: 854 dr. 3 ob.; the fourth, weight: 600+ dr.

[ἐκ τ]οῦ Μετρώιου παρακαταθήκη· χερ[νιβεῖον ---
σταθμὸν --] ΔΓⱵ· τοῦτο οὐχ ὑγιές· ἐξαγίστ[ο ---
σεσημασμένα τ]ῇ δημοσίᾳ σφραγῖδι· τοῖν θ[εοῖν ---
ο]ὐχ ὑγιεῖς, σταθμὸν πρώτη ΓΗΗ [--- δευτέρα ---
τρί]τη ΓΗΗΗᚠⱵⱵⱵΙΙΙ· τετάρτη ΓΗ---.

IG II², 1445 lines 24–8 (376/5)


CONTAINERS OTHER THAN VASES

29.                 A stone container[9]
                    κυλιχνὶς λιθίνη
                        IG II², 1448 line 8 (397/6)

30.                 In an ivory container ---
                    ἐν κυλιχνίδι ἐλεφαντίνη---
                        IG II², 1448 line 2 (397/6)

31.                 From the box from Brauron: equestrian head-gear, reins,
                    which Xenotimos, son of Karkinos, dedicated
                    ἐκ τῆς κιβωτοῦ τῆς Βραυρωνόθεν· ἱππικὸς κεκρύφαλος
                    ἐχήνια Ξενότιμος Καρκίνου ἀνέθηκε
                        IG II², 1388 lines 73–4 (398/7)
                            1400 lines 61–2 (390/89)
                            1447 lines 28–9 (before 371/0)
                            1451 lines 27–8 (after 365/4)
                            1452 lines 8–9 (before 350)
                            1455 lines 25–7 (341/0)
                            1459 lines 1–2 (after 340/39)

32.                 From the fifth container ---
                    --- πέμπτης θήκης ---
                        EM 12392 [Hesperia 7 (1938) 272–4] line 3 (402/1 or
                            401/0)

33.                 [In the fifth container] a silver [---] in a box ---
                    --- ος ἀργυροῦς ἐν κοίτῃ ---
                        EM 12392 [Hesperia 7 (1938) 272–4] line 4 (402/1 or
                            401/0)

33.                 From the sixth container ---
                    ἐκ τῆς ἕκτης θήκης ---

---

[9] Cf. Hesych. κυλιχνίδες· πυξίδες. See Thompson (1965) 230-1.

EM 12392 [*Hesperia* 7 (1938) 272–4] line 3 (402/1 or 401/0)

35. From the seventh container ---

ἐκ τῆς ἑβδόμης θήκης ---

IG II², 1399 lines 4–5 (403/2)

36. In a box, two chains, a necklace, two pairs of earrings, these are of gilt wood; bellows, two gilt-wood apples, eight iron rings, of which one is set in unfired gold, a glass seal, five tin earrings

ἐν κιβωτίῳ ὅρμω δύο ὑποδερὶς διοπῶν δύο ζεύγει ταῦτα ὑπόξυλα κατακεχρυσωμένα· φυσητὸν μήλω δύο ὑποξύλω κατακεχρυσωμένω δακτύλιοι σιδηροῖ ὀκτὶ πρὸς ἑνὶ χρυσίον ἄπυρον πρόσεστιν σφραγὶς ὑαλίνη καττιτέρινα ἐνῴδια πέντε

IG II², 1388 lines 75–9 (398/7)
1400 lines 62–4 (390/89)
1447 lines 10–13 (before 371/0)
1450 lines 9–12 (after 366/5)
1451 lines 10–13 (after 365/4)
1449 line 9 (397/6) [glass seal only]
1455 lines 27–32 (341/0)
1457 lines 1–3 (after 316/5)

37. (IV.32; V.164) In a painted box, which Kleito, wife of Aristokrates, son of Oulios, son of Kimon, dedicated, in which box there is a container in which there is a sealstone set in a gold ring, which Dexilla dedicated. A neckband having 12 gold pieces on it, and another one having 12 gold pieces, and another having 7 gold pieces. A choker having 10 gold pieces including some unfired. Two coloured glass seals having golden chains, an onyx having a gold ring, a jasper seal having a gold ring, a glass seal set in gold having a gold ring, a jasper seal set in gold, two seals having silver rings, seven coloured glass seals set in gold, a seal set in gold, a necklace ---

ἐν κιβωτίῳ ποικίλῳ ὃ Κλειτὼ Ἀριστοκράτους τοῦ, Ὀυλίου Κίμωνος γυνὴ ἀνέθηκεν· ἐγ κυλιχνίδι ἑνὶ ἐν τῷ κιβωτίῳ σφραγὶς χρυσοῦν δακτύλιον ἔχουσα· Δέξιλλα ἀνέθηκεν· ὄχθοιβος χρυσία ἔχων δώδεκα· ἕτερος ὄχθοιβος χρυσία ἔχων δώδεκα· ἕτερος ὄχθοιβος χρυσία ἔχων ἑπτά· χλιδὼν χρυσία ἔχων δέκα σὺν τῷ ἀπύρῳ· σφραγῖδε ὑαλίνα ποικίλα

δύο· περικεχρυσωμέναι ἁλύσεις χρυσᾶς ἔχουσαι·
ὄνυξ χρυσοῦν δακτύλιον ἔχων· σφραγὶς ἴασπις
χρυσοῦν δακτύλιον ἔχουσα· σφραγὶς ὑαλίνη
περικεχρυσωμένη χρυσοῦν δακτύλιον ἔχουσα·
σφραγὶς ἴασπις περικεχρυσωμένη· σφραγῖδες δύο
ἀργυροῦς δακτυλίους ἔχουσαι· σφραγῖδες ὑάλιναι
ἑπτὰ ποικίλαι περικεχρυσωμέναι· σφραγὶς
περίχρυσος· ὑποδερίς---

IG II², 1396 lines 23–4 (beg. 4th cent.) [Hekatompedon]
[λίθιναι for ὑάλιναι]
1398 lines 11–12 (399/8) [λίθιναι for ὑάλιναι]
1388 lines 81–91+1408 lines 21–2 (398/7)
**1400 lines 65–71 (390/89) [Opisthodomos]**
1417 line 9 (after 385/4)
1418 lines 18–19 (after 385/4)
1447 lines 15–17 (before 371/0)
1451 lines 15–18 (after 365/4)
1455 lines 33–5 (341/0)
1459 lines 7–8 (after 340/39)
1457 lines 6–7 (after 316/5)

**38.**            Six bronze baskets, corroded.

κανᾶ χαλκᾶ διακεκομμένα ΓΙ

IG II², **1453 lines 6–7 (before 350)**

**39. (V.189)**   In a leather bag: articles in silver, bronze, overlaid wood,
gilt, and silver overlay; weight: 1650 dr. Sealed with the
public seal[10]

ταῦτα μὲν ἐν τῷ φασκώλῳ· ἀργυρία καὶ χαλκία καὶ
ὑπόξυλα καὶ ἐπίχρυσα καὶ ἐπάργυρα σταθμὸν
ΧΡΗϜ σεσήμανται τῇ δημοσίᾳ σφραγῖδι

IG II², 1408 lines 15–16 (398/7) [Hekatompedon]
1409 lines 8–9 (395/4) [Hekatompedon]
**1445 lines 22–4 (376/5)**
1453 lines 8–11 (before 350)

FIGURINES

**40.**            Ivory figurines from the thrones

ζῴδια ἐλεφάντινα ἀπὸ τῶν θρόνων

IG II², **1424a line 116 (371/0)**
1438 line 47 (349/8)
1466 line 9 (321/0)

---

[10] The last phrase, 'sealed with the public seal' was added in *IG* II², 1445 and 1453.

41.　Two ivory hands
χεῖρε ἐλεφαντίνα δύο
　　*IG* II², 1424a line 117 (371/0)

42.　Half a silver serpent
ὄφεως ἀργυροῦ ἥμισυ
　　*IG* II², 1414, add. p. 799, line 21 (after 385/4)
　　1424a line 118 (371/0)

JEWELLERY (see also **36, 37** above)

43.　Two pairs of earrings in gilt wood
διοπῶν ζεύγη δύο ὑπόξυλα κατακεχρυσωμένα
　　*IG* II², 1447 lines 11–12 (before 371/0)
　　1450 lines 10–11 (after 366/5)
　　1451 lines 11–12 (after 365/4)

44.　Two seals having silver rings, sacred to Artemis Brauronia
Ἀρτέμιδος Βραυρωνίας σφραγῖδε δύο ἀργυροῦς
δακτυλίους ἔχουσαι
　　*IG* II², 1447 lines 26–7 (before 371/0)
　　1451 lines 25–7 (after 365/4)

45.　A stone seal bound in silver, of Artemis Brauronia
Ἀρτέμιδος Βραυρωνίας σφραγὶς λιθίνη ἀργυρίῳ
δεδεμένη
　　*IG* II², 1447 lines 25–6 (before 371/0)
　　1452 lines 4–5 (before 350)

46.　A jasper seal of Artemis Brauronia
Ἀρτέμιδος Βραυρωνίας σφραγὶς ἴασπις
　　*IG* II², 1447 lines 24–5 (before 371/0)
　　1451 lines 24–5 (after 365/4)

47.　2 gold earrings; weight: ---
ἐνῳδίω δύο χρυσὼ σταθμὸν ---
　　*IG* II², 1448 line 10 (before 397/6)

48.　2 silver earrings overlaid with gold ---
ἐνῳδίω ἀργυρὼ ‖ ἐπιχρύσω κα[---
　　*IG* II², 1445 line 14 (before 376/5)

49.　A sard sealstone with ring
σφραγίδιον σάρδιον δακτυλι[---

IG II², 1445 line 20 (before 376/5)

50.            Two silver gilt rings
               δακτύλιοι ΙΙ ὑπάργυροι
                       IG II², 1445 line 21 (before 376/5)

51.            A circular silver ring
               δακτύλιος ἀργυροῦς ἀπείρων
                       IG II², 1436 line 71 (350/49)
                               1455 line 32 (341/0)
                               1457 line 5 (after 316/5)
                               1459 lines 5–6 (shortly after 340/39)
                               1478 lines 29–30 (after 316/5)

52.            A gold ring in a container
               δακτύλιος χρυσοῦς ἐγ κυλιχνίδι
                       IG II², 1445 line 40 (376/5)
                               1447 line 3 (before 371/0)

53.            [Seals] without rings, in a container
               σφραγῖδες [---] ἄνευ δακτυλίων ἐγ κυλιχνίδι
                       IG II², 1445 lines 44–5 (376/5)
                               1447 lines 7–8 (before 371/0)

54.            A headband with ornament
               χλιδώνιον τέττιγα ἔχον
                       IG II², 1455 lines 35–6 (341/0)
                               1459 line 9 (after 340/39)
                               1457 line 8 (after 316/5)

55.            2 headbands having gold pieces
               χλιδωνίω δύο χρυσία ἔχοντε
                       IG II², 1449 lines 3–4 (397/6)
                               1445 line 46 (376/5)
                               1447 line 9 (after 371/0)

56. (V.159)    A sard seal having a silver ring
               σφραγίδιον σάρδιον δακτύλιον ἀργυροῦν ἔχουσα
                       IG II², 1408 lines 8–9 (398/7) [Hekatompedon]
                               1409 line 3 (395/4)
                               1424a line 112 (371/0)
                               1425 line 107 (368/7)

57. (V.159)    Two sards set in silver
               σάρδια δύο ἀργυρίω δεδεμένα
                       IG II², 1455 lines 34–5 (341/0) [Opisthodomos]

1459 line 8 (shortly after 340/39)

**1457 lines 7–8 (after 316/5)**

58.    Two seals having silver rings

σφραγῖδες δύο ἀργυροῦς δακτυλίος ἔχουσαι

**IG II², 1338 lines 89–90+1408 lines 21–2 (398/7)**

1400 line 70 (390/89)

1409 line 12 (395/4)

1447 line 17 (before 371/0)

1451 line 17 (after 365/4)

1457 lines 6–7 (after 316/5)

1459 lines 7–8 (shortly after 340/39)

MISCELLANEOUS

59.    Of the doors of the Opisthodomos ---

τῶν θυρῶν τοῦ ὀπισθοδόμου ---

**IG II², 1471 line 60 (after 318/7)**

60. (V.203)    The doors, the ones in the Hekatompedon, are lacking these parts, and are not complete. Around the lion's head is missing 1 of the leaves, and around the front part of the ram 5 of the smaller leaves are missing. Around the front part of the gorgon's head is missing a strip of moulding about eight dactyls long. The nails in the lowest row of the door are lacking three poppy-heads, two on one side, one on the other. These are in the care of the treasurers in the transfer. Starting from the first nail of the right door some gold has fallen off, to a length of ten dactyls, eleven dactyls across, and two dactyls in depth. The right door-jamb [---] lacks 48, the left door-jamb lacks 44 [small bosses]. In the Hekatompedon ---

αἱ θύραι αἱ ἐν τῷ ἑκατομπέδῳ τῶνδε δέονται μὴ ἐντελεῖς εἶναι· περὶ τὴν τοῦ λέοντος κεφαλὴν ἐλλείπει τῶν φύλλων Ι περὶ δὲ τὴν τοῦ κριοῦ προτομὴν φύλλων ἐλλείπει τῶν ἐλαττόνων Γ περὶ τὴν τοῦ γοργονείου ἐλλείπει τοῦ κυματίου ὅσον ἐπὶ ὀκτὼ δακτύλους· οἱ ἦλοι οἱ ἐν τοῖς κατωτάτω ζυγοῖς τῶν θυρῶν δέονται κωδυῶν τριῶν· ἐμ μὲν τῷ δυοῖν, ἐν δὲ τῷ μιᾶς· αὗταί εἰσι παρὰ τοῖς ταμίαις ἐν τῇ παραδόσει· ἀπὸ τοῦ πρώτου ἤλου τῆς δεξιᾶς θύρας τοῦ χρυσίου ἀποπέπτωκεν μῆκος οἷον ἐπὶ δέκα δακτύλους·

πλάτος ἐπὶ δακτύλους ἔνδεκα· κάτωθεν ἐπὶ δύο
δακτύλους· ἡ δεξιὰ παραστὰς --- δεῖται ΔΔΔΔΓΙΙΙ
ἡ ἀριστερὰ παραστὰς πο[μφολύγων] δεῖται
ΔΔΔΔΙΙΙΙ· ἐν τῷ Ἑκατομπέδῳ ---

*IG* II², 1455 lines 36–49 (341/0)
1457 lines 9–20 (after 316/5)

61.        These things are gilt wood: a seal ---

           ταῦτα ὑπόξυλα κατακεχρυσωμένα· σφραγίς ---

           *IG* II², 1445 lines 28–9 (341/0)
           1457 line 2 (after 316/5)

62.        A purple snood

           μίτρα ἁλουργής

           *IG* II², 1448 line 4 (397/6)

63.        --- corroded, [wrapped] in linen ---

           --- κεκομμένον ἐν ὀθονίῳ---

           *IG* II², 1433 line 22 (between 384/3 and 378/7)
           1455 line 31 (341/0)
           **1457 line 4 (after 316/5)**
           1459 lines 4–5 (340/39)

64.        A *pentorobos* silver-plated, of Artemis Brauronia ---
           another one, broken, silver-plated

           Ἀρτέμιδος Βραυρωνίας πεντώροβος ἐπάργυρος ---
           ἄλλος διερρωγὼς ἐπάργυρος

           *IG* II², 1447 lines 29–30 (before 371/0)
           1451 lines 29–30 (after 365/4)
           1452 line 7 (before 350)

65.        [Something] stone to the Two Goddesses [Demeter and
           Kore], unweighed

           λιθίνη τοῖν θεοῖν ἄστατος

           *IG* II², 1447 line 21 (before 371/0)
           1451 lines 19–20 (after 365/4)

66.        [Something] which Sophokles of Kolonos, son of Iophon,
           dedicated

           Σοφοκλῆς Ἰοφῶντος ἐκ Κολωνοῦ ἀνέθηκε

           *IG* II², 1445 lines 37–8 (376/5)

67.        Weighing-beam with silver-gilt scales

           ζυγὸν ὑπαργύρους ἐπιχρύσους πλάστιγγας ἔχον

           *IG* II², 1448 line 7 (397/6)

EM 12963 [*Hesperia* 41 (1972) 423–4] line 4 (397/6)
*IG* II², 1447 lines 18–19 (before 371/0)
    1451 lines 18–19 (after 365/4)

MUSICAL INSTRUMENTS

68.    An ivory aulos-case, gilt
       συβήνη ἐλεφαντίνη κατάχρυσος
       *IG* II², 1388 line 75 (398/7)
           1400 line 62 (390/89)

69.    An ivory aulos-case, without gold, unusable
       συβήνη ἐλεφαντίνη ἄχρυσος ἄχρηστος
       *IG* II², 1447 line 10 (before 371/0)
           1450 lines 8–9 (after 366/5)
           1451 lines 9–10 (after 365/4)
           1461 line 8 (after 330/29)

70.    An ivory aulos-case
       συβήνη ἐλεφαντίνη
       *IG* II², 1461 line 13 (after 330/29)

71.    These things Thaumarete, wife of Timonides, dedicated;
       in a box: an ivory lyre and an ivory plectrum.
       ταῦτα Θαυμαρέτη ἀνέθηκεν Τιμωνίδου γυνὴ ἐγ
       κιβωτίῳ· λύριον ἐλεφάντινον καὶ πλῆκτρον
       *IG* II², 1388, add. p. 798 lines 79–80 (398/7)
           1400 lines 64–5 (390/89)
           1421 line 119 (374/3)
           1447 line 14 (before 371/0)
           1424a line 304 (371/0)
           1443 line 202 (344/3)
           1451 lines 13–15 (after 365/4)
           1460 lines 19–21 (after 330/29)

TOOLS

72.    A sling
       σφενδόνη
       *IG* II², 1448 line 3 (397/6)

73.    A gold muzzle
       κημὸς χρυσοῦς
       *IG* II², 1448 line 11 (397/6)

74.            4 iron anvils, 2 hammers, 22 dies.

ἄκμονες σιδηροῖ ΙΙΙΙ· σφῦραι ΙΙ· χαρακτῆρες ΔΔΙΙ.

IG II², 1424a line 119 (371/0)

75.            A box: 299 arrows, and 20 more this year.

κιβωτός· σώρακοι τοξευμάτων ΗΗϜΔΔΔΔΓΙΙΙΙ
ἐπετείου ΔΔ.

IG II², 1424a lines 121–2 (371/0)

76.            Two bronze nails overlaid with silver and gold; weight:
---

ἧλοι χαλκοῖ δύο ἐπάργυροι ἐπίχρυσοι σταθμὸν ---

IG II², 1453 lines 3–4 (before 350)

77.            Two nails, overlaid with silver and gold; weight: 2 dr.
3 ob.

ἧλοι ἐπάργυροι ἐπίχρυσοι σταθμὸν ϜϜΙΙΙ

IG II², 1453 lines 4–5 (before 350)

VASES

78.            A silver wine-jug
οἰνοχόη ἀργυρᾶ

IG II², 1401 lines 19–20 (394/3)
1400 line 36 (390/89)
1404 line 2 (393/2?)

79.            A silver wine-jug, sacred to Demeter
οἰνοχόη ἀργυρᾶ ἱερὰ Δήμητρος

IG II², 1445 line 9 (376/5)

80.            A silver wine-jug, sacred; weight: 200 + dr.
οἰνοχόη ἀργυρᾶ ἱερὰ σταθμὸν ΗΗ---

IG II², 1445 line 12 (376/5)

81.            A silver wine-jug, broken
οἰνοχόη ἀργυρᾶ κατεαγυῖα

IG II², 1445 line 29 (376/5)

82. (V.351)    Gold phialai of Artemis Brauronia
Ἀρτέμιδος Βραυρωνίας χρυσίδες

IG II², 1386 lines 4–5 (401/0) [Hekatompedon]
1388 lines 49–50 (398/7)
1400 line 39 (390/89)

1447 lines 22–4 (before 371/0) [Opisthodomos]
1451 lines 22–4 (after 365/4)

83. (V.302)    A tin phiale

φιάλη καττιτερίνη

IG II², 1455 line 31 (341/0)
**1457 line 4 (after 316/5)**
1459 line 5 (after 340/39)

84.    Silver phialai --- first shelf 20 phialai; weight: 1926 dr.
Second shelf 20 phialai; weight: 1931 dr. Third shelf
---

ἀργυραῖ φιάλαι --- πρῶτος ῥυμὸς φιάλαι ΔΔ
σταθμὸν ΧΡΗΗΗΗΔΔΓΙ· δεύτερος ῥυμὸς φιάλαι
ΔΔ σταθμὸν ΧΡΗΗΗΗΔΔΔΙ· τρίτος ῥυμὸς
φιάλαι ---

IG II², 1445 lines 31–4 (376/5)

85.    Two phialai

φιάλαι δύο

IG II², 1445 line 36 (376/5)

86.    A phiale dedicated in the archonship of Alkisthenes
[372/1]; weight: 100 dr.

ἐπὶ Ἀλκισθένους φιάλη σταθμὸν Η

**Akropolis 18/5/89 line 6 (after 360/59)**

87.    A phiale dedicated in the archonship of Phrasikleides
[371/0]; weight ---

ἐπὶ Φρασικλείδου φιάλη σταθμὸν ---

IG II², 1451 line 5 (after 365/4)
**Akropolis 18/5/89 line 7 (after 360/59)**

88.    A phiale dedicated in the archonship of Lysistratos
[369/8], unmarked; weight: 181 dr. 3 ob.

ἐπὶ Λυσιστράτου φιάλη ἄσημον σταθμὸν ΗϜΔΔΔΗΙΙΙ

**Akropolis 18/5/89 line 8 (after 360/59)**
**Robinson Coll. [AJP 58 (1937) 43] lines 2–3**
**(after 352/1)**

89.    A phiale dedicated in the archonship of Nausigenes
[368/7]; weight: 100 dr.

ἐπὶ Ναυσιγένους φιάλη σταθμὸν Η

Akropolis 18/5/89 line 9 (after 360/59)
**Robinson Coll. [AJP 58 (1937) 43] lines 4–5**
**(after 352/1)**

90. A phiale dedicated in the archonship of Polyzelos [367/6]; weight: 100 dr.

ἐπὶ Πολυζήλου φιάλη σταθμὸν Η

> *IG* II², 1450 line 5 (after 366/5)
> 1451 line 7 (after 365/4)
> **Akropolis 18/5/89 line 9 (after 360/59)**
> Robinson Coll. [*AJP* 58 (1937) 43] lines 6–7 (after 352/1)

91. A phiale, dedicated in the archonship of Kephisodoros [366/5]; weight: 100 dr.

ἐπὶ Κηφισοδώρου φιάλη σταθμὸν Η

> *IG* II², 1450 lines 5–6 (after 366/5)
> **Akropolis 18/5/89 line 10 (after 360/59)**
> Robinson Coll. [*AJP* 58 (1937) 43] line 8 (after 352/1)

92. A phiale dedicated in the archonship of Chion [365/4]; weight: 163 dr. 3 ob.

ἐπὶ Χίωνος φιάλη σταθμὸν ΗϜΔΗΗΙΙΙ

> *IG* II², 1451 line 9 (after 365/4)
> **Akropolis 18/5/89 lines 10–11 (after 360/59)**

93. A phiale dedicated in the archonship of Timokrates [364/3]; weight: ---

ἐπὶ Τιμοκράτους φιάλη σταθμὸν ---

> **Akropolis 18/5/89 lines 11–12 (after 360/59)**

94. A phiale dedicated in the archonship of Charikleides [363/2]; weight: 100 dr.

ἐπὶ Χαρικλείδου φιάλη σταθμὸν Η

> **Akropolis 18/5/89 line 12 (after 360/59)**

95. A phiale dedicated in the archonship of Molon (362/1); weight: ---

ἐπὶ Μόλωνος φιάλη σταθμὸν ---

> **Akropolis 18/5/89 lines 12–13 (after 360/59)**

96. A phiale dedicated in the archonship of Kallimedes [360/59]; weight: 100 dr. 1 ob.

ἐπὶ Καλλιμήδους φιάλη σταθμὸν ΗΙ

> **Akropolis 18/5/89 line 14 (after 360/59)**

97. A phiale; weight: 80+ dr.

φιάλη σταθμὸν ϜΔΔΔ---

> *IG* II², 1450 lines 6–7 (after 366/5)

98.          A [phiale;] weight: 88 dr.

--- σταθμὸν ⊢ΔΔΔΓⱶⱶ

IG II², 1450 lines 7–8 (after 366/5)

99.          Gold phiale

χρυσίς

IG II², 1445 line 13 (376/5)

100.         A silver washbasin, broken

χερνιβεῖον ἀργυροῦν κατεαγώς

IG II², 1445 line 30 (376/5)

## OBSERVATIONS

Most of the objects inventoried in the Opisthodomos are made of gold and silver. These were valuable for their material and would have been useful in case an emergency minting was required. The precious metals were kept in the Opisthodomos to supplement the financial resources of Athens. In addition to minted coins, the anvils, hammers, and dies used for minting were kept in the Opisthodomos (74).

In contrast to the Hekatompedon and Erechtheion, no wreaths were kept in the Opisthodomos. Wreaths may have been given to Athena only on the occasion of an annual festival, and were not a part of the traditions associated with the treasures of the other gods: IG II², 2311 lists wreaths given as prizes to the athletes at the Panathenaia, and some of these may have become votive offerings.

There were many more sealstones in the Opisthodomos than in any other building on the Akropolis (36–7, 44–6, 49, 53, 56–8). The seals identified as coming from the Opisthodomos were in precious stones, glass, gold, and silver, sometimes with rings or chains or set in gold or silver, amounting to over thirty-eight in number.

The seven seals in the Opisthodomos (38) were inventoried in different years both as λίθιναι and ὑάλιναι, which suggests that they were rock crystal. Perhaps the treasurers in various years could not tell the difference between the glass and rock crystal, or, alternatively, this may be evidence that ὑάλινος means 'rock crystal' in the fourth century. Boardman noted that the adjective ψίλαι, tentatively given as 'bare' above (6), may be an indication either that the seals had no device engraved on them, or that they were unmounted ring-stones.[11]

Only in the Opisthodomos do we have any tin items, the five earrings (36). The eight iron rings (also 36) were kept in the Opisthodomos and belonged to the Treasurers of the Other Gods. Linders noted that the iron rings were kept in the same box as gold rings and other valuables, and that the term δακτύλιοι (lit. 'finger-rings') is used for them.[12]

These inventories give more information about the methods of storage than the other inventories of the Akropolis. Specific references are made to boxes and baskets which were used to store smaller items—for example, the numbered containers used to keep silver wine-jugs and the like (32–5), or the baskets used to store 'ivories' (9, 10, 15). These ivories may be slivers or pieces from the cult statue or from ivory furniture and musical instruments that had separated from the original objects. For a clear example of this note the 'ivory figurines from the thrones' (40).

A few baskets were identified by the decorations on their exterior, notably Zeus and Apollo, either depicted or possibly inscribed on the exterior of bronze and gold chests (3, 4). Others contained personal dedications, such as the ivory lyre with plectrum dedicated by Thaumarete, wife of Timonides (71), or the variety of jewellery given by Kleito and Dexilla (37). In addition to boxes and baskets, a leather bag is inventoried, containing miscellaneous pieces of value, and sealed with the public seal (39). Many other such sacks were probably used but not inventoried. Leather bags may have been the principal type of container used to store coinage or collect taxes. There may be another example, though not explicit, in 97.

Wooden chests were unweighed, but those of bronze weighed thousands of drachmas. Wood was not given value based on weight, so there was no point in weighing wooden objects. In the entry recording 299 arrows (72) it is stated that twenty more were added that year (371/0). This raises many questions: were the arrows used or new? In storage or dedicated? And was this a regular annual practice or just occasional? What were the historical circumstances for the use of these weapons in 371/0? Finally, this entry does suggest that there may have been many more items inside the Opisthodomos than were listed in the inventories. This in turn

---

[11] Boardman (1970) 429.       [12] Linders (1975).

raises the crucial issue of the inventories: if an inventory is not thorough or complete, then what is its purpose?

Many other inventories record broken or useless items. This is especially apparent in those of Delos, but may be found elsewhere such as in the recently published inventory from Miletos.[13] Such examples demonstrate that all items kept in sanctuaries need not have been valuable or complete; evidence for repairs to pottery and statues in sanctuaries indicates this as well.[14]

There were a number of vases, of which the principal shapes were the phiale and oinochoe (wine-jug). Does this suggest that libations of wine were made in this room, or that the objects were stored together for ritual use? Whereas the Erechtheion had one incense burner, of gold, set into the floor of the temple, the Opisthodomos had four which were transferred to the Hekatompedon at the beginning of the fourth century (9–12). Perhaps they were in storage for ceremonies performed by the priests of the other gods; or was the Opisthodomos also a sacred building with rituals involving incense?

The majority of items were vases made of precious metals, silver and gold. In the fifth-century lists of the treasures kept in the Parthenon, the terms φιάλη and ἀργυρίς were virtually interchangeable. Phialai averaging 100 drachmas in weight were kept as reserve bullion. One particularly important entry in this regard is **82**, where the phialai were collected and weighed together and referred to as 'the first group of 20', and there are a minimum of three such groups listed in the inventory of 376/5.[15] The vases kept in the Opisthodomos tend not to be decorative pieces composed of gold and silver, but were solid and capable of yielding unadulterated coin when melted. There were fewer ritual shapes (krateres, lustral basins, incense-burners), and more phialai than any other type. This also suggests that the vases kept in the Opisthodomos were there for the intrinsic value of their metal and less for their functional application in festivals or as votive offerings. This would lead one to expect that the phialai dedicated by freedmen or paid as part of fines in civil suits should appear in the Akropolis inventories. They may have been stored in sacks or chests, but are not mentioned at all unless it is in this instance (**22**).

---

[13] See Günther (1988).

[14] Cf. Harris (1992) for broken bronze statues on the Akropolis in the 4th cent.

[15] *IG* II², 1445 lines 31–4 (376/5).

# PART III

# The Treasures of the Proneos

## THE FUNCTION OF THE PRONEOS

The Parthenon has some architectural peculiarities which suggest that the interior was designed with its function as a treasury in mind. The Proneos is deeper than the Opisthodomos, and has a sculpted Lesbian cyma plus an Ionic frieze over the cross-wall and door between the Proneos and Hekatompedon.[1] All of the walls had wall-crowns, but most were painted, rather than sculpted, with Lesbian leaf.[2] The door into the Opisthodomos was larger than that leading into the Proneos, with the height of the former cutting into the level of the entablature.[3]

It is a well-known fact that no two temples are identical in plan. Where differences are seen, they may be due to cult function, or to the architect's personal style.[4] Both the Parthenon and the temple of Zeus at Olympia share the feature of having a large portion of the interior space devoted to the cult statue and reflecting pond.[5] Yet the interior of the Parthenon is far larger than that of the temple of Zeus. The outer stylobate is the same, but an effort was made in the case of the Parthenon to reduce the space occupied by the columns on the inside and create a generous interior. At Olympia the statue looked squeezed in; in the Parthenon Athena was placed within an appropriate architectural frame. There were two large windows in the east wall of the temple, aligned with the side aisles of the interior cella.[6] The evidence of the moulding and frieze inside the Proneos, the elaborate door leading into the Hekatompedon, the two-storeyed Π-shaped interior colonnade, the reflecting pond, and the decorated wall-crowns of the interior all point to one con-

---

[1] Korres and Bouras (1983) 668–9.
[2] Korres (1989) 9.
[3] Korres (pers. comm. 1990).
[4] Corbett (1970) 152. An example of the adjustment of architectural design to cult needs may be seen in the Erechtheion, where the building incorporates the olive-tree, the trident-mark, the grave of Kekrops, and other shrines into one temple.
[5] Corbett (1970) 152.
[6] Korres and Bouras (1983) 668; Korres (1989) 9.

clusion: the architecture of the Parthenon was as concerned with the interior space as with outward appearance.

The Proneos of the Parthenon differed from the traditional Doric temple plan in having a hexastyle colonnade across the entrance, instead of just two columns before the *antae*. The six columns were grilled, with metal screens which prevented access except at the centre. The central passage into the main cella was a double door which swung inwards and locked. The marble threshold is worn down considerably and semicircular gashes in the floor preserve the memory of the swinging doors. On some sides of the lower courses of the column drums, flattened and chiselled marks indicate the placement of the grilled screens. Any treasures kept inside the Proneos may have been partially visible through the screens, gleaming as sunlight reflected off the silver and gold.

In comparison with traditional temple plans, the Proneos of this temple was wider and yet more shallow in proportion to the temple as a whole. The *antae* barely stretch beyond the cella, reducing the length of the Proneos and creating an exaggerated sense of the breadth, as opposed to the traditional axial plan. The extra width would have been useful in storing and stacking treasures at the sides while allowing for a relatively unimpeded passage to the doors leading into the main cella.

The treasures grew by small amounts each year from 434/3 to 408/7. After the melting at the end of the Peloponnesian war, the Proneos was no longer used for storing treasures, and therefore no more lists were published.[7] In the last inventory of the Proneos only one item remained: 'gold wreath; weight of this 33 dr. 3 obols' (**III.41** below).

### THE TREASURES OF THE PRONEOS

Below are listed the treasures kept in the Proneos from 434/3 to 408/7. They are all vase shapes, and the Proneos is therefore very different from the other rooms in the temple, lacking the variety of types of objects.

1.          A small (goblet) in a small box, gilt wood
            καρχήσιον μικρὸν ἐγ καλιάδι ὑπόξυλον κατάχρυσον

[7] Cf. Dinsmoor and Ferguson (1933).

IG I³, 292 line 13 (434/3)
    293 lines 22–3 (433/2)
    **294 lines 33–4 (432/1)**

2.    3 silver drinking-horns; weight of these 528 dr.

κέρατα ἀργυρᾶ ΙΙΙ σταθμὸν τούτων ΓΔΔΓΗΗ

IG I³, 292 lines 7–8 (434/3)
    293 line 20 (433/2)
    294 line 32 (432/1)
    295 line 43 (431/0)
    **296 line 7 (430/29)**
    297 lines 18–19 (429/8)
    298 lines 31–2 (428/7)
    299 lines 44–5 (427/6)
    300 line 8 (426/5)
    301 line 20 (425/4)
    302 line 32 (424/3)
    303 line 43 (423/2)
    305 lines 8–9 (418/7)
    306 line 28 (417/6)
    307 line 49 (416/5)
    308 line 69 (415/4)
    309 line 6 (414/3)
    310 line 22 (413/2)
    311 line 39 (412/1)
    312 line 56 (411)
    313 line 75 (411/0)
    314 lines 5–6 (409/8)
    315 lines 32–3 (408/7)

3.    A silver wine cup; unweighed

κύλιξ ἀργυρᾶ ἄσταθμος

IG I³, 306 lines 40–1 (417/6)
    307 line 61 (416/5)
    308 line 80 (415/4)
    **309 line 16 (414/3)**
    310 line 32 (413/2)
    **311 line 49 (412/1)**
    313 line 85 (411/0)

4.    A silver lamp; weight of this: 38 dr.

λύχνος ἀργυροῦς σταθμὸν τούτου ΔΔΔΓΗΗ

IG I³, 292 line 9 (434/3)
    293 lines 21–2 (433/2)
    **294 line 33 (432/1)**
    295 line 44 (431/0)
    296 line 9 (430/29)

297 lines 19–20 (429/8)
298 lines 32–3 (428/7)
299 line 46 (427/6)
300 line 9 (426/5)
301 line 21 (425/4)
302 line 33 (424/3)
303 line 44 (423/2)
305 lines 9–10 (418/7)
306 line 29 (417/6)
307 line 50 (416/5)
308 line 70 (415/4)
309 line 7 (414/3)
310 line 23 (413/2)
311 line 40 (412/1)
312 lines 56–7 (411)
313 lines 75–6 (411/0)
314 lines 6–7 (409/8)
315 lines 33–4 (408/7)

5.    A silver lamp; weight of this: 22 dr.

λύχνος ἀργυροῦς σταθμὸν τούτου ΔΔͰͰ

IG I³, 303 line 49 (423/2)
**305 line 16 (418/7)**
**306 lines 35–6 (417/6)**
307 lines 56–7 (416/5)
308 lines 75–6 (415/4)
309 line 12 (414/3)
310 line 28 (413/2)
311 line 45 (412/1)
313 line 81 (411/0)
314 line 15 (409/8)
315 line 42 (408/7)

6.    A gold phiale from which lustrations are made; unweighed

φιάλη χρυσᾶ ἐξ ἧς ἀπορραίνονται ἄσταθμος

IG I³, 292 lines 6–7 (434/3)
293 lines 18–19 (433/2)
294 lines 30–1 (432/1)
295 lines 50–1 (431/0)
**296 line 6 (430/29)**
297 line 17 (429/8)
298 lines 30–1 (428/7)
299 lines 43–4 (427/6)
300 line 7 (426/5)
301 line 19 (425/4)
302 line 31 (424/3)

303 line 42 (423/2)
305 line 7 (418/7)
306 lines 26–7 (417/6)
307 lines 47–8 (416/5)
308 line 68 (415/4)
309 line 5 (414/3)

In the following list of phialai, note that the base number grows each year with the addition of a few more, and a running tally of phialai is recorded.

7.          104 silver phialai; weight of these 10,500+ dr.
            φιάλαι ἀργυραῖ ΗΙΙΙΙ σταθμὸν τούτων ΜΓ---
            *IG* I³, 292 line 7 (434/3)

8.          9 silver phialai; weight of these: 970+ dr.
            φιάλαι ἀργυραῖ ΓΙΙΙΙ σταθμὸν τούτων ΡΗΗΗΗϜΔΔ---
            *IG* I³, 292 line 12 (434/3) [total = 113 phialai]

9.          113 silver phialai; weight of these: 11,500+ dr.
            φιάλαι ἀργυραῖ ΗΔΙΙΙ σταθμὸν τούτων ΜΧΓ---
            *IG* I³, 293 lines 19–20 (434/3)

10.         2 silver phialai; weight of these: --- dr.
            φιάλα ἀργυρᾶ ΙΙ σταθμὸν τούτοιν ---
            *IG* I³, 293 line 24–5 (433/2) [total = 115 phialai]

11.         115 silver phialai; weight of these: --- dr.
            φιάλαι ἀργυραῖ ΗΔΓ σταθμὸν τούτων ---
            *IG* I³, 294 line 31 (432/1)

12.         3 silver phialai; weight of these: --- dr.
            φιάλαι ἀργυραῖ ΙΙΙ σταθμὸν τούτων ---
            *IG* I³, 294 lines 35–6 (432/1) [total = 118 phialai]

13.         118 silver phialai; weight of these: 2 talents+
            φιάλαι ἀργυραῖ ΗΔΓΙΙΙ σταθμὸν τούτων ΤΤ---
            *IG* I³, 295 line 42 (432/1)

14.         3 silver phialai; weight of these: --- dr.
            φιάλαι ἀργυραῖ ΙΙΙ σταθμὸν τούτων ---
            *IG* I³, 295 lines 45–6 (431/0) [total = 121 phialai]

15.         121 silver phialai; weight of these: 2 talents 432 dr.

φιάλαι ἀργυραῖ ΗΔΔΙ σταθμὸν τούτων
ΤΤΗΗΗΗΔΔΔΗ

    *IG* I³, 296 lines 6–7 (430/29)
          297 lines 17–18 (429/28)
          298 line 31 (428/7)
          299 line 44 (427/6)
          300 lines 7–8 (426/5)
          301 lines 19–20 (425/4)
          302 lines 31–2 (424/3)
          303 lines 42–3 (423/2)
          305 lines 7–8 (418/7)
          306 lines 27–8 (417/6)
          307 lines 48–9 (416/5)
          308 lines 68–9 (415/4)
          309 lines 5–6 (414/3)
          310 line 22 (413/2)
          311 lines 38–9 (412/1)
          312 lines 55–6 (411)
          313 lines 74–5 (411/0)
          314 lines 4–5 (409/8)
          315 lines 31–2 (408/7)

16.        7 silver phialai; weight of these: 700 dr.

    φιάλαι ἀργυραῖ ΓΙΙ σταθμὸν τούτων ΡΗΗ

    *IG* I³, 297 line 22 (429/8)
          298 lines 33–4 (428/7)
          299 lines 46–7 (427/6)
          300 line 9 (426/5)
          301 lines 21–2 (425/4)
          302 line 33 (424/3)
          303 line 44 (423/2)
          305 line 10 (418/7)
          306 lines 29–30 (417/6)
          307 lines 50–1 (416/5)
          308 lines 70–1 (415/4)
          309 line 7 (414/3)
          310 lines 23–4 (413/2)
          311 line 40 (412/1)
          312 line 57 (411)
          313 line 76 (411/0)
          314 lines 7–8 (409/8)
          315 lines 34–5 (408/7)

17.        2 silver phialai; weight of these: 200 dr.

    φιάλα ἀργυρᾶ ΙΙ σταθμὸν τούτοιν ΗΗ

    *IG* I³, 298 lines 35–6 (428/7)
          299 lines 47–8 (427/6)

300 line 10 (426/5)
301 line 22 (425/4)
302 line 34 (424/3)
303 line 45 (423/2)
305 line 11 (418/7)
306 lines 30–1 (417/6)
307 lines 51–2 (416/5)
308 lines 71–2 (415/4)
309 line 8 (414/3)
310 lines 24–5 (413/2)
311 line 41 (412/1)
312 line 58 (411)
313 line 77 (411/0)
314 line 9 (409/8)
315 line 36 (408/7)

18.    4 silver phialai; weight of these: 329 dr.

φιάλαι ἀργυραῖ ΙΙΙΙ σταθμὸν τούτων ΗΗΗΔΔΓⱵⱵⱵⱵ

IG I³, 299 line 50 (427/6)
300 lines 10–11 (426/5)
301 line 23 (425/4)
302 line 34 (424/3)
303 line 45 (423/2)
305 lines 11–12 (418/7)
306 line 31 (417/6)
**307 line 52 (416/5)**
308 line 72 (415/4)
309 lines 8–9 (414/3)
310 line 25 (413/2)
311 lines 41–2 (412/1)
312 line 58 (411)
313 line 77 (411/0)
314 lines 9–10 (409/8)
315 lines 36–7 (408/7)

19.    7 silver phialai; weight of these: 920 dr. [dedicated in 426/5]

φιάλαι ἀργυραῖ ΓΙΙ σταθμὸν τούτων ΓΗΗΗΗΔΔ

IG I³, 300 line 12 (426/5)
301 line 24 (425/4)
**302 line 35 (424/3)**
303 line 46 (423/2)
305 lines 12–13 (418/7)
306 line 32 (417/6)
307 line 53 (416/5)
308 line 73 (415/4)
309 lines 9–10 (414/3)

310 line 26 (413/2)
311 lines 42–3 (412/1)
312 line 59 (411)
313 line 78 (411/0)
314 line 11 (409/8)
315 line 38 (408/7)

20.    4 silver phialai; weight of these: 420 dr.

φιάλαι ἀργυραῖ ΙΙΙΙ σταθμὸν τούτων ΗΗΗΗΔΔ

*IG* I³, 301 lines 25–6 (425/4)
302 lines 35–6 (424/3)
303 lines 46–7 (423/2)
**305 line 13 (418/7)**
306 lines 32–3 (417/6)
**307 lines 53–4 (416/5)**
308 line 73 (415/4)
309 line 10 (414/3)
310 line 26 (413/2)
311 line 43 (412/1)
312 lines 59–60 (411)
313 lines 78–9 (411/0)
314 lines 12–13 (409/8)
315 lines 39–40 (408/7)

21.    7 silver phialai; weight of these: 643 dr. 2 ob.

φιάλαι ἀργυραῖ ΓΙΙ σταθμὸν τούτων ΡΗΔΔΔΔΗΗΙΙ

*IG* I³, **302 lines 36–7 (424/3)**
303 lines 47–8 (423/2)
305 lines 14–15 (418/7)
**306 line 34 (417/6)**
307 lines 54–5 (416/5)
308 line 74 (415/4)
309 lines 10–11 (414/3)
310 line 27 (413/2)
311 line 44 (412/1)
312 lines 60–1 (411)
313 lines 79–80 (411/0)
314 line 13 (409/8)
315 lines 40–1 (408/7)

22.    3 silver phialai; weight of these: 251 dr.

φιάλαι ἀργυραῖ ΙΙΙ σταθμὸν τούτων ΗΗΓⱵ

*IG* I³, 303 lines 48–9 (423/2)
**305 line 15 (418/7)**
306 lines 34–5 (417/6)
307 lines 55–6 (416/5)
308 lines 74–5 (415/4)

309 line 11 (414/3)
310 lines 27–8 (413/2)
311 line 44 (412/1)
312 line 61 (411)
**313 line 80 (411/0)**
314 lines 13–14 (409/8)
315 line 41 (408/7)

23.        3 silver phialai; weight of these: 294 dr.

φιάλαι ἀργυραῖ ΙΙΙ σταθμὸν τούτων ΗΗΓΔΔΔΔΗΗΗ

*IG* I³, 305 lines 16–17 (418/7)
306 line 36 (417/6)
307 line 57 (416/5)
**308 line 76 (415/4)**
309 lines 12–13 (414/3)
310 line 29 (413/2)
311 lines 45–6 (412/1)
313 line 81 (411/0)
314 lines 15–16 (409/8) [reads ἀργυρίδες]
315 lines 42–3 (408/7) [reads ἀργυρίδες]

24.        5 silver phialai; weight of these: 413 dr.

φιάλαι ἀργυραῖ Γ σταθμὸν τούτων ΗΗΗΗΔΗΗΗ

*IG* I³, 304 line 15 (419/8)
305 line 17 (418/7)
306 lines 36–7 (417/6)
307 lines 57–8 (416/5)
308 lines 76–7 (415/4)
**309 line 13 (414/3)**
310 line 29 (413/2)
311 line 46 (412/1)
313 lines 81–2 (411/0)
314 lines 16–17 (409/8) [reads ἀργυρίδες]
315 lines 43–4 (408/7) [reads ἀργυρίδες]

25.        1 silver piece [phiale?]; weight of this: 112 dr.

ἀργυρίς Ι σταθμὸν ταύτης ΗΔΗΗ

*IG* I³, 304 lines 15–16 (419/8)
305 lines 17–18 (418/7)
**306 line 37 (417/6)**
307 line 58 (416/5)
308 line 77 (415/4)
309 line 13 (414/3)
310 lines 29–30 (413/2)
311 lines 46–7 (412/1)
313 line 82 (411/0)
314 line 17 (409/8)

315 line 44 (408/7)

26.      1 silver piece [phiale?]; weight of this: 60 dr.

ἀργυρὶς 1 σταθμὸν ταύτης ⊢Δ

> *IG* I³, 304 lines 16–17 (419/8)
> 305 lines 18–19 (418/7)
> **306 line 38 (417/6)**
> 307 line 59 (416/5)
> 308 lines 77–8 (415/4)
> 309 line 14 (414/3)
> 310 lines 30–1 (413/2)
> 311 line 47 (412/1)
> 313 line 83 (411/0)
> 314 line 18 (409/8)
> 315 line 45 (408/7)

27.      1 silver piece [phiale?]; weight of this: 153 dr.

ἀργυρὶς 1 σταθμὸν ταύτης Η⊢⊦⊦⊦

> *IG* I³, 305 lines 19–20 (418/7)
> 306 line 39 (417/6)
> **307 line 60 (416/5)**
> 308 lines 78–9 (415/4)
> 309 lines 14–15 (414/3)
> 310 line 31 (413/2)
> 311 line 48 (412/1)
> 313 lines 83–4 (411/0)
> 314 line 19 (409/8)
> 315 line 46 (408/7)

28.      4 silver pieces [phialai?]; weight of these: 386 dr.

ἀργυρίδες ΙΙΙΙ σταθμὸν τούτων ΗΗΗ⊢ΔΔΔΓ⊦

> *IG* I³, 306 line 40 (417/6)
> **307 line 61 (416/5)**
> 308 lines 79–80 (415/4)
> 309 lines 15–16 (414/3)
> 310 line 32 (413/2)
> 311 line 49 (412/1)
> 313 lines 84–5 (411/0)
> 314 line 20 (409/8)
> 315 lines 47–8 (408/7)

29.      A silver phiale; weight of this: 194 dr.

φιάλη ἀργυρᾶ σταθμὸν ταύτης Η⊢ΔΔΔΔ⊦⊦⊦

> *IG* I³, **307 line 62 (416/5)**
> 308 line 80 (415/4)
> 309 line 16 (414/3)
> 310 lines 32–3 (413/2)

311 lines 49–50 (412/1)
313 line 85 (411/0)
**314 lines 20–1 (409/8)** [reads ἀργυρίς]
**315 line 48 (408/7)** [reads ἀργυρίς]

30.        4 silver pieces [phialai?]; weight of these: 788 dr.
           ἀργυρίδες ΙΙΙΙ σταθμὸν τούτων ΓΗΗϜΔΔΔΓΗΗ

           *IG* I³, **302 lines 80–1 (415/4)**
                  309 lines 16–17 (414/3)
                  310 line 33 (413/2)
                  311 line 50 (412/1)
                  313 lines 85–6 (411/0)
                  314 lines 21–2 (409/8)
                  315 lines 48–9 (408/7)

31.        3 silver pieces [phialai?]; weight of these: 718 dr.
           ἀργυρίδες ΙΙΙ σταθμὸν τούτων ΓΗΗΔϜΗΗ

           *IG* I³, 309 line 17 (414/3)
                  310 lines 33–4 (413/2)
                  311 lines 50–1 (412/1)
                  **313 line 86 (411/0)**
                  314 line 22 (409/8)
                  315 line 49 (408/7)

32.        A silver piece [phiale?]; weight of this: --- dr.
           ἀργυρὶς σταθμὸν ταύτης ---

           *IG* I³, 310 line 34 (413/2)
                  311 line 51 (412/1)
                  312 line 68 (411)
                  313 line 86 (411/0)
                  **314 line 23 (409/8)**
                  315 line 50 (408/7)

33.        3 silver drinking-cups; weight of these: ---
           ποτήρια ἀργυρᾶ ΙΙΙ σταθμὸν τούτων ---

           *IG* I³, 292 lines 8–9 (434/3)
                  293 line 21 (433/2)
                  **294 lines 32–3 (432/1)**
                  295 line 43 (431/0)

34.        4 silver drinking-cups; weight of these: 142 dr.
           ποτήρια ἀργυρᾶ ΙΙΙΙ σταθμὸν τούτων ΗΔΔΔΔΗ
           *IG* I³, 296 lines 7–8 (430/29)
                  **296 lines 10–11 (430/29)** [adds another cup to
                      the group]

35.        5 silver drinking-cups; weight of these: 167 dr.

ποτήρια ἀργυρᾶ Γ σταθμὸν τούτων ΗϜΔΓⱵ

    *IG* I³, **297 line 19–20 (429/8)**
        298 line 32 (428/7)
        299 lines 45–6 (427/6)
        300 line 8 (426/5)
        301 lines 20–1 (425/4)
        302 lines 32–3 (424/3)
        303 lines 43–4 (423/2)
        305 line 9 (418/7)
        306 lines 28–9 (417/6)
        307 lines 49–50 (416/5)
        308 lines 69–70 (415/4)
        309 lines 6–7 (414/3)
        310 line 23 (413/2)
        311 lines 39–40 (412/1)
        312 line 56 (411)
        313 line 75 (411/0)
        314 line 6 (409/8)
        315 line 33 (408/7)

36.      A silver drinking-cup from Chalkis; weight of this: 40 dr.

      ποτήριον ἀργυροῦν Χαλκιδικόν, σταθμὸν τούτου
      ΔΔΔΔ

        *IG* I³, **299 lines 50–1 (427/6)**
            **300 line 11 (426/5)**
        301 lines 23–4 (425/4)
        302 line 35 (424/3)
        303 lines 45–6 (423/2)
        305 line 12 (418/7)
        306 lines 31–2 (417/6)
        307 lines 52–3 (416/5)
        308 lines 73–4 (415/4)
        309 line 10 (414/3)
        310 line 25 (413/2)
        311 line 42 (412/1)
        312 line 59 (411)
        313 lines 77–8 (411/0)
        314 lines 10–11 (409/8)
        315 lines 37–8 (408/7)

37.      A silver drinking-cup; weight of this: 40 dr.

      ποτήριον ἀργυροῦν σταθμὸν τούτου ΔΔΔΔ

        *IG* I³, 301 lines 25–6 (425/4)
        **302 line 36 (424/3)**
        303 line 47 (423/2)
        305 lines 13–14 (418/7)
        306 lines 33–4 (417/6)

307 line 54 (416/5)
308 lines 73–4 (415/4)
309 line 10 (414/3)
310 lines 26–7 (413/2)
311 lines 43–4 (412/1)
312 line 60 (411)
313 line 79 (411/0)
314 lines 11–12 (409/8)
315 line 39 (408/7)

38.  A silver drinking-cup; weight of this: 66 dr.

ποτήριον ἀργυροῦν σταθμὸν τούτου ⅠⅮΓⱵ

IG I³, 303 lines 48–9 (423/2)
305 lines 15–16 (418/7)
306 line 35 (417/6)
307 line 56 (416/5)
308 line 75 (415/4)
309 lines 11–12 (414/3)
310 line 28 (413/2)
311 line 45 (412/1)
313 lines 80–1 (411/0)
314 lines 14–15 (409/8)
315 lines 41–2 (408/7)

39.  A silver drinking-cup; weight of this: 39 dr.

ποτήριον ἀργυροῦν σταθμὸν τούτου ΔΔΔΓⱵⱵⱵⱵ

IG I³, 304 line 17 (419/8)
305 line 19 (418/7)
306 lines 38–9 (417/6)
307 lines 59–60 (416/5)
308 line 78 (415/4)
309 line 14 (414/3)
310 line 31 (413/2)
311 lines 47–8 (412/1)
313 line 83 (411/0)
314 lines 18–19 (409/8)
315 lines 45–6 (408/7)

40.  A silver drinking-cup; weight of this: 30 dr.

ποτήριον ἀργυροῦν σταθμὸν τούτου ΔΔΔ

IG I³, 305 lines 19–20 (418/7)
306 lines 39–40 (417/6)
307 lines 60–1 (416/5)
308 line 79 (415/4)
309 line 15 (414/3)
310 lines 31–2 (413/2)
311 lines 48–9 (412/1)

313 line 84 (411/0)
314 lines 19–20 (409/8)
315 lines 46–7 (408/7)

41.  A gold wreath; weight of this: 33 dr. 3 ob.

στέφανος χρυσοῦς σταθμὸν τούτου ΔΔΔⱵⱵΙΙΙ

*IG* I³, 297 lines 22–3 (429/8)
298 line 34 (428/7)
299 lines 47–8 (427/6)
300 lines 9–10 (426/5)
301 line 22 (425/4)
302 lines 33–4 (424/3)
303 lines 44–5 (423/2)
305 lines 10–11 (418/7)
306 line 30 (417/6)
307 line 51 (416/5)
308 line 71 (415/4)
309 lines 7–8 (414/3)
310 line 24 (413/2)
311 lines 40–1 (412/1)
312 lines 57–8 (411)
313 lines 76–7 (411/0)

*IG* I³, 314 lines 8–9 (409/8) [in a round box]
315 lines 35–6 (408/7) [in a round box]
316 line 68 (407/6?) [in a round box]

*Note.* This is the only object inventoried in the Proneos after the melting at the end of the Peloponnesian war.

## OBSERVATIONS

The total number of objects kept in the Proneos in 412 BC, at its greatest, is as follows:

phialai: 1 gold, 118 silver     gold wreaths: 1
drinking-cups: 10               kylix: 1
drinking-horns: 3               *karchēsion*: 1
lamps: 2

All items dedicated in the Proneos were silver or gold vases. Each item was dedicated as an *epeteion*. The most common vase shape placed in the Proneos was the phiale, with the drinking-cup a distant second. By 411 BC there were 188 silver phialai and 11 drinking-cups in the Proneos. One of the cups (**III. 36**) is specifically called Chalkidian, dedicated in the year 427/6. This one might be war booty or a dedication somehow acquired during battle. Likewise, in the Hekatompedon certain items are specified as having been taken from Methymna and Lesbos; these too were dedicated in 427/6.[8]

The phiale as a vase shape is Near Eastern in origin and came to Greece in the Iron Age as is demonstrated by a ninth-century Phoenician bronze phiale excavated in the Kerameikos, in a Middle Geometric grave (42), which came perhaps from a Phoenician colony on Cyprus.[9] The use of the phiale-type bowl was common in Phrygia, Assyria, and Phoenicia, and eighth-century examples were found in the Greek sanctuaries of Delphi and Olympia, Delos and Athens, as well as on Crete.[10] Such an early presence of Near Eastern phialai in Greek sanctuaries during the period of their infancy suggests that the function and use of such objects may also have been borrowed.

The use of a phiale made for sprinkling has a remarkable parallel in Old Babylonian ritual: 'Ritual songs are sung, jugglers and wrestlers perform, and when they have finished, the king takes his seat. Water is sprinkled three times in various specific parts of the shrine, and then water in metal cups is held out, "ready for the needs for the ecstatics".'[11] The Old Babylonian sprinkling vessel and metal cups may be compared to the items inside the Proneos of the Parthenon in the first year in which the treasurers recorded their inventories. The phiale for making libations (**III.6**) and the 104 silver phialai (**III.7**) may correspond to the cult practice at Mari.

Some evidence is present in these lists to suggest that the phialai were not only viewed as ritual vases, but were also a kind of standard weight. In the lists of 409/8 silver phialai were called ἀργυρίδες, 'silver pieces', as if the phiale shape equalled a standard silver piece (see **III.25–32**). The phialai listed above do seem to have been crafted on a weight standard of roughly 100 dr. In the accompanying table the phialai kept in the Proneos are paired with their weights in drachmas. For the 42 phialai which entered the Proneos between 429/8 and 419/8, the total weight is 4170 dr. 2 obols, which yields an average weight per phiale of 99 dr. 1¾ obols.

A comparison of the average weight of the phialai above (approx. 99 dr.) with the silver pieces in the second table shows that they too

    [8] Cf. Camp (1978).
    [9] Coldstream (1977) 58–60 and fig. 15; cf. Mansfield (1985) 161 n. 28. For the phiale, see Luschey (1939) 31–7; Boardman (1980) 68 and 270 n. 110.
    [10] Boardman (1980) 68, 270 n. 110 with references.
    [11] Dalley (1984) 136; cf. Bottero (1957) 46 no. 119.

were on a 100-drachma scale, but could be made in denominations of 50, 100, 150, and even 200 drachmas.

| Silver Phialai | Weight | |
|---|---|---|
| | Total | Average |
| 7 (III.16) | 700 dr. | 100 dr. |
| 2 (III.17) | 200 dr. | 100 dr. |
| 4 (III.18) | 329 dr. | 82 dr. 1½ ob. |
| 7 (III.19) | 920 dr. | 131 dr 2½ ob. |
| 4 (III.20) | 420 dr. | 105 dr. |
| 7 (III.21) | 643 dr. 2 ob. | 92 dr. ¼ ob. |
| 3 (III.22) | 251 dr. | 83 dr. 4 ob. |
| 3 (III.23) | 294 dr. | 98 dr. |
| 5 (III.24) | 413 dr. | 82 dr. 3½ ob. |

| Silver Pieces [ἀργυρίδες] | Weight | |
|---|---|---|
| | Total | Average |
| 1 (III.25) | 112 dr. | 112 dr. |
| 1 (III.26) | 60 dr. | 60 dr. |
| 1 (III.27) | 153 dr. | 153 dr. |
| 4 (III.28) | 386 dr. | 96 dr. 3 ob. |
| 1 (III.29) | 194 dr. | 194 dr. |
| 4 (III.30) | 788 dr. | 197 dr. |
| 3 (III.31) | 718 dr. | 239 dr. 2 ob. |

The ἀργυρίδες or 'silver pieces' in the table are more variable in weight than the phialai. The first in the list may be taken as a rough approximation to 100 dr. The second is somewhat more than half a phiale in value, the third is close to 1.5 times the value; the next entry of four pieces produces a close average of 96.5 dr.; the next two entries yield individual weights of twice the average phiale; and the last entry is approximately 2.5 times the size.

Who paid for these expensive vessels to be contributed to the temple? Considering that the average wage of a labourer in Athens was two drachmai per day, these vases were quite valuable. No decrees have been preserved on stone to suggest that the *dēmos* or the *boulē* voted to dedicate such vases to Athena each year. Yet these are not likely to have been individually owned and privately dedicated. They are listed as *epeteia*, yearly offerings of the Treasurers of Athena, presumably on behalf of all Athena's worshippers. The treasurers may have paid for these themselves, with funds gained through the rental of sacred property, fines and levies, and private contributions. Or the vases dedicated may represent any surplus left over at the end of the treasurers' year of office, after expenses such as sacrifices and construction on the Akropolis had been paid.

# PART IV

# The Treasures of the Parthenon

### THE TREASURES

The term 'Parthenon' in this chapter refers specifically to the west cella of the temple. The treasurers had access only from the western doors. Passing through the back chamber into the 'Parthenon' would have been possible only by breaking the seals on the Opisthodomos grills and gate. The chamber itself had four Ionic columns supporting the superstructure. The Treasures would have been seen only by the treasurers and priests; it was not open to the public and no cult statue stood inside. This room, then, was a chamber devoted to the storage of Athena's treasures in the fifth century. There is no evidence that cult veneration took place in the room.

The term 'Parthenon' is derived from the rooms where unmarried women slept in private houses. Thus, the western cella was Athena's private bedroom, her parthenōn.[1] The western cella was called the Parthenon, but the temple as a whole became known as the 'Hekatompedos Parthenon'; 'Hekatompedon' was its original name and 'Parthenon' a nickname. The fifth-century inventories indicate that the treasures were kept in four distinct places: the Proneos, the Hekatompedon, the Parthenon, and the Opisthodomos. Some stelai from the fifth century contain the heading ἐν τῷ Παρθενῶνι, and the contents of these inscriptions are listed below as treasures which were certainly kept in the western chamber. It may have continued to contain treasures in the fourth century, but the inventory lists do not mention objects kept in that chamber specifically. In the fourth-century inventories all treasures are listed as 'In the Hekatompedon' (ἐν τῷ Ἑκατομπέδῳ), which must refer to the whole temple without differentiating the rooms within it.

Plutarch, in *Perikles* 13. 4, calls the temple 'the Parthenon with its one-hundred-foot cella', and in *Cato* 5. 3 he says, 'when the Athenians were building the Parthenon'. Likewise, in the Strasburg

[1] Bruno (1974) 67–8.

Papyrus (c.AD 100) the whole building is called τὸν Παρθενῶνα. The building accounts for the temple do not preserve the heading, which would indicate its name during the period of its construction.[2] Only one contract payment contains the attribute which certifies that the accounts belong to the Parthenon and to no other building on the Akropolis, namely, the sculpted pediments: ἀγαλματοποιοῖς ἐναιετίων μισθός.[3]

The treasures are a mix of furniture, weapons, jewellery, wreaths, and vases. There are no named dedicants associated with any of these items, nor are there many indications of private worship. The objects from Lesbos may be war booty from the campaign against Mytilene in 428/7.[4] The Persian daggers could be relics of the Persian wars, or acquired at the Eurymedon or any number of other skirmishes during the fifth century. There does seem to be a large number of couches and stools for a room which is supposed not to have been used for cult activities. Perhaps the furniture was in storage in this room; or, alternatively, the room was indeed used for worship in spite of the lack of literary evidence.

One remarkable item is the gilt kore on a stele (**IV.19**): there was another in the Hekatompedon accounts (**V.90**). What their function was is not known.

ARMS AND WEAPONS

1.                    6 Persian daggers overlaid with gold

                     ἀκινάκαι περίχρυσοι ΓΙ

                     *IG* I³, 343 line 8 (434/3)
                            344 line 24 (433/2)
                            **346 line 59 (431/0)**
                            350 line 70 (427/6)
                            351 line 9 (422/1)
                            352 lines 33–4 (421/0)
                            353 lines 56–7 (420/19)
                            354 line 76 (419/8)
                            355 lines 9–10 (414/3)
                            **356 line 36 (413/2)**
                            357 line 62 (412/1)

**2. (V.1)**          1 Persian dagger overlaid with gold; unweighed

                     ἀκινάκης ἐπίχρυσος Ι ἄσταθμος

   [2] *IG* I³, 436–50.
   [3] *IG* I³, 446 line 338; 447 line 360; 448 line 368; 449 lines 401–2.
   [4] See Camp (1978) for a spear-point excavated in the Athenian Agora inscribed as war booty from Lesbos. cf. Thuc. 3. 2.

IG I³, 349 lines 58–9 (428/7) [Parthenon]
350 line 79 (427/6)
351 line 17 (422/1)
353 line 64 (420/19)
**354 line 81 (419/8)**
355 line 18 (414/3)
356 lines 44–5 (413/2)
357 lines 70–1 (412/1)
IG II², 1373 line 15 (403/2)
1376 line 16 (402/1 or 401/0)
1377, add. p. 797 line 26 (399/8)
[Hekatompedon]
1394 line 11 (397/6)
1395 line 27 (395/4)

Ag. I 5363 [Hesperia 32 (1963) 165–8] line 3 (before 385/4)
IG II², 1424a line 336 (371/0)
1425 lines 268–9 (368/7)
1428 line 222 (367/6)

3.            A gold-plated helmet
κυνῆ ἐπίχρυσος

IG I³, 343 line 12 (434/3)
344 line 27 (433/2)
345 line 45 (432/1)
346 line 62 (431/0)
349 line 53 (428/7)
350 line 74 (427/6)
351 lines 12–13 (422/1)
352 line 37 (421/0)
**353 line 60 (420/19)**
354 line 78 (419/8)
355 line 13 (414/3)
356 line 40 (413/2)
357 lines 65–6 (412/1)

4. (V.14)     3 bronze helmets
κράνη χαλκᾶ III

IG I³, 343 line 15 (434/3) [Parthenon]
344 lines 30–1 (433/2)
345 line 48 (432/1)
346 lines 65–6 (431/0)
349 line 56 (428/7)
350 line 77 (427/6)
351 line 15 (422/1)
**353 line 63 (420/19)**
354 line 80 (419/8)
355 line 16 (414/3)

356 line 43 (413/2)
357 line 69 (412/1)
*IG* II², 1373 line 1 (403/2)
1380 line 10 (after 390) [Hekatompedon]
1424a line 330 (371/0)
1425 line 259 (368/7)

5. (V.10)   A bronze Illyrian helmet, from Lesbos

κράνος ἐγ Λέσβου Ἰλλυρικὸν χαλκοῦν

*IG* I³, 350 lines 80–3 (427/6) [Parthenon]
**351 line 19 (422/1)**
**353 lines 66–7 (420/19)**
354 line 82 (419/8)
355 line 20 (414/3)
356 lines 46–7 (413/2)
357 line 73 (412/1)
358 line 2 (411 or 411/0)
*IG* II², **1373 lines 3–4 (403/2)**
**1424a line 331 (371/0)** [Hekatompedon]
1425 line 261 (368/7)
1428 line 211 (367/6)
1434 line 13 (*c.*367/6)

6a. (V.5)   14 breast-plates

θώρακες ΔΙΙΙΙ

*IG* I³, 343 line 13 (434/3) [Parthenon]
**344 line 29 (433/2)**
345 line 46 (432/1)
346 line 64 (431/0)

6b.   16 breast-plates

θώρακες ΔΓΙ

*IG* I³, 349 line 54 (428/7)
350 line 75 (427/6)
351 line 14 (422/1)
**353 line 61 (420/19)**
354 line 79 (419/8)
355 line 14 (414/3)
356 line 41 (413/2)
357 line 67 (412/1)
*IG* II², 1433 line 6 (between 384/3 and 378/7)
[Hekatompedon]
1424a line 328 (371/0)
1425 line 256 (368/7)
1428 line 205 (367/6)

7. (V.28)   31 brazen shields

ἀσπίδες ἐπίχαλκοι ΔΔΔΙ

IG I³, 343 line 14 (434/3) [Parthenon]
344 line 29 (433/2)
345 line 47 (432/1)
346 line 64 (431/0)
349 line 55 (428/7)
350 line 76 (427/6)
351 line 14 (422/1)
353 line 61 (420/19)
354 line 79 (419/8)
355 lines 14–15 (414/3)
356 line 41 (413/2)
357 line 67 (412/1)

8a.    Six shields with blazons
ἀσπίδες ἐπίσημοι ΓΙ

IG I³, 343 line 13 (434/3)
344 line 29 (433/2)
345 line 46 (432/1)
346 line 64 (431/0)
349 lines 54–5 (428/7)
350 line 75 (427/6)
351 line 14 (422/1)
353 line 61 (420/19)
354 line 79 (419/8)
355 line 14 (414/3)
356 line 41 (413/2)
357 line 67 (412/1)

8b.    33 shields with blazons
ἀσπίδες ἐπίσημοι ΔΔΔΙΙΙ

IG II², 1433 line 13 (between 384/3 and 378/7)
[Hekatompedon]

8c.    33 shields with blazons, of these three are inscribed
ἀσπίδες ἐπίσημοι ΔΔΔΙΙΙ τούτων τρεῖς γεγραμμέναι

IG II², 1424a lines 338–9 (371/0)

8d.    33 shields with blazons, of these five are not inscribed
ἀσπίδες ἐπίσημοι ΔΔΔΙΙΙ τούτων Γ οὐ γεγραμμέναι

IG II², 1425 lines 272–4 (368/7)

8e.    Shields with blazons
ἀσπίδες ἐπίσημοι

IG II², 1463 line 6? (349/8)

8f.    Shields with blazons --- [one] has letters
ἀσπίδες ἐπίσημοι --- γράμματα ἔχει

IG II², 1443 lines 219–20? (344/3)

8g.                     33 shields with blazons, of these three are inscribed

ἀσπίδες ἐπίσημοι ΔΔΔΙΙΙ τούτων γεγραμμέναι τρεῖς

*IG* II², 1501 lines 20–1? (after 330)

9a.                     13 shields, gilt wood

ἀσπίδες ἐπίχρυσοι ὑπόξυλοι ΔΙΙΙ

*IG* I³, 343 line 12 (434/3)

344 **lines 27–8 (433/2)**

344 **line 32 (433/2)** [one more added]

9b.                     14 shields, gilt wood

ἀσπίδες ἐπίχρυσοι ὑπόξυλοι ΔΙΙΙΙ

*IG* I³, 345 **line 45 (432/1)**

346 line 63 (431/0)

9c.                     15 shields, gilt wood

ἀσπίδες ἐπίχρυσοι ὑπόξυλοι ΔΓ

*IG* I³, 349 **line 53 (428/7)**

350 line 74 (427/6)

351 line 13 (422/1)

352 line 37 (421/0)

353 line 60 (420/19)

354 line 78 (419/8)

355 line 13 (414/3)

356 line 40 (413/2)

357 line 66 (412/1)

10. (V.20)              1 shield with blazon, from Lesbos

ἀσπὶς ἐγ Λέσβου ἐπίσημος Ι

*IG* I³, 350 lines 80–3 (427/6) [Parthenon]

351 **line 19 (422/1)**

353 line 66 (420/19)

354 line 82 (419/8)

355 line 20 (414/3)

356 line 46 (413/2)

357 line 73 (412/1)

358 line 2 (411 or 411/0)

*IG* II², 1373 line 3 (403/2)

1414 line 24 (385/4) [Hekatompedon]

1424a line 331 (371/0)

1425 lines 261–2 (368/7)

1428 line 213 (367/6)

11.                     2 shields, gilt wood

ἀσπίδε ἐπιχρύσω ὑποξύλω ΙΙ

*IG* I³, 349 line 58 (428/7)

350 lines 78–9 (427/6)

351 line 17 (422/1)
353 line 64 (420/19)
**354 line 81 (419/8)**
355 lines 17–18 (414/3)
356 line 44 (413/2)
357 line 70 (412/1)

12a. (V.19)    A bronze light shield

πέλτη χαλκῆ

IG I³, 349 line 57 (428/7) [Parthenon]
350 lines 77–8 (427/6)
351 line 16 (422/1)
353 line 63 (420/19)
354 line 80 (419/8)
355 line 16 (414/3)
356 line 43 (413/2)
357 line 69 (412/1)

IG II², 1373 lines 1–2 (403/2) [as restored in *JHS* 58
(1938) 71]
1380 line 9 (after 390) [Hekatompedon]
1414 line 23 (385/4)
1433 lines 6–7 (between 384/3 and 378/7)
1424a line 328 (371/0)
1425 line 257 (368/7)
1428 line 208 (367/6)
**1434, add. p. 809 line 8 (c.367/6)**[5]

12b.    Light shield overlaid with gold, complete

πέλτη ἐπίχρυσος ἐντελής

IG II², 1473 lines 9–10 (304/3)

BASKETS AND CONTAINERS

13.    2 gilt-wood baskets

κανὼ ὑποξύλω καταχρύσω ΙΙ

IG I³, 343 line 9 (434/3)
344 lines 24–5 (433/2)
**346 line 60 (431/0)**
350 line 71 (427/6)
**351 line 10 (422/1)**
352 line 34 (421/0)
353 line 57 (420/19)
354 lines 76–7 (419/8)
355 line 10 (414/3)
356 line 37 (413/2)

---

[5] See Woodward (1940) 390 for the restoration of πέλτη instead of πήληξ.

357 line 63 (412/1)

**14. (V.35)**    A gilt-wood box

κοίτη ὑπόξυλος κατάχρυσος

         *IG* I³, 343 line 10 (434/3) [Parthenon]
               344 lines 25–6 (433/2)
               346 line 61 (431/0)
               350 line 72 (427/6)
               **351 line 11 (422/1)**
               352 line 35 (421/0)
               353 line 58 (420/19)
               354 line 77 (419/8)
               **355 line 11 (414/3)**
               356 line 38 (413/2)
               357 line 64 (412/1)
         *IG* II², 1380 line 5 (after 390) [Hekatompedon]
               1433 lines 12–13 (between 384/3 and 378/7)
               1424a line 338 (371/0)
               1425 lines 271–2 (368/7)
               1428 line 226 (367/6)

COINS

**15.**    A gold tetradrachm; weight of this: 7 dr. 2½ ob.

τετράδραχμον χρυσοῦν σταθμὸν τούτου ΓϜϜΙΙϹ

         *IG* I³, **351 line 23 (422/1)**
               352 lines 47–8 (421/0)
               **353 lines 70–1 (420/19)**
               354 lines 84–5 (419/8)
               355 lines 24–5 (414/3)
               356 lines 50–1 (413/2)
               357 lines 77–8 (412/1)
               358 line 6 (411 or 411/0)
               359 lines 2–3 (410/9 or 409/8)

**16.**    Two gold pieces; weight of these: ---

χρυσίω δύο σταθμὸν τούτοιν ---

         *IG* I³, **355 lines 26–7 (414/3)**
               356 lines 52–3 (413/2)
               357 line 79 (412/1)
               358 line 7 (411 or 411/0)
               **359 line 5 (410/9 or 409/8)**

**17.**    Unmarked gold; weight of this: 1 dr. 4 ob.

χρυσίον ἄσημον σταθμὸν τούτου ϜΙΙΙΙ

         *IG* I³, 343 line 5 (434/3)

344 lines 20–1 (433/2)
346 line 56 (431/0)
350 lines 66–7 (427/6)
**351 line 6 (422/1)**
352 line 30 (421/0)
353 line 53 (420/19)
354 line 74 (419/8)
355 line 6 (414/3)
356 lines 32–3 (413/2)
**357 lines 58–9 (412/1)**

18.    Unmarked gold; weight of this: 7 dr.

χρυσίον ἄσημον σταθμὸν τούτου ΓΗΗ

*IG* I³, **355 line 25 (414/3)**
356 lines 51–2 (413/2)
357 line 78 (412/1)

19.    Unmarked gold; weight of this: ---

χρυσίον ἄσημον σταθμὸν τούτου ---

*IG* I³, **357 line 80 (412/1)**
358 line 8 (411 or 411/0)

FIGURINES AND STATUES

20.    A gilt kore on a base

κόρη ἐπὶ στήλης κατάχρυσος

*IG* I³, 343 line 10 (434/3)
344 line 25 (433/2)
346 lines 60–1 (431/0)
350 line 72 (427/6)
**351 line 11 (422/1)**
352 line 35 (421/0)
353 line 58 (420/19)
354 line 77 (419/8)
355 line 11 (414/3)
356 line 38 (413/2)
357 lines 63–4 (412/1)

21. (V.102)    A gorgoneion, gilt monster-figures

γοργόνειον· κάμπη ἐπίχρυσα

*IG* I³, 343 lines 10–11 (434/3) [Parthenon]
344 line 26 (433/2)
346 line 61 (431/0)
350 lines 72–3 (427/6)
351 line 11 (422/1)
352 lines 35–6 (421/0)

353 lines 58–9 (420/19)
354 line 77 (419/8)
**355 lines 11–12 (414/3)**
**356 line 38 (413/2)**
357 line 64 (412/1)
*IG* II², 1380 line 6 (after 390?)
1414 line 22 (385/4) [Hekatompedon]
1426 line 25 (375/4)
1424a line 324 (371/0)
1425 line 251 (368/7)
1428 lines 198–9 (367/6)

22. (V.103)  Horse, griffin, griffin's protome, large griffin, lion's head, flowery chain, snake, all these gilt

ἵππος· γρύψ· γρυπὸς προτομή· γρὺψ μέγας· λέοντος κεφαλή· ὅρμος ἀνθέμων· δράκων· ἐπίχρυσα ταῦτα

*IG* I³, 343 lines 11–12 (434/3) [Parthenon]
344 lines 26–7 (433/2)
346 lines 61–2 (431/0)
349 lines 52–3 (428/7)
350 lines 73–4 (427/6)
**351 lines 11–12 (422/1)**
352 lines 36–7 (421/0)
353 lines 59–60 (420/19)
354 lines 77–8 (419/8)
355 lines 12–13 (414/3)
356 line 39 (413/2)
357 lines 64–5 (412/1)
*IG* II², 1380 lines 6–7 (after 390?)
1414 line 22 (385/4) [Hekatompedon]
1426 lines 25–6 (375/4)
1424a lines 324–6 (371/0)
**1425 lines 252–4 (368/7)**
1428 lines 199–202 (367/6)

23. (V.109)  Golden wheat: 12 stalks

λήιον περίχρυσον στάχυες ΔΙΙ

*IG* I³, 343 line 9 (434/3) [Parthenon]
344 line 24 (433/2)
346 lines 59–60 (431/0)
350 lines 70–1 (427/6)
**351 line 10 (422/1)**
**352 line 34 (421/0)**
353 line 57 (420/19)
354 line 76 (419/8)
355 line 10 (414/3)
356 lines 36–7 (413/2)

357 lines 62–3 (412/1)
IG II², 1379 lines 8–9 (402/1 or 401/0)
1426 lines 31–2 (375/4) [Hekatompedon]
1424a line 333 (371/0)
1425 line 264 (368/7)
1428 line 215 (367/6)
1485, add. p. 810 line 55 (304/3)

24.    A mask, silver-gilt; weight of this: 116 dr.

πρόσωπον ὑπάργυρον κατάχρυσον σταθμὸν τούτου
ΗΔΓⱶ

IG I³, 343 line 7 (434/3)
344 lines 22–3 (433/2)
346 line 58 (431/0)
350 line 69 (427/6)
**351 line 8 (422/1)**
352 lines 32–3 (421/0)
353 lines 55–6 (420/19)
354 lines 75–6 (419/8)
355 line 8 (414/3)
356 line 35 (413/2)
357 line 61 (412/1)

FURNITURE

25. (V.113)    7 Chian couches

κλῖναι Χιουργεῖς ΓΙΙ

IG I³, 343 line 12 (434/3) [Parthenon]
344 line 28 (433/2)
345 line 45 (432/1)
**346 line 63 (431/0)**
349 lines 53–4 (428/7)
350 lines 74–5 (427/6)
351 line 13 (422/1)
353 line 60 (420/19)
354 line 78 (419/8)
355 lines 13–14 (414/3)
356 line 40 (413/2)
357 line 66 (412/1)
IG II², 1424a line 326 (371/0) [Hekatompedon]
1425 lines 254–5 (368/7)
1428 line 203 (367/6)

26. (V.115)    10 Milesian couches

κλῖναι Μιλησιουργεῖς Δ

IG I³, 343 line 13 (434/3) [Parthenon]

344 line 28 (433/2)
345 line 46 (432/1)
346 line 63 (431/0)
349 line 54 (428/7)
350 line 75 (427/6)
351 line 13 (422/1)
353 lines 60–1 (420/19)
**354 line 79 (419/8)**
355 line 14 (414/3)
356 lines 40–1 (413/2)
357 lines 66–7 (412/1)

*IG* II², 1379 lines 3–4 (402/1 or 401/0)
1394 line 18 (397/6) [Hekatompedon]
1380 line 1 (after 390)
1413 line 34 (between 384/3 and 378/7)
**1421 lines 109–10 (374/3)** [in need of repair;
ἐπισκευῆς δεόμεναι]
1424a line 299 (371/0) [in need of repair;
ἐπισκευῆς δεόμεναι]
1425 lines 217–18 (368/7) [in need of repair;
ἐπισκευῆς δεόμεναι]

**27.**          4 stools
δίφροι ||||

*IG* I³, 343 line 14 (434/3)
344 line 29 (433/2)
**345 line 47 (432/1)**
346 lines 64–5 (431/0)
349 line 55 (428/7)
350 line 76 (427/6)
351 line 14 (422/1)
353 line 62 (420/19)
354 line 79 (419/8)
355 line 15 (414/3)
356 lines 42 (413/2)
357 line 68 (412/1)

**28.**          13 feet for couches, overlaid with silver
κλινῶν πόδες ἐπάργυροι Δ|||

*IG* I³, 343 lines 15–16 (434/3)
344 line 31 (433/2)
345 line 48 (432/1)
346 line 66 (431/0)
349 lines 56–7 (428/7)
350 line 77 (427/6)
351 lines 15–16 (422/1)
**353 line 63 (420/19)**
354 line 80 (419/8)

355 line 16 (414/3)
356 line 43 (413/2)
357 line 69 (412/1)

29a. (V.119) 9 campstools

ὀκλαδίαι ΓΙΙΙΙ

*IG* I³, 343 line 14 (434/3) [Parthenon]
344 lines 29–30 (433/2)
345 line 47 (432/1)
346 line 65 (431/0)
349 line 55 (428/7)
350 line 76 (427/6)
351 lines 14–15 (422/1)
**353 line 62 (420/19)**
354 line 79 (419/8)
355 line 15 (414/3)
356 line 42 (413/2)
357 line 68 (412/1)

29b. Ten campstools

ὀκλαδίαι δέκα

*IG* II², 1421 line 111 (374/3) [Hekatompedon]
**1424a line 300 (371/0)**
1425 line 218 (368/7)
1428 line 141 (367/6)
1460 lines 9–10 (after 330/29)

30. (V.121) An ivory-inlaid table

τράπεζα ἠλεφαντωμένη

*IG* I³, 343 line 15 (434/3) [Parthenon]
344 line 30 (433/2)
345 line 48 (432/1)
346 line 65 (431/0)
349 line 56 (428/7)
350 line 77 (427/6)
351 line 15 (422/1)
353 line 62 (420/19)
**354 line 80 (419/8)**
355 line 16 (414/3)
356 lines 42–3 (413/2)
357 lines 68–9 (412/1)
*IG* II², 1421 line 112 (374/3) [Hekatompedon]
1424a line 300 (371/0)
1425 line 219 (368/7)
1460 lines 4–5 (after 330/29)

31. 6 thrones

θρόνοι ΓΙ

IG I³, 343 line 14 (434/3)
344 line 29 (433/2)
345 line 47 (432/1)
**346 line 64 (431/0)**
349 line 55 (428/7)
350 line 76 (427/6)
351 line 14 (422/1)
353 line 61 (420/19)
354 line 79 (419/8)
355 line 15 (414/3)
356 lines 41–2 (413/2)
357 line 68 (412/1)
IG II², 1379 line 1 (402/1 or 401/0)
1394 line 16 (397/6)

JEWELLERY

**32. (V.146)** An onyx having a gold ring; unweighed

ὄνυξ τὸν δακτύλιον χρυσοῦν ἔχων ἄσταθμος

IG I³, 351 lines 23–4 (422/1) [Parthenon]
352 line 48 (421/0)
**353 line 71 (420/19)**
354 line 85 (419/8)
355 line 25 (414/3)
356 line 51 (413/2)
357 line 78 (412/1)
358 line 6 (411 or 411/0)
359 lines 3–4 (410/9 or 409/8)
IG II², 1373 line 4 (403/2)
1377, add. p. 797 lines 26–7 (399/8)
1388 lines 62–3 (398/7) [Hekatompedon]

**33.** Eight gilt seals and two stone griffins; weight of these: 40+ dr.

σφραγῖδες ὀκτὼ περίχρυσοι καὶ γρῦπε διαλίθω δύο σταθμὸν τούτων ΔΔΔΔ ---

**IG I³, 361 lines 4–5 (407/6?)**
IG II², 1373 lines 12–13 (403/2)
1376 lines 11–13 (402/1 or 401/0)
**1377 lines 17–18 (399/8)**
1394 lines 1–2 (397/6)
1395 lines 18–20 (395/4)

**34.** 2 chains and a golden olive branch; weight of these: 35 dr. 3 ob.

ὁρμίσκω ΙΙ καὶ θαλλὸς χρυσοῦς· σταθμὸν τούτων
ΔΔΔΓΙΙΙ

IG I³, 355 line 26 (414/3)
356 line 52 (413/2)
357 line 79 (412/1)
358 lines 6–7 (411 or 411/0)
359 **lines 4–5 (410/9 or 409/8)**
360 lines 1–2 (408/7?)

35. (V.139)  Wide collars set with stones attached to a leather band, five in number; weight of these: 55 dr.

ὅρμοι πλατεῖς διάλιθοι καὶ σκῦτος προσὸν ἀριθμὸς πέντε· σταθμὸν τούτων ϜΓ

IG I³, 361 lines 2–3 (407/6?) [Parthenon]
IG II², 1373 lines 10–11 (403/2)
**1376 lines 8–10 (402/1 or 401/0)**
**1377 lines 15–16 (399/8)** [Hekatompedon]
1395 lines 16–17 (395/4)

36.  100+ earrings ---

ἐνῴδια χρυσᾶ Η---

IG I³, 357 **line 81 (412/1)**

37. (V.132)  Two gold earrings set with stones; weight of these: 21 dr.

ἐνῳδίω διαλίθω χρυσὼ ἀριθμὸς δύο σταθμὸν τούτοιν ΔΔϜ

IG I³, 361 lines 3–4 (407/6?) [Parthenon]
IG II², 1373 lines 11–12 (403/2)
**1376 lines 10–11 (402/1 or 401/0)**
**1377 lines 16–17 (399/8)** [Hekatompedon]
1395 lines 17–18 (395/4)

38.  A gold belt

ζώνη χρυσῆ

IG I³, 360 line 3 (408/7?)

39. (V.136)  The smaller gold necklace set with stones, having 20 rosettes; weight of this: ---

ὅρμος χρυσοῦς διάλιθος ὁ μικρὸς ῥόδων ἀριθμὸς ΔΔ σταθμὸν τούτου ---

IG I³, 360 line 6 (408/7?) [Parthenon] [reads ὁ ἐλάττων]
IG II², 1373 lines 7–9 (403/2) [reads ὁ ἐλάττων]
**1376 lines 5–6 (402/1 or 401/0)**
**1377 lines 11–13 (399/8)** [Hekatompedon]
1395 lines 12–13 (395/4)

40. (V.137)    The larger gold necklace set with stones, having 20 rosettes, and 1 ram's head; weight of these: 30 dr.

ὅρμος χρυσοῦς διάλιθος ὁ μείζων ἀριθμὸς ῥόδων ΔΔ καὶ κριοῦ κεφαλὴ Ι σταθμὸν τούτου ΔΔΔ

       *IG* I³, 360 lines 4–5 (408/7?) [Parthenon]

       *IG* II², 1373 lines 5–6 (403/2)

            **1376 lines 1–3 (402/1 or 401/0)**

            1377 lines 10–11 (399/8) [Hekatompedon]

            1395 lines 10–12 (395/4)

MUSICAL INSTRUMENTS

41. (V.191)    The gilded ivory aulos-case from Methymna

συβήνη ἐλεφαντίνη ἡ παρὰ Μηθυμναίων ἐπίχρυσος

       *IG* I³, 350 lines 80–2 (427/6) [Parthenon]

            351 lines 18–19 (422/1)

            353 lines 65–6 (420/19)

            **354 line 82 (419/8)**

            355 lines 19–20 (414/3)

            356 line 46 (413/2)

            357 line 72 (412/1)

            358 lines 1–3 (411 or 411/0)

       *IG* II², 1373 lines 2–3 (403/2)

            1377 lines 25–6 (399/8) [Hekatompedon]

            1394 lines 10–11 (397/6)

            1395+Ag. I 1182 [*Hesperia* 5 (1936) 390] lines 26–7 (395/4)

       Ag. I 5363 [*Hesperia* 32 (1963) 165–8] lines 2–3 (before 385/4)

       *IG* II², 1412 line 8 (382/1)

            1421 lines 105–6 (374/3)

            1424a lines 296–7 (371/0)

            1425 lines 213–14 (368/7)

            1428 line 139 (367/6)

            1463 line 11 (349/8)

42. (V.192)    A gilt lyre

λύρα κατάχρυσος

       *IG* I³, 343 line 14 (434/3) [Parthenon]

            344 line 30 (433/2)

            345 line 47 (432/1)

            346 line 65 (431/0)

            349 line 55 (428/7)

            350 line 76 (427/6)

            351 line 15 (422/1)

353 line 62 (420/19)
354 line 79 (419/8)
355 line 15 (414/3)
356 line 42 (413/2)
357 line 68 (412/1)
IG II², 1380 line 9 (after 390?)
1414 line 23 (385/4) [Hekatompedon]
1433 line 7 (between 384/3 and 378/7)
1426 line 29 (375/4)
1424a line 328 (371/0)
1425 line 257 (368/7)
1428 line 209 (367/6)
1434 line 8 (c.367/6)
1457 line 27 (after 316/5) [reads λύριον χρυσοῦν]

**43a. (V.195)**   3 ivory lyres

λύραι ἐλεφάντιναι III

IG I³, 343 lines 14–15 (434/3) [Parthenon]
344 line 30 (433/2)
**345 lines 47–8 (432/1)**
**345 line 50 (432/1)** [1 lyre added; λύρα
ἐλεφαντίνη]

**43b.**   4 ivory lyres

λύραι ἐλεφάντιναι IIII

*IG* I³, **346 line 65 (431/0)**
349 lines 55–6 (428/7)
350 lines 76–7 (427/6)
351 line 15 (422/1)
353 line 62 (420/19)
354 lines 79–80 (419/8)
355 lines 15–16 (414/3)
356 line 42 (413/2)
357 line 68 (412/1)
IG II², 1424a line 329 (371/0) [Hekatompedon]
1425 line 258 (368/7)
1428 line 210 (367/6)
1434 line 9 (c.367/6)

**44a. (V.197)**   4 wooden lyres

λύραι ξύλιναι IIII

*IG* I³, 343 line 15 (434/3) [Parthenon]
344 line 30 (433/2)
345 line 48 (432/1)
346 line 65 (431/0)
349 line 56 (428/7)
350 line 77 (427/6)

351 line 15 (422/1)
353 line 62 (420/19)
354 line 80 (419/8)
355 line 16 (414/3)
356 line 42 (413/2)
357 line 68 (412/1)
*IG* II², **1424a line 329 (371/0)** [Hekatompedon]
1434 lines 10–11 (*c.*367/6)

**44b.**  5 wooden lyres

λύραι ξύλιναι Γ

*IG* II², **1425 lines 258–9 (368/7)**
1428 line 210 (367/6)

TOOLS

**45. (V.208)**  9 sabres

ξιφομάχαιραι ΓΙΙΙΙ

*IG* I³, 343 line 13 (434/3) [Parthenon]
344 line 28 (433/2)
345 line 46 (432/1)
346 lines 63–4 (431/0)
349 line 54 (428/7)
350 line 75 (427/6)
351 lines 13–14 (422/1)
**353 line 61 (420/19)**
354 line 79 (419/8)
355 line 14 (414/3)
356 line 41 (413/2)
357 line 67 (412/1)
*IG* II², 1380 line 8 (after 390) [Hekatompedon]
1424a line 327 (371/0)
1425 line 255 (368/7)
1428 line 203 (367/6)

**46a.**  4 swords

ξίφη ΙΙΙΙ

*IG* I³, 343 line 13 (434/3)
344 line 28 (433/2)
**345 line 46 (432/1)**
346 line 64 (431/0)

**46b.**  Five swords

ξίφη πέντε

349 line 54 (428/7)
350 line 75 (427/6)
**351 line 14 (422/1)**

353 line 61 (420/19)
354 line 79 (419/8)
355 line 14 (414/3)
356 line 41 (413/2)
357 line 67 (412/1)

47.  Two nails, silver gilt; weight of these: 184 dr.

ἥλω δύο ὑπαργύρω καταχρύσω σταθμὸν τούτοιν
ΗϜΔΔΔΙΙΙΙ

*IG* I³, 343 lines 6–7 (434/3)
344 line 22 (433/2)
346 lines 57–8 (431/0)
350 lines 68–9 (427/6)
**351 lines 7–8 (422/1)**
352 lines 31–2 (421/0)
353 lines 54–5 (420/19)
354 line 75 (419/8)
355 lines 7–8 (414/3)
356 lines 34–5 (413/2)
357 lines 60–1 (412/1)

VESSELS

48a.  --- silver phialai; weight of these: 723+ dr.

φιάλαι ἀργυραῖ --- σταθμὸν τούτων --- ΓΗΗΔΔΙΙΙΙ

*IG* I³, **343 line 8 (434/3)**
344 lines 23–4 (433/2)
346 lines 58–9 (431/0)

48b.  138 silver phialai, a silver drinking-horn; weight of these:
2 talents 3307 dr.

φιάλαι ἀργυραῖ ΗΔΔΔΓΙΙΙ κέρας ἀργυροῦν σταθμὸν
τούτων ΤΤΧΧΧΗΗΗΓΙΙ

*IG* I³, 350 lines 69–70 (427/6)
**351 lines 8–9 (422/1)**
352 line 33 (421/0)
353 line 56 (420/19)
354 line 76 (419/8)
355 line 9 (414/3)
356 lines 35–6 (413/2)
357 lines 61–2 (412/1)[6]

49.  8 silver phialai; weight of these: 807 dr.

φιάλαι ἀργυραῖ ΓΙΙΙ σταθμὸν τούτων ΓΗΗΗΓΙΙ

*IG* I³, 350 line 81 (427/6)

---

[6] See W. E. Thompson (1965a) 229–30 for the relationship between **48a** and **48b**.

351 lines 17–18 (422/1)
**353 lines 64–5 (420/19)**
354 line 81 (419/8)
355 lines 18–19 (414/3)
356 line 45 (413/2)
357 line 71 (412/1)

50.        5 gold phialai; weight of these: 782 dr.

φιάλαι ἀργυραῖ Γ σταθμὸν τούτων ΓΗΗℲΔΔΔΗⵑ

*IG* I³, 343 line 4 (434/3)
344 line 20 (433/2)
345 line 49 (432/1)
346 lines 55–6 (431/0)
350 line 66 (427/6)
351 lines 5–6 (422/1)
352 lines 29–30 (421/0)
353 line 53 (420/19)
**354 line 74 (419/8)**
355 lines 5–6 (414/3)
356 line 32 (413/2)
357 line 58 (412/1)

51.        Two silver phialai; two silver goblets; weight of these:
580 dr.

φιάλα ἀργυρᾶ· καρχησίω ἀργυρὼ σταθμὸν τούτων
ΓℲΔΔΔ

*IG* I³, 350 lines 83–4 (427/6)
**351 lines 19–20 (422/1)**
353 line 67 (420/19)
354 lines 82–3 (419/8)
355 lines 20–1 (414/3)
356 line 47 (413/2)
357 lines 73–4 (412/1)
358 lines 2–3 (411 or 411/0)

52.        4 silver phialai, 2 silver containers, a silver horse; weight
of these: 900 dr.

φιάλαι ἀργυραῖ ΙΙΙΙ κυλιχνίω ἐπαργύρω ΙΙ ἵππος
ἀργυροῦς σταθμὸν τούτων ΓΗΗΗΗ

*IG* I³, 349 lines 57–8 (428/7)
350 line 78 (427/6)
**351 lines 16–17 (422/1)**
353 lines 63–4 (420/19)
354 lines 80–1 (419/8)
355 line 17 (414/3)
356 lines 43–4 (413/2)
357 lines 69–70 (412/1)

53. A gold *karchesion* (goblet) having a silver base, sacred to Herakles in Elaious; weight of this: 138 dr.

καρχήσιον χρυσοῦν τὸμ πυθμένα ὑπάργυρον ἔχων ἱερὸν τοῦ Ἡρακλέους τοῦ ἐν Ἐλαιεῖ σταθμὸν τού- του ΗΔΔΔΓΗΗ

> IG I³, 343 lines 5–6 (434/3)
> 344 lines 21–2 (433/2)
> 346 lines 56–7 (431/0)
> 350 lines 67–8 (427/6)
> **351 lines 6–7 (422/1)**
> 352 lines 30–1 (421/0)
> 353 lines 53–4 (420/19)
> 354 lines 74–5 (419/8)
> 355 lines 6–7 (414/3)
> 356 lines 33–4 (413/2)
> 357 lines 59–60 (412/1)

54. (V.265) An incense-burner, gilt wood

θυμιατήριον ὑπόξυλον κατάχρυσον

> IG I³, 343 lines 9–10 (434/3) [Parthenon]
> 344 line 25 (433/2)
> 346 line 60 (431/0)
> 350 lines 71–2 (427/6)
> 351 lines 10–11 (422/1)
> 352 lines 34–5 (421/0)
> 353 lines 57–8 (420/19)
> **354 line 77 (419/8)**
> 355 lines 10–11 (414/3)
> 356 line 37 (413/2)
> 357 line 63 (412/1)
> IG II², 1379 lines 2–3 (402/1 or 401/0)
> 1394 lines 17–18 (397/6) [Hekatompedon]

55. 4 silver Chalkidian drinking-cups; weight of these: 124 dr.

ποτήρια Χαλκιδικὰ ἀργυρᾶ ΙΙΙΙ σταθμὸν τούτων ΗΔΔΗΗΗ

> IG I³, 350 lines 81–2 (427/6)
> **351 line 18 (422/1)**
> 353 line 65 (420/19)
> 354 lines 81–2 (419/8)
> 355 line 19 (414/3)
> 356 lines 45–6 (413/2)
> 357 lines 71–2 (412/1)
> 358 line 1 (411 or 411/0)

56.                 3 silver Lesbian cups; weight of these: 370 dr.

Λέσβιοι κότυλοι ἀργυροῖ ΙΙΙ σταθμὸν τούτων
ΗΗΗϜΔΔ

*IG* I³, 350 line 84 (427/6)
           351 lines 20–1 (422/1)
           **353 lines 67–8 (420/19)**
           **354 line 83 (419/8)**
           355 lines 21–2 (414/3)
           356 lines 47–8 (413/2)
           357 line 74 (412/1)
           358 line 3 (411 or 411/0)

WREATHS

57.                 A gold wreath; weight of this: 60 dr.

στέφανος χρυσοῦς σταθμὸν τούτου ϜΔ

*IG* I³, 343 line 4 (434/3)
           344 lines 19–20 (433/2)
           346 line 55 (431/0)
           350 lines 65–6 (427/6)
           351 line 5 (422/1)
           352 line 29 (421/0)
           353 line 52 (420/19)
           **354 line 74 (419/8)**
           355 line 5 (414/3)
           356 line 32 (413/2)
           357 line 58 (412/1)

58.                 A gold wreath; weight of this: 18 dr. 3 ob.

στέφανος χρυσοῦς σταθμὸν τούτου ΔΓΗΗΙΙΙ

*IG* I³, **351 line 21 (422/1)**
           353 line 68 (420/19)
           354 line 83 (419/8)
           355 line 22 (414/3)
           356 line 48 (413/2)
           357 lines 74–5 (412/1)
           358 line 4 (411 or 411/0)

59.                 A gold wreath, weight of this 29 dr.

στέφανος χρυσοῦς σταθμὸν τούτου ΔΔΓΗΗΗ

*IG* I³, 351 line 21 (422/1)
           **353 lines 68–9 (420/19)**
           354 lines 83–4 (419/8)
           355 line 22 (414/3)
           356 lines 48–9 (413/2)
           357 line 75 (412/1)

358 line 4 (411 or 411/0)

60.      A gold wreath of Athena Nike; weight of this: 29 dr.

Ἀθηναίας Νίκης στέφανος χρυσοῦς σταθμὸν τούτου
ΔΔΓⱵⱵⱵ

> *IG* I³, 351 lines 21–2 (422/1)
> 353 line 69 (420/19)
> **354 line 84 (419/8)**
> 355 lines 22–3 (414/3)
> 356 line 49 (413/2)
> 357 lines 75–6 (412/1)
> 358 lines 4–5 (411 or 411/0)

61.      A gold wreath; weight of this: 33 dr.

στέφανος χρυσοῦς σταθμὸν τούτου ΔΔΔⱵⱵ

> *IG* I³, 351 line 22 (422/1)
> 353 lines 69–70 (420/19)
> 354 line 84 (419/8)
> 355 lines 23–4 (414/3)
> 356 lines 49–50 (413/2)
> 357 line 76 (412/1)
> 358 line 5 (411 or 411/0)
> **359 line 1 (410/9 or 409/8)**

62.      A gold wreath of Athena Nike; weight of this: 33 dr.

Ἀθηναίας Νίκης στέφανος χρυσοῦς σταθμὸν τούτου
ΔΔΔⱵⱵ

> *IG* I³, **351 lines 22–3 (422/1)**
> 352 lines 46–7 (421/0)
> **353 line 70 (420/19)**
> 354 line 84 (419/8)
> 355 line 24 (414/3)
> 356 line 50 (413/2)
> 357 lines 76–7 (412/1)
> 358 lines 5–6 (411 or 411/0)
> 359 lines 1–2 (410/9 or 409/8)

# PART V

# *The Treasures of the Hekatompedon*

## OBSERVATIONS

The Hekatompedon became the principal repository for the treasures after the fall of Athens to Sparta at the end of the fifth century.[1] The name 'Hekatompedon' (one-hundred-foot cella) was used to mean the main (eastern) cella with its double Doric interior peristyle and cult statue, or alternatively referred to the temple as a whole. It was also the name of the temple's sixth-century predecessor, and was perhaps used for that part of the south side of the Akropolis in the period between the Persian sack and the beginning of construction in the time of Perikles.

The most numerous category of items was formed by the gold wreaths. As silver wreaths were the official prize for some events in the Panathenaia, and all save one wreath listed in the inventories were gold, that cannot have been the source. Who dedicated these wreaths, and how were they paid for? Some were honorific, awarded by the city to an individual and then returned to her as a dedication. Take, for example, the honorific decree proposed by Androtion in praise of the Spartokidai of the Bosporan kingdom, *IG* II², 212 (346/5). The decree orders the *Athlothetai* to make gold wreaths for them in the year of the Greater Panathenaia, and then prescribes that the wreaths must be dedicated in the temple of Athena Polias with an inscription. Remarkable as it seems, the Assembly dictated how the label on the dedicated wreath should read:

And when they dedicate their wreaths to Athena Polias, then let the *athlothetai* place the wreaths in her temple, with the inscription 'Spartokos

---

[1] The term Ἑκατόμπεδος Νεώς in the masculine gender is found in Hesychios; *Sudo*; Plut. *De glor. Ath.* 7. 8 ; *De soll. anim.* 13, *Cato* 5. 3; and in Aristeides 51. 61. It appears as a neuter noun in Harpokration, the *Glossa Patmia* frag. of Lykourgos, and the inventory lists. Cf. W. B. Dinsmoor (1947) 123 n: 74; Jahn and Michaelis (1901) 54 n. 32*. The term 'Parthenon' is used for the whole temple in Aelian *De nat. anim.* 6. 48; Dem. 22. 13; Himerios *Ecl.* 31. 8; Pliny *NH* 22. 44; Plut. *Per.* 13, *Sulla* 13; Strabo 9. 1. 16; Paus. 8. 41. 9. Cf. Jahn and Michaelis (1901) 54 n. 32**.

and Pairisades sons of Leukon dedicated these wreaths to Athena having been presented with them by the *demos* of Athens.'

ἐπειδὴ δὲ τοὺς στεφάνους ἀνατιθέασι τῇ Ἀθηνᾷ τῇ Πολιάδι τοὺς ἀθλοθέτας εἰς τὸν νεὼ ἀνατιθέναι τοὺς στεφάνους ἐπιγράψαντας· Σπάρτοκος καὶ Παιρισάδης Λεύκωνος παῖδες ἀνέθεσαν τῇ Ἀθηναίᾳ στεφανωθέντες ὑπὸ τοῦ δήμου τοῦ Ἀθηναίων.

A wreath was in fact listed in the inventories of the Hekatompedon by Spartokos of Pontos, dedicated to 'the *demos* of Athens'. Unfortunately, the earliest listing of Spartokos' wreath is in the last decade of the fourth century BC, so that we cannot confirm that they are one and the same.[2]

The inscriptions on the wreaths were a source of pride for the Athenians, according to Demosthenes:

You all, I suppose, used to see the words written under the circlets of the wreaths: 'The Allies crowned the Athenian people for valour and righteousness', or 'The Allies dedicated to the Goddess of Athens a prize of victory'; or, from the several states of the Alliance, 'such-and-such a city crowned the People by whom they were delivered' or 'the liberated Euboeans', for example, 'crowned the People,' or again 'Conon from the sea-fight with the Lacedaemonians,' 'Chabrias from the sea-fight off Naxos.' Such, I say, were the inscriptions on the wreaths.'[3]

When would the Athenians have all had a chance to see such objects? Demosthenes must be referring to a festival day when these items would be brought out and displayed or paraded in public.

After the battle of the Granikos, Alexander sent back to Athens an offering of 300 panoplies.[4] Arrian records the dedicatory inscription attached to them as follows: 'Alexander, son of Philip, and the Greeks (except the Lakedaimonians) dedicate these spoils, taken from the Persians who dwell in Asia.' The Treasurers of Athena apparently did not make an inventory of these panoplies, although they did record gifts of jewellery offered by Alexander's Bactrian queen, Roxane (**V.141**).

Likewise, the Harpalos affair implied that much treasure accumulated during Alexander's campaigns was sent to Athens—yet there is no record in the inventories of the cash or any treasures of gold or

---

[2] *IG* II[2], 1486 lines 14–16 (after 307/6); 1485 lines 21–4 (304/3).

[3] *Dem.* 24. 180–1, trans. J. H. Vince. The only inscription remotely resembling those Demosthenes recalled is the wreath in honour of Konon. He and other members of his family dedicated items on the Acropolis for a century, and their statues could be seen on the Akropolis and in the Agora; see the discussion in Part VII.

[4] Arr. *Anab.* 1. 16. 7.

silver entering the inventory lists in the years 330 and following. Harpalos served as Alexander's imperial treasurer, and was stationed in Ecbatana and then in Babylon, living with Pythionike, an Athenian woman, for whom he later built a costly tomb on the Sacred Way to Eleusis. In Ecbatana alone he was left responsible for a treasury which amounted to 180,000 talents.[5] After much graft, when caught, he directed an Athenian revolt against Alexander, funding it with 5000 talents' worth of treasures he had brought from Persia.[6] Harpalos is alleged to have deposited 305 talents on the Akropolis in the year 324 BC, but none of it was recorded in the inventory lists or accounts.[7]

There are two mentions of the deposit of counterfeit coinage in the temple. One case involved twenty-five silver pieces 'from Eleusis' (II.26=V.58). In the second case, some counterfeit staters were 'sealed in a box by Lakon' (V.66).[8] The earliest records of both are in the inventories for the year 398/7. Perhaps this could indicate a rise in counterfeit coinage during the financial crisis at the end of the Peloponnesian war and the internal political crisis which followed. Stroud identified a law of 375/4 concerning counterfeit coinage, stipulating that the only coinage which should be accepted was that bearing the official stamp of the Athenian mint and made of good silver.[9] A hoard of plated drachmai was excavated at Eleusis which may have been from the issue minted in 406/5 and withdrawn from circulation in 394/3.[10] If so, some of these same coins may have been deposited in the temple to keep them out of circulation.

Several items associated with the minting of coins and testing for counterfeit appear in the inventories. First, there are the anvils, hammers, and dies (V.34): 'A wooden box in which are kept the dies and little anvils'. Then there are the *dokimeia* or test pieces (V.87, 88). They may have been the specimens to be used for testing the gold that went into the new oinochoe of Athena, the oinochoe of the gods, the phialai, the incense-burners, and even a throne (V.38, 45). Their small weights indicate that they were not

[5] Diod. Sic. 17. 80; Strabo. 15. 3. 9; Arr. *Anab.* 3. 19. 7.

[6] Berve no. 143; Arr. *Anab.* 3. 19. 7; Diod. Sic. 17. 108. 1–8; Curt. 10. 2. 2–3; Just. 13. 5. 9; Plut. *Demosthenes* 25. 1–6. See also Badian (1961) 16–43; Wilcken (1932) 207, 341.

[7] Hyperid. on Demosthenes fr. 1 col. II, 5; *Vit. X orat.* 846B; Phot. *Bibl.* 265 p. 491a; cf. Jahn and Michaelis (1901) 18 no. 187.

[8] Alessandri (1982).

[9] Stroud (1974) 157–88; cf. Giovannini (1975) 193.

[10] E. S. G. Robinson (1960) 8–13; M. Thompson, Mørkholm, and Craay (1973) no. 46; cf. Giovannini (1975) 189.

full size. The *dokimeia* were kept in boxes in the Hekatompedon.[11] What exactly these items were is still not clear. An official magistrate of fourth-century Athens was called the *dokimastēs*, or public tester, and had responsibility for distinguishing good Athenian coins from forged counterfeits. According to the decree, he was to test silver coins, and if they were counterfeit cut and confiscate them.[12] After confiscation, where would they go? Perhaps they went back into the melting-pot. But if it were not pure silver, and not of sufficient quality to melt down, the temple would be a suitable location in which to keep such coins permanently out of circulation.

Some items in the inventories are of a personal nature, but were not listed with the name of their dedicant. These objects occur in the categories of jewellery and clothing, the sort of article which an individual would be most likely to dedicate. There is very little personal clothing in the inventories. The few garments listed are of luxurious material: fine cotton, linen, and imported muslin, at least one example of which was dyed purple. These may have been particularly fine clothes, and for that reason were inscribed in the lists. Or else they may have been dedicated as a way of getting rid of articles which were either illegal or might have incurred jealousy from fellow citizens.[13] Items of clothing include a robe of the type called a *xustis* (**V.51**); a linen chiton (**V.49**); something made of fine muslin (**V.52**); a purple-dyed snood (**II.62**); and two boxes of boots or heavy sandals (**V.53**).

War booty must have formed a major component of Athena's wealth. War revenue often included slaves, property, and money raised from the sale of booty; as Pritchett has remarked, 'without wars, few of the temples and other sacred buildings of Greece would have been built. The custom of giving to the gods a war tithe resulted in some of civilization's most treasured fruits.'[14] Most war booty would have arrived at a sanctuary in its original form, as armour stripped from the enemy on the battlefield.[15] In the time of Pausanias a few famous pieces of war booty were on display on the Akropolis, for example, the corslet of Masistios and the sword (ἀκινάκης) of Mardonios.[16] But relatively few items of military equipment found their way into the inventories of the Parthenon.

Pritchett noted that as early as Homer's *Iliad* Athena was recognized as the patron deity of war booty (*Il.* 10. 460), 'and sacrifices

[11] Ferguson (1932) 119.    [12] *Hesperia*, 43 (1974) 157–88 lines 8–13.
[13] This practice is well attested; cf. Mills (1984) 255–65.
[14] Pritchett (1971) 96–100.    [15] Burkert (1985) 69.    [16] Paus. 1. 27. 1; Hdt. 9. 22. 10.

were offered to her in this capacity at Olympia (Paus. 5. 14. 5)'.[17] Much war booty must be unrecognizable as such in the inventories, since the tithes may have been in the form of money to the treasury, uninventoried, or in the form of vessels and objects purchased with that money and not labelled as booty. It has been conjectured that the golden Nikai of the fifth century represent the money gained from the sale of war-booty.[18] *Laphyropōlai* or booty-traders were appointed after battles to exchange the booty for money through trade, and once it was transformed into money it could be dedicated directly or used to purchase a dedication.[19] Both forms of dedication would be unrecognizable in the treasury without a tag indicating that they derived from war booty. The Treasurers of Athena do not often note the name of the dedicant, much less the function or purpose of the dedication.

We thus have no certain example of a dedication of war booty. Clearly once the treasurers determined to admit an article into the temple, the purpose of its dedication was forgotten. The distinction may not have been an important one to the treasurers, since once a vase or object taken as war booty was acquired, it could have been put to use in ceremonies like any other ceremonial utensil. That it does not appear more frequently is also testimony to the lack of interest that the treasurers had in distinguishing the origin of an object. Once it was dedicated to Athena, there was little purpose in maintaining the categories which Thucydides observed in 2. 13. 4: 'The uncoined gold and silver in offerings made either by individuals or by the state; sacred vessels and furniture used in processions and games, and the spoils taken from the Persians.'

Objects of a military nature may have been gathered from a battlefield after the trophy was erected, and a contribution sent to the Akropolis. However, it is equally likely that such dedications were valuable personal gifts to Athena. The lists below show that there was not enough armour in the Parthenon to make up a tithe (10 per cent) of military victories. Dedication of a tithe must not have been a regular practice. However, the following lists do not include armour in the Chalkotheke, which served as a repository for arms of all sorts, including war booty; tithes may have been kept there. Items of armour that ended up in the Parthenon were

---

[17] Pritchett (1971) 54 n. 5.
[18] D. B. Thompson (1944) 176; Pritchett (1971) 97.
[19] References to λαφυροπῶλαι (booty-sellers) may be found in Pritchett (1971) 90.

usually made of bronze, silver, or gold, and were often under-sized or miniature, surely a sign of their votive nature.

Greaves did not form a major type of treasure in the Parthenon. The texts in which they appear are mostly records of the Chalkotheke, but a few do occur in inventories of the Parthenon. These include **V.6, 7,** and **18**, with at least ten pairs over the course of the 135 years of inventories. Fourteen breastplates were dedicated simultaneously (**V.5**), first appearing in the lists in 434/3. Two more were added in 428/7; the only other was in the panoply dedicated by Alexander son of Polyperchon in the list of 304/3 (**V.18**). Helmets were more commonly dedicated. One miniature helmet with gold and ivory first appears in an inventory of 374/3 (**V.13**). The rest, of full size, numbering at least thirty, were dedicated over the entire span of the fourth century.[20] Of interest is the Illyrian helmet (**V.10**), which first entered the inventory in 427/6 and was probably captured in battle, as it is said to have come from Lesbos and the Athenians were fighting there that year. This type of helmet came into vogue shortly after the Persian wars.[21]

Shields were the most common form of armour dedicated in the temple. Seven were miniature votive shields.[22] The rest must be presumed to be full-sized, of which there were at least 138, not necessarily all present at the same time.[23] This total does not include shields in the Chalkotheke, Erechtheion, and Opisthodomos. Some of the shields were said to have blazons or emblems, and of the few which specify the design of the emblem, only the gorgoneion is ever named.[24]

The storage and display of all of these shields in the temple are matters for conjecture. If they were hung on the walls, the surviving wall-blocks ought to provide an indication, either with peg-holes for mounting or at least ghost outlines and weathering marks where the shields protected the wall from lamp-smoke and dust. No trace of such marks has been reported.

Some weapons were kept in the temple. The ἀκινάκης, a Persian type of dagger, may have been among war relics captured or left behind in the Persian wars. Six were dedicated in the Parthenon in 434/3, and one more joined the inventories in 428/7.[25] In the

---

[20] V.8–12, 14–16, and 18.
[21] Snodgrass (1967) 95; Schroeder (1912) 317–44.
[22] For these see V.21, 23, 97.
[23] See V.18–32, 97.
[24] Gorgoneia appear as blazons on the following shields: V.21–2, 31–2, 102.
[25] The six gold Persian daggers appear in IV.1 in the inventories of the Parthenon.

fourth-century inventories only two ἀκινάκαι appear, the golden one which entered in 428/7 (**V.1**) and an iron one (**V.2**). Detailed information was given in the latter case: 'An iron Persian dagger, having a gold grip, a sheath of ivory and gold, and a knob (πυγλίον) of gold.'

Dorothy Thompson suggested that a number of relics and items of booty from the Persian wars were kept in the Parthenon and displayed in Athens.[26] The number of objects she attributed to the Persians was generous; today it is difficult to ascribe any to the Persians, with the possible exception of those which have Persian names, such as the ἀκινάκαι. Only a few items are labelled as Persian: an aulos-case Μηδική (**V.190**), a copper-coloured phiale βαρβαρική which Kleon dedicated (**V.315**), ten Persian shekels (**V.60**) kept in the Parthenon between 405 and 389 BC, and some gold Darics dedicated to Demeter and Kore mentioned in the inventories of 394 and 390 (**V.57**). In the Chalkotheke there were other items listed as Persian or indeed Lakedaimonian, which were most certainly war booty: e.g. 86 Persian bridles (χαλινοὶ Μηδικοὶ ͰΔΔΔΓΙ).[27]

Most spears were stored in the Chalkotheke, but 110 spear-points were kept in the Parthenon (**V.4**).[28] The Erechtheion housed silver spears which were under-sized and clearly votive rather than true armour. Eight and a half boxes of 'rotten and useless arrows' were kept in the Parthenon (**V.3**). There is no apparent reason for this unless they were gathered up from a battlefield of some significance. The fact that they were rotten by 370 BC may indicate that they were of considerable age, perhaps dating from the time of the Peloponnesian or even Persian war. These appear under the rubric 'from the Parthenon' among a group of objects which had been in the treasury longer than most other items. Everything under that rubric had been kept in the western chamber, the Parthenon proper, prior to the collection of all items together in the Hekatompedon.

The variety of furniture is quite remarkable; in the year 368/7 the complete inventory list *IG* II², 1425, records twenty-six couches (**V.112–15**), ten camp-stools (**V.119**), five stools (δίφροι) (**V.116–17**), nine thrones (**V.122–4**), and a table (**V.121**). How all of these were arranged in relation to the cult statue and interior colonnade cannot be determined. The couches could have been

[26] D. B. Thompson (1956).

[27] *IG* II², 1424a line 135.

[28] Spears in the Chalkotheke: nine, *IG* II², 1414 line 8; 38, *IG* II², 1424a line 132; 48, *IG* II², 1425 line 392; 3, *IG* II², 1465 line 2; unspecified no., *IG* II², 1491 line 7.

arranged around the Parthenon room where they were kept in the fifth century, albeit awkwardly, since the door is not off-centre, or they may have been stored there to be used out of doors on festival days. Milesian and Chian couches were considered to be of the finest quality. That they were commissioned for the temple as the furniture for the Parthenon room may be ascertained by the fact that they appear in the first inventory of 434 BC (*IG* I³, 343 lines 12–13). The only items of furniture that we know to have been used in the Panathenaic processions were the *diphroi*.[29] The *diphrophoroi* were the stool-carriers on these occasions, and appear on the frieze of the Parthenon.[30] Shapiro has recently shown that the *diphros* was a modest but appropriate seat for Athena and is associated with the goddess in vase-painting.[31] The function of the rest of the furniture is not known. Thrones were seats of honour used for prominent statesmen; couches were for sleeping, eating, and funerals.[32] Why were these kept in the temple? Who was supposed to sit on the thrones and couches? What was the table used for?[33]

Many of the types of furniture also appeared on the Attic Stelai recording the sale of the confiscated property of the Hermokopidai (415 BC). Milesian couches (V.114–15) were listed in the Attic Stelai (n. 1, 229 and 11, 244). Eleven of them sold for 90 dr., one for 7 dr. 3 ob. Athenaios praised Chian and Milesian couches very highly.[34] Some of the furniture seems to have been in disrepair (V.123–4) and may have been discarded in subsequent reorganizations, since there is no mention of most of the couches and stools after 367/6.[35]

A few dedications were kept on a *bathron*, which may be loosely defined as a base but could also be a backless seat, a footstool, or a bench.[36] Golden earrings, two gold rings, and a gem set in gold were on the *bathron*, unweighed (V.156); a gold helmet was inventoried as having come from the *bathron* (V.13). In both cases the *bathron* could be an offering-table or bench. Another way in which the

---

[29] The δίφρος is discussed in Pritchett and Amyx (1956) 215–16. They appear on the frieze of the Parthenon on east slabs **IV–VI**.

[30] Ancient sources for the διφροφόροι are collected in Michaelis (1871) 329–30. These include Ar. *Av.* 1549; Hesych. s.v.

[31] Shapiro (1989) 31 pls. 10–11.

[32] Richter (1987) 371.

[33] There may be some significance to the fact that only one table ever appeared in the inventories. Most temples had offering-tables which played an important role in the cult. See Aleshire (1989) 308; D. H. Gill (1974) 117–37; Dow and Gill (1965) 103–14.

[34] Athen. 1. 28 B. Cf. Pritchett and Amyx (1956) 228.

[35] Only the ivory table (121), ten camp-stools (119), two diphroi (117), and four thrones (123) reappeared in inscriptions later than 367/6.

[36] Pritchett and Amyx (1956) 215. Cf. Leipen (1971) 27.

word *bathron* is used in the inventories is in reference to the chryselephantine cult-statue base. Another example is 'a gold piece,
which Aristokles from --- recovered, from the base of the statue;
weight: 100+ dr.' (**V.80**). The word βάθρον here was qualified with
the genitive ἀγάλματος following, to distinguish this βάθρον from
any others. But the others should be presumed to have been similar
in form in order for the same term to have been used.

Evidence for shelving, probably in the form of open cases or cupboards, rather than shelves attached to the marble cella walls, can be
found in these inventories, where the vases are assigned specific locations.[37] Gold wreaths would not have been kept on the floor, and
since they are inventoried in the order of their dedication by archon
year, it would be reasonable to think that they were kept on shelves.
They could also have been hung on the walls, but Korres has
not found any peg-holes in the walls in his thorough study of
the Parthenon for the new restoration. The shelving would have
been placed against the cella walls behind the interior colonnade
surrounding the cult statue and reflecting pond, rendering that
area closed to traffic.[38] Chests were also used for keeping smaller
valuables.

The musical instruments stored in the Parthenon were lyres and
auloi. It is no coincidence that these two instruments are known
from literary sources to have accompanied the rites of Athena.
Perikles himself is said to have initiated musical contests at the
Panathenaic festival: 'Again eager for honour, Perikles had a resolution passed establishing a musical contest in the Panathenaic festival.
And he himself, having been selected as judge (*athlothetēs*), arranged
how the competitors should play the aulos and sing and play
the *kithara*. And it was in the Odeion that they used to view the
musical contests, both at that time and at other times.'[39] The frieze
on the Parthenon depicts auletes and kitharodes.[40] The lyres were
made of wood and ivory, the wood probably being *kernos*-oak.[41]
There are fifteen lyres listed in the inventories, not all in the temple
at the same time.

The only allusion to an aulos in the inventories is to the case for
the instrument called a συβήνη. These were made of wood, ivory,

[37] For depictions of shelving in Greek art see Richter (1966) 78–9.

[38] Korres, the architect of the recent restoration of the Parthenon, agrees with this suggestion.

[39] Plut. *Per.* 13. 11.

[40] Rotroff (1977). The panels showing these musicians are north frieze, nos. 20–7; south frieze, nos.
102–4.

[41] Theophr. *Hist. Pl.* 5. 7. 6.

and gold and were more valuable than the instrument itself, it would seem. The two recorded aulos-cases were both foreign products, one from Methymna which was taken to Athens in the year of the conflict on Lesbos (428/7 BC), the other said to be Persian (Μηδική).[42]

Lyres and auloi were the earliest musical instruments in Greece, to judge from the Cycladic figurines of the harpist and double aulos (third millennium BC). Plutarch (*Per.* 13. 11) suggests that musical contests were not a regular event in the Panathenaia until they were introduced under Perikles, necessitating the construction of the Odeion. Vase representations of musical contests on Panathenaic amphoras, however, attest to musical competitions earlier than the mid-fifth century.[43] The musical categories included singing and recitation by rhapsodes. The competition for recitation of Homer's epic poems may have been the earliest feature. *IG* II², 2311, lists the winners of four musical competitions, who received gold wreaths and a cash prize of silver.[44] The contests mentioned in this inscription included the youths playing the kithara (παῖδες κιθαρισταί), adult singers to the kithara (κιθαρῳδοί), adult male kithara-players (ἄνδρες κιθαρισταί), adult aulos-players (αὐληταί), and male voices accompanied by the aulos (ἄνδρες αὐλῳδοί). The instruments kept in the Parthenon could have been used in the competitions at the Panathenaia, if the kithara and the lyre are considered to be equivalent terms. They would have left the temple and been brought down the slope to the Odeion, a procedure which would require that the instruments be inventoried and returned to the temple after the festival.

A wide variety of shapes of vases were kept in the Parthenon, the majority of them in gold and silver. Twenty-seven silver hydriai, each weighing close to 1000 dr., appear regularly in the lists from 402/1 (**V.260**). Between 384/3 and 378/7 three new hydriai were added to the Parthenon for Athena (**V.255**). Aphrodite, the Dioskouroi (Kastor and Poludeukes), Athena Nike, Demeter and Kore, and Artemis Brauronia each had their own hydriai, bringing the total to fifty (**V.252, 254, 256, 257, 259**). In the last quarter of the fourth century at least thirteen more were commissioned by the

---

[42] **V.191; V.190**.

[43] Shapiro (1989) 41–2; Davison (1958) 36–41.

[44] The prizes are described in *Ath. Pol.* 60. 3 and supported by *IG* II², 2311. Literary sources for the musical contests include rhapsodic competitions: Diog. Laert. 1. 57; Isoc. *Paneg.* 159; Lycurg. *Leok.* 102, *Hipparchos* 228 B; Plato *Ion* 530 B. Auletes: Σ Pindar *Pyth.* 12. 6–8; [Plut.] *De Musica* 8; *Per.* 13. 11. Cithara: Ar. *Nub.* 969–71; Σ Ar. *Av.* 11; *Souda* s.v. Φρῦνις.

treasurers for the temple (V.215–18, 251, 253, 258). In addition, there were seven hydriai made of gold (V.244–9, 261). Hydriai were certainly carried in the Panathenaic festival, as depicted on the Ionic frieze of the Parthenon.[45]

Silver phialai are noticeably absent from the inventories of the Hekatompedon in the fourth century, and seem to have been more common in the Erechtheion. It will be remembered that there were many silver and gold phialai in the fifth-century inventories of the Proneos, but these were all melted down at the end of the Peloponnesian war.[46] Silver phialai were probably kept in the Parthenon, but were for some reason uninventoried. Shortly after 320/19 some silver hydriai were listed as having been made from the silver phialai of freedmen (*IG* II², 1469 lines 12–17); the lists of silver phialai (*IG* II², 1553–78, *c.*330 BC) recorded those about to be melted down which had been in the treasury but had remained uninventoried. Gold phialai, however, were quite numerous, with groups of them listed for Athena (V.325–8) and many individual phialai (V.211, 219, 220, 223, 304, 309, 310, 319, 320, 323, 324, 330, 331, 339, 341, 342), numbering at least thirty-three.

One certain category of ritual vessel was the *skaphē* or *skaphion,* the ceremonial tray. A hundred *skaphai* were listed from 405/4 to at least 385/4.[47] The *skaphēphoroi*, who carried the *skaphai* in the Panathenaic procession, were metics and ephebes.[48] These may also be depicted in the frieze of the Parthenon.[49] Photios attests that metics carried the bronze and silver trays in the Panathenaic procession, and that the trays were filled with Phoenician garments.[50]

One of the largest groups of vessels inventoried is comprised by the incense-burners. There were probably many more of these than were required for the rites of Athena. There were at least ten silver ones, and six gilt.[51] We must imagine the smell of sweet burning incense emanating from the gold and silver *thymiatēria* inventoried in the temple. During the procession it is possible that participants swung the incense-burners as they marched, adding to the festive

[45] North frieze slab VI, figs 16–19. For the ancient sources on the ὑδριαφόροι, see Michaelis (1871) 329–30.

[46] *IG* I³, 292–316.

[47] See V.228, 229.

[48] Ancient sources are assembled in Michaelis (1871) 329–30. These include Photios s.v. σκάφας; Hesychios and Harpokration s.v. σκαφηφόροι.

[49] North slab V, figs. 13–15.

[50] Photios s.v. σκάφας.

[51] For silver incense-burners see V.222, 262–3, 273–6. Gilt ones are listed as V.265–6, 268–9, 271–2.

atmosphere a scent associated with Athena's rites. Four silver wash-basins, or *chernibeia* were kept in the temple, and they may have had a ritual function.[52] Oinochoai, kylikes, *karchesia, pinakes, ekpōmata, kymbia,* and other vase-shapes appear more or less frequently in the inventories, as indicated in the following catalogue.

The catalogue below includes items kept in the Opisthodomos or in the Parthenon chamber in the fifth-century inventories but listed in inventories of the Hekatompedon at the beginning of the fourth century BC. These are in the form of cross-references to Parts II and IV respectively.

### THE TREASURES

ARMS AND WEAPONS

1. (IV.2)

2. An iron Persian dagger, having a gold grip, a sheath of ivory and gold, and a knob of gold

   ἀκινάκης σιδηροῦς τὴν λαβὴν χρυσῆν ἔχων τὸ δὲ κολεὸν ἐλεφάντινον περίχρυσον τὸ δὲ πυγλίον χρυσοῦν

   > *IG* II², 1413 line 28 (after 385/4)
   > 1421 lines 27–30 (374/3)
   > **1424a lines 77–80 (371/0)**
   > 1425 lines 75–8 (368/7)
   > 1460 lines 12–15 (after 330/29)

3. 8½ boxes of rotten and useless arrows

   σώρακοι ΓΙΙΙ καὶ ἡμισωράκιον τοξευμάτων σαπρῶν ἀχρήστων

   > *IG* II², **1424a lines 344–5 (371/0)**
   > 1425 lines 280–2 (368/7)
   > 1428 line 217 (367/6)

4. 110 spear–points

   στύρακες ΗΔ

   > *IG* II², **1424a line 344 (371/0)**
   > 1425 line 280 (368/7)

5. (IV.6)

---

[52] References to χερνιβεῖα (wash-basins) are listed as **V.221, 230–3**. Silver on a χερνιβεῖον is listed as **V.233**.

6.            Pairs of greaves
κνημίδων ζεύγη
     *IG* II², 1473 line 2 (304/3)

7.            6 pairs of greaves
κνημίδων ζεύγη ΓΙ
     *IG* II², 1424a line 342 (371/0)
         1425 line 278 (368/7)

8.            Achaian helmets
κράνη Ἀχαϊκά
     *IG* II², 1463 line 7 (349/8)
         1473 line 3 (304/3)

9.            Achaian helmets
κράνη Ἀχαϊκά
     *IG* II², 1463 line 9 (349/8)

10. (IV.5)

11.          A bronze helmet
κυνῆ χαλκῆ
     *IG* II², 1415 line 22 (375/4)

12.          One bronze helmet, covered with gold
κυνῆ χαλκῆ ἐπίχρυσος μία
     *IG* II², 1380 line 4 (after 390?)
         1421 line 94 (374/3)
         **1424a line 290 (371/0)**
         1425 lines 202–3 (368/7)
         1443 line 203 (344/3)

13.          A small helmet from the base, having a gold cheekpiece and an ivory crest
κρανίδιον μικρὸν ἀπὸ τοῦ βάθρου παρειὰς χρυσᾶς ἔχον καὶ λόφον ἐλεφάντινον
     *IG* II², 1421 lines 123–5 (374/3)
         1424a lines 319–21 (371/0)
         1425 lines 245–7 (368/7)
         1443 lines 208–9 [without cheekpieces]
         1455 lines 10–11 [without cheekpieces]

14. (IV.4)

15.         4 bronze helmets
κράνη χαλκᾶ ΙΙΙΙ

*IG* II², 1425 line 259 (368/7)
1428 line 211 (367/6)
1434 line 11 (*c*.367/6)

16. 26 helmets, upper parts bronze

κυναῖ χαλκαῖ ἄνω ΔΔΓΙ

*IG* II², 1424a line 343 (371/0)
1425 line 279 (368/7) [17]
1433 line 18 (between 384/3 and 374/3) [17]

17. Small ivory javelins

ἀκόντια ἐλεφάντινα

*IG* II², 1461 lines 33–4 (after 330/29)

18. A panoply, which Alexander, son of Polyperchon, dedicated: a complete ceremonial breast-plate, a complete light shield, gilt, bronze greaves with silver work

πανοπλία ἣν Ἀλέξανδρος ὁ Πολυπέρχοντος ἀνέθηκεν·
θώραξ πομπικὸς ἐντελής· πέλτη ἐπίχρυσος ἐντελής·
κνημῖδες χαλκαῖ ἀργυρωταί

*IG* II², 1473 lines 6–11 (304/3)

19. (IV.12)

20. (IV.10)

21. A gilt [shield?] having Athena as a shield blazon [---]
Another miniature gilt-wood shield, having a gorgoneion as a blazon

--- ἐπίχρυσος [---] ἐπίσημον ἔχουσα Ἀθηνᾶν [---]
ἑτέρα ἀσπιδίσκη ξυλίνη ἐπίχρυσος ἐπίσημον
ἔχουσα γοργόνειον

*IG* II², 1476 lines 42–6 (308/7 or 306/5)

22. Two smooth shields, gilt; a third gilt shield having a gorgoneion

ἀσπίδες ἐπίχρυσοι λεῖαι δύο· τρίτη ἀσπὶς ἐπίχρυσος
γοργόνειον ἔχουσα

*IG* II², 1421 lines 31–3 (374/3)
**1424a lines 80–2 (371/0)**
1425 lines 78–9 (368/7)
1460 lines 3–4 (after 330/29)

23. Four miniature shields, silver-gilt

ἀσπιδίσκαι ἐπίχρυσοι ὑπάργυροι τέτταρες

*IG* II², 1421 lines 25–6 (374/3)

1424a lines 76–7 (371/0)
1425 lines 74–5 (368/7)

24.        10 bronze shields, from the Panathenaia
           ἀσπίδες ἐκ Παναθηναίων ἐπίχαλκοι Δ

           *IG* II², 1433, add. p. 809 line 9 (between 384/3 and
           378/7)
           **1424a line 332 (371/0)**
           1425 lines 262–3 (368/7)
           1428 line 214 (367/6)

25.        15 shields, wood overlaid with bronze
           ἀσπίδες ἐπίχαλκοι ὑπόξυλοι ΔΓ

           *IG* II², **1380 lines 4–5 (after 390)**
           **1424a line 330 (371/0)**
           1433, add. p. 809 lines 7–8 (between 384/3 and
           378/7)
           1434 lines 12–14 (*c*.367/6)

26.        17 bronze shields
           ἀσπίδες ἐπίχαλκοι ΔΓΙΙ

           *IG* II², **1424a line 340 (371/0)**
           1425 lines 274–5 (368/7)
           1462 line 24? (after 318/7)

27.        25 shields, gilt wood emblazoned; of these, one lacks a
           blazon
           ἀσπίδες ἐπίχρυσοι ὑπόξυλοι ΔΔΓ ἐπίσημοι τούτων
           μία οὐκ ἔχει τὸ ἐπίσημον

           *IG* II², 1421 lines 113–15 (374/3)
           **1424a lines 301–2 (371/0)**
           1425 line 260 (368/7)

28. (IV.7)

29.        Gold leaf from the shield from in front of the temple;
           weight with its silver: 3 dr. 5 ob.
           χρυσίον ἐπίτηκτον ἀπὸ τῆς ἀσπίδος τῆς πρὸς τῷ
           νεῷ σταθμὸν σὺν τῷ ἀργυρίῳ ⊢⊢ΙΙΙΙΙ

           *IG* II², 1423 line 4 (374/3)
           **1424a lines 108–9 (371/0)**
           1425 lines 103–4 (368/7)
           1428 lines 122–3 (367/6)
           1429 lines 32–3 (*c*.367/6)
           1435 line 4 (before 350)
           **1436 lines 63–4 (350/49)**

30.        A gorgoneion, silver gilt, from the shield from the temple

γοργόνειον χρυσοῦν ὑπάργυρον ἀπὸ τῆς ἀσπίδος
τῆς ἀπὸ τοῦ νεώ

    *IG* II², 1388 lines 52–3 (398/7)
        1393 lines 32–3 (397/6)
        1401 lines 38–9 (394/3)
        1400 line 53 (390/89)
        1407 lines 44–5 (385/4)
        1415 lines 22–3 (375/4)
        1421 lines 22–4 (374/3)
        1424a lines 74–6 (371/0)
        1425 lines 72–5 (368/7)

31.    Lintels, a gorgoneion from a shield, worked with silver overlay; weight: 390 dr.

ἐπιθύριοι· γοργόνειον ἀσπίδος· ἐπίτηκτα ἐπάργυρα
σταθμὸν ΗΗΗϜΔΔΔΔ

    *IG* II², 1408 lines 20–1 (398/7)
        1409 lines 11–12 (395/4)

BOXES, CHESTS, CONTAINERS

32.    A case for alabaster ornaments, having a silver chain

ἀλαβαστοθήκη ἄλυσιν ἀργυρᾶν ἔχουσα

    *IG* II², 1414 line 25 (385/4)
        1433 line 10 (between 384/3 and 378/7)
        **1424a lines 333–4 (371/0)**
        1425 lines 265–6 (368/7)
        1428 lines 218–9 (367/6)

33.    A wooden case for alabaster ornaments

ἀλαβαστοθήκη ξυλίνη

    *IG* II², 1408, add. p. 799 line 11 (398/7)
        1409, add. p. 799 line 4 (395/4)
        1433 line 12 (between 384/3 and 378/7)
        **1424a lines 337–8 (371/0)**
        1425 line 271 (368/7)
        1428 lines 225–6 (367/6)

34.    A box in which are kept the dies and little anvils on which they stamped the gold, marked with the public seal

κιβωτὸς ἐν ἧ οἱ χαρακτῆρες καὶ ἀκμονίσκοι εἰσὶν ἐφ’
ὧν τοὺς χρυσοῦς ἔκοπτον σεσήμανται τῆ δημοσίαι
σφραγῖδι

    *IG* II², **1408, add. p. 799 lines 11–13 (398/7)**
        1409, add. p. 799 lines 4–6 (395/4)

35. (IV.14)

36.                    30 empty bronze boxes, one without a cover

κοῖται κεναὶ χαλκαῖ ΔΔΔ μία ἄνευ ἐπιθήματος

IG II², 1408 line 14 (398/7) [Hekatompedon]
                 1409 line 7 (395/4)
                 1440 line 49 (349/8) [Chalkotheke]

37.                    Silver container[53]

κυλιχνὶς ἀργυρᾶ

IG II², 1405 line 3 (beg. 4th cent.)

38.                    [Something] in a little ivory container

--- ἐν κυλιχνίδι ἐλεφαντίνῃ

IG II², 1443 line 184 (344/3)
                 1456 line 51 (after 314/3)

39.                    A basket, gilt wood, having bronze frame supports

κανοῦν κατάχρυσον ὑπόξυλον χαλκᾶ διερείσματα
          ἔχον

IG II², 1421 lines 38–9 (374/3)
                 **1424a lines 85–6 (371/0)**
                 1425 lines 82–3 (368/7)
                 1460 lines 10–12 (after 330/29)

40–3. (II.1–4)

44.                    A silver basket, on which is inscribed 'the *boulē* in the
                       archonship of Archippos of Rhamnous [318/7] dedi-
                       cated this to Athena'; weight: ---

κανοῦν ἀργυροῦν ἐφ᾿ ᾧ ἐπιγέγραπται ἡ βουλὴ ἡ ἐπ᾿
          Ἀρχίππου ραμνουσίου ἄρχοντος τῇ Ἀθηνᾷ
          ἀνέθηκεν σταθμὸν ---

IG II², 1474 lines 10–13 (after 318/7)

45.                    Two baskets, gilt wood

κανὼ ὑποξύλω καταχρύσω δύο

IG II², 1379 lines 1–2 (402/1 or 401/0)
                 **1394 lines 16–17 (397/6)**

46.                    3 bronze baskets

κανᾶ χαλκᾶ ΙΙΙ

IG II², 1424a line 343 (371/0)

47.                    A bronze basket ---

---

[53] Hesych. κυλιχνίδες· πυξίδες; cf. W. E. Thompson (1965*c*).

κανοῦν χαλκοῦν ---

*IG* II², 1443 lines 160–1 (344/3)

48. (II.7)

CLOTHES

49. A coarsely-woven linen chiton

χιτὼν στύππινος

*IG* II², 1414 line 26 (385/4)

50. A purple-dyed *chitoniskos*

χιτωνίσκος ἀλουργής

*IG* II², 1475 line 7 (after 318/7)

51. A robe which Pharnabazos dedicated

ξυστὶς ἣν Φαρνάβαζος ἀνέθηκεν

*IG* II², 1412 line 11 (382/1)
1421 line 118 (374/3)
1424a line 303 (371/0)
1428 line 143 (367/6)

52. [Something made] of fine muslin cloth

--- σινδόνων ---

*IG* II², 1478 line 17 (after 316/5)

53. Two boxes: boots [or heavy sandals]

κιβωτίω δύο ὀπισθοκρηπῖδες

*IG* II², 1424a lines 336–7 (371/0)
1425 lines 269–70 (368/7)
1428 lines 222–3 (367/6)

COINS

54. A gold half-obol and two Aiginetan staters, given by
Thrasyllos of Euonymon

Θράσυλλος Εὐωνυμεὺς χρυσοῦν C στατῆρε II
Αἰγιναίω

*IG* II², 1388 lines 69–70 (398/7)
1407 line 46 (?) (385/4)

55. Gold from Boiotia ---

χρυσοῦν Βοιωτι---

*IG* II², 1407 line 48 (385/4)

56.          Corinthian staters
             Κορίνθιοι στατῆρες
                  *IG* II², 1414 line 9 (385/4)

57.          43 gold Darics for the Two Goddesses [Demeter and
             Kore]
             χρυσίου Δαρεικοὶ τοῖν θεοῖν ϘϘϘϘϹΣΣ
                  *IG* II², 1401 line 27 (394/3)
                        1400 line 43 (390/89)

58. (=II. 94)

59.          Staters of Kyzikene gold
             Κυζικηνοῦ χρυσίου στατῆρες
                  *IG* I³, 341 line 11 (406/5)

60a.         10 silver Persian shekels
             σίγλοι Μηδικοὶ ἀργυροῖ Δ
                  *IG* I³, 342 lines 11–12 (405/4)

60b.         11 silver Persian shekels
             σίγλοι Μηδικοὶ ἀργυροῖ ΔΙ
                  *IG* II², 1384 line 7 (403/2)
                        **1386 line 15 (401/0)**
                        1390 lines 3–4 (399/8)
                        1388 line 43 (398/7)
                        1393 lines 23–4 (397/6)
                        1389 line 4 (391/0)
                        1400 lines 19–20 (390/89)

61.          One gold Phokaian *hekte*
             ἕκτη χρυσῆ Φωκαῖς μία
                  *IG* I³, 342 line 19 (405/4)
                  *IG* II², 1390 line 5 (399/8)
                        1388 lines 44–5 (398/7)
                        1393 lines 24–5 (397/6)
                        1389 line 5 (391/0)
                        **1400 lines 20–1 (390/89)**

62.          Three Phokaian *hektai*
             ἕκται Φωκαΐδες τρεῖς
                  *IG* II², 1400 **line 44 (390/89)**

63.          12 Phokaian gold *hektai*
             ἕκται Φωκαΐδες χρυσαῖ ΔΙΙ
                  *IG* I³, 342 line 10 (405/4)

1384 line 6 (403/2)
**1386 lines 14–15 (401/0)**
1390 line 3 (399/8)
1388 lines 42–3 (398/7)
1408 line 7 (398/7)
1393 line 23 (397/6)
1389 line 4 (391/0)
1400 line 19 (390/89)

64. 2 Phokaian staters

Φωκαϊκὼ στατῆρε ΙΙ

*IG* I³, 342 lines 9–10 (405/4)
1384 lines 5–6 (403/2)
1386 line 14 (401/0)
1390 line 3 (399/8)
**1388 line 42 (398/7)**
1393 line 23 (397/6)
1409 lines 14–15 (395/4)
1389 line 4 (391/0)
1400 line 19 (390/89)

65. A gold half-obol

χρυσοῦν ἡμιωβέλιον

*IG* II², **1414 line 6 (385/4)**
1428 line 144 (367/6)

66. Counterfeit staters in a box, stamped with the public seal by Lakon

στατῆρες κίβδηλοι ἐν κιβωτίῳ παρὰ Λάκωνος σεσημασμένοι τῇ δημοσίαι σφραγῖδι

*IG* II², 1388 lines 61–2 (398/7)
1401 lines 44–5 (394/3)
1400 line 57 (390/89)
1407 line 43 (385/4)
1415 lines 19–20 (375/4)
**1424a line 311 (371/0)**
1428 line 149 (367/6)
1443 lines 207–8 (344/3)

67. From the unmarked silver set aside for the Stratiotic Fund we have received from Nikeratos of Kydantidai, the treasurer of the Stratiotic Fund, by weight. First shelf, labelled A, first bar: 1203 dr.; second: 1200 dr. 3 ob.; third: 1199 dr. 3 ob.; fourth: 1201 dr.; fifth: 1202 dr. 3 ob. Second shelf, labelled B, first bar: 1196 dr.; second: 1198 dr.; third: 1205 dr. 3 ob.; fourth: 1193 dr.; fifth: 1202 dr. 3 ob. Third shelf, labelled Γ, first bar: 1197 dr.;

second: 1200 dr. 3 ob.; third: 1200 dr.; fourth: 1198 dr. 3 ob.; fifth: 1200 dr. 3 ob. Fourth shelf, labelled Δ, first bar: 1208 dr. 3 ob.; second: 1201 dr.; third: 1203 dr.; fourth: 1202 dr. 3 ob.; fifth: 1201 dr. 3 ob. Fifth shelf, labelled E, first bar: 1196 dr. 3 ob.; second: 1200 dr. 3 ob.; third: 1199 dr.; fourth: 1202 dr. 3 ob.; fifth: 1202 dr. Sixth shelf, labelled Z, first bar: 1206 dr.; second: 1201 dr.; third: 1203 dr.; fourth: 1201 dr.; fifth:1207 dr. 3 ob. Seventh shelf, labelled H, first bar: 1197 dr.; second: 1203 dr. 3 ob.; third: 1197 dr.; fourth: 1191 dr.; fifth: 1200 dr. Eighth shelf, labelled Θ, first bar: 1208 dr. 3 ob.; second:1199 dr.; third: 1199 dr.; fourth: 1202 dr.; fifth: 1203 dr. Ninth shelf, labelled I, first bar: 1184 dr. 3 ob.; second: 1200 dr. 3 ob.; third: 1197 dr.; fourth: 1201 dr. 3 ob.; fifth: 1198 dr. 3 ob. Tenth shelf, labelled K, first bar: 1197 dr.; second: 1197 dr.; third: 1203 dr.; fourth: 1200 dr. 3 ob.; fifth: 1201 dr. Eleventh shelf, labelled Λ, first bar: 1189 dr. 3 ob.; second: 1197 dr. 3 ob.; third: 1198 dr.; fourth: 1203 dr.; fifth: 1204 dr. 3 ob. Twelfth shelf, labelled M, first bar: 1195 dr. 3 ob.; second: 1197 dr. 3 ob.; third: 1205 dr. 3 ob.; fourth: 1196 dr. 3 ob.; fifth: 1205 dr. 3 ob. Thirteenth, labelled N, first bar: 1200 dr. 3 ob.; second: 1198 dr. 3 ob.; third: 1206 dr. 3 ob.; fourth: 1197 dr.; fifth: 1203 dr. 3 ob. Fourteenth, labelled Ξ, first bar: 1204 dr.; second: 1199 dr.; third: 1210 dr.; fourth: 1196 dr.; fifth: 1204 dr. 3 ob. Fifteenth, labelled O, first bar: 1202 dr.; second: 1199 dr.; third: 1196 dr.; fourth: 1203 dr.; fifth: 1203 dr. 3 ob. Sixteenth, labelled Π, first bar: 1192 dr. 3 ob.; second: 1200 dr.; third: 1203 dr. 3 ob.; fourth: 1198 dr. 3 ob.; fifth:1205 dr. 3 ob. Seventeenth, labelled P, first bar: 1205 dr. 3 ob.; second: 1201 dr. 3 ob.; third: 1200 dr.; fourth: 1197 dr.; fifth: 1202 dr. Eighteenth, labelled Σ, first bar: 1201 dr.; second: 1204 dr. 3 ob.; third: 1197 dr. 3 ob.; fourth: 1208 dr.; fifth: 1195 dr. Nineteenth, labelled T, first bar: 1192 dr.; second: 1198 dr. 3 ob.; third: 1201 dr. 3 ob.; fourth: 1202 dr. 3 ob.; fifth: 1202 dr. 3 ob. Twentieth shelf, labelled Y, first bar: 1201 dr.; second: 1206 dr. 3 ob.; third: 1203 dr. 3 ob.; fourth: 1203 dr. 3 ob.; fifth: 1184 dr. Twenty-first, labelled Φ, first bar: 1200 dr.; second: 1199 dr.; third: 1201 dr. 3 ob.; fourth: 1198 dr.; fifth: 1204 dr. Twenty-second, labelled X, first bar: 1199 dr.; second: 1202 dr. From the beginning, another set: first shelf, labelled AA, first

bar: 1194 dr.; second: 1198 dr. 3 ob.; third: 1200 dr. 3
ob.; fourth: 1183 dr. 3 ob.; fifth: 1204 dr. Second shelf,
labelled BB, first bar: 1191 dr.; second: 1199 dr. 3 ob.;
third: 1200 dr. 3 ob.; fourth: 1204 dr.; fifth: 1197 dr.
Third shelf, labelled ΓΓ, first bar: 1198 dr. 3 ob.;
second: 1192 dr.; third: 1191 dr. 3 ob.; fourth: 1197 dr.
3 ob.; fifth: 1199 dr. Fourth shelf, labelled ΔΔ, first bar:
1200 dr.; second: 1187 dr. 3 ob.; third: 1195 dr. 3 ob.;
fourth: 1191 dr. 3 ob.; fifth: 1193 dr. 3 ob. Fifth shelf,
labelled EE, first bar: 1199 dr.; second: 1199 dr.; third:
1201 dr. 3 ob.; fourth: 1198 dr. 3 ob.; fifth: 1196 dr. 3
ob. Sixth shelf, labelled ZZ, first bar ---

ἀσήμου ἀργυρίου τοῦ εἰς τὰ στρατιωτικὰ
ἐξαιρεθέντος παρὰ ταμίου στρατιωτικῶν
παρελάβομεν Νικηράτου Κυδαντίδου σταθμῷ
πρῶτος ῥυμὸς ἵνα τὸ Α πρῶτος φθοῖς ΧΗΗΗΗ
δεύτερος ΧΗΗΙΙΙ τρίτος ΧΗΡΔΔΔΔΓΗΗΗΙΙΙ
τέταρτος ΧΗΗΗ πέμπτος ΧΗΗΗΗΙΙΙ· δεύτερος ῥυμὸς
ἵνα τὸ Β πρῶτος φθοῖς ΧΗΡΔΔΔΔΓΗ δεύτερος
ΧΗΔΔΔΔΓΗΗΗ τρίτος ΧΗΗΓΙΙΙ τέταρτος
ΧΗΡΔΔΔΔΗΗΗ πέμπτος ΧΗΗΗΗΙΙΙ· τρίτος ῥυμὸς ἵνα
τὸ Γ πρῶτος φθοῖς ΧΗΡΔΔΔΔΓΗΗ δεύτερος ΧΗΗΙΙΙΙ
τρίτος ΧΗΗ τέταρτος ΧΗΡΔΔΔΔΓΗΗΗΙΙΙ πέμπτος
ΧΗΗΙΙΙ· τέταρτος ῥυμὸς ἵνα τὸ Δ πρῶτος φθοῖς
ΧΗΗΓΗΗΗΙΙΙ δεύτερος ΧΗΗΗ τρίτος ΧΗΗΗΗΗ
τέταρτος ΧΗΗΗΗΙΙΙ πέμπτος ΧΗΗΗΙΙΙ· πέμπτος
ῥυμὸς ἵνα τὸ Ε πρῶτος φθοῖς ΧΗΡΔΔΔΔΓΗΙΙΙ
δεύτερος ΧΗΗΙΙΙ τρίτος ΧΗΡΔΔΔΔΓΗΗΗΗ τέταρτος
ΧΗΗΗΗΙΙΙ πέμπτος ΧΗΗΗΗ· ἕκτος ῥυμὸς ἵνα τὸ Ζ
πρῶτος φθοῖς ΧΗΗΓΗ δεύτερος ΧΗΗΗ τρίτος
ΧΗΗΗΗΗ τέταρτος ΧΗΗΗ πέμπτος ΧΗΗΓΗΗΙΙΙ·
ἕβδομης ῥυμὸς ἵνα τὸ Η πρῶτος φθοῖς
ΧΗΡΔΔΔΔΓΗΗ δεύτερος ΧΗΗΗΗΗΙΙΙ τρίτος
ΧΗΡΔΔΔΔΓΗΗ τέταρτος ΧΗΡΔΔΔΔΗ
πέμπτος ΧΗΗ· ὄγδοος ῥυμὸς ἵνα τὸ Θ πρῶτος
φθοῖς ΧΗΗΓΗΗΗΙΙΙ δεύτερος ΧΗΡΔΔΔΔΓΗΗΗΗ τρίτος
ΧΗΡΔΔΔΔΓΗΗΗΗ τέταρτος ΗΗΗΗ πέμπτος ΧΗΗΗΗΗ·
ἔνατος ῥυμὸς ἵνα τὸ Ι πρῶτος φθοῖς
ΧΗΡΔΔΔΗΗΗΗΙΙΙ δεύτερος ΧΗΗΙΙΙ τρίτος
ΧΗΡΔΔΔΔΓΗΗ τέταρτος ΧΗΗΗΙΙΙ πέμπτος
ΧΗΡΔΔΔΔΓΗΗΗΗΙΙΙ δέκατος ῥυμὸς ἵνα τὸ Κ πρῶτος
φθοῖς ΧΗΡΔΔΔΔΓΗΗ δεύτερος ΧΗΡΔΔΔΔΓΗΗ τρίτος
ΧΗΗΗΗΗ τέταρτος ΧΗΗΙΙΙΙ πέμπτος ΧΗΗΗ·
ἐνδέκατος ῥυμὸς ἵνα τὸ Λ πρῶτος φθοῖς

ΧΗϜΔΔΔΓΗΗΗΙΙΙ δεύτερος ΧΗϜΔΔΔΔΓΗΗΙΙΙ τρίτος
ΧΗϜΔΔΔΔΓΗΗ τέταρτος ΧΗΗΗΗ πέμπτος
ΧΗΗΗΗΗΙΙΙ· δωδέκατος ῥυμὸς ἵνα τὸ Μ πρῶτος
φθοῖς ΧΗϜΔΔΔΔΓΙΙΙ δεύτερος ΧΗϜΔΔΔΔΓΗΗΙΙ
τρίτος ΧΗΗΓΙΙΙ τέταρτος ΧΗϜΔΔΔΔΓΗΙΙΙ πέμπτος
ΧΗΗΓΙΙΙ· τρίτος καὶ δέκατος ἵνα τὸ Ν πρῶτος
φθοῖς ΧΗΗΙΙΙ δεύτερος ΧΗϜΔΔΔΔΓΗΗΗΙΙΙ τρίτος
ΧΗΗΓΗΙΙΙ τέταρτος ΧΗϜΔΔΔΔΓΗΗ πέμπτος
ΧΗΗΗΗΗΙΙΙ· τέταρτος καὶ δέκατος ἵνα τὸ Ξ πρῶτος
φθοῖς ΧΗΗΗΗΗ δεύτερος ΧΗϜΔΔΔΔΓΗΗΗΗ τρίτος
ΧΗΗΔ τέταρτος ΧΗϜΔΔΔΔΓΗ πέμπτος
ΧΗΗΗΗΗΙΙΙ· πέμπτος καὶ δέκατος ἵνα τὸ Ο πρῶτος
φθοῖς ΧΗΗΗΗ δεύτερος ΧΗϜΔΔΔΔΓΗΗΗΗ τρίτος
ΧΗϜΔΔΔΔΓΗ τέταρτος ΧΗΗΗΗΗ πέμπτος
ΧΗΗΗΗΗΙΙΙ· ἕκτος καὶ δέκατος ἵνα τὸ Π πρῶτος
φθοῖς ΧΗϜΔΔΔΔΗΙΙΙ δεύτερος ΧΗΗ τρίτος
ΧΗΗΗΗΗΙΙΙ τέταρτος ΧΗϜΔΔΔΔΓΗΗΗΙΙΙ πέμπτος
ΧΗΗΓΙΙΙ· ἕβδομος καὶ δέκατος ἵνα τὸ Ρ πρῶτος
φθοῖς ΧΗΗΓΙΙΙ δεύτερος ΧΗΗΗΙΙΙ τρίτος ΧΗΗ
τέταρτος ΧΗϜΔΔΔΔΓΗΗ πέμπτος ΧΗΗΗΗ· ὄγδοος
καὶ δέκατος ἵνα τὸ Σ πρῶτος φθοῖς ΧΗΗΗΗ δεύτερος
ΧΗΗΗΗΗΗΙΙΙ τρίτος ΧΗϜΔΔΔΔΗΙΙΙ τέταρτος
ΧΗΗΓΗΗΗ πέμπτος ΧΗϜΔΔΔΔΓ· ἔνατος καὶ
δέκατος ἵνα τὸ Τ πρῶτος φθοῖς ΧΗϜΔΔΔΔΗ
δεύτερος ΧΗϜΔΔΔΔΓΗΗΗΙΙΙ τρίτος ΧΗΗΗΙΙΙ
τέταρτος ΧΗΗΗΗΙΙΙ πέμπτος ΧΗΗΗΗΙΙΙ· εἰκοστὸς
ῥυμὸς ἵνα τὸ Υ πρῶτος φθοῖς ΧΗΗΗ δεύτερος
ΧΗΗΓΗΙΙΙ τρίτος ΧΗΗΗΗΗΙΙΙ τέταρτος ΧΗΗΗΗΗΙΙΙ
πέμπτος ΧΗϜΔΔΔΗΗΗΗ· εἷς καὶ εἰκοστὸς ἵνα τὸ Φ
πρῶτος φθοῖς ΧΗΗ δεύτερος ΧΗϜΔΔΔΔΓΗΗΗΗ
τρίτος ΧΗΗΗΙΙΙ τέταρτος ΧΗϜΔΔΔΔΓΗΗ πέμπτος
ΧΗΗΗΗΗ· δεύτερος καὶ εἰκοστὸς ἵνα τὸ Χ πρῶτος
φθοῖς ΧΗϜΔΔΔΔΓΗΗΗΗ δεύτερος ΧΗΗΗΗ· ἐξ ἀρχῆς
ἕτερον· πρῶτος ῥυμὸς ἵνα τὸ ΑΑ πρῶτος φθοῖς
ΧΗϜΔΔΔΔΗΗΗΗ δεύτερος ΧΗϜΔΔΔΔΓΗΗΗΙΙΙ τρίτος
ΧΗΗΗΙΙΙ τέταρτος ΧΗϜΔΔΔΗΗΗΙΙΙ πέμπτος
ΧΗΗΗΗΗΗ· δεύτερος ῥυμὸς ἵνα τὸ ΒΒ πρῶτος φθοῖς
ΧΗϜΔΔΔΔΗ δεύτερος ΧΗϜΔΔΔΔΓΗΗΗΗΙΙΙ τρίτος
ΧΗΗΗΙΙΙ τέταρτος ΧΗΗΗΗΗΗ πέμπτος
ΧΗϜΔΔΔΔΓΗΗ· τρίτος ῥυμὸς ἵνα τὸ ΓΓ πρῶτος
φθοῖς ΧΗϜΔΔΔΔΓΗΗΗΙΙΙ δεύτερος ΧΗϜΔΔΔΔΗΗ
τρίτος ΧΗϜΔΔΔΔΗΙΙΙ τέταρτος ΧΗϜΔΔΔΔΓΗΗΙΙΙ
πέμπτος ΧΗϜΔΔΔΔΓΗΗΗΗ· τέταρτος ῥυμὸς ἵνα τὸ
ΔΔ πρῶτος φθοῖς ΧΗΗ δεύτερος ΧΗϜΔΔΔΓΗΗΙΙΙ

τρίτος ΧΗϜΔΔΔΓΙΙΙ τέταρτος ΧΗϜΔΔΔΔΗΙΙΙ
πέμπτος ΧΗϜΔΔΔΔΗΗΙΙΙ· πέμπτος ῥυμὸς ἵνα τὸ
ΕΕ πρῶτος φθοῖς ΧΗϜΔΔΔΔΓΗΗΗ δεύτερος
ΧΗϜΔΔΔΔΓΗΗΗ τρίτος ΧΗΗΗΙΙΙ τέταρτος
ΧΗϜΔΔΔΔΓΗΗΙΙΙ πέμπτος ΧΗϜΔΔΔΔΓΗΙΙ· ἕκτος
ῥυμὸς ἵνα τὸ ΖΖ πρῶτος φθοῖς ---

*IG* II², 1443 lines 12–88 (344/3)

68.  Mixed silver, unmarked; weight: 8 dr. 3 ob.

ἀργύριον σύμμεικτον ἄσημον σταθμὸν ΓΗΗΙΙΙ

*IG* II², 1388 lines 71–2 (398/7)
1400 line 61 (390/89)
1414 line 4 (385/4)

69.  Mixed silver with overlay; weight: 10 dr. 2 ob.

ἀργύριον σύμμεικτον καὶ ἐπίτηκτον σταθμὸν ΔΙΙ

*IG* II², 1393 lines 28–9 (397/6)
**1401 line 34 (394/3)**
1400 line 49 (390/89)

70.  Of the deposit of silver plate made by Meletades of Erchia, the weight is: 30 dr.

ἀργυρίου ἐπιτήκτου παρακαταθήκη Μελητάδου
Ἐρχιεὺς σταθμὸν ΔΔΔ

*IG* II², 1393 line 29 (397/6)
**1401 line 35 (394/3)**
1400 lines 49–50 (390/89)
1415 lines 18 (375/4)
**1421 lines 71–2 (374/3)**

71. (II.22)

72.  Gold; weight: 1 dr.

χρυσὸς σταθμὸν Η

*IG* II², 1408 line 21 (398/7)
1409 line 12 (395/4)

73.  Andron of Elaious provided a first-fruit offering; 2 gold dr.

Ἄνδρων Ἐλαιούσιος ἀπήρξατο χρυσᾶς ΗΗ

*IG* II², 1388 line 69 (398/7)

74.  [Some things] silver gilt, 2, deposited from Sounion

--- χρυσοῖ ὑπάργυροι ΙΙ ἀπὸ Σουνίου παρακαταθήκη

*IG* II², 1400 lines 47–8 (390/89)

75.            An unstamped gold piece; weight: 3 dr.

χρυσίον ἄσημον σταθμὸν ⊢⊢⊢

    *IG* II², 1388 lines 72–3 (398/7)

76.            A piece of gold-plate from the *akroteria* of the Temple of
        Nike; weight: 6 dr. 3 ob.

χρυσίον ἐπίτηκτον ἀπὸ τῶν ἀκροτηρίων τοῦ νεὼ τῆς
Νίκης σταθμὸν Γ⊢III

    *IG* II², 1412 lines 27–8 (382/1)
          1415 line 8 (375/4)
          1421 lines 59–61 (374/3)
          1423 lines 1–3 (374/3)
          **1424a lines 106–7 (371/0)**
          1425 lines 101–2 (368/7)
          1428 lines 125–6 (367/6)
          1435 line 7 (before 350)
          1436 line 65 (350/49)

77.            Another gold piece from the *akroteria*; weight: 13 dr.

ἕτερον χρυσίον ἀπὸ τῶν ἀκρωτηρίων σταθμὸν Δ⊢⊢⊢

    *IG* II², 1415 line 8 (375/4)
          1423 lines 7–8 (374/3)
          **1424a lines 110–11 (371/0)**
          1425 lines 105–6 (368/7)
          1428 lines 126–7 (367/6)
          1435 line 7 (before 350)
          1436 lines 66–67 (350/49)

78. (II.27)

79.            Gold piece, which was found at [the house of?]
        Aristarchos; weight: 7 dr. 1 ob.

χρυσίον ὃ παρὰ Ἀριστάρχῳ ηὑρέθη σταθμὸν Γ⊢⊢

    *IG* II², 1421 lines 8–9 (374/3)
          1424a lines 42–3 (371/0)
          **1425 lines 37–8 (368/7)**
          1435 line 5 (before 350)

80.            The gold piece, which Aristokles from --- recovered, the
        one from the base of the statue; weight: 100+ dr.

χρυσίον ὃ Ἀριστοκλῆς ὁ ἀπὸ ---ης ἀπήνεγκεν τὸ
ἀπὸ τοῦ βάθρου τοῦ ἀγάλματος σταθμὸν Η---

    *IG* II², 1388 lines 64–5 (398/7)
          1401, add. p. 799 line 46 (394/3)

81.            Another gold piece, found at the goldsmith's shop;

weight: 3½ ob.

ἕτερον χρυσίον ὃ παρὰ τῷ χρυσοχόῳ ηὑρέθη
σταθμὸν ΙΙΙC

> *IG* II², 1388 lines 65–6 (398/7)

82. An unfired gold piece; weight of this: 3½ ob.

χρυσίον ἄπυρον σταθμὸν τούτου ΙΙΙC

> *IG* I³, 342 lines 10–11 (405/4)
> 1384 lines 6–7 (403/2)
> 1405 line 5 (beg. 4th cent.)
> 1408 line 7 (398/7)
> 1393 lines 12–13 (397/6)
> **1400 line 13 (390/89)**

83. Two gold pieces, unfired; total weight: 21 dr. 5 ob.

χρυσίω ἄπυρω δύο σταθμὸν ἄγει ΔΔΗΙΙΙΙ

> *IG* II², 1396 lines 33–4 (beg. 4th cent.)
> 1378+1398, add. p. 797 lines 16–17 (399/8)

84. Gold pieces set with precious stones, a mixture of small
bricks and cicadas; weight of these: 58 dr.

χρυσίδια διάλιθα σύμμικτα πλινθίων καὶ τεττίγων
σταθμὸν τούτων ⋔ΓΗΗΗ

> *IG* II², 1373 lines 6–7 (403/2)
> 1376 lines 3–5 (402/1 or 401/0) [56 dr. 2 ob.]
> **1377 lines 13–14 (399/8)**
> 1395 lines 13–15 (395/4)

85. Ivory tokens

σημεῖα ἐλεφάντινα

> *IG* II², 1459 line 12 (340/39)
> **1457 line 25 (after 316/5)**

86. 12 bronze weights

σταθμία χαλκᾶ ΔΙΙ

> *IG* I³, 342 line 24 (405/4?)
> *IG* II², 1381+1386, add. p. 798 line 19 (401/0)
> 1390 line 7 (399/8)
> 1388 line 46 (398/7)
> 1393 line 26 (397/6)
> 1401 lines 2–3 (394/3)
> 1389 line 6 (391/0)
> 1407 lines 40–1 (385/4)
> 1412 line 27 (382/1)
> 1415 lines 8–9 (375/4)
> 1421 line 83+1423 line 10 (374/3)

1424a line 247 (371/0)
1425 line 193 (368/7)

87.                Forty-six smooth gold test pieces; weight: 89 dr. 5 ob.

δοκιμεῖα λεῖαι χρυσαῖ τετταράκοντα ἒξ σταθμὸν
ͰΔΔΔΓͰͰͰΙΙΙΙ

IG II², 1421 lines 6–7 (374/3)
1424a lines 40–1 (371/0) [89 dr. 3 ob.]
1425 lines 35–6 (368/7) [89 dr. 3 ob.]
1436 lines 58–9 (350/49)
Ag. I 2260 [*Hesperia* 25 (1956) 103] lines 19–20 (after
346/5)

88.                A test-piece for the wine-jug of the Two Goddesses
[Demeter and Kore]; weight: 1¾ gold ob., in a box. A
gold test-piece for the wine-jug of Athena; weight: 1¾
ob., in a box. A test-piece for the gold to be used for
the phialai, in a box; weight: 1½ ob. A test-piece for
the gold to be used for the incense-burners, in a box;
weight: 1¾ ob. A test-piece for the throne, lacking any
inscription; weight: 1½ ob.

δοκιμεῖον τῆς οἰνοχόης τοῖν θεοῖν σταθμὸν χρυσίου
ΙϹΤ ἐν κιβωτίῳ· δοκιμεῖον τῆς οἰνοχόης τῆς Ἀθηνᾶς
χρυσίου σταθμὸν ΙϹΤ ἐγ κιβωτίῳ· δοκιμεῖον τοῦ
χρυσίου τοῦ εἰς τὰς φιάλας ἐγ κιβωτίῳ σταθμὸν
ΙϹ· δοκιμεῖον τοῦ χρυσίου τοῦ εἰς τὰ θυμιατήρια ἐγ
κιβωτίῳ σταθμὸν ΙϹΤ· δοκιμεῖον τοῦ θρόνου οὐκ
ἐπεγέγραπτο οὐδὲν σταθμὸν ΙϹ

IG II², 1415 lines 10–14 (375/4)
1424a lines 313–19 (371/0)
1425 lines 235–44 (368/7)
1428 lines 152–8 (367/6)

FIGURINES AND STATUES[54]

89.                The golden statue, the one in the Hekatompedon, and the
shield and the base, we received intact, according to the
bronze stele, the one kept in the Parthenon

ἄγαλμα χρυσοῦν τὸ ἐν τῷ Ἑκατομπέδῳ καὶ ἡ ἀσπὶς
καὶ τὸ βάθρον παρελάβομεν ἐντελὲς κατὰ τὴν
στήλην τὴν χαλκῆν τὴν ἐν τῷ Παρθενῶνι

IG II², 1407 lines 5–6 (385/4)
1410 lines 7–8 (377/6)
1443 lines 10–11 (344/3)

[54] See also 'Boxes, Chests, and Containers' above.

1468 lines 6–8 (321/0)
1477 lines 12–14 [*Hesperia* 40 (1971) 449–50]
(304/3)

90.     A gold kore on a base; unweighed

κόρη χρυσῆ ἐπὶ στήλης ἄσταθμος

**IG I³, 317 line 5 (434/3)**
318 line 13 (433/2)
319 line 18 (432/1)
320 line 26 (431/0)
321 line 33 (430/29)
322 lines 40–1 (429/8)
323 line 49 (428/7)
324 line 61 (427/6)
325 line 6 (422/1)
326 lines 17–18 (421/0)
327 line 29 (420/19)
328 lines 41–2 (419/8)
329 line 6 (418/7)
330 lines 20–1 (417/6)
331 lines 35–6 (416/5)
332 lines 50–1 (415/4)
333 line 5 (414/3)
334 line 19 (413/2)
336 line 47 (411)
339 line 6 (409/8)
340 lines 23–4 (408/7)

91.     The other Nike, first shelf: head, circlet, chain, earrings, necklace, two gold pins, left hand, bracelets, small gold pieces; weight: 2044 dr. 2 ob. Second shelf: torso, chestband, neckband, two garments, small gold pieces; weight: 1948 dr. Third shelf: drapery folds, two brooches, two feet, small gold pieces; weight: 1939 dr. 3 ob. Fourth shelf: right hand, bracelets, two ribbons, wreath, small gold pieces; weight: 1994 dr. Fifth shelf: back part of a wing, two legs, small gold pieces; weight: 4002 dr. 3 ob.

τῆς ἑτέρας Νίκης πρῶτος ῥυμός· κεφαλὴ στεφάνη ὅρμος ἐνώδια, ὑποδερὶς ἥλω δύο χρυσῶ χεὶρ ἀριστερὰ ἀμφιδέα χρυσία μικρὰ σταθμὸν ΧΧΔΔΔΔΓΗΗΙΙ· δεύτερος ῥυμός· θώραξ στρόφιον περιτραχηλίδιον στολίδε δύο χρυσία μικρὰ σταθμὸν ΧΓΗΗΗΗΔΔΔΓΗΗ· τρίτος ῥυμός· ἀπόπτυγμα περόναι δύο πόδε δύο χρυσία μικρὰ σταθμὸν ΧΓΗΗΗΗΔΔΔΓΗΗΗΙΙΙ· τέταρτος ῥυμός·

χεὶρ δεξιά ἀμφιδέα κατωρίδε δύο στέφανος χρυσία
μικρά σταθμὸν ΧΡΗΗΗΗϜΔΔΔΔΙΙΙΙ· πέμπτος
ῥυμός· ἀκρωτήριον ὀπίσθιον σκέλη δύο σταθμὸν
ΧΧΧΧΙΙΙΙΙ·

*IG* II², 1371 lines 6–11 (403/2)
　　　　1386+1381+Ag. I 4508, add. p. 798 [*Hesperia* 9
　　　　　　(1940) 310–11] lines 2–7 (401/0)
　　　　1388, add. p. 798 lines 16–24 (398/7)
　　　　1393 lines 6–11 (397/6)
　　　　1400 lines 8–12 (390/89)
　　　　1407 lines 8–11 (385/4)
　　　　**1424a lines 5–21 (371/0)**
　　　　**1428 lines 26–40 (367/6)**
　　　　1431 lines 5–13 (*c*.367/6)

92.　　　The Nike made in the archonship of Sokratides [374/3],
　　　　first shelf: head, the circlet, the wreath on her head,
　　　　earrings, neckband, chain, both hands, two bracelets;
　　　　weight: 3077 dr. 4 ob. Second shelf: torso, two
　　　　brooches, belt, gold from the rear part; weight: 3391 dr.
　　　　3 ob. Third shelf: both legs and two ribbons; weight:
　　　　3288 dr. Fourth shelf: drapery folds, two feet, brooches,
　　　　(one is closed); weight: 2141 dr. 3 ob.

τῆς Νίκης τῆς ἐπὶ Σωκρατίδου ἄρχοντος πρῶτος
ῥυμός· κεφαλὴ στεφάνη στέφανος ὁ ἐπὶ τῇ κεφαλῇ
ἐνῴδια ὑποδερὶς ὅρμος χεῖρες ἀμφότεραι ἀμφιδέαι
δύο σταθμὸν ΧΧΧϜΔΔΓΙΙΙΙΙ· δεύτερος ῥυμός·
θώραξ περόνα ζωνίον χρυσίον ὀπίσθιον σταθμὸν
ΧΧΧΗΗΗϜΔΔΔΔΙΙΙΙ· τρίτος ῥυμός· σκέλη
ἀμφότερα καὶ κατωρίδε δύο σταθμὸν
ΧΧΧΗΗϜΔΔΔΓΙΙΙ· τέταρτος ῥυμός· ἀπόπτυγμα
πόδε δύο περονίδες μία κατακλείεται σταθμὸν
ΧΧΗΔΔΔΔΙΙΙΙ

*IG* II², **1424a lines 50–62 (371/0)**
　　　　1425 lines 45–62 (368/7)
　　　　1428 lines 9–24 (367/6)

93.　　　--- wing, gold from the rear part, two legs, small gold
　　　　pieces; weight: 4035 dr.

--- ἀκρωτήριον χρυσίον ὀπίσθιον σκέλη δύο χρυσίδια
μικρὰ σταθμὸν ΧΧΧΧΔΔΔΓ

*IG* II², **1425 lines 14–16 (368/7)**
　　　　1431 lines 1–4 (*c*.367/6)

94.　　　The gold wreath, which the Nike on the hand of the
　　　　golden statue has on her head; unweighed

στέφανος χρυσοῦς ὃν ἡ Νίκη ἔχει ἐπὶ τῆς κεφαλῆς ἡ
ἐπὶ τῆς χειρὸς τοῦ ἀγάλματος τοῦ χρυσοῦ
ἄστατος

> IG I³, 342 lines 2–4 (405/4)=IG II², 1382
> IG II², 1384 lines 1–3 (403/2)
> **1386 lines 12–14 (401/0)**
> 1390 lines 1–2 (399/8)
> 1388 lines 40–2 (398/7)
> 1393 lines 22–3 (397/6)
> 1389 lines 3–4 (391/0)
> 1400 lines 18–19 (390/89)
> 1407 line 31 (385/4)
> 1413 lines 11–12 (between 384/3 and 378/7)
> 1415 lines 14–15 (375/4)
> 1424a lines 48–9 (371/0)
> 1425 lines 43–5 (368/7)
> Ag. I 4527 [*Hesperia* 9 (1940) 320] lines 6–9 (*c.*367/6)
> IG II², 1468 lines 8–9 (321/0)
> 1476 lines 7–12? (308/7 or 306/5)
> 1477 lines 14–19 [*Hesperia* 40 (1971) 449–50]
> (304/3)

95.    Four gold olive-leaves from the wreath worn by the Nike
       on the hand of the statue; weight of these: 6 dr. 2 ob.

πέταλα θαλλοῦ χρυσᾶ τέτταρα ἀπὸ τοῦ στεφάνου ὃν
ἡ Νίκη ἔχει ἡ ἐπὶ τῆς χειρὸς τοῦ ἀγάλματος
σταθμὸν τούτων ΓΗΙΙ

> IG II², 1376 lines 19–21 (402/1 or 401/0)
> **1377 lines 22–4 (399/8)**
> 1394 lines 5–8 (397/6)
> 1395+Ag. I 1182 [*Hesperia* 5 (1936) 390] lines
> 22–4 (395/4)
> 1414 lines 10–11 (385/4)

96.    The gold wreath which the Nike has; weight of this: 60
       dr.

στέφανος χρυσοῦς ὃν ἡ Νίκη ἔχει σταθμὸν τούτου ϜΔ

> IG I³, 323 lines 51–2 (428/7)
> 324 lines 62–3 (427/6)
> **325 line 7 (422/1)**
> 326 line 19 (421/0)
> 327 lines 30–1 (420/19)
> 328 line 43 (419/8)
> 329 line 7 (418/7)
> 330 line 22 (417/6)
> 331 lines 36–7 (416/5)

333 lines 6–7 (414/3)
334 line 20 (413/2)
336 lines 48–9 (411)
339 lines 7–8 (409/8)
340 line 25 (408/7)

97.    A gold and ivory Palladion and a gilded shield, both dedicated by Archias, (a metic) living in Peiraieus

παλλάδιον ἐλεφάντινον ἐπίχρυσον καὶ ἡ ἀσπὶς ἐπίχρυσος ὢ Ἀρχίας ἐμ Πειραιεῖ οἰκῶν ἀνέθηκεν

*IG* II², **1388 lines 67–9 (398/7)**
1400 lines 58–9 (390/89)
1407 line 44 (385/4)
1420 line 4 (after 385/4)
1415 lines 20–2 (375/4)
1421 lines 89–91 (374/3)
1424a lines 252–3 (371/0)
1425 lines 199–201 (368/7)
1443 lines 200–2 (344/3)
1460 lines 17–19 (after 330/29)

98.    Ivory figures: a young man setting up a trophy; Apollo holding a gilded bow; Dionysos upon a leopard

σημεῖα ἐλεφάντινα· νεανίσκος τρόπαιον ἱστάς· Ἀπόλλων τόξον ἔχων ἐπίχρυσον· Διόνυσος ἐπὶ παρδάλεως

*IG* II², 1459 lines 12–14 (after 340/39)
**1457 lines 25–7 (after 316/5)**

99.    A bronze flower covered with gold overlay

ἀνθέμιον χαλκοῦν ἐπιτήκτῳ περικεχρυσωμένον

*IG* II², 1421 lines 34–5 (374/3)
**1424a lines 82–3 (371/0)**
1425 lines 80–1 (368/7)
1443 lines 198–9 (344/3)
1460 lines 15–16 (after 330/29)

100.   An ivory cow figurine

βοίδιον ἐλεφάντινον

*IG* II², **1388 line 54 (398/7)**
1393 line 34 (397/6)
1401 line 39 (394/3)
1400 lines 53–4 (390/89)
1407 line 43 (385/4)

101.   Ivory cow figurine, which Smikythe dedicated

βοίδιον ἐλεφάντινον ὃ Σμικύθη ἀνέθηκεν

> *IG* II², 1415 lines 18–19 (375/4)
> 1421 lines 87–8 (374/3)
> 1423 lines 14–15 (374/3)
> 1424a lines 250–1 (371/0)
> 1425 lines 197–8 (368/7)
> 1443 lines 199–200 (344/3)
> 1460 lines 16–17 (after 330/29)

102–3 (IV.21–2)

104.　A knobby piece of gold to the Two Goddesses [Demeter and Kore], weight: 93 dr.

τοῖν θεοῖν χρυσὶς κονδυλωτὴ σταθμὸν ⊢ΔΔΔΔⅠⅠⅠ

> *IG* II², 1401 line 19 (394/3)
> **1400 line 36 (390/89)**

105.　--- three gold pieces (phialai?) and one knobby piece [of gold], belonging to Athena, which Stephanos of Lamptrai dedicated; weight of these: 649 dr.

--- Ἀθηναίας χρυσίδες τρεῖς καὶ κονδυλωτὸν Στέφανος Λαμπτρεὺς ἀνέθηκεν σταθμὸν τούτων ΓΗΔΔΔΔΓⅠⅠⅠⅠ

> *IG* II², 1386 lines 10–12 (401/0)
> 1390 line 1 (399/8)
> EM 6790+*IG* II², 1388+1403+1408 [*JHS* 51 (1931)
> 140–1] lines 50–2 (398/7)
> *IG* II², 1401 lines 23–4 (394/3)
> **1400 line 40 (390/89)**
> 1407 lines 24–5 (385/4)

106.　A protome of a ram from the wooden throne with ivory inlay

κριοῦ προτομὴ ἀπὸ θρόνου ξυλίνου περιηλεφαντωμένη

> *IG* II², 1485 lines 42–4 (304/3)

107.　A gilt-wood *rhumbos*

ῥύμβος ξύλινος ἐπίχρυσος

> *IG* II², 1456 lines 49–50 (after 314/3)

108.　--- of a silver serpent ---

--- ὄφεως ἀργυροῦ ---

> *IG* II², 1414 line 21 (385/4)

109. (IV.23)

110. A figurine --- and ivory figurine --- ivory; a little ivory
figurine; a figurine --- of ivory [for] Dionysos --- of
ivory

ζωίδιον --- ζωίδιον ἐλεφάντινον --- ἐλεφάντινον·
ζωίδιον ἐλεφάντινον μικρόν· ζωίδιον --- ἐλεφάντινον Διονυσο --- ἐλεφαντίνη

*IG* II², 1456 lines 43–8 (after 314/3)

111. Wooden figurines

ζωίδια ξύλινα

*IG* II², 1461 line 24 (after 330/29)

FURNITURE

112. Two couches

κλινίδες δύο

*IG* II², 1424a line 342 (371/0)
1425 line 278 (368/7)

113. (IV.25)

114. 7 Milesian couches

κλῖναι Μιλησιουργεῖς ΓΙΙ

*IG* II², 1424a line 341 (371/0)
1425 line 277 (368/7)

115. (IV.26)

116. A broken stool, and two in good condition

δίφρος κατεαγὼς ὑγιεῖς δύο

*IG* II², 1424a lines 297–8 (371/0)
1425 line 215 (368/7)
1428 line 140 (367/6)

117. 2 stools

δίφροι ΙΙ

*IG* II², 1424a line 345 (371/0) [Hekatompedon]
1425 line 282 (368/7)
1428 line 221 (367/6)
1443 line 191 (344/3)
1460 line 6 (after 330/29)
1464 line 5 (after 316/5) [Chalkotheke]

118. 5 round-footed stools, one with silver feet

δίφροι στρογγυλόποδες Γ ἀργυρόπους εἷς

*IG* II², 1394 lines 13–14 (397/6)
1414 lines 12–13 (385/4)
1412 lines 4, 9 (382/1)

119. (IV.29)

120.      Camp-stools having ivory backs

ὀκλαδίαι ἀνακλίσεις ἠλεφαντωμένας ἔχοντες

*IG* II², 1379 lines 4–5 (402/1 or 401/0)
1394 lines 18–19 (397/6)
1413 line 30 (between 384/3 and 378/7)

121. (IV.30)

122.      A Thessalian throne

θρόνος Θετταλικός

*IG* II², 1414 line 8 (385/4)
**1421 line 104 (374/3)**
1424a line 296 (371/0)
1425 line 212 (368/7)
1428 line 138 (367/6)

123.      Three large thrones, not in good condition, having backs
inlaid with ivory; another throne not having a back

θρόνοι μεγάλοι τρεῖς οὐχ ὑγιεῖς ἀνακλίσεις ἔχοντες
ἠλεφαντωμένας· ἕτερος θρόνος ἀνάκλισιν οὐκ ἔχον

*IG* II², 1412 line 3 (382/1)
1415 lines 26–7 (375/4)
1421 lines 97–100 (374/3)
**1424a lines 292–4 (371/0)**
1425 lines 206–8 (368/7)
1443 lines 191–3 (344/3)
1460 lines 6–9 (after 330/29)

124a.      Four thrones, three are in good condition

θρόνοι τέτταρες οἱ τρεῖς ὑγιεῖς

*IG* II², **1421 line 108 (374/3)**

124b.      Four thrones, of these one is broken

θρόνοι τέτταρες τούτων κατεαγὼς εἷς

*IG* II², **1424a line 298 (371/0)**
1425 line 216 (368/7)

125.      Thrones inlaid with ivory

θρόνοι ἠλεφαντωμένοι

*IG* II², 1412 line 3 (382/1)

126.   5 pieces of ivory from the thrones ---
ἐλεφάντινα ἀπὸ τῶν θρόνων Γ ---

> *IG* II², **1438 line 47 (349/8)**
> 1456 line 43 (after 314/3)
> 1461 line 26 (after 330/29)
> 1466 line 9 (321/0)

JEWELLERY

127.   Weight of foreign silver with the two bracelets: 83 dr. 3
ob.
ξενικοῦ ἀργυρίου σὺν τοῖν ἀμφιδειδίοιν σταθμὸν
ⱵΔΔΔⱵⱵΙΙΙ

> *IG* II², 1449 lines 1–2 (397/6)
> 1421 lines 75–6 (374/3)
> **1424a lines 183–4 (371/0)**
> 1428 lines 75–6 (367/6)
> 1436 lines 56–7 (350/49)

128. (II.5)

129.   Gold earrings of Artemis Brauronia; weight: 3 dr. 5 ob.
εἱλικτῆρες Ἀρτέμιδος Βραυρωνίας χρυσοῖ σταθμὸν
ⱵⱵΙΙΙΙΙ

> *IG* II², 1421 lines 10–11 (374/3)
> **1424a lines 44–5 (371/0)**
> 1425 lines 39–40 (368/7)
> 1428 line 146 (367/6)
> 1436 line 55 (350/49)
> Ag. I 2260 [*Hesperia* 25 (1956) 103] line 18 (after 346/5)

130.   2 fine gold bracelets, which Polyippe, daughter of
Meleteon of Acharnai, dedicated; weight of these: 1 dr.
4 ob.
ἀμφιδέαι χρυσαῖ λεπταὶ ΙΙ Πολυίππη Μελετέωνος
Ἀχαρνέως ἀνέθηκεν σταθμὸν τούτοιν ⱵΙΙΙΙ

> *IG* II², **1388 lines 27–8 (398/7)**
> 1393 lines 13–14 (397/6)
> 1400 lines 13–14 (390/89)
> 1393+1406+1448+1449+*Hesperia* 41 (1972) 423
> no. 55+426 no. 58 lines 13–14 (385/4)

131.   2 gold earrings of Artemis Brauronia, which [---]os dedicated; weight: 3½ ob.
ἐνῳδίω χρυσῶ ΙΙ Ἀρτέμιδος Βραυρωνίας ---ος

ἀνέθηκεν ΙΙΙC

    *IG* II², 1388 lines 60–1 (398/7)
        1401 lines 43–4 (394/3)
        1400 line 56 (390/89)

132. (IV.37)

133.        Miscellaneous gold pieces set with stones and an earring; weight: 100 dr.

        χρυσία σύμμεικτα διάλιθα καὶ ἐνῴδιον σταθμὸν Η

        *IG* II², 1388 line 63 (398/7)
          1401, add. p. 799 lines 45–6 (394/3)
          1400 lines 57–8 (390/89)

134.        A small necklace, gilt wood

        ὑποδερίδιον ξύλινον ἐπίχρυσον

        *IG* II², 1421 lines 36–7 (374/3)
          **1424a line 84 (371/0)**
          1425 lines 81–2 (368/7)

135.        A necklace, silver gilt; weight: 58 dr. 4 ob.

        στρεπτὸν περίχρυσον ὑπάργυρον σταθμὸν ϜΓΗΗΙΙΙΙ

        *IG* II², 1386 lines 1–2 (401/0)
          **1388 lines 28–9 (398/7)**
          1393 line 14 (397/6)
          1400 line 14 (390/89)
          1407 line 39 (385/4)

136–7. (IV.39–40)

138.        A worn piece of gold having a gold chain, dedicated to Artemis Brauronia, which Kallion, wife of Aristokles, dedicated; weight: 2 dr. 1 ob.

        Ἀρτέμιδος Βραυρωνίας χρυσῆ θριπήδεστος ἄλυσιν ἔχουσα χρυσῆν ἣν ἀνέθηκεν Κάλλιον Ἀριστοκλέους γυνὴ σταθμὸν ΗΙ

        *IG* II², 1402, add. p. 799 lines 7–8 [*EAC* 3 (1965)
          60–1 lines 34–6] (402/1)
          1381 +1386, add. p. 798 lines 24–6 (401/0)
        EM 6790+1388+1403+1408 [*JHS* 51 (1931) 140–1] lines
          53–5 (398/7)
          1401 lines 25–6 (394/3)
          1400 lines 41–2 (390/89)

139. (IV.35)

140.        Two gold chains with a protome of a ram set with stones

ὅρμοι χρυσοῖ σὺν κριοῦ κεφαλῇ δύο διάλιθοι
*IG* II², 1418 line 7 (after 385/4)

141. Gold necklaces which Roxane, wife of King Alexander, dedicated to Athena Polias; weight: ---

περιτραχήλια χρυσᾶ --- ἀνέθηκεν βασιλέως
Ἀλεξάνδρου γυνὴ Ῥωξάνη Ἀθηνᾷ Πολιάδι στα---
*IG* II², 1492 lines 54–7 (305/4?)[55]

142. An onyx; weight: 276 dr. ½ ob.
ὄνυξ σταθμὸν ΗΗΓΔΔΓΗC
*IG* II², 1407 line 30 (385/4)

143. A large onyx
ὄνυξ μέγας
*IG* II², 1400 line 57 (390/89)

144. A large onyx, broken
ὄνυξ μέγας κατεαγώς
*IG* II², 1415 line 20 (375/4)
    1421 line 101 (374/3)
    1424a line 294 (371/0)
    1428 line 136 (367/6)
    1455 line 8 (341/0)
    1460 lines 23–4 (after 330/29)

145. A large onyx depicting a priapic goat-stag; weight: 32 dr.
ὄνυξ μέγας τραγελάφου πριαπίζοντος σταθμὸν
ΔΔΔΗ
*IG* II², 1388, add. p. 798 lines 62–3 (398/7)
    1401 line 45 (394/3)

146. (IV.32)

147. An onyx in a bronze container without a ring
ὄνυξ ἐν χαλκῇ κυλιχνίδι ἄνευ δακτυλίου
*IG* II², 1394 lines 11–12 (397/6)
    1395+Ag. I 1182 [*Hesperia* 5 (1936) 390] lines
    27–8 (395/4)
    1421 lines 116–17 (374/3)
    **1424a lines 302–3 (371/0)**
    1428 line 142 (367/6)

148. A gold ring, which Axiothea, wife of Sokles, dedicated; weight: 1 dr. 3 ob.

---

[55] See also V.358.

χρυσοῦς δακτύλιος ὃν Ἀξιοθέα Σωκλέους γυνή
ἀνέθηκε σταθμὸν ⊢ΙΙΙ

IG II², 1402 line 7? (402/1)
1388 lines 70–1 (398/7)

149.     A gold ring, which Dorkas, (a metic) living in Peiraieus,
dedicated to Artemis Brauronia

δακτύλιος χρυσοῦς ὃν Δορκὰς ἐμ Πειραιεῖ οἰκοῦσα
ἀνέθηκε Ἀρτέμιδι Βραυρωνίαι

IG II², 1403 lines 11–12 (398/7)
1401 lines 32–3 (394/3)
1400 lines 46–7 (390/89)

150.     A circular ring made of gold, which E[---] dedicated

δακτύλιος ἀπείρων χρυσοῦς ὃν Ε[--- ἀνέθηκε

IG I³, 341 lines 3–4 (406/5)

151.     A gold ring on a platter, which Kleinomache dedicated to
Artemis Brauronia.

δακτύλιος χρυσοῦς ἐν πινακίῳ ὃν Κλεινομάχη ἀνέθηκε
Ἀρτέμιδι Βραυρωνίᾳ

IG II², 1388 lines 57–8 (398/7)
1393 lines 36–7 (397/6)
1401 lines 41–2 (394/3)
1400 lines 55–6 (390/89)

152.     A circular gold ring, which Platthis of Aigina dedicated;
weight of this: 1½ ob.

δακτύλιος ἀπείρων χρυσοῦς ὃν Πλάτθις Αἰγινήτης
ἀνέθηκε σταθμὸν τούτου ΙC

IG II², 1386 lines 9–10 (401/0)
1388 lines 39–40 (398/7)
1393 lines 21–2 (397/6)
1389 lines 2–3 (391/0)

153.     A gold ring of Artemis Brauronia

Ἀρτέμιδος Βραυρωνίας δακτύλιος χρυσοῦς

IG II², 1400 line 60 (390/89)

154.     A twisted gold ring of Artemis Brauronia; weight: 1 dr. 5
ob.

δακτύλιος χρυσοῦς στρεπτὸς Ἀρτέμιδος Βραυρωνίας
σταθμὸν ⊢ΙΙΙΙΙ

IG II², 1377, add. p. 797 lines 24–5 (399/8)
1394 lines 8–9 (397/6)

1395+Ag. I 1182 [*Hesperia* 5 (1936) 390] lines
24–6 (395/4)
Ag. I 5363 [*Hesperia* 32 (1963) 165–8] line 4 (before
385/4)
*IG* II², 1418 line 12? (after 385/4?)

155.     A gold ring and unfired gold bound in silver, which
Phryniskos of Thessaly dedicated; weight of these: 2+
dr.

δακτύλιος χρυσοῦς καὶ χρυσίον ἄπυρον ἀργυρίω
δεδεμένον ὂν Φρυνίσκος Θετταλὸς ἀνέθηκε σταθμὸν
τούτων ---ΗΗ

*IG* II², 1388 lines 58–60 (398/7)
1393 lines 37–8 (397/6)
1401 lines 42–3 (394/3)[56]

156.     Glyke, daughter of Archestratos, dedicated [---] earrings,
two gold rings, a set stone, these gold things upon the
base, unweighed.

Γλύκη Ἀρχεστράτου ἀνέθηκεν --- εἱλικτῆρες δακτυλίω
χρυσῶ δύο διάλιθον χρυσᾶ ταῦτα ἐπὶ τοῦ βάθρου
ἄστατα

*IG* II², 1393 line 31 (397/6)
1401 lines 37–8 (394/3)
1400 lines 51–2 (390/89)

157.     An ivory seal having a gold ring

σφραγίδιον ἐλεφάντινον δακτύλιον ἔχον

*IG* II², 1424a lines 308–9 (371/0)
1428 lines 147–8 (367/6)
1443 lines 206–7 (344/3)
1455 lines 9–10 (341/0)
1460 lines 26–7 (after 330/29)

158.     Sards ---

σαρδία ---

*IG* II², 1457 line 31 (after 316/5)

159. (II.56, 57)

160.     Two seals, one gold and one overlaid with silver, having
two silver rings

σφραγῖδε δύο ἀργυρὼ δακτυλίω ἔχουσαι χρυσᾶ καὶ
ἐπάργυρος

*IG* II², 1408 lines 21–2 (398/7)

[56] Cf. **VI.46.**

1409 line 12 (395/4)
1447 line 17 (before 371/0)
1451 line 17 (after 365/4)
1457 lines 6–7 (after 316/5)

161.   A seal, jasper bound in silver

σφραγὶς ἴασπις ἀργυρίῳ ἐνδεδεμένη

IG II², 1409 lines 3–4 (395/4)

162.   A signet bound in silver, dedicated by the treasurers in the
year of Kephisodoros [366/5]

σφραγίδιον ἀργυρίῳ δεδεμένον ὃ ἀνέθεσαν οἱ ταμίαι
οἱ ἐπὶ Κηφισοδώρου

IG II², 1443 lines 212–14 (344/3)
1455 lines 14–15 (341/0)
1460 lines 28–9 (after 330/29)

163.   Two stone seals, of which one has a gold ring, the other
a silver one

δύο σφραγῖδε λιθίνω χρυσοῦν ἔχουσα τὸν δακτύλιον
ἡ δὲ ἑτέρα ἀργυροῦν

IG I³, 342 lines 21–4 (405/4?)
IG II², 1386, add. p. 798 lines 17–19 (401/0)
1390 lines 5–6 (399/8)
**1388 lines 45–6 (398/7)**
1393 line 25 (397/6)
1389 lines 5–6 (391/0)
1400 line 21 (390/89)
1407 lines 39–40 (385/4)
1415 lines 15–16 (375/4)

164. (II.37)

165.   8 gold seals and two gold griffins set with stones; weight
of these: 40+ dr.

σφραγῖδες περίχρυσοι ΓΙΙΙ καὶ γρῦπε διαλίθω χρυσώ
ΙΙ σταθμὸν τούτων ΔΔΔΔ ---

IG II², 1373 lines 12–13 (403/2)
**1376 lines 11–13 (402/1 or 401/0)**
1377 lines 17–18 (399/8)
1394 lines 1–2 (397/6)
1395+Ag. I 1182 [*Hesperia* 5 (1936) 390] lines
18–20 (395/4)
1418 lines 11–12 (after 385/4)

166. (II.6)

MISCELLANEOUS

167.    An ivory writing-stick in a container, not in good condition, not complete

γραφεῖον ἐλεφάντινον ἐν ἐλύτρῳ οὐχ ὑγιὲς οὐδ' ἐντελές

   *IG* II², 1485 lines 52–4 (304/3)

168.    A writing tablet from the *boulē* of the Areopagos, sealed

γραμματεῖον παρὰ τῆς βουλῆς τῆς ἐξ Ἀρείου πάγου σεσημασμένον

   *IG* II², 1412 lines 1–2 (382/1)
          1424a lines 290–1 (371/0)
          **1425 lines 203–5 (368/7)**
          1428 lines 158–9 (367/6)
          1443 lines 203–4 (344/3)
          1455 lines 7–8 (341/0)
          1460 lines 22–3 (after 330/29)

169.    Bronze [objects]

χαλκ ---

   *IG* II², 1379 line 11 (402/1 or 401/0)
          1414 line 41 (385/4)
          1469 line 50 (after 320/19)
          1462 line 4 (after 318/7)
          1478 line 13 (after 315/4)
          1478 line 15 (after 315/4)
          1478 line 19 (after 315/4)
          1478 line 21 (after 315/4)
          1483 line 7 (after 313/2)
          1483 line 13 (after 313/2)
          1467 lines 5–6 (304/3)
          1467 lines 6–7 (304/3)
          1473 lines 17–18 (304/3)

170.    A gilded bridle

χαλινὸς κεχρυσωμένος

   *IG* II², 1424a line 335 (371/0)
          1425 line 267 (368/7)
          1433 line 11 (between 384/3 and 378/7)

171a.   A gold [object]

--- ἐπίχρυσον ---

   *IG* II², 1443 lines 195–6 (344/3)
          1443 lines 197–8 (344/3)

171b.   Gold [objects]

--- ἐπίχρυσοι ---

> IG II², 1379 line 6 (402/1 or 401/0)
> 1379 line 8 (402/1 or 401/0)
> 1412 line 5 (382/1)
> 1476 line 42 (308/7 or 306/5)

171c.      --- gold [objects] not in good condition

--- ἐπίχρυσοι οὐχ ὑγιεῖς

> IG II², 1481 line 8 (end of 4th cent.)

171d.      A gilt wood [object]

--- ἐπίχρυσος ὑπόξυλος

> IG II², 1443 line 162 (344/3)
> 1461 line 3 (after 330/29)

171e.      A silver gilt [object]

--- ἐπάργυρος ἐπίχρυσος ---

> IG II², 1409 line13 (395/4)

171f.      A silver [object], gilt

ἀργυροῦν ἐπίχρυσον ---

> IG II², 1456 lines 54–5 (after 314/3)

171g.      Bronze gilt [objects]

--- ἐπίχρυσος ὑπόχαλκος ---

> IG II², 1443 line 211 (344/3)
> 1455 line 13 (341/0)

171h.      Gold leaf [object]

--- περίχρυσον ---

> IG II², 1379 line 9 (402/1 or 401/0)
> 1414 line 6 (385/4)
> 1414 line 10 (385/4)

171i.      Gold leaf [objects]

--- περίχρυσα ---

> IG II², 1458 line 4 (after 316/5)

171j.      Gold leaf [objects]

--- περίχρυσοι ---

> IG II², 1409 lines 2–3 (395/4)

171k.      Gold plated [objects]

--- κατάχρυσοι ---

> IG II², 1380 line 3 (after 390?)

172.      A solid gold piece and a meniskos

χρυσίον στέριφον καὶ μηνίσκος

IG II², 1436 line 60 (350/49)

173.      A gold [object], which Demeas [dedicated]

--- χρυσοῦς ὂν Δημέας [--- ἀνέθηκεν]

IG II², 1412 line 16 (382/1)

174.      Three iron objects and one ---

σιδηρᾶ τρία καὶ ἕν---

IG II², 1464 line 7 (after 316/5)

175.      Ivory weaving-blades

σπάθαι ἐλεφάντιναι

IG II², 1464 line 18 (after 316/5)

176.      Small gleaming ivories

ἐλεφάντινα ἀργὰ μικρά

IG II², 1438 line 49 (349/8)

177a.     An ivory [object]

ἐλεφαντίνη(ν) ---

IG II², 1413 line 27 (after 385/4)
           1443 line 191 (344/3)

177b.     An ivory [object]

ἐλεφάντινον ---

IG II², 1461 line 34 (after 330/29)
           1464 line 19 (after 316/5)
           1464 line 24 (after 316/5)
           1456 line 41 (after 314/3)
           1509 lines 9–10 (after 313/2)

177c.     Ivory [objects]

ἐλεφάντινα ---

IG II², 1469 line 32 (after 320/19)
           1509 lines 7–8 (after 313/2)
           1466 line 12 (321/0)

177d.     Ivory [objects]

ἐλεφαντινοι ---

IG II², 1491 lines 2–3 (307/6)

177e.     Ivory [object(s)]

ἐλεφαντιν---

IG II², 1469 line 110 (after 320/19)
           1458 line 9 (after 316/5)
           1464 line 26 (after 316/5)
           1456 line 40 (after 314/3)

        1509 lines 1–2 (after 313/2)
        1509 lines 3–4 (after 313/2)
        1467 lines 42–3 (304/3)
        1485 line 40 (304/3)

**177f.**     [An object] with ivory inlay

ἠλεφαντωμέν ---

        *IG* II², 1464 line 20 (after 316/5)
        1463 line 4 (349/8)
        1466 line 15 (321/0)

**178.**     [Containers] of ivory shavings are sealed with the public seal

--- ἐλεφαντίνων περιπρισμάτων σεσήμανται τῆ δημοσίαι σφραγῖδι

        *IG* II², 1408 lines 13–14 (398/7)
        **1409 lines 6–7 (395/4)**
        1414 lines 17–18 (385/4)
        1412 lines 32–3 (382/1)

**179a.**     Silver [objects]

ἀργυρ---

        *IG* II², 1409 line 13 (395/4)
        1414 line 3 (385/4)
        1433 line 3 (between 384/3 and 378/7)
        1432 line 16 (after 350/49)
        1474 lines 24–5 (after 318/7)
        1457 line 32 (after 316/5)

**179b.**     Silver [objects]

ἀργυρᾶ

        *IG* II², 1413 line 15 (between 384/3 and 378/7)
        1473 lines 18–19 (304/3)
        1458 line 8 (after 316/5)

**179c.**     A silver [object]

ἀργυροῦς

        *IG* II², 1432 line 14 (after 350/49)
        1455 line 19 (341/0)
        1483 line 12 (after 313/2)

**179d.**     [An object] bound in silver

ἀργυρίῳ δεδεμέν---

        *IG* II², 1458 lines 4–5 (after 316/5)

**179e.**     [Objects] silver-gilt

ὑπάργυροι

*IG* II², 1393 line 27 (397/6)
1404 line 4 (393/2)
1443 line 189 (344/3)

180a.           Wooden [objects]
ξυλ---

*IG* II², 1414 line 16 (385/4)
1417 line 7 (after 385/4)

180b.           Wooden [objects]
ξύλιναι

*IG* II², 1461 line 21 (after 330/29)
1456 line 49 (after 314/3)
1461 line 21 (after 330/29)

180c.           Wooden [object(s)]
ξύλινο---

*IG* II², 1490 line 6 (304/3)

180d.           Wooden [objects]
ξύλινοι

*IG* II², 1461 line 14 (after 330/29)

180e.           Wooden [objects] with overlay
ὑποξυλ---

*IG* II², 1379 line 7 (402/1 or 401/0)

180f.           A wooden object belonging to Artemis Brauronia
ξυλίνη Ἀρτέμιδος Βραυρωνίας

*IG* II², 1461 line 28 (after 330/29)

181.            [Something] of wood, turned on a lathe
--- ξύλινον τετορνευμένον

*IG* II², 1456 lines 53–4 (after 314/3)

182.            A gold-like stone on a wooden column.
χρυσῖτις λίθος ἐπὶ κίονος ξυλίνου

*IG* II², 1415 line 22 (375/4)
1421 lines 92–3 (374/3)
1424a line 254 (371/0)
1425 lines 201–2 (368/7)

183.            A silver [object]; weight: 41 dr.
ἀργυρίου ΔΔΔΔⱶ

*IG* II², 1457 line 23 (after 316/5)

184.            [The phiale] with silver core weighs: 104 dr. 3 ob.

ἄγει ἡ ὑπάργυρος ΗϜϜϜΙΙΙ

*IG* II², 1400 line 39 (390/89)
1407 lines 23–4 (385/4)

185. [Something] with silver core; weight: 816 dr.

--- ὑπάργυρος σταθμὸν ΓΗΗΗΔΓⱵ

*IG* II², 1407 lines 22–3 (385/4)

186. Weight of a silver-gilt (object): 5+ dr.

ὑπαργύρου χρυσίου σταθμὸν Γ---

*IG* II², 1401 line 27 (394/3)
**1400 line 43 (390/89)**

187. A piece of silver overlaid with gold; weight: 4 dr. 4 ob.

χρυσίον ἐπίτηκτον ὑπάργυρον σταθμὸν ϜϜϜΙΙΙΙ

*IG* II², 1421 lines 57–8 (374/3)
**1424a lines 104–5 (371/0)**
1425 lines 99–100 (368/7)
1428 line 124 (367/6)

188. (A gold or silver piece); weight of this: --- dr.

[χρυσὶς or ἀργυρὶς] σταθμὸν ταύτης ---

*IG* I³, 333 line 14 (414/3)
334 line 28 (413/2)
336 line 56 (411)

189. (II.39)

MUSICAL INSTRUMENTS

190. A Persian aulos-case

συβήνη Μηδική

*IG* II², 1424a line 337 (371/0)
1425 line 270 (368/7)
1428 line 225 (367/6)

191–2 (IV.41–2)

193. An ivory lyre with gold overlay, in a leather bag

λύριον ἐλεφάντινον ἔχον τὸ σκῦτος ἐπίτηκτον
ἐπίχρυσον

*IG* II², 1421 lines 119–21 (374/3)

194. A wooden lyre having ivory horns, and in a case, not in
good condition

λύριον ξύλινον ἐν ἐλύτρῳ τοὺς πήχεις ἐλεφαντίνους

             ἔχον οὐχ ὑγιής

             *IG* II², 1460 lines 19–21 (after 330/29)

**195. (IV.43)**

**196.**           5 wooden lyres

             λύραι ξύλιναι Γ

             *IG* II², 1425 lines 258–9 (368/7)

                1428 line 210 (367/6)[57]

**197. (IV.44)**

NAILS

**198.**           5 bronze nails, covered with silver and gold

             ἧλοι χαλκοῖ ἐπάργυροι ἐπίχρυσοι Γ

             *IG* II², 1419 lines 3–4 (after 385/4)

**199.**           10 bronze nails, covered with silver and gold; 150 marked
             ones

             ἧλοι χαλκοῖ ἐπάργυροι ἐπίχρυσοι Δ· ἐπίσημοι ΗΓ̄

             *IG* II², 1408 lines 19–20 (398/7)

                1409 lines 10–11 (395/4)

**200.**           Bronze nails covered with silver; number: 21

             ἧλοι χαλκοῖ ἐπάργυροι ἀριθμὸς ΔΔΙ

             *IG* II², 1408 lines 18–19 (398/7)

                1409 lines 9–10 (395/4)

                1419 line 2 (after 385/4)

**201.**           40 bronze nails covered with silver and gold

             ἧλοι χαλκοῖ ἐπάργυροι ἐπίχρυσοι ΔΔΔΔ

             *IG* II², 1408 line 18 (398/7)

                1409 line 10 (395/4)

                1419 lines 2–3 (after 385/4)

**202.**           Gold foil from a nail on the door of the Hekatompedon;
             unweighed

             φύλλον ἀπὸ τῆς θύρας ἀπὸ τοῦ Ἐκατομπέδου
             χρυσοῦν ἀπὸ τοῦ ἥλου ἄστατον

             *IG* II², 1414 lines 3–4 (385/4)

                **1424a lines 46–7 (371/0)**

                1425 lines 41–2 (368/7)

                1428 line 129 (367/6)

                Ag. I 4527 [*Hesperia* 9 (1940) 320] lines 3–5 (c.367/6)

[57] May be the same collection as V.197, with the addition of an extra instrument.

IG II², 1443 lines 194–5 (344/3)

203. (II.76)

RITUAL EQUIPMENT[58]

204.     A silver lustral basin; unweighed
         ἀπορραντήριον ἀργυροῦν ἄσταθμον
             *IG* II², 317 line 5 (434/3)
                 318 line 13 (433/2)
                 319 line 19 (432/1)
                 320 line 27 (431/0)
                 321 lines 33–4 (430/29)
                 322 line 41 (429/8)
                 323 lines 49–50 (428/7)
                 324 line 61 (427/6)
                 325 line 6 (422/1)
                 326 line 18 (421/0)
                 327 lines 29–30 (420/19)
                 328 line 42 (419/8)
                 329 line 6 (418/7)
                 330 line 21 (417/6)
                 331 line 36 (416/5)
                 333 line 5 (414/3)
                 334 line 19 (413/2)
                 336 line 47 (411)
                 339 line 6 (409/8)
                 340 line 24 (408/7)

205.     A sacrificial knife entirely of iron
         μάχαιρα ὁλοσίδηρος
             *IG* II², 1481 line 5 (end 4th cent.)

206.     Bronze ritual knife in an ivory sheath
         μάχαιρα χαλκῆ ἐν ἐλύτρῳ ἐλεφαντίνῳ
             *IG* II², 1424a lines 334–5 (371/0)
                 1425 lines 266–7 (368/7)
                 1428 line 220 (367/6)

207.     An iron sacrificial knife having an ivory sheath, which the
         *boulē* dedicated in the archonship of Antigenes [407/6]
         μάχαιρα σιδηρᾶ ἐλεφάντινον κολεὸν ἔχουσα ἣν ἡ
         βουλὴ ἀνέθηκεν ἡ ἐπὶ Ἀντιγένους ἄρχοντος
             *IG* I³, 342 lines 16–19 (405/4?)
             *IG* II², 1386+1381, add. p. 798 lines 19–21 (401/0)

[58] Includes all references to items inscribed 'Sacred to . . .'.

1390 lines 7–9 (399/8)
1388 lines 46–8 (398/7)
1401 lines 3–4 (394/3)
1389 lines 6–7 (391/0)
1400 line 22 (390/89)
1415 lines 16–18 (375/4)
1421 lines 84–6 (374/3)
1423 lines 11–13 (374/3)
**1424a lines 248–50 (371/0)**
1425 lines 194–6 (368/7)

208. **(IV.45)**

209.      Ivory sheath for a surgical knife

κολεὸν μαχαίρας ἰατρικῆς ἐλεφάντινον

     *IG* II², **1424a lines 340–1 (371/0)**
     1425 lines 275–6 (368/7)

210.      A dagger; 5 swords

ἐγχειρίδιον· ξίφη Γ

     *IG* II², 1373 line 3 (403/2)
     **1424a line 327 (371/0)**
     1425 line 256 (368/7)
     1428 line 204 (367/6)

*Sacred to Artemis*

211.      A gold phiale, marked ---, inscribed 'Sacred to Artemis Brauronia' ---

φιάλη χρυσῆ ἐφ' ᾗ τὸ --- ἐφ' ᾗ ἐπιγέγραπται ἱερὰ Ἀρτέμιδος Βραυρωνίας ---

     *IG* II², 1475 lines 27–8 (after 318/7)
     **1476 lines 32–5 (308/7 or 306/5)**

212.      Silver phialai, inscribed 'Sacred to Artemis'

φιάλαι ἀργυραῖ ἐφ' αἷς ἐπιγέγραπται ἱεραὶ τῆς Ἀρτέμιδος

     *IG* II², 1492 lines 88–90 (305/4)

213.      3 silver phialai, sacred to Artemis Brauronia; weight of these: 503+ dr. 1 ob.

Ἀρτέμιδος Βραυρωνίας χρυσίδες φιάλαι ΙΙΙ τούτων σταθμὸν Γ--ΗΗΗ

     *IG* II²,·1388+EM 6790 [*JHS* 51 (1931) 140–1] lines 49–50 (398/7)

*Sacred to Asklepios*

214. A silver basket, inscribed 'Sacred to Asklepios'; weight: 2906 dr. 4 ob.

κανοῦν ἀργυροῦν ἐφ' ᾧ ἐπιγέγραπται ἱερὸν Ἀσκληπιοῦ σταθμὸν ΧΧΓΗΗΗΗΓΗΙΙΙΙ

*IG* II², 1474 lines 8–10 (after 318/7)

215. A silver hydria, inscribed 'Sacred to Asklepios; Nikokrates of Kolonos made me'; weight: 1000 dr.

ὑδρία ἀργυρᾶ ἐφ' ᾗ ἐπιγέγραπται ἱερὰ Ἀσκληπιοῦ· Νικοκράτης ἐκ Κολωνοῦ ἐποίησεν· στα(θμὸν) Χ

*IG* II², 1492 lines 24–7 (305/4)

216. A silver hydria, inscribed 'Sacred to Asklepios; Nikokrates of Kolonos made me'; weight: 1004 dr.

ὑδρία ἀργυρᾶ ἐφ' ᾗ ἐπιγέγραπται ἱερὰ Ἀσκληπιοῦ· Νικοκράτης ἐκ Κολωνοῦ ἐποίησεν· στα(θμὸν) ΧΗΗΗΗ

*IG* II², 1492 lines 22–4 (305/4)

217. A silver hydria, marked Ε, inscribed 'Sacred to Asklepios; Nikokrates of Kolonos made me in the archonship of Simonides [311/0]'; weight: 1050 dr.

ὑδρία ἀργυρᾶ ἐφ' ᾗ τὸ Ε ἐφ' ᾗ ἐπιγέγραπται ἱερὰ Ἀσκληπιοῦ· Νικοκράτης ἐκ Κολωνοῦ ἐποίησεν· ἄρχων Σιμωνίδης· στα(θμὸν) ΧϜ

*IG* II², 1492 lines 32–5 (305/4)

218. Silver hydria, marked Γ, inscribed 'Sacred to Asklepios, Nikokrates of Kolonos made me'; weight: 1004 dr. 2 ob.

ὑδρία ἀργυρᾶ ἐφ' ᾗ τὸ Γ ἐφ' ᾗ ἐπιγέγραπται ἱερὰ Ἀσκληπιοῦ· Νικοκράτης ἐκ Κολωνοῦ ἐποίησεν· στα(θμὸν) ΧΗΗΗΗΙΙ

*IG* II², 1492 lines 27–9 (305/4)

219. Gold phiale, marked ---, on which is inscribed 'Sacred to Asklepios'; weight: 146+ dr.

φιάλη χρυσῆ ἐφ' ᾗ τὸ . ἐφ' ᾗ ἐπιγέγραπται ἱερὰ Ἀσκληπιοῦ· σταθμὸν ΗΔΔΔΔΓΗ---

*IG* II², 1475 lines 22–4 (after 318/7)

220. 2 gold phialai, marked ---, inscribed 'Sacred to Asklepios'; weight: 205+ dr.

φιάλαι χρυσαῖ ΙΙ ἐφ' αἷς τὸ . ἐφ' αἷς ἐπιγέγραπται

ἱεραὶ Ἀσκληπιοῦ· σταθμὸν ΗΗΓ---

*IG* II², 1475 lines 24–7 (after 318/7)

*Sacred to Athena*

221.   A silver washbasin, inscribed 'Sacred to Athena Polias; Nikokrates of Kolonos made me in the archonship of Archippos of Rhamnous [318/7]'; weight:---

χερνιβεῖον ἀργυροῦν ἐφ' ᾧ ἐπιγέγραπται ἱερὸν Ἀθηνᾶς Πολιάδος· Νικοκράτης ἐποίσεν ἐπὶ Ἀρχίππου Ῥαμνουσίου ἄρχοντος· σταθμὸν ---

*IG* II², 1474 lines 18–22 (after 318/7)

222.   Another silver-plated incense-burner, sacred to Athena Nike, having bronze supports; weight: 2120 dr.

ἕτερον ἐπάργυρον θυμιατήριον ἱερὸν Ἀθηνᾶς Νίκης χαλκᾶ διερείσματα ἔχον σταθμὸν ΧΧΗΔΔ

*IG* II², 1436 lines 46–8 (350/49)
Ag. I 2260 [*Hesperia* 25 (1956) 103] lines 14–15 (after 346/5) [not in good condition]

223.   10+ silver phialai, inscribed 'Sacred to Athena'; weight: --- 13 silver phialai, inscribed 'Sacred to Asklepios'; weight:--- [?] silver phialai, inscribed 'sacred to Artemis Brauronia; weight: 1708 dr.

φιάλαι ἀργυραῖ ἐφ' αἷς ἐπιγέγραπται ἱεραὶ Ἀθηνᾶς Δ --- στα(θμὸν) --- φιάλαι ἀργυραῖ ἐφ' αἷς ἐπιγέγραπται ἱεραὶ Ἀσκληπιοῦ ΔΙΙΙ· στα(θμὸν) --- φιάλαι ἀργυραῖ ἐφ' αἷς ἐπιγέγραπται ἱεραὶ Ἀρτέμιδος Βραυρωνίας --- στα(θμὸν) ΧΓΗΗΓΗΗ

*IG* II², 1492 lines 73–80 (305/4)

224.   [?] silver phialai, inscribed 'Sacred to ---'; weight: 900+ dr. 8 silver phialai ---; weight: 500+ dr. [?] silver phialai, inscribed 'Sacred to ---'

φιάλαι ἀργυραῖ ἐφ' αἷς ἐπιγέγραπται ἱεραὶ --- στα--- ΓΗΗΗΗ· φιάλαι ἀργυραῖ --- ΓΙΙΙ στα(θμὸν) Γ--- φιάλαι ἀργυραῖ ἐφ' αἷς ἐπιγέγραπται ἱεραὶ ---

*IG* II², 1492 lines 80–4 (305/4)

225.   A silver platter, on which is inscribed 'Sacred to Athena Polias, Nikokrates [of Kolonos] made me in the archonship of Archippos of Rhamnous [318/7]'; weight: 1410(?) dr.

πίναξ ἀργυροῦς ἐφ' ᾧ ἐπιγέγραπται ἱερὸς Ἀθηνᾶς

Πολιάδος· Νικοκράτης ἐποίησεν ἐπὶ Ἀρχίππου
Ῥαμνουσίου ἄρχοντος· σταθμὸν Χ.ΗΗΗΔ

IG II², 1474 lines 14–18 (after 318/7)

*Sacred to Demeter and Kore*

226.  A silver duck from the incense-burner, sacred to the Two
Goddesses; weight: 11 dr. 3 ob.

νῆττα ἀργυρᾶ ἀπὸ τοῦ θυμιατηρίου τοῖν θεοῖν
σταθμὸν ΔΗΙΙΙ

IG II², 1421, add. p. 799 lines 77–8 (374/3)
1424a lines 185–6 (371/0)
1428 lines 77–8 (367/6)
1436 line 53 (350/49)

*Sacred to Zeus*

227.  Silver phialai, inscribed 'sacred to Zeus'.

φιάλαι ἀργυραῖ ἐφ' αἷς ἐπιγέγραπται ἱεραὶ Διός

IG II², 1492 lines 86–7 (305/4)

*Offering-Trays*

228.  A bronze offering-tray

σκάφιον χαλκοῦν

IG II², 1467 lines 5–6 (304/3)

229.  One-hundred bronze offering trays.

σκάφαι χαλκαῖ Η

IG I³, 342 line 24 (405/4?)
IG II², 1381+1386, add. p. 798 line 19 (401/0)
1390 line 7 (399/8)
1388 line 46 (398/7)
1393 lines 25–6 (397/6)
1401 line 2 (394/3)
1389 line 6 (391/0)
1407 line 27 (385/4)

VESSELS

230.  A silver washbasin; weight: ---

χερνιβεῖον ἀργυροῦν σταθμὸν ---

IG II², 1372+1402+EM 13409 [*EAC* 3 (1965) 60–1]
lines 27–8 (402/1)
IG II², 1449 lines 7–8 (397/6)
1401 line 25 (394/3)

1400 line 41 (390/89)
1413 line 1 (between 384/3 and 378/7)

231.  A silver washbasin; weight: 1050 dr. Another silver washbasin; weight: 940 dr.

χερνιβεῖον σταθμὸν ΧϜ· χερνιβεῖον σταθμὸν
ΓΗΗΗΗΔΔΔΔ

    IG II², 1385 [JHS 58 (1938) 87] lines 15–16
        1388+1403+1408+EM 6790 [EAC 3 (1965) 75]
        line 53 (398/7) [1 only]
    IG II², 1415 lines 2–3 (375/4)
    **1424a lines 174–5 (371/0)**
    1428 lines 66–8 (367/6)
    1430 lines 8–10 (c.367/6)
    **1432 lines 9–10 (after 350/49)**
    1444 lines 27–9 (341/0) [not in good condition]

232.  A silver washbasin, a silver incense-burner; unweighed

χερνιβεῖον ἀργυροῦν θυμιατήριον ἀργυροῦν ἄστατα

    **IG II², 1400 lines 50–1 (390/89)**

233.  100 dr. weight of silver overlay which --- of Sounion put against the base of the washbasin

ἀργυρίου ἐπ[ιτήκτου, ὃ κατέ]βαλε πρὸς τὸ [βάθρον]
τοῦ χερνιβείου --- Σουνιεὺς σταθμὸν Η

    IG II², 1421 lines 67–9 (374/3)

234.  A gold stand; unweighed

ὑπόστατον χρυσοῦν ἄστατον

    IG I³, 342 lines 12–13 (405/4)
    IG II², 1384 lines 7–8 (403/2)
        1386 line 16 (401/0)
        1390 line 4 (399/8)
        1388 lines 43–4 (398/7)
        1393 line 24 (397/6)
        1389 lines 4–5 (391/0)
        **1400 line 20 (390/89)**
        1413 lines 9–10 (between 384/3 and 378/7)[59]

235.  A krater-stand, gilt bronze

ὑπόστατον κρατῆρος ὑπόχαλκον ἐπίχρυσον

    IG II², 1421 lines 20–1 (374/3)
        1424a lines 73–4 (371/0)
        **1425 lines 71–2 (368/7)**
        1428 line 61 (367/6)

[59] For the crater see V.236.

236.　　A krater, silver gilt; unweighed

κρατὴρ ὑπάργυρος ἐπίτηκτος ἄσταθμος

　　　IG II², 1384 lines 8–9 (403/2)
　　　　1386 lines 16–17 (401/0)
　　　　1390 lines 4–5 (399/8)
　　　　**1388 line 44 (398/7)**
　　　　1393 line 24 (397/6)
　　　　1389 lines 4–5 (391/0)
　　　　1400 line 20 (390/89)
　　　　1407 lines 25–6 (385/4)
　　　　1421 lines 18–19 (374/3)
　　　　1424a line 72 (371/0)
　　　　1425 line 70 (368/7)
　　　　1428 line 60 (367/6)

237.　　The small gold krater; weight: 2569 dr. 3 ob.

κρατὴρ χρυσοῦς ὁ μικρὸς σταθμὸν XXΓ𐅅ΔΓⱵⱵⱵⱵΙΙΙ

　　　**IG II², 1396 lines 19–20 (beg. 4th cent.)**
　　　　1398 lines 7–9 (399/8)
　　　　1415 line 6 (375/4)

238.　　The smaller gold krater; weight: 17+ dr. 2 ob.

κρατὴρ χρυσοῦς ὁ ἐλάττων σταθμὸν ---ΔΓⱵΙΙ

　　　IG II², 1424a lines 22–3 (371/0)
　　　　**1425 lines 17–18 (368/7)**

239.　　--- from the large krater, which comes from the hand of the Nike

--- τοῦ κρατῆρος τοῦ μεγάλου ἀπὸ τῆς χειρὸς τῆς Νίκης

　　　**IG II², 1407 lines 26–7 (385/4)**
　　　　1413 line 14 (between 384/3 and 378/7)

240.　　A drinking-horn, a silver drinking-cup, and the silver band around it; weight: 210 dr.

κέρας ἔκπωμα ἀργυροῦν καὶ περισκελὶς πρόσεστιν ἀργυρᾶ σταθμὸν ΗΗΔ

　　　IG II², 1382 line 13 (405/4?)
　　　　**1408 lines 16–17 (398/7)**
　　　　1409 line 9 (395/4)
　　　　1407 line 38 (385/4)

241.　　A silver drinking-cup, a silver protome of Pegasos, these the Athenians dedicated to (Athena) Polias; weight: 118 dr.

ἔκπωμα ἀργυροῦν· πηγάσου προτομή· τούτω

Ἀθηναῖοι ἀνέθεσαν Πολιάδι· σταθμὸν ΗΔΓΗΗ

IG I³, 342 lines 14–16 (405/4)

242.     A bronze brazier

ἐσχάρα χαλκᾶ

IG II², 1414 line 41 (385/4)

243.     A bronze jug

ἐπίχυσις χαλκῆ

IG II², 1475 line 8 (after 318/7)

244.     A gold hydria; weight: 78+ dr. 4 ob.

ὑδρία χρυσῆ σταθμὸν ---ϜΔΔΓΗΗΙΙΙΙ

IG II², 1425 line 19 (368/7)

245.     A gold hydria; weight: 1200 dr. 3 ob.

ὑδρία χρυσῆ σταθμὸν ΧΗΗΙΙΙ

IG II², 1424a line 63 (371/0)

246.     A gold hydria; weight: 1174 dr. 4 ob. A gold hydria; weight: 1201 dr.

ὑδρία χρυσῆ σταθμὸν ΧΗϜΔΔΗΗΗΙΙΙΙ· ὑδρία χρυσῆ σταθμὸν ΧΗΗΗ

IG II², 1424a lines 24–5 (371/0)

247.     A gold hydria; weight: 1100 dr. 5 ob.

ὑδρία χρυσῆ σταθμὸν ΧΗΙΙΙΙΙ

IG II², 1425 line 63 (368/7)

248.     A gold hydria of Athena; weight: 49 dr. 3 ob.

τῆς Ἀθηνᾶς ὑδρία χρυσῆ σταθμὸν ΔΔΔΔΓΗΗΗΙΙΙ

IG II², 1415 lines 7–8 (375/4)
1425 line 20? (368/7)

249.     A gold hydria, which An[--- dedicated]; weight: 100 dr.

ὑδρία χρυσῆ Η ἦν Ἀν[--- ἀνέθηκε]

IG II², 1463 line 14 (349/8)

250.     The smooth glass hydria [dedicated] in the archonship of Dysniketos [370/69]; weight: 48+ dr.

ὑδρία λεία ὑαλίνη ἡ ἐπὶ Δυσνικήτου σταθμὸν ---
ΔΔΔΔΓΗΗ

IG II², 1425 line 117 (368/7)

251.     A silver hydria, marked Δ, inscribed 'Nikokrates of

Kolonos made me'; weight: 1437 dr.

ὑδρία ἀργυρᾶ ἐφ' ᾗ τὸ Δ ἐφ' ᾗ ἐπιγέγραπται
Νικοκράτης ἐκ Κολωνοῦ ἐποίησε· στα(θμὸν)
ΧΗΗΗΗΔΔΔΓΗ

IG II², 1492 lines 29–32 (305/4)

252.     One silver hydria of Aphrodite; [weight]: 950 dr.

Ἀφροδίτης ὑδρία ἀργυρᾶ μία ΓΗΗΗΗΓ

IG II², 1424a line 246 (371/0)
1425 line 192 (368/7)
1429 lines 20–1 (367/6)
1437 line 66 (after 350/49)
1444 line 18 (341/0)

253.     Three silver hydriai which the treasurers in the archonship
of Archippos [321/0] had made from the phialai of the
freedmen, which Diomedon --- made. The one
marked A; weight: 1489 dr.

ὑδρίαι ἀργυραῖ τρεῖς ἃς ἐποιήσαντο ταμίαι οἱ ἐπὶ
Ἀρχίππου ἄρχοντος ἐκ τῶν φιαλῶν τῶν
ἐξελευθερικῶν ἃς Διομέδων --- ἐποίησεν· ἐφ' ᾗ τὸ Α
σταθμὸν ΧΗΗΗΗΓΔΔΔΓΗΗ

IG II², 1469 lines 3–12 (after 320/19)

254.     Silver hydriai of the Dioskouroi: The first: 883 dr.; the
second: 895 dr. 3 ob.; the third: 932 dr.

Ἀνάκοιν ὑδρίαι ἀργυραῖ· πρώτη ΓΗΗΗΓΔΔΔΗΗ
δευτέρα ΓΗΗΗΓΔΔΔΓΙΙΙ τρίτη ΓΗΗΗΗΔΔΔΗΗ

IG II², 1412 line 20 (382/1)
1413 lines 21–2 (between 384/3 and 378/7)
**1424a lines 237–40 (371/0)**
1425 lines 182–5 (368/7)
1429 lines 10–13 (c.367/6)
1437 lines 67–72 (after 350/49) [adding a fourth]
1444 lines 19–22? (341/0)

255.     New silver hydriai [of Athena Polias]. The first: 893 dr.;
the second: 907 dr.; the third: 900 dr. 3 ob.

ὑδρίαι ἀργυραῖ καιναί· πρώτη ΓΗΗΗΓΔΔΔΔΗΗ
δευτέρα ΓΗΗΗΗΓΗΗ τρίτη ΓΗΗΗΗΙΙΙ

IG II², 1413 lines 17–18 (between 384/3 and 378/7)
**1424a lines 220–3 (371/0)**
1425 lines 165–8 (368/7)
1428 lines 104–7 (367/6)
1437 lines 73–4 (after 350/49)

Part V

**256.** Hydriai of Athena Nike. The first: 960 dr.; the second: 982 dr.; the third: 1001 dr.; the fourth: 992 dr.

Ἀθηνᾶς Νίκης ὑδρίαι· πρώτη ΓΗΗΗΗΓΔ δευτέρα
ΓΗΗΗΗΓΔΔΔΗ τρίτη ΧΗ τετάρτη
ΓΗΗΗΗΓΔΔΔΔΗ

IG II², 1412 lines 17–18 (382/1)
1413 lines 18–19 (between 384/3 and 378/7)
**1424a lines 224–8 (371/0)**
1425 lines 169–73 (368/7)
1429 line 1 (c.367/6)
1437 lines 42–8 (after 350/49) [adding a fifth]
1444 lines 8–12 (341/0)

**257.** Silver hydriai of Demeter and Kore. First: 924 dr. 3 ob. Second: 988 dr. Third: 928 dr. 3 ob. Fourth: 988 dr. Fifth: 959 dr.

Δήμητρος καὶ Κόρης ὑδρίαι ἀργυραῖ· πρώτη
ΓΗΗΗΗΔΔΗΗΗΙΙΙ δευτέρα ΓΗΗΗΗΓΔΔΔΓΗΗΗ
τρίτη ΓΗΗΗΗΔΔΓΗΗΗΙΙΙ τετάρτη
ΓΗΗΗΗΓΔΔΔΓΗΗΗ πέμπτη ΓΗΗΗΗΓΓΗΗΗΗ

IG II², 1412 lines 24–5 (382/1)
1413 lines 24–7 (between 384/3 and 378/7)
**1424a lines 241–5 (371/0)**
1425 lines 186–91 (368/7)
1429 lines 14–19 (c.367/6)
1437 lines 58–65 (after 350/49)
1444 lines 14–17 (341/0)

**258.** Silver hydriai, which the treasurers in the archonship of Neaichmos [320/19] had made from the phialai of the freedmen, which Nikokrates of Kolonos made. The one marked Δ, weight: 1474 dr. Of this, the tag weighs 3 dr. The one marked E; weight: 1485 dr. Of this, the tag weighs 4 dr. The one marked Z; weight: 1483 dr. Of this the tag weighs 4 dr. The one marked H, which Archephon of Erchia made; weight: 1479 dr. Of this the tag weighs 4 dr. The one marked Θ, which Nikokrates of Kolonos made; weight: 120+ dr. Of this the tag weighs ---

ὑδρίαι ἀργυραῖ ἃς ἐποιήσαντο ταμίαι οἱ ἐπὶ
Νεαίχμου ἄρχοντος ἐκ τῶν φιαλῶν τῶν
ἐξελευθερικῶν ἃς Νικοκράτης ἐκ Κολωνοῦ ἐποίησεν·
ἐφ᾽ ᾗ τὸ Δ σταθμὸν ΧΗΗΗΗΓΔΔΗΗΗ τούτου
κόλλα ΗΗΗ ἐφ᾽ ᾗ τὸ E σταθμὸν ΧΗΗΗΗΓΔΔΔΓ
τούτου κόλλα ΗΗΗ ἐφ᾽ ᾗ τὸ Z σταθμὸν

ΧΗΗΗΗΡΔΔΔⱵⱵ τούτου κόλλα ⱵⱵⱵⱵ ἐφ᾽ ᾗ τὸ Η
ἦν Ἀρχεφῶν Ἐρχι(εύς) ἐποίησε σταθμὸν
ΧΗΗΗΗΡΔΔΓⱵⱵⱵⱵ τούτου κόλλα ⱵⱵⱵⱵ ἐφ᾽ ᾗ τὸ Θ
ἦν Νικοκράτης ἐκ Κολωνοῦ ἐποίησεν σταθμὸν
---Η.ΔΔ. τούτου κόλλα ---

IG II², 1469 lines 12–26 (after 320/19)

259. Silver hydriai of Artemis Brauronia. The first: 979 dr.; the second: 882 dr. ; the third: 987 dr.; the fourth: 992 dr.; the fifth: 922 dr.; the sixth: 922 dr.; the seventh: 959 dr.

Ἀρτέμιδος Βραυρωνίας ὑδρίαι ἀργυραῖ· πρώτη
ΡΗΗΗΗΡΔΔΓⱵⱵⱵⱵ δευτέρα ΡΗΗΗΡΔΔΔⱵⱵ τρίτη
ΡΗΗΗΗΡΔΔΔΓⱵⱵ τετάρτη ΡΗΗΗΗΡΔΔΔΔⱵⱵ
πέμπτη ΡΗΗΗΗΔΔⱵⱵ ἕκτη ΡΗΗΗΗΔΔⱵⱵ ἑβδόμη
ΡΗΗΗΗΡΓⱵⱵⱵⱵ

IG II², 1412 lines 19–21 (382/1)
     1413 lines 15–18, 21–4 (between 384/3 and 378/7)
     **1424a lines 229–36 (371/0)**
     1425 lines 174–81 (368/7)
     1437 lines 49–57 (after 350/49)
     1444 lines 9–13 (341/0)

260. Silver hydriai of Athena Polias: The first: 998 dr.; the second: 991 dr.; the third: 982 dr.; the fourth: 989 dr.; the fifth: 1003 dr. 3 ob.; the sixth: 997 dr. 3 ob.; the seventh: 993 dr.; the eighth: 995 dr. 3 ob.; the ninth: 1001 dr. 3 ob.; the tenth: 991+ dr.; the eleventh: 995 dr. 3 ob.; the twelfth: 990 dr.; the thirteenth: 992 dr. 4 ob.; the fourteenth: 990 dr. 4 ob.; the fifteenth: 993 dr.; the sixteenth: 999 dr. 3 ob.; the seventeenth: 991 dr.; the eighteenth: 994 dr.; the nineteenth: 994 dr. 3 ob. the twentieth: 992 dr.; the twenty-first: 1004 dr. 1 ob.; the twenty-second: 992 dr. 4 ob.; the twenty-third: 1002 dr. 1 ob.;[60] the twenty-fourth: 991 dr.; the twenty-fifth: 1000 dr.; the twenty-sixth: 1009 dr. 4 ob.; the twenty-seventh: 1000 dr. 3 ob.

ὑδρίαι ἀργυραῖ Ἀθηνᾶς Πολιάδος· πρώτη
ΡΗΗΗΗΡΔΔΔΓⱵⱵⱵ δευτέρα ΡΗΗΗΗΡΔΔΔΔⱵ
τρίτη ΡΗΗΗΗΡΔΔⱵⱵ τετάρτη
ΡΗΗΗΗΡΔΔΔΓⱵⱵⱵⱵ πέμπτη ΧⱵⱵⱵ ἕκτη
ΡΗΗΗΗΡΔΔΔΓⱵⱵΙΙΙ ἑβδόμη ΡΗΗΗΗΡΔΔΔΔⱵⱵⱵ
ὀγδόη ΡΗΗΗΗΡΔΔΔΓΙΙΙ ἐνάτη ΧⱵΙΙΙ δεκάτη
ΡΗΗΗΗΡΔΔΔΔⱵ --- ἑνδεκάτη ΡΗΗΗΗΡΔΔΔΔΓΙΙΙ

---

[60] Or 1001 dr. 206.

δωδεκάτη ΓΗΗΗΗϜΔΔΔΔ τρίτη καὶ δεκάτη
ΓΗΗΗΗϜΔΔΔΔΗΙΙΙΙ τετάρτη καὶ δεκάτη
ΓΗΗΗΗϜΔΔΔΔΙΙΙΙ πέμπτη καὶ δεκάτη
ΓΗΗΗΗϜΔΔΔΔΗΗ ἕκτη καὶ δεκάτη
ΓΗΗΗΗϜΔΔΔΔΓΗΗΗΙΙΙ ἑβδόμη καὶ δεκάτη
ΓΗΗΗΗϜΔΔΔΔΗ ὀγδόη καὶ δεκάτη
ΓΗΗΗΗϜΔΔΔΔΗΗΗ ἐνάτη καὶ δεκάτη
ΓΗΗΗΗϜΔΔΔΔΗΗΗΙΙΙ εἰκοστὴ ΓΗΗΗΗϜΔΔΔΔΗΗ
μία καὶ εἰκοστὴ ΧΗΗΗΙ δευτέρα καὶ εἰκοστὴ
ΓΗΗΗΗϜΔΔΔΔΗΙΙΙΙ τρίτη καὶ εἰκοστὴ ΧΗΗΙ
τετάρτη καὶ εἰκοστὴ ΓΗΗΗΗϜΔΔΔΔΗ πέμπτη καὶ
εἰκοστὴ Χ ἕκτη καὶ εἰκοστὴ ΧΓΗΗΗΗΙΙΙΙ ἑβδόμη καὶ
εἰκοστὴ ΧΙΙΙ

> *IG* II², 1372 lines 7–10+EM 13409 [*EAC* 3 (1965) 60–1]
> lines 10–26 (402/1)
> 1386+1381, add. p. 798 lines 27–30 (401/0)
> 1388+1408+EM 6790 [*EAC* 3 (1965) 75] lines
> 56–67 (398/7)
> 1406 lines 1–9+EM 12961 [*Hesperia* 41 (1972)
> 426– 7] lines 1–7 (397/6)
> 1401 lines 4–14 (394/3)
> 1389, add. p. 799 line 8 (391/0)
> 1400 lines 23–32 (390/89)
> 1407 lines 14–20 (385/4)
> 1414 line 46 (385/4)
> 1412 lines 12–13 (382/1)
> **1424a lines 192–219 (371/0)**
> 1425 lines 137–64 (368/7)
> 1439 lines 10–16 (between 366/5 and 353/2)
> 1437 lines 38–41 (after 350/49)
> 1444 lines 1–8 (341/0)

261.  A gold hydria, inscribed 'Sacred to Artemis; Nikokrates of
Kolonos made me'; weight: 20+ dr.

ὑδρία χρυσῆ ἐφ' ᾗ ἐπιγέγραπται ἱερὰ Ἀρτέμιδος
Νικοκράτης ἐκ Κολωνοῦ ἐποίησεν· στα(θμὸν) ---ΔΔ

*IG* II², 1492, add. p. 810 lines 17–20 (305/4?)

262.  A silver incense-burner

θυμιατήριον ἀργυροῦν

*IG* II², 1474 lines 22–3 (after 318/7)

263.  A silver incense-burner

θυμιατήριον ἀργυροῦν

*IG* II², 1425 line 134 (368/7)

264.  A silver incense-burner; weight of this: 1000 dr.

θυμιατήριον ἀργυροῦν σταθμὸν τούτου Χ

> IG II² 328 line 49 (419/8)
> **329 line 13 (418/7)**
> **330 lines 27–8 (417/6)**
> 331 lines 42–3 (416/5)
> 333 line 11 (414/3)
> 334 line 25 (413/2)
> 336 line 53 (411)
> 339 line 13 (409/8)

**265. (IV.54)**

**266.**    Incense-burner, gilt bronze ---

θυμιατήριον χρυσοῦν ὑπόχαλκον ---

> *IG* II², 1412 lines 29–30 (382/1)

**267.**    An incense-burner, silver over wood; weight of this: 1357 dr. 2 ob.

θυμιατήριον ἀργυροῦν ὑπόξυλον σταθμὸν
ΧΗΗΗ𐅄ΓΗΙΙ

> *IG* II², 1378+1398, add. pp. 797–8 lines 14–15 (399/8)
> 1396 lines 4–6 (beg. 4th cent.?)
> 1392 lines 17–18 (398/7)

**268–9. (II.9–10)**

**270. (II.12)**

**271.**    An incense-burner, gilt bronze, sealed with an A; weight including the bronze nails: 3400 dr.

θυμιατήριον ἐπίχρυσον ὑπόχαλκον ἵνα τὸ ἄλφα
παρασεσήμανται σταθμὸν σὺν τοῖς ἥλοις τοῖς
χαλκοῖς ΧΧΧΗΗΗΗ

> *IG* II², 1421 lines 50–3 (374/3)
> **1424a lines 98–100 (371/0)**
> 1425 lines 94–6 (368/7)
> 1428 lines 113–15 (367/6)
> 1429 lines 28–9 (367/6)
> **1443 lines 154–5 (344/3)**

**272.**    An incense-burner, gilt bronze, sealed with a B; weight: 3160 dr. 2 ob.

θυμιατήριον ἐπίχρυσον ὑπόχαλκον ἵνα τὸ βῆτα
παρασεσήμανται σταθμὸν ΧΧΧΗ𐅅ΔΙΙ

> *IG* II², 1421 lines 54–6 (374/3)
> **1424a lines 101–3 (371/0)**
> 1425 lines 97–8 (368/7)

1428 lines 116–7 (367/6)
1429 lines 30–1 (367/6)
1443 lines 155–6 (344/3)

273.    A silver incense-burner, having bronze supports, which Aristokritos of Anakaia dedicated; weight: 2330 dr.

θυμιατήριον ἀργυροῦν χαλκᾶ διερείσματα ἔχον ὃ Ἀριστόκριτος Ἀνακαιεὺς ἀνέθηκεν σταθμὸν ΧΧΗΗΗΔΔΔ

*IG* II², **1413 lines 3–4 (after 385/4)**
1412 line 14 (382/1)
**1424a lines 162–4 (371/0)**
**1425 lines 110–12 (368/7)**
1436 lines 43–5 (350/49)

274.    A silver incense-burner, which Kleostrate, daughter of Nikeratos, dedicated, having bronze supports; weight of this: 1300 dr.

θυμιατήριον ἀργυροῦν ὃ Κλεοστράτη ἀνέθηκεν Νικεράτου χαλκᾶ διερείσματα ἔχον σταθμὸν τούτου ΧΗΗΗ

*IG* I³, 342 lines 4–7 (405/4)
*IG* II², 1384 lines 3–5 (403/2)
**1388 lines 24–6 (398/7)**
1393 lines 11–12 (397/6)
1400 lines 12–13 (390/89)
1407 lines 11–12 (385/4)
1413 lines 4–5 (between 384/3 and 378/7)
1424a lines 167–9 (371/0)
1425 lines 115–16 (368/7) [1320 dr.]
1428 lines 132–4 (367/6)
1436 lines 41–2 (350/49)
Ag. I 2260 [*Hesperia* 25 (1956) 103] lines 8–12 (after 346/5)

275.    An incense-burner, having bronze supports; weight: 2428 dr.

θυμιατήριον χαλκᾶ διερείσματα ἔχων σταθμὸν ΧΧΗΗΗΗΔΔΓⱵⱵⱵ

*IG* II², 1413 lines 2–3 (between 384/3 and 378/7)
**1424a lines 165–6 (371/0)**
1425 lines 113–14 (368/7)
Ag. I 2260 [*Hesperia* 25 (1956) 103] lines 7–8 (after 346/5)

276.    Three silver incense-burners, not in good condition near the table; unweighed

θυμιατήρια ἀργυρᾶ τρία οὐχ ὑγιᾶ παρὰ τὴν
τράπεζαν ἄστατα

> Ag. I 2260 [*Hesperia* 25 (1956) 103] line 6 (after
> 346/5)

277.    Gold from the incense-burners, which was recovered at
[the house of] Kallimachos; weight: ---

ἀπὸ τῶν θυμιατηρίων χρυσίον ὃ παρὰ Καλλιμάχῳ
ηὑρέθη σταθμὸν ---

> *IG* II², 1421 lines 16–17 (374/3)

278.    A silver goblet; weight of this: 200 dr.

καρχήσιον ἀργυροῦν σταθμὸν τούτου ΗΗ

> *IG* I³, 323 line 53 (428/7)
> 324 lines 63–4 (427/6)
> 325 line 8 (422/1)
> 326 line 20 (421/0)
> 327 line 31 (420/19)
> 328 line 44 (419/8)
> 329 line 8 (418/7)
> **330 line 23 (417/6)**
> 331 lines 37–8 (416/5)
> 333 line 7 (414/3)
> 334 line 21 (413/2)
> 336 line 49 (411)
> 339 line 8 (409/8)
> 340 lines 25–6 (408/7)

279.    A goblet; weight: 1198 dr. 4 ob.

καρχήσιον σταθμὸν ΧΗℲΔΔΔΔΓΗΗΗΙΙΙΙ

> *IG* II², 1414 lines 4–5 (385/4)

280.    Silver *karchesion* of Zeus Polieus; weight: 200 dr.

καρχήσιον ἀργυροῦν Διὸς Πολιῶς σταθμὸν τούτου
ΗΗ

> *IG* I³, 323 lines 53–4 (428/7)
> 324 line 64 (427/6)
> 325 lines 8–9 (422/1)
> 326 line 20 (421/0)
> 327 lines 31–2 (420/19)
> 328 lines 44–5 (419/8)
> 329 lines 8–9 (418/7)
> **330 lines 23–4 (417/6)**
> 331 line 38 (416/5)
> 333 lines 7–8 (414/3)
> 334 lines 21–2 (413/2)

336 lines 49–50 (411)
339 lines 8–9 (409/8)
342 lines 13–14 (405/4?)=IG II², 1382 lines
12–13 [199 dr.]
IG II², 1388 lines 48–9 (398/7)
1401 line 4 (394/3)
1400 lines 22–3 (390/89)

281.        A silver and glass vessel; weight: 50 dr. 3 ob.

ὑάλινον ἀργυροῦν σταθμὸν τούτου ⱵΙΙΙ

IG II², 1373 lines 15–16 (403/2)
**1376 line 18 (402/1 or 401/0)**
1377 lines 21–2 (399/8)
1394 lines 4–5 (397/6?)
1395+Ag. I 1182 [*Hesperia* 5 (1936) 390] lines
21–2 (395/4)

282.        A silver *kyathos* for sweet oil; unweighed

κύαθος μυρηρὸς ἀργυροῦς ἄστατος

**IG II², 1424a line 321 (371/0)**
1425 lines 247–8 (368/7)
1428 line 161 (367/6)

283.        A silver wine-cup; weight: 105 dr.

κύλιξ ἀργυρᾶ σταθμὸν ΗⱵ

IG II², 1403 line 2 (398/7)
1401 line 20 (394/3)
**1400 line 37 (390/89)**

284.        A gold wine-cup; weight: ---

κύλιξ χρυσῆ σταθμὸν ---

IG II², 1401 line 20 (394/3)
**1400 line 37 (390/89)**

285.        A gold cup; weight: 27 dr. 1¼ ob.

κυμβίον χρυσοῦν σταθμὸν ΔΔⱵΗΗƆ

IG II², 1424a line 37 (371/0)
**1425 line 32 (368/7)**

286.        33 smooth gold cups; weight of these: 44 dr.

κυμβία λεῖα χρυσᾶ ΔΔΔΙΙΙ σταθμὸν τούτων
ΔΔΔΔⱵⱵⱵⱵ

IG II², 1373 lines 13–14 (403/2)
**1376 lines 13–15 (402/1 or 401/0)**
1377 lines 19–20 (399/8)
1408 lines 5–6 (398/7)

1394 lines 2–3 (397/6)

1395+Ag. I 1182 [*Hesperia* 5 (1936) 390] line 20 (395/4)

Ag. I 5363 [*Hesperia* 32 (1963) 165–8] line 5 (before 385/4)

287.  A silver wine-jug; weight: 108+ dr.

οἰνοχόη ἀργυρᾶ σταθμὸν Η---ΓϜϜ[61]

*IG* II², 1401 lines 19–20 (394/3)
1400 line 36 (390/89)

288.  A silver wine-jug; weight: 652 dr.

οἰνοχόη ἀργυρᾶ σταθμὸν ΓΗϜϜ

*IG* II², 1407 line 23 (385/4)
1415 line 3 (375/4)
1421 line 81 (374/3)
**1424a line 180 (371/0)**
1428 line 72 (367/6)
1430 line 14 (*c.*367/6)
1432 line 6 (after 350/49)
1444 line 23 (341/0)

289.  A gold wine-jug; weight: 67 dr. 3 ob.

οἰνοχόη χρυσῆ σταθμὸν ϜΔΓϜΙΙΙ

*IG* II², 1424a line 26 (371/0)
1443 line 124 (344/3)

290.  A gold wine-jug; weight: 2+ dr. 1 ob.

οἰνοχόη χρυσῆ, σταθμὸν --- ϜΙ

*IG* II², 1425 line 21 (368/7)

291.  Gold wine-jug; weight: 60+ dr. 2 ob.+

οἰνοχόη χρυσῆ σταθμὸν ϜΔ.ΙΙ---

*IG* II², 1443 line 124 (344/3)

292.  Another gold wine-jug, not in good condition; weight: 2500+ dr.

ἑτέρα οἰνοχόη χρυσῆ οὐχ ὑγιὴς σταθμὸν ΧΧΓ---

*IG* II², 1443 line 125 (344/3)

293.  A gold wine-jug, ribbed

οἰνοχόη χρυσῆ ῥαβδωτή

*IG* II², 1412 line 32 (382/1)
1413 line 6 (between 384/3 and 378/7)

---

[61] As restored by Clinton (1984) 55–60.

**294. (II.13)**

295.        A wine-jug; which --- handed over ---

οἰνοχόη ἦν παρέδωκεν ---

*IG* II², 1480 line 5 (after 313/2)

296.        A wine-jug, which the treasurers in the archonship of Nikodoros [314/3] had made from the phialai of the freedmen, made by Nikokrates of Kolonos, marked . ; weight: 1438 dr.

οἰνοχόη ἦν ἐποιήσαντο ταμίαι οἱ ἐπὶ Νικοδώρου ἄρχοντος ἐκ τῶν φιαλῶν τῶν ἐξελευθερικῶν ἣν Νικοκράτης ἐκ Κολωνοῦ ἐποίησεν ἐφ᾽ ᾗ τὸ .
σταθμὸν ΧΗΗΗΗΔΔΔΓ⊦⊦[62]

*IG* II², 1480 [*Hesperia* 57 (1988) 355] lines 8–11 (after 313/2)

297.        Three silver wine-jugs; weight: 1382 dr. 2 ob.

οἰνοχόαι ἀργυραῖ τρεῖς σταθμὸν ΧΗΗΗℾΔΔΔ⊦⊦II

*IG* II², 1372+1402+EM 13409 [*EAC* 3 (1965) 60–1] lines 28–9 (402/1)
1388 lines 30–1 (398/7)
1393 lines 15–16 (397/6)
1401 line 14 (394/3?)
1400 line 32 (390/89)
1407 line 22 (385/4)
1415 lines 3–4 (375/4)
1421 line 64 (374/3)
1424a line 177 (371/0)
**1428 lines 69–70 (367/6)**
1430 lines 11–12 (367/6)
1432 line 7 (after 350/49)
1444 line 24 (341/0)

298.        Silver wine-jugs ---

οἰνοχόαι ἀργυραῖ ---

*IG* II², 1492 line 85 (305/4)

299.        Silver wine-jugs; weight of these: 1405 dr.

οἰνοχόαι ἀργυραῖ --- σταθμὸν τούτων ΧΗΗΗΗΓ

*IG* II², 1392 line 18 (398/7)

300.        A silver phiale ---

φιάλη ἀργυρᾶ ---

*IG* I³, 342 line 7 (405/4)

[62] As restored in Harris (1988) 35.

301. An ivory phiale

φιάλη ἐλεφαντίνη

IG II², 1464 lines 20–1 (after 316/5)

302. (II.83)

303. A small bronze phiale

φιάλιον χαλκοῦν

IG II², 1421, add. p. 799 line 127 (374/3)
**1424a line 322 (371/0)**
1425 line 249 (368/7)
1428 line 163 (367/6)
1443 line 210 (344/3)
1455 line 12 (341/0)

304. A gold phiale; weight: ---

φιάλη χρυσῆ σταθμὸν ---

IG II², 1443 line 126 (344/3)

305. A silver phiale; weight: 930 dr.

φιάλη ἀργυρᾶ σταθμὸν ΓΗΗΗΗΔΔ

IG II², 1415 lines 6–7 (375/4)

306. A silver phiale; weight: 105 dr. Another silver phiale; ---
Another silver phiale; weight: 100 dr.

φιάλη ἀργυρᾶ σταθμὸν ΗΓ ἑτέρα φιάλη ἀργυρᾶ ---
ἑτέρα φιάλη ἀργυρᾶ σταθμὸν Η

IG II², 1415 lines 3–5 (375/4)

307. Deposit from Sounion: a silver phiale ---

ἀπὸ Σουνίου παρακαταθήκη· φιάλη ἀργυρᾶ ---

IG II², 1400 line 48 (390/89)
1421 line 70 (374/3)

308. A silver-gilt phiale with acorn-ornament; weight: 101 dr.
5 ob.

φιάλη ὑπάργυρος ἀκυλωτὴ σταθμὸν ΗΓΙΙΙΙΙ

IG II², 1421 lines 48–9 (374/3)
**1424a line 97 (371/0)**
1425 line 93 (368/7)
1428 lines 120–1 (367/6)

309. A smooth gold phiale, on which is inscribed its weight:
199 dr. 2 ob.

φιάλη χρυσῆ λεία ἄγουσα σταθμὸν ὃ ἐπιγέγραπται

*Part V*

ἐπὶ τῆ φιάλη ΗϜΔΔΔΔΓⱵⱵⱵⱵΙΙ

*IG* II², 1441 line 20 (347/6)
1443 lines 130–1 (344/3)

310. A gold phiale, not in good condition, on which is inscribed its weight: --- dr. 2+ ob.

φιάλη χρυσῆ --- οὐχ ὑγιὴς σταθμὸν ὃ ἐπιγέγραπται ἐπὶ τῆ φιάλη ---ΙΙ---

*IG* II², 1443 lines 133–5 (344/3)

311. A silver phiale, which Aristola dedicated; weight ---

φιάλη ἀργυρᾶ ἣν Ἀριστόλα ἀνέθηκε σταθμὸν ---

*IG* II², 1393 lines 28–9 (397/6)
1401 lines 31–2 (394/3)
1403 lines 10–11 (398/7)
1407 line 35 (385/4)

312. Silver phialai, which Eutrephes, son of Eumnemon --- dedicated; weight: 500+ dr.

φιάλαι ἀργυραῖ ἃς Εὐτρέφης Εὐμνήμονος --- ἀνέθηκε σταθμὸν τούτων Γ ---

*IG* I³, 341 lines 6–7 (406/5)=*IG* II², 1383 line 7
342 lines 19–21 (405/4)

313. Bronze phiale, which Kallias of Plotheia dedicated

φιάλη χαλκῆ ἣν Καλλίας Πλωθειεὺς ἀνέθηκεν

*IG* II², 1412 line 6 (382/1)
1421 lines 102–3 (374/3)
1424a line 295 (371/0)
1425 lines 210–11 (368/7)
1428 line 137 (367/6)
1443 lines 205–6 (344/3)
1455 lines 8–9 (341/0)
1460 lines 24–5 (after 330/29)

314. Silver phiale dedicated by Kallistratos, son of Kalliades, of Acharnai; weight of this: 100+ dr.

φιάλη ἀργυρᾶ ἣν Καλλίστρατος Καλλιάδου Ἀχαρνεὺς ἀνέθηκεν σταθμὸν ταύτης Η---

*IG* II², 1403+1388+EM 6790+1408 [*EAC* 3 (1965) 75] lines 9–10 (398/7)
1401 lines 30–1 (394/3)
1400 lines 45–6 (390/89)

315. Copper-topped (?) phiale, Persian, which Kleon dedicated; weight: 167 dr. 5 ob.

φιάλη χαλκοκρὰς βαρβαρικὴ ἦν Κλέων ἀνέθηκε
σταθμὸν ΗϜΔΓΗΙΙΙΙ

    *IG* II², 1421 lines 46–7 (374/3)
       **1424a lines 95–6 (371/0)**
       1425 lines 91–2 (368/7)
       1428 lines 118–19 (367/6)

316. A silver phiale, which Leokrates, son of Aischron, of
Phaleron, dedicated; weight of this: 110 dr.

φιάλη ἀργυρᾶ ἦν Λεωκράτης Αἰσχρωνος Φαληρεὺς
ἀνέθηκε σταθμὸν ταύτης ΗΔ

    *IG* II², **1388 lines 54–5 (398/7)**
       1393 lines 34–5 (397/6)
       1401 lines 39–40 (394/3)
       1400 line (390/89)
       1407 lines 35–6 (385/4)
       1414 line 7 (after 385/4)

317. A silver phiale, which Lysimache, mother of Telemachos,
dedicated; on which is the gorgoneion; weight: 3+ dr.

φιάλη ἀργυρᾶ ἦν Λυσιμάχη Τηλεμάχου μήτηρ
ἀνέθηκε ἐν ᾗ τὸ γοργόνειον σταθμὸν --- ΗΗΗ

    *IG* II², **1388 lines 55–7 (398/7)**
       1393 lines 35–6 (397/6)
       1401 lines 40–1 (394/3)
       1400 lines 54–5 (390/89)
       1407 lines 36–7 (385/4)

318. A silver phiale unweighed, which the wife of Speuson
dedicated

[φιάλη ἀργυρᾶ ἄστατος ἦν Σπεύ]σωνος [γυ]νὴ
[ἀνέθηκ]εν[63]

    *IG* II², **1414 lines 26–27 (385/4)**

319. Gold phiale, which Stephanos, son of Thallos, dedicated;
weight: 198 dr.

φιάλη χρυσῆ ἦν Στέφανος Θάλλου ἀνέθηκεν σταθμὸν
ΗϜΔΔΔΔΓΗΗ

    *IG* II², **1424a lines 32–3 (371/0)**
       1425 lines 27–8 (368/7)

320. Gold phialai, which the treasurers in the archonship of
Neaichmos [320/19] had made from the money which
Archippos collected as archon [321/0] for the 1 per
cent tax, on each of which is inscribed 'Nikokrates of

---

[63] As restored by Woodward (1940) 390.

Kolonos made me'. The three marked Σ; weight: 590 dr. 3+ ob. Three gold phialai which Archephon of Erchia made, marked 'Τ'; weight: 550+ dr.

φιάλαι χρυσαῖ ἃς ἐποιήσαντο ταμίαι οἱ ἐπὶ Νεαίχμου ἄρχοντος ἐκ τῶν χρημάτων ἃ ἀνεκόμισεν Ἄρχιππος ἄρχων ἑκατοστὴν ἐφ' αἷς ἐπιγέγραπται Νικοκράτης ἐκ Κολωνοῦ ἐποίησεν· τρεῖς ἐφ' αἷς τὸ Σ σταθμὸν ΓϜΔΔΔΔΙΙΙ---· φιάλαι χρυσαῖ τρεῖς ἃς Ἀρχεφῶν Ἐρχιεὺς ἐποίησεν ἐφ' αἷς τὸ Τ σταθμὸν ΓϜ---[64]

> *IG* II², 1471 lines 10–15 (after 318/7)

321.      A phiale of Ammon; weight: 802 dr.

Ἄμμωνος φιάλη σταθμὸν ΓΗΗΗΗΙΙ

> *IG* II², 1424a line 176 (371/0)
> 1428 lines 73–4 (367/6)

322.      Belonging to Artemis Brauronia: a small silver phiale, a small wine-cup . . .

Ἀρτέμιδος Βραυρωνίας φιάλη μικρὰ ἀργυρᾶ· κύλιξ μικρὰ ---

> *IG* II², 1403 lines 7–8 (398/7)
> **1401 lines 29–30 (394/3)**
> 1400 line 45 (390/89)

323.      A gold phiale of Athena Nike; weight: ---

φιάλη χρυσῆ Ἀθηνᾶς Νίκης σταθμὸν ---

> *IG* II², 1443 lines 126–7 (344/3)

324.      Gold phialai of Athena --- not in good condition; weight: ---

φιάλαι χρυσαῖ --- οὐχ ὑγιεῖς Ἀθηνᾶς σταθμὸν ---

> *IG* II², 1443 lines 129–30 (344/3)

325.      Gold phialai of the goddess: first shelf, eight phialai; weight: 1405 dr. 3 ob.

χρυσίδες φιάλαι τῆς θεοῦ πρῶτος ῥυμὸς φιάλαι ὀκτὼ σταθμὸν ΧΗΗΗΗΓΙΙΙ

> *IG* II², 1396 lines 26–8 (beg. 4th cent.?)
> 1378+1398, add. pp. 797–8 line 15 (399/8)
> Ag. I 5363 [*Hesperia* 32 (1963) 165–8] lines 1–2 (before 385/4)
> *IG* II², 1441 line 21 (347/6)

---

[64] As restored in Harris (1988) 329–30.

326.     Gold phialai: second shelf, three phialai; weight: ---

φιάλαι χρυσαῖ δεύτερος ῥυμὸς φιάλαι τρεῖς σταθμὸν ---

*IG* II², 1401 line 21 (394/3)
**1400 line 38 (390/89)**

327.     Gold phialai marked A, inscribed 'Sacred to Athena'; weight: 1300+ dr. Gold phialai marked B, inscribed 'Sacred to Athena'; weight: 808 dr. Gold phialai marked Γ, 7, inscribed 'Sacred to Athena'; weight: --- Gold phialai marked Δ, inscribed, 'Sacred to Athena'; weight: 319 dr. 3 ob. Gold phialai marked K, inscribed 'Sacred to Athena'; weight: 2+ dr. 3 ob.

φιάλαι χρυσαῖ ἐφ' αἷς τὸ A, ἐφ' αἷς ἐπιγέγραπται ἱεραὶ Ἀθηνᾶς σταθμὸν ΧΗΗΗ---φιάλαι χρυσαῖ ἐφ' αἷς τὸ B ἐφ' αἷς ἐπιγέγραπται ἱεραὶ Ἀθηνᾶς σταθμὸν ΓΗΗΗΓΗΗ φιάλαι χρυσαῖ ἐφ' αἷς τὸ Γ ΓΙΙ ἐφ' αἷς ἐπιγέγραπται ἱεραὶ Ἀθηνᾶς σταθμὸν --- φιάλαι χρυσαῖ ἐφ' αἷς τὸ Δ ἐφ' αἷς ἐπιγέγραπται ἱεραὶ Ἀθηνᾶς σταθμὸν ΗΗΗΔΓΗΗΗΙΙΙ φιάλη χρυσῆ ἐφ' ᾗ τὸ K ἐφ' ᾗ ἐπιγέγραπται ἱεραὶ Ἀθηνᾶς σταθμὸν ---ΗΙΙΙ

*IG* II², 1475 lines 9–22 (after 318/7)

328.     Silver phialai belonging to the Two Goddesses [Demeter and Kore]; first shelf of 20 phialai, weight of these: 2022 dr. Second shelf of 20 phialai, weight of these: 2022 dr. Third shelf of 20 phialai, weight of these: 1000+ dr. Fourth shelf of 20 phialai, weight of these: 2008 dr. Fifth shelf of 20 phialai, weight of these: 1748 dr. Sixth shelf of 20 phialai, weight of these: 1008+ dr.

τοῖν θεοῖν φιάλαι ἀργυραῖ· πρῶτος ῥυμὸς φιάλαι ΔΔ σταθμὸν τούτων ΧΧΔΔΗ δεύτερος ῥυμὸς φιάλαι ΔΔ σταθμὸν τούτων ΧΧΔΔΗ τρίτος ῥυμὸς φιάλαι ΔΔ σταθμὸν τούτων Χ--- τέταρτος ῥυμὸς φιάλαι ΔΔ σταθμὸν τούτων ΧΧΓΗΗ πέμπτος ῥυμὸς φιάλαι ΔΔ σταθμὸν τούτων ΧΡΗΗΔΔΔΔΓΗΗ ἕκτος ῥυμὸς φιάλαι ΔΔ σταθμὸν τούτων Χ---ΓΗΗ

*IG* II², 1375+EM 12951+13410 [BSA 70 (1975) 183]
lines 1–9 (400/399)
*IG* II², 1401 lines 15–19 (394/3)
**1400 lines 33–6 (390/89)**

329.     Gold phiale of the Other Gods, crushed, weight: 35+ dr.

φιάλη χρυσῆ τῶν ἄλλων θεῶν συντεθλασμένη

σταθμὸν ---ΔΔΔΓ

    *IG* II², 1443 lines 141–2 (34/3)

330.    Gold phialai of the other gods, on which are inscribed their weights: a phiale ---

φιάλαι χρυσαῖ τῶν ἄλλων θεῶν ἄγουσαι σταθμὸν ὃ ἐπιγέγραπται ἐπὶ ταῖς φιάλαις· φιάλη ---

    *IG* II², 1443 lines 139–40 (344/3)

331.    Two silver phialai; weight: 208 dr.

φιάλαι ἀργυραῖ δύο σταθμὸν ΗΗΓΗΗ

    *IG* II², 1421 lines 65–6 (374/3)
          1428 line 71 (367/6)
          1430 line 13 (*c.*367/6)
          1432 line 8 (after 350/49)

332.    Two silver phialai; weight of one: 100 dr.

φιάλαι ἀργυραῖ δύο σταθμὸν τῆς ἑτέρας Η

    *IG* II², 1424a lines 178–9 (371/0)[65]

333.    A gold phiale; weight of this: 724 dr.

φιάλη χρυσῆ σταθμὸν ταύτης ΓΗΗΔΔΗΗΗ

    *IG* I³, 333 line 15 (414/3)
          334 line 29 (413/2)
          336 line 57 (411)

334.    2 gold phialai; weight of these: 1344 dr.

φιάλα χρυσᾶ ΙΙ σταθμὸν τούτοιν ΧΗΗΗΔΔΔΔΗΗΗ

    *IG* I³, 317 lines 4–5 (434/3)

335.    A gold phiale; weight of this: 1200 dr.

φιάλη χρυσῆ σταθμὸν ταύτης ΧΗΗ

    *IG* I³, 317 lines 7–8 (434/3)

336.    3 gold phialai; weight of these: 2544 dr.

φιάλαι χρυσαῖ ΙΙΙ σταθμὸν τούτων ΧΧΓΔΔΔΔΗΗΗ

    *IG* I³, 318 line 12 (433/2)
          319 line 18 (432/1)
          320 line 26 (431/0)
          321 lines 32–3 (430/29)
          322 line 40 (429/8)
          323 lines 48–9 (428/7)
          324 lines 60–1 (427/6)
          325 lines 5–6 (422/1)

[65] Probably part of the preceding entry.

326 line 17 (421/0)
327 lines 28–9 (420/19)
328 line 41 (419/8)
329 lines 5–6 (418/7)
**330 line 20 (417/6)**
331 line 35 (416/5)
332 line 50 (415/4)
333 lines 4–5 (414/3)
334 lines 18–19 (413/2)
335 line 32 (412/1)
336 lines 46–7 (411)
339 lines 5–6 (409/8)
340 line 23 (408/7)

337.  Four Aithiopian phialai; weight: 805 dr. 3 ob.

φιάλαι Αἰθιοπίδες τέτταρες σταθμὸν ΓΗΗΗΓΙΙΙ

> *IG* II², 1413 lines 6–7 (between 384/3 and 378/7)
> 1424a lines 30–1 (371/0)
> **1425 line 25 (368/7)**
> 1443 line 127 (344/3)

338.  These are from the shrine of the Dioskouroi: 7 large silver phialai, two small ones, one silver *karchesion*, weight of this: 268+ dr.

τάδε ἐκ τοῦ Ἀνακίου· φιάλαι ἀργυραῖ μεγάλαι ΓΙΙ μικραὶ δύο· καρχήσιον ἀργυροῦν ἕν σταθμὸν τούτου ΗΗΓΔΓΗΗ ---

> *IG* II², 1403 lines 6–7 (398/7)
> **1401 lines 28–9 (394/3)**
> 1400 lines 44–5 (390/89)

339.  Eight gold --- phialai; weight: 860 dr.

φιάλαι χρυσαῖ --- ὀκτὼ σταθμὸν ΓΗΗΗΓΔ

> *IG* II², 1443 lines 136–7 (344/3)

340.  8 silver phialai; weight of these: 800 dr.

φιάλαι ἀργυραῖ ΓΙΙΙ σταθμὸν τούτων ΓΗΗΗ

> *IG* I³, 323 lines 52–3 (428/7)
> 324 line 63 (427/6)
> **325 lines 7–8 (422/1)**
> 326 lines 19–20 (421/0)
> 327 line 31 (420/19)
> 328 lines 43–4 (419/8)
> 329 lines 7–8 (418/7)
> 330 lines 22–3 (417/6)
> 331 line 37 (416/5)
> 333 line 7 (414/3)

334 lines 20–1 (413/2)
336 line 49 (411)
339 line 8 (409/8)
340 line 25 (408/7)

341.  Six phialai, with feathered decoration; weight: 1036 dr.
φιάλαι πτιλωταὶ ἕξ σταθμὸν ΧΔΔΔΓⱵ
    *IG* II², 1424a line 29 (371/0)
        1425 line 24 (368/7)
        **1443 lines 135–6 (344/3)**

342.  Gold phialai marked 'A', weight: ---
φιάλαι χρυσαῖ --- ἔχουσαι σημεῖον Α σταθμὸν ---
    *IG* II², 1443 lines 137–8 (344/3)

343.  A silver phiale; weight of this: 192 dr.
ἀργυρὶς σταθμὸν ταύτης ΗℲΔΔΔΔⱵⱵ
    *IG* I³, 328 lines 48–9 (419/8)
        **329 lines 12–13 (418/7)**
        330 line 27 (417/6)
        331 line 42 (416/5)
        333 line 11 (414/3)
        334 line 25 (413/2)
        336 line 53 (411)
        339 line 12 (409/8)

344.  A gold phiale; weight of this: 138 dr. 2 ob.
χρυσὶς σταθμὸν ταύτης ΗΔΔΔΓⱵⱵⱵΙΙ
    *IG* I³, 325 line 12 (422/1)
        326 line 23 (421/0)
        327 line 34 (420/19)
        328 line 47 (419/8)
        329 line 11 (418/7)
        **330 line 26 (417/6)**
        331 line 41 (416/5)
        333 line 10 (414/3)
        334 line 24 (413/2)
        336 line 52 (411)
        339 line 11 (409/8)

345.  1 gold phiale; weight of this: 119 dr.
χρυσὶς Ι σταθμὸν ταύτης ΗΔΓⱵⱵⱵⱵ
    *IG* I³, 326 line 24 (421/0)
        327 lines 34–5 (420/19)
        328 lines 47–8 (419/8)
        **329 line 12 (418/7)**
        330 line 26 (417/6)

331 line 41 (416/5)
333 line 10 (414/3)
334 line 24 (413/2)
336 line 52 (411)
339 line 12 (409/8)

346.  A gold phiale, which Paapis E--- dedicated; weight of this: --- dr.

χρυσὶς ἦν Πάαπις E--- ἀνέθηκε σταθμὸν ταύτης ---

*IG* I³, 341 line 6 (406/5?)=*IG* II², 1383 line 6

347.  2 small gold phialai; weight: 2+ ob.

χρυσίδια ΙΙ σταθμὸν ---ΙΙ

*IG* II², 1457 line 29 (after 316/5)

348.  Two gold phialai; weight of these: 293 dr. 3 ob.

χρυσίδε δύο σταθμὸν τούτοιν ΗΗΓ𐅄ΔΔΔΗΗΙΙΙ

*IG* I³, 325 lines 11–12 (422/1)
326 lines 22–3 (421/0)
327 line 34 (420/19)
328 line 47 (419/8)
**329 line 11 (418/7)**
**330 lines 25–6 (417/6)**
331 lines 40–1 (416/5)
333 lines 9–10 (414/3)
334 lines 23–4 (413/2)
336 lines 51–2 (411)
339 line 11 (409/8)

349.  Two gold phialai, weight of both: 274 dr.

χρυσίδε δύο σταθμὸν τούτοιν ΗΗΓ𐅄ΔΔΗΗΗΗ

*IG* II², 1373 lines 14–15 (403/2)
**1376 lines 15–16 (402/1 or 401/0)**
**1377 line 20 (399/8)**
1408 lines 6–7 (398/7)

350.  Three gold phialai; weight of these: 480 dr.

χρυσίδες τρεῖς σταθμὸν τούτων ΗΗΗΗΓ𐅄ΔΔΔ

*IG* II², 1402 line 5 [ÉAC 3 (1965) 60–1] lines 33–4
(402/1) [494 dr. 5½ ob.]
**1381+1386, add. p. 798 lines 23–4 (401/0)**
1385 lines 16–17 (400/399)[66]
1388 line 50 (398/7)[67]

---

[66] As restored by West and Woodward (1938) 87.
[67] As restored by West and Woodward (1931) 140.

351. (II.82)

352.    Bosses from two phialai; weight: 150 dr.
        ὀμφαλοὶ φιαλῶν δυοῖν σταθμὸν ΗϜ
            *IG* II², 1421 **lines 79–80 (374/3)**
                1424a line 187 (371/0) [6 dr.]
                1425 line 133 (368/7)
                1428 line 79 (367/6)
                1439 line 7 (between 366/5 and 353/2)
                1436 line 54 (350/49)
            Ag. I 2260 [*Hesperia* 25 (1956) 103] lines 17–18 (after
                346/5)

353.    A silver platter
        πίναξ ἀργυροῦς
            *IG* II², 1470 line 6 (321/0)

354.    A silver platter; weight: 1093 dr. 3 ob.
        πίναξ ἀργυροῦς σταθμὸν ΧϜΔΔΔΔΙΗΗΙΙΙ
            *IG* II², 1372+1402+EM 13409 [*EAC* 3 (1965) 60–1]
                line 27 (402/1)
                1385 [*JHS* 58 (1938) 87] lines 13–14 (400/399)
                1388+1403+1408+EM 6790 [*JHS* 51 (1931)
                140–1] lines 52–3 (398/7)
                **1401 lines 24–5 (394/3)**

355.    A silver platter; weight: 2128 dr. Another platter; weight:
        2027 dr. 3 ob. Another platter; weight: 719 dr. 3 ob.
        πίναξ ἀργυροῦς σταθμὸν ΧΧΗΔΔΓΗΗ πίναξ ἕτερος
        σταθμὸν ΧΧΔΔΓΗΗΙΙΙ πίναξ ἕτερος σταθμὸν
        ΓΗΗΔΓΗΗΗΙΙΙ
            *IG* II², 1415 lines 1–2 (375/4)
                1424a lines 170–3 (371/0) [2027 dr. 3 ob., 1028
                dr., 719 dr. 3 ob.]
                **1428 lines 62–5 (367/6)** [2028 dr., 1028 dr. 3
                ob., 719 dr. 3 ob.]
                1430 lines 4–7 (*c.*367/6)
                1432 lines 11–13 (after 350/49)
                1444 lines 31–2 (341/0) [not in good condition]

356.    Silver platters ---
        πίνακες ἀργυροῖ ---
            *IG* II², 1470 line 7 (321/0)

357.    Slivers from silver platters; weight: 49 dr. 2 ob.
        πινάκων ἀργυρῶν περιτμήματα σταθμὸν
        ΔΔΔΔΓΗΗΗΙΙ

        *IG* II², 1428 lines 80–1 (367/6)
            1439 lines 8–9 (between 366/5 and 353/2)
            **1436 lines 61–2 (350/49)**

358.      A gold rhyton --- which Roxane, wife of King Alexander, dedicated to Athena Polias; weight: ---

ῥυτὸν χρυσοῦν --- ἀνέθηκεν βασιλέως Ἀλεξάνδρου γυνὴ Ῥωξάνη Ἀθηνᾷ Πολιάδι στα(θμὸν) ---

        *IG* II², 1492 lines 51–3 (305/4?)[68]

WREATHS

359.      A silver wreath

στέφανος ἀργυροῦς

        **IG II², 1407+1414 line 30 (385/4)**
           1420 line 5 (after 385/4?)

360.      A gold wreath

στέφανος χρυσοῦς

        **IG II², 1471 line 31 (after 318/7)**

361.      Gold wreath; weight of this: 3+ dr. 2 ob.

στέφανος χρυσοῦς σταθμὸν τούτου ---ⲦⲦΙΙ

        *IG* I³, 325 line 9 (422/1)
           326 lines 20–1 (421/0)
           327 line 32 (420/19)
           328 line 45 (419/8)
           329 line 9 (418/7)
           **330 line 24 (417/6)**
           331 lines 38–9 (416/5)
           333 line 8 (414/3)
           334 line 22 (413/2)
           336 line 50 (411)
           339 lines 9–10 (409/8)

362.      A gold wreath; weight of this: 18 dr. 3 ob.

στέφανος χρυσοῦς σταθμὸν τούτου ΔΓⲦⲦΙΙΙ

        *IG* I³, 325 line 11 (422/1)
           326 line 22 (421/0)
           327 lines 33–4 (420/19)
           328 line 46 (419/8)
           **329 lines 10–11 (418/7)**
           330 line 25 (417/6)
           331 line 40 (416/5)
           333 line 9 (414/3)

          [68] See also V.141.

334 line 23 (413/2)
336 line 51 (411)
339 lines 10–11 (409/8)

363.    A gold wreath; weight of this: 26 dr. 3 ob.
        στέφανος χρυσοῦς σταθμὸν τούτου ΔΔΓΗΙΙ
            IG I³, 328 line 48 (419/8)
                329 line 12 (418/7)
                **330 lines 26–7 (417/6)**
                331 lines 41–2 (416/5)
                333 lines 10–11 (414/3)
                334 lines 24–5 (413/2)
                336 lines 52–3 (411)
                339 line 12 (409/8)

364.    A gold wreath; weight of this: 1+ dr.
        στέφανος χρυσοῦς σταθμὸν τούτου ---Ͱ
            IG I³, 329 line 14 (418/7)
                **330 lines 28–9 (417/6)**
                331 lines 43–4 (416/5)
                333 line 12 (414/3)
                334 line 26 (413/2)
                336 line 54 (411)

365.    A gold wreath; weight of this: 35 dr.
        στέφανος χρυσοῦς σταθμὸν τούτου ΔΔΔΓ
            IG I³, 329 lines 14–15 (418/7)
                330 line 29 (417/6)
                331 line 44 (416/5)
                333 line 12 (414/3)
                334 line 26 (413/2)
                336 line 54 (411)

366.    A gold wreath; weight of this: 1250 dr.
        στέφανος χρυσοῦς σταθμὸν τούτου ΧΗΗϜ
            IG I³, 329 lines 13–14 (418/7)
                330 line 28 (417/6)
                331 line 43 (416/5)
                333 lines 11–12 (414/3)
                334 lines 25–6 (413/2)
                336 lines 53–4 (411)

367.    A gold wreath; weight of this: --- dr.
        στέφανος χρυσοῦς σταθμὸν τούτου ---
            IG I³, 331 lines 44–5 (416/5)
                **333 line 13 (414/3)**
                334 line 27 (413/2)

336 line 55 (411)

368.  A gold wreath; weight of this: --- dr.

στέφανος χρυσοῦς σταθμὸν τούτου ---

IG I³, 332 line 60 (415/4)
**333 lines 13–14 (414/3)**
334 line 27 (413/2)
336 lines 55–6 (411)

369.  A gold wreath; weight of this: --- dr.

στέφανος χρυσοῦς σταθμὸν τούτου ---

IG I³, **333 lines 14–15 (414/3)**
334 line 28 (413/2)
336 line 56 (411)

370.  A gold wreath; weight of this: 20+ dr.

στέφανος χρυσοῦς σταθμὸν τούτου ΔΔ---

IG I³, **339 line 14 (409/8)**

371.  A gold wreath, the archon was not inscribed; weight: 34 dr. 4 ob.

στέφανος χρυσοῦς ἄρχων οὐχ ἐπεγέγραπτο σταθμὸν τούτου ΔΔΔⱵⱵⱵIIII

IG II², 1437 [*Hesperia* 7 (1938) 288] **line 35 (after 350/49)**

372.  A gold wreath, a dedication; weight: 40 dr.

στέφανος χρυσοῦς ἀνάθημα σταθμὸν ΔΔΔΔ

IG II², **1437 line 36 (after 350/49)**
1438 line 26 [*Hesperia* 7 (1938) 284] line 27 (349/8)

373.  A gold wreath set with stones; weight of this: 46 dr.

στέφανος χρυσοῦς διάλιθος σταθμὸν τούτου ΔΔΔΔΓⱵ

IG II², **1373 line 9 (403/2)**
**1377 lines 14–15 (399/8)**
1395 lines 15–16 (395/4)

374.  A gold circlet; weight of this: 63 dr.

στεφάνη χρυσῆ σταθμὸν ταύτης ⊢ΔⱵⱵ

IG I³, 325 lines 9–10 (422/1)
326 line 21 (421/0)
327 lines 32–3 (420/19)
328 lines 45–6 (419/8)
**329 lines 9–10 (418/7)**
330 line 24 (417/6)

                    331 line 39 (416/5)
                    333 lines 8–9 (414/3)
                    334 line 22 (413/2)
                    336 line 50 (411)
                    339 line 10 (409/8)

375.        2 gold wreaths; weight of these: 80 dr.
            στεφάνω χρυσὼ ΙΙ σταθμὸν τούτοιν ⅍ΔΔΔ

                *IG* I³, 319 line 20 (432/1)
                    320 line 27 (431/0)
                    321 line 34 (430/29)
                    322 line 41 (429/8)
                    323 line 50 (428/7)
                    324 lines 61–2 (427/6)
                    325 lines 6–7 (422/1)
                    326 lines 18–19 (421/0)
                    327 line 30 (420/19)
                    328 lines 42–3 (419/8)
                    **329 lines 6–7 (418/7)**
                    **330 lines 21–2 (417/6)**
                    331 line 36 (416/5)
                    333 line 6 (414/3)
                    334 line 20 (413/2)
                    336 line 48 (411)
                    339 line 7 (409/8)
                    340 lines 24–5 (408/7)
                    342 lines 1–2 (405/4?)=*IG* II², 1382

376.        2 gold wreaths; weight of these: 53 dr.
            στεφάνω χρυσὼ ΙΙ σταθμὸν τούτοιν ⅍ΗΗ

                *IG* I³, **330 lines 29–30 (417/6)**
                    331 line 44 (416/5)
                    333 line 13 (414/3)
                    334 lines 26–7 (413/2)
                    336 line 55 (411)

377.        4 gold wreaths; weight of these: 135 dr. 2 ob.
            στέφανοι χρυσοῖ ΙΙΙΙ σταθμὸν τούτων ΗΔΔΔΓΙΙ

                *IG* I³, 325 line 10 (422/1)
                    326 lines 21–2 (421/0)
                    327 line 33 (420/19)
                    328 line 46 (419/8)
                    329 line 10 (418/7)
                    **330 lines 24–5 (417/6)**
                    331 lines 39–40 (416/5)
                    333 line 9 (414/3)
                    334 lines 22–3 (413/2)

336 lines 50–1 (411)
339 line 10 (409/8)

378.
Number of wreaths: 84

ἀριθμὸς τῶν στεφάνων ⲄΔΔΔΙΙΙΙ

IG II², 1474 lines 4–5 (after 318/7)

379.
A wreath marked A, which the Ephesians dedicated as a prize-dedication to Athena; weight: 198 dr. 4 ob.

στέφανος ἐφ' ᾧ τὸ A ὃν ἀνέθεσαν οἱ Ἐφέσιοι ἀριστεῖον τῇ Ἀθηνᾷ· στα(θμὸν) ΗⲄΔΔΔΔΓⲎⲎⲎΙΙΙΙ

IG II², 1486 lines 5–7 [Lewis (1988) 307] (after 307/6)
1485 lines 8–11 (304/3)

380.
Wreath marked B, which the *dēmos* of the Tenedians gave to the *dēmos* of the Athenians; weight: 197 dr. 3 ob.

στέφανος ἐφ' ᾧ τὸ B, Τενεδίων ὁ δῆμος τὸν δῆμον τὸν Ἀθηναίων σταθμὸν ΗⲄΔΔΔΔΓⲎⲎ

IG II², 1486 lines 7–10 [Lewis (1988) 307] (after 307/6)
1485 lines 11–14 (304/3)

381.
A wreath marked Γ, which the *dēmos* of the Peparethians gave to the *dēmos* of the Athenians; weight: 100+ dr. 2+ ob.

στέφανος ἐφ' ᾧ τὸ Γ ὁ δῆμος ὁ Πεπαρηθίων τὸν δῆμον τὸν Ἀθηναίων σταθμὸν Η---ΙΙ---

IG II², 1486 lines 10–12 [Lewis (1988) 307] (after 307/6)
1485 lines 14–17 (304/3)

382.
A wreath marked 'Δ', which the *dēmos* of (Lemnian) Myrrina gave to the *dēmos* of the Athenians; weight: 1+ dr.

στέφανος ἐφ' ᾧ τὸ Δ Μυριναίων ὁ δῆμος τὸν δῆμον τὸν Ἀθηναίων σταθμὸν ---Ⱶ---

IG II², 1486 lines 12–14 [Lewis (1988) 307] (after 307/6)
1485 lines 18–21 (304/3)

383.
A wreath marked E, which Spartokos of Pontos gave to the *dēmos* of the Athenians; weight: 189 dr.

στέφανος ἐφ' ᾧ τὸ E Σπάρτοκος ἐκ τοῦ Πόντου τὸν δῆμον τὸν Ἀθηναίων σταθμὸν ΗⲄΔΔΔΓⲎⲎⲎⲎ

IG II², 1486 lines 14–16 [Lewis (1988) 307] (after
307/6)
1485 lines 21–4 (304/3)

384.     A wreath marked Z, which the *dēmos* of the Milesians gave
to the *dēmos* of the Athenians; weight: 265+ dr.

στέφανος ἐφ' ᾧ τὸ Ζ ὁ δῆμος ὁ Μιλησίων τὸν δῆμον
τὸν Ἀθηναίων σταθμὸν ΗΗℲΔΓ---

IG II², 1485 lines 25–7 (304/3)

385.     Gold wreath Η, which the *dēmos* of the Athenians gave to
Lysimachos; weight: ---

στέφανος ἐφ' ᾧ τὸ Η ὁ δῆμος ὁ Ἀθηναίων Λυσίμαχον
σταθμὸν ---

IG II², 1485 lines 27–30 (304/3)

386.     Gold wreath Θ, which the *dēmos* of the inland --- gave the
*dēmos* of the Athenians; weight: ---

στέφανος ἐφ' ᾧ τὸ Θ ---ίων τῶν μεσογαίων ὁ δῆμος
τὸν δῆμον τὸν Ἀθηναίων σταθμὸν ---

IG II², 1485 lines 31–3 (304/3)

387.     A wreath marked ΤΤ, which the *dēmos* of the Athenians
gave to ---leides of Gargettos; weight: 86 dr. 1 ob.

στέφανος ἐφ' ᾧ τὰ δύο [ΤΤ ὁ δῆμος ὁ Ἀθηναίων
--]λείδην Γαργήττιον σταθμὸν ℲΔΔΔΓΗ

IG II², 1486 [Lewis (1988) 307] lines 1–2 (after
307/6)
1485 lines 2–3 (304/3)

388.     Gold wreaths, which were handed over to us by the
treasurers in the archonship of Euxenippos [305/4],
who recorded neither the archon in the year they were
dedicated nor the names of the dedicants. The wreath
marked A, weight: 300 dr. The wreath marked B;
weight: 300 dr. The wreath marked Γ; weight: 300 dr.
The wreath marked Δ; weight: 252 dr. The wreath
marked E; weight: 89 dr. 4 ob. The wreath marked Z;
weight: 100 dr. The wreath marked Η; weight: 100 dr.
The wreath marked Θ; weight: --- The wreath marked
Ι; weight: --- The wreath marked Κ, weight: --- dr. 4+
ob. The wreath marked Λ; weight: 100 dr. The wreath
marked Μ; weight: 90+ dr. The wreath marked Ν;
weight: --- The wreath marked Ξ; weight: --- The
wreath marked Ο; weight: 1+ dr. The wreath marked

Π, weight: 5+ dr. The wreath marked Ρ; weight: ---
The wreath marked Σ, weight: 4+ ob. The wreath
marked Τ; weight: 49 dr. 3 ob. The wreath marked Υ;
weight: 100 dr. The wreath marked Φ; weight: 49 dr.
3 ob. The wreath marked Χ; weight: 40+ dr. The
wreath marked Ψ, weight: --- The wreath marked Ω;
weight: ---

στέφανοι χρυσοῖ οὓς παρέδοσαν ἡμῖν ταμίαι οἱ ἐπ'
Εὐξενίππου ἄρχοντος οὐχ ἐπιγράψαντες οὔτε τὸν
ἄρχοντα ἐφ' οὗ ἀνετέθησαν οὔτε τὸν ἀναθέντα·
στέφανος ἐφ' ᾧ τὸ Α στα(θμὸν) ΗΗΗ· στέφανος
ἐφ' ᾧ τὸ Β στα(θμὸν) ΗΗΗ· στέφανος ἐφ' ᾧ τὸ Γ
στα(θμὸν) ΗΗΗ· στέφανος ἐφ' ᾧ τὸ Δ, στα(θμὸν)
ΗΗ⊦ΗΗ· στέφανος ἐφ' ᾧ τὸ Ε στα(θμὸν)
⊦ΔΔΔΓΗΗΙΙΙΙ· στέφανος ἐφ' ᾧ τὸ Ζ στα(θμὸν) Η·
στέφανος ἐφ' ᾧ τὸ Η στα(θμὸν) Η· στέφανος ἐφ' ᾧ
τὸ Θ στα(θμὸν) ---· στέφανος ἐφ' ᾧ τὸ Ι
στα(θμὸν) ---· στέφανος ἐφ' ᾧ τὸ Κ στα(θμὸν) ---
ΙΙΙΙ· στέφανος ἐφ' ᾧ τὸ Λ στα(θμὸν) Η· στέφανος
ἐφ' ᾧ τὸ Μ στα(θμὸν) ⊦ΔΔΔΔ---· στέφανος ἐφ' ᾧ
τὸ Λ στα(θμὸν) Η· στέφανος ἐφ' ᾧ τὸ Ν στα(θμὸν)
---· στέφανος ἐφ' ᾧ τὸ Ξ στα(θμὸν) ---· στέφανος
ἐφ' ᾧ τὸ Ο στα(θμὸν) ---⊦· στέφανος ἐφ' ᾧ τὸ Π
στα(θμὸν) ---Γ· στέφανος ἐφ' ᾧ τὸ Ρ στα(θμὸν)
---· στέφανος ἐφ' ᾧ τὸ Σ στα(θμὸν) ---ΙΙΙΙ·
στέφανος ἐφ' ᾧ τὸ Τ σταθμὸν ΔΔΔΔΓΗΗΗΙΙΙ·
στέφανος ἐφ' ᾧ τὸ Υ στα(θμὸν) Η· στέφανος ἐφ' ᾧ
τὸ Φ στα(θμὸν) ΔΔΔΔΓΗΗΗΙΙΙ· στέφανος ἐφ' ᾧ τὸ
Χ στα(θμὸν) ΔΔΔ---· στέφανος ἐφ' ᾧ τὸ Ψ
στα(θμὸν) ---· στέφανος ἐφ' ᾧ τὸ Ω στα(θμὸν) ---

> *IG* II², 1476 lines 12–27 (308/7 or 306/5)
> 1477 [*Hesperia* 40 (1971) 449–50] lines 19–50
> (304/3)

389. A wreath in the year of Euboulides [394/3]
ἐπ' Εὐβουλίδου στέφανος
*IG* II², 1407 line 28 (385/4)

390. A wreath in the year of Demostratos [390/89]
ἐπ' Δημοστράτου στέφανος
*IG* II², 1407 line 28 (385/4)

391. A wreath, a prize-dedication in the year of Phrasikleides
[371/0]; weight: 232 dr. 2 ob.

ἀριστεῖον ἐπὶ Φρασικλείδου στέφανος σταθμὸν
ΗΗΔΔΔΗΙΙ

*IG* II², 1436 lines 9–10 (350/49)
1438 line 2 (349/8)

392.    A gold wreath in the archonship of Lysistratos [369/8];
weight: 36 dr.

ἐπὶ Λυσιστράτου ἄρχοντος στέφανος χρυσοῦς
σταθμὸν ΔΔΔΓΗ

*IG* II², 1438 lines 3–4 (349/8)

393.    A wreath in the archonship of Polyzelos [367/6]; weight:
38 dr.

ἐπὶ Πολυζήλου ἄρχοντος στέφανος σταθμὸν ΔΔΔΓΗΗ

*IG* II², 1436 line 17 (350/49)
1438 line 5 (349/8)

394.    A gold wreath in the archonship of Kephisodoros [366/5];
weight: 38 dr. 5½ ob.

ἐπὶ Κηφισοδώρου ἄρχοντος στέφανος χρυσοῦς
σταθμὸν ΔΔΔΓΗΗΙΙΙΙΙΣC

*IG* II², 1436 line 18 (350/49)
1438 lines 5–6 (349/8)

395.    A gold wreath in the archonship of Chion [365/4];
weight: 38 dr. 5 ob.

ἐπὶ Χίωνος ἄρχοντος στέφανος χρυσοῦς σταθμὸν
ΔΔΔΓΗΗΙΙΙΙΙ

*IG* II², 1436 line 19 (350/49)
1438 lines 6–7 (349/8)

396.    A wreath in the archonship of Timokrates [364/3];
weight: 39 dr. 3 ob.

ἐπὶ Τιμοκράτους ἄρχοντος στέφανος σταθμὸν
ΔΔΔΓΗΗΗΙΙΙ

*IG* II², 1436 line 20 (350/49)
1438 line 7 (349/8)

397.    Gold wreath, a prize-dedication in the archonship of
Charikleides [363/2]; weight: 250 dr.

ἐπὶ Χαρικλείδου ἄρχοντος στέφανος χρυσοῦς
ἀριστεῖον σταθμὸν ΗΗϜ

*IG* II², 1436 lines 21–2 (350/49)
1438 lines 7–8 (349/8)

398.  A gold wreath in the same archonship; weight: 39 dr. 3 ob.

ἐπὶ τοῦ αὐτοῦ ἄρχοντος στέφανος χρυσοῦς σταθμὸν
ΔΔΔΓΗΗΗΙΙΙ

> *IG* II², 1436 line 23 (350/49)
> 1438 lines 8–9 (349/8)

399.  A wreath in the archonship of Molon [362/1]; weight: 39 dr. 3 ob.

ἐπὶ Μόλωνος ἄρχοντος στέφανος σταθμὸν
ΔΔΔΓΗΗΗΙΙΙ

> *IG* II², 1436 line 24 (350/49)
> 1438 line 9 (349/8)

400.  A gold wreath, a prize-dedication in the archonship of Nikophemos [361/0]; weight: 250 dr.

ἐπὶ Νικοφήμου ἄρχοντος στέφανος χρυσοῦς ἀριστεῖον
σταθμὸν ΗΗℙ

> *IG* II², 1436 lines 25–6 (350/49)
> 1438 lines 9–10 (349/8)

401.  A gold wreath in the same archonship; weight of this: 40 dr.

ἐπὶ τοῦ αὐτοῦ ἄρχοντος στέφανος χρυσοῦς· σταθμὸν
τούτου ΔΔΔΔ

> *IG* II², 1438 lines 10–11 [*Hesperia* 7 (1938) 284] lines
> 11–12 (349/8)

402.  A wreath in the archonship of Kallimedes [360/59]; weight: 40 dr. ¾ ob.

ἐπὶ Καλλιμήδους ἄρχοντος στέφανος σταθμὸν
ΔΔΔΔСΤ

> *IG* II², 1436 line 27 (350/49)
> 1438 line 11 (349/8)

403.  A gold wreath in the archonship of Eucharistos [359/8], weight: 40 dr. 1 ob.

ἐπὶ Εὐχαρίστου ἄρχοντος στέφανος χρυσοῦς σταθμὸν
ΔΔΔΔΙ

> *IG* II², 1436 line 28 (350/49)
> 1438 lines 11–12 [*Hesperia* 7 (1938) 284] lines
> 12–13 (349/8)

404.  A wreath in the archonship of Kephisodotos [358/7]; weight: 40 dr. 3 ob.

ἐπὶ Κηφισοδότου ἄρχοντος στέφανος σταθμὸν
ΔΔΔΔΙΙΙ

> *IG* II², 1436 line 29 (350/49)
> 1438 line 12 (349/8)

405.　　A wreath in the archonship of Agathokles [357/6];
weight: 41 dr. 3 ob.

ἐπὶ Ἀγαθοκλέους ἄρχοντος στέφανος σταθμὸν
ΔΔΔΔΗΙΙΙ

> *IG* II², 1436 line 30 (350/49)
> 1438 lines 12–13 (349/8)

406.　　In the archonship of Agathokles [357/6], a wreath;
weight: 243 dr.

ἐπὶ Ἀγαθοκλέους ἄρχοντος στέφανος σταθμὸν
ΗΗΔΔΔΗΗΗ

> *IG* II², 1436 lines 31–2 (350/49)
> 1437 lines 4–5 (after 350/49)
> **1438 lines 13–14 (349/8)**

407.　　A wreath in the archonship of Elpines [356/5], weight: 41
dr. 3 ob.

ἐπὶ Ἐλπίνου ἄρχοντος στέφανος σταθμὸν ΔΔΔΔΗΙΙΙ

> *IG* II², 1436 line 33 (350/49)
> 1437 line 7 (after 350/49)
> 1438 line 14 (349/8)

408.　　A wreath in the archonship of Kallistratos [355/4]; weight:
41 dr. 1 ob.

ἐπὶ Καλλιστράτου ἄρχοντος στέφανος σταθμὸν
ΔΔΔΔΗ

> *IG* II², 1436 line 34 (350/49)
> **1437 lines 8–9 (after 350/49)**
> 1438 lines 14–15 (349/8)

409.　　A gold wreath in the archonship of Thoudemos [353/2]
　　　　　---

στέφανος χρυσοῦς ἐπὶ Θουδήμου ἄρχοντος ---

> *IG* II², 1438 line 27 [*Hesperia* 7 (1938) 284] lines
> 27–8 (349/8)

410.　　A gold wreath of Athena Nike in the archonship of
Thoudemos [353/2]; weight: 34 dr. 4 ob.

ἐπὶ Θουδήμου ἄρχοντος στέφανος χρυσοῦς Ἀθηνᾶς
Νίκης σταθμὸν τούτου ΔΔΔΗΗΗΙΙΙΙ

*IG* II², 1438 line 21 [*Hesperia* 7 (1938) 284] lines
26-7 (349/8)

411. A wreath in the archonship of Theophilos [348/7]; ---
[στέφανος] ἐπὶ Θεοφίλου ἄρχοντος ---
*IG* II², 1441 line 5 (347/6)

412. A wreath in the archonship of Themistokles [347/6]; ---
[στέφανος] ἐπὶ Θεμιστοκλέους ἄρχοντος ---
*IG* II², 1441 line 4 (347/6)

413. Gold wreaths, which were awarded for the tragedies at the
Dionysia in the archonship of Philokles [322/1]. A
wreath, which the *dēmos* of the Athenians [gave at the]
Panathenaia; weight: ---. A wreath, which the *dēmos* of
the Athenians [gave ---]; weight: ---. A wreath, which
the *dēmos* of the Athenians gave; weight: 95 dr.

στέφανοι χρυσοῖ οἱ ἀναρρηθέντες Διονυσίων
τραγῳδοῖς ἐπὶ Φιλοκλέους ἄρχοντος· στέφανος ὃν
ὁ δῆμος ὁ Ἀθηναίων --- Παναθήναια σταθμὸν ---
στέφανος --- ὁ δῆμος ὁ Ἀθηναίων --- σταθμὸν ---
στέφανος --- ὁ δῆμος ὁ Ἀθηναίων --- σταθμὸν
ⵊΔΔΔΔΓ

*IG* II², 1468 lines 12–19 (321/0)

414. The gold wreath which was announced at the tragedies of
the Greater Dionysia, with which the *dēmos* of the
Athenians crowned the hipparchs in the archonship of
Archippos [321/0]; weight: ---

στέφανος χρυσοῦς ὁ ἀνακηρυχθεὶς Διονυσίων τῶν
μεγάλων τραγῳδοῖς, ᾧ ἐστεφάνωσεν ὁ δῆμος ὁ
Ἀθηναίων τοὺς ἱππάρχους τοὺς ἐπὶ Ἀρχίππου
ἄρχοντος σταθμὸν ---

*IG* II², 1479 lines 8–11 (after 315/4)

415. These things the treasurers in the archonship of
Anaxicrates [307/6] handed over to the treasurers in the
archonship of Koroibos [306/5]: the gold wreaths,
which were announced at the tragedies of the Greater
Dionysia, in the archonship of Anaxicrates [307/6].
The wreath marked AA, with which the Boiotian
League crowned ---

Τάδε παρέδοσαν ταμίαι οἱ ἐπ᾽ Ἀναξικράτους
ἄρχοντος ταμίαις τοῖς ἐπὶ Κοροίβου ἄρχοντος·
στεφάνους χρυσοῦς τοὺς ἀνακηρυχθέντας

Διονυσίων τραγῳδοῖς ἐπ' Ἀναξικράτους ἄρχοντος·
στέφανος ἐφ' ᾧ τὰ δύο ΑΑ ᾧ ἐστεφάνωσεν τὸ
κοινὸν τὸ Βοιωτῶν ---

IG II², 1491 lines 8–15 (305/4?)

416. A gold olive-wreath, which the city gave as the prize for
singing to the kithara, weight of this: 85 dr.

στέφανος χρυσοῦς θαλλοῦ ὃν ἡ πόλις ἀνέθηκε τὰ
νικητήρια τοῦ κιθαρῳδοῦ σταθμὸν ⱵΔΔΔΓ

IG II², 1402 lines 2–3 [EAC 3 (1965) 60–61] lines 30–1
(402/1)
1385 lines 17–19 (400/399)
1388 lines 36–7 (398/7)
1393 lines 19–20 (397/6)
1389 line 1 (391/0)
**1400 line 17 (390/89)**
1407 lines 33–4 (385/4)

417. A gold wreath, a prize-dedication from the Panathenaia;
weight of this: 273 dr. 3½ ob.

στέφανος χρυσοῦς ἀριστεῖον ἐκ Παναθηναίων σταθμὸν
τούτου ΗΗⱵΔΔⱵⱵΙΙΙC

IG II², 1402 lines 1–2 [EAC 3 [1965] 60–1] lines
29–30 (402/1)

418. A gold wreath, a prize-dedication from the Panathenaia in
the archonship of Dysniketos [370/69]; weight: 200 dr.

ἐπὶ Δυσνικήτου ἄρχοντος στέφανος χρυσοῦς
ἀριστεῖον ἐκ Παναθηναίων σταθμὸν ΗΗ

IG II², 1425 lines 121–2 (368/7)
1436 lines 13–14 (350/49)
**1438 lines 2–3 (349/8)**

419. A gold wreath, a prize-dedication from the Panathenaia in
the archonship of Nausinikos [378/7]; weight: 193 dr.
4 ob.

στέφανος χρυσοῦς ἀριστεῖον ἐκ Παναθηναίων τῶν ἐπὶ
Ναυσινίκου ἄρχοντος σταθμὸν ΗⱵΔΔΔΔⱵⱵΙΙΙΙ

IG II², 1424a lines 34–6 (371/0) [197 dr. 5 obols]
1425 lines 29–31 (368/7) [198 dr. 4 obols]
1436 lines 11–12 (350/49)
**1438 [Hesperia 7 (1938) 281] lines 1–3 (349/8)**

420. The gold wreath which was announced at the Greater
Panathenaia for the athletic contest [318/7], with
which the *dēmos* of the Athenians crowned Konon, of

Anaphlystos, son of Timotheos; weight: 100 dr.

στέφανος χρυσοῦς ὁ ἀνακηρυχθεὶς Παναθηναίων τῶν
μεγάλων τῷ γυμνικῷ ἀγῶνι ᾧ ἐστεφάνωσεν ὁ
δῆμος ὁ Ἀθηναίων Κόνωνα Τιμοθέου Ἀναφλύστιον
σταθμὸν Η

IG II², 1479 lines 18–21 (after 315/4)

421.    1 gold tiara on a wooden mount, which Aspasia dedicated

στλεγγὶς Ι χρυσῆ ἐπὶ ξύλου ἣν Ἀσπασία ἀνέθηκε

IG II², 1409 [*JHS* 58 (1938) 77] line 14 (395/4)
        1400 line 50 (390/89)
        1419 line 15 (after 385/4)

422.    A wreath, dedicated by ---, the archon was not inscribed;
        weight: 89 dr. 2 ob.

στέφανος ὃν ---οι ἀνέθεσαν ἄρχων οὐχ ἐπεγέγραπτο
σταθμὸν ⊢ΔΔΔΓ⊦⊦⊦ΙΙ

IG II², 1436 lines 39–40 (350/49)
        **1437 lines 32–3 (after 350/49)**
        1438 lines 17–18 (349/8)

423.    A gold wreath in the archonship of Thoudemos [353/2],
        a prize-dedication dedicated by ---, weight of this: 79
        dr. 4½ ob.

ἐπὶ Θουδήμου ἄρχοντος στέφανος χρυσοῦς ἀριστεῖον
ὃν --- ἀνέθηκεν σταθμὸν τούτου ⊢ΔΔΓ⊦⊦⊦ΙΙΙC

IG II², 1437 lines 28–9 (after 350/49)
        **1438 line 21** [*Hesperia* 7 (1938) 284] **line 22**
        **(349/8)**

424.    A gold olive-wreath, which Aristomache daughter of
        Aristokles dedicated, weight of this: 36 dr. 3 ob.

στέφανος θαλλοῦ χρυσοῦς ὃν Ἀριστομάχη
Ἀριστοκλέους ἀνέθηκε σταθμὸν τούτου ΔΔΔΓ⊦ΙΙΙ

IG II², 1402, add. p. 799 lines 3–5 [*EAC* 3 (1965) 60–1]
        lines 31–2 (402/1)
        1385 [*JHS* 58 (1938) 87] lines 20–1 (400/399)
        **1388 lines 37–9 (398/7)**
        1393 lines 20–1 (397/6)
        1389 lines 1–2 (391/0)
        1400 lines 17–18 (390/89)

425.    A wreath, dedicated by Aristophon; weight of this: 83 dr.;
        the archon was not inscribed

στέφανος ὃν Ἀριστοφῶν ἀνέθηκεν σταθμὸν τούτου

ϜΔΔΔΗΗ ἄρχων δὲ οὐκ ἐπεγέγραπτο

*IG* II², 1436 lines 37–8 (350/49)
1437 lines 30–1 (after 350/49)
**1438 lines 16–17** [*Hesperia* 7 (1938) 284, lines
17–18] **(349/8)**

426.   A gold olive-wreath, which Gelon of Pellana, son of
Tlesonides, dedicated; weight of this: 17 dr. 3 ob.

στέφανος θαλλοῦ χρυσοῦς ὃν Γέλων Τλησωνίδου
Πελληνεὺς ἀνέθηκε σταθμὸν τούτου ΔΓΗΗΙΙΙ

*IG* II², 1386 lines 6–7 (401/0)
**1388 lines 33–4 (398/7)**
1393 lines 17–18 (397/6)
1400 lines 15–16 (390/89)
1407 lines 32–3 (385/4)

427.   A gold olive-wreath, which Hierokles of Phaselis
dedicated; weight of this: 59 dr.

στέφανος θαλλοῦ χρυσοῦς ὃν Ἱεροκλῆς Φασηλίτης
ἀνέθηκε σταθμὸν τούτου ϜΓΗΗΗ

*IG* II², 1386 lines 7–9 (401/0)
**1388 lines 34–6 (398/7)**
1393+EM 12963+EM 12961 [*Hesperia* 41 (1972)
423 no. 55, 426 no. 58] lines 18–19 (397/6)
1400 line 16 (390/89)
1407 line 33 (385/4)

428.   A gold wreath, which Lysander of Sparta, son of
Aristokritos dedicated to Athena; weight: 66 dr. 5 ob.

στέφανος χρυσοῦς ὃν Λύσανδρος Ἀριστοκρίτου
Λακεδαιμόνιος Ἀθηναίαι ἀνέθηκε σταθμὸν τούτου
ϜΔΓΗΙΙΙΙ

*IG* II², 1386 lines 2–4 (401/0)
**1388 lines 31–3 (398/7)**
1393 lines 16–17 (397/6)
1400 lines 14–15 (390/89)
1407 lines 31–2 (385/4)

429.   A wreath, with which the *dēmos* [of the Athenians]
crowned the *boulē*, in the archonship of Archias [346/5]
dedicated; weight: 10+ dr.

ἐπ᾽ Ἀρχίου στέφανος ᾧ ὁ δῆμος ὁ [τῶν Ἀθηναιῶνᵐ]
ἐστεφάνωσεν τὴν βουλὴν σταθμὸν Δ

*IG* II², 1443 lines 102–3 (344/3)

430.   A wreath, which --- gave to the *dēmos* of the Athenians

in the archonship of Themistokles [347/6]; weight: ---

ἐπὶ Θεμιστοκλείους ἄρχοντος στέφανος ᾧ ---
ἐστεφάνωσαν τὸν δῆμον τὸν Ἀθηναίων σταθμὸν
---

*IG* II², 1443 lines 104–6 (344/3)

431. A wreath, which --- gave the *dēmos* of the Athenians in the archonship of Archias [346/5]; weight: ---

ἐπὶ Ἀρχίου ἄρχοντος στέφανος ᾧ ὁ δῆμος ὁ ---
ἐστεφάνωσεν τὸν δῆμον τὸν Ἀθηναίων σταθμὸν
---

*IG* II², 1443 lines 100–2 (344/3)

432. The gold wreath from the Abderans; weight: 39+ dr. 2 ob.

στέφανος χρυσοῦς ὁ παρ' Ἀβδηριτῶν σταθμὸν ---
ΔΔΔΓΗΗΗΙΙ

*IG* II², 1425 lines 119–20 (368/7)

433. The gold wreath from the Andrians to the *boulē* in the archonship of Nausigenes [368/7]; weight: 129 dr. 2 ob.

στέφανος χρυσοῦς ὁ παρὰ Ἀνδρίων τῇ βουλῇ τῇ ἐπὶ
Ναυσιγένους ἄρχοντος σταθμὸν ΗΔΔΓΗΗΗΙΙ

*IG* II², 1425 lines 221–3 (368/7)
1428 line 56 (367/6)

434. A wreath, which the Arethousians dedicated; weight: 36 dr. 2 ob.

στέφανος ὃν Ἀρεθούσιοι ἀνέθεσαν σταθμὸν ΔΔΔΓΗΙΙ

*IG* II², 1437 lines 18–19 (after 350/49)
1438 line 22 [*Hesperia* 7 (1938) 284] line 23
(349/8)

435. A gold wreath, from the sixth prytany-period in the archonship of Diotimos [354/3], which the Kálchedonians dedicated; weight: 56 dr. 2 ob.

ἕκτη τῆς πρυτανείας ἐπὶ Διοτίμου ἄρχοντος στέφανος
χρυσοῦς ὃν Καλχηδόνιοι ἀνέθεσαν σταθμὸν τούτου
ϜΓΗΙΙ

*IG* II², 1437 lines 16–17 (after 350/49)
1438 line 20 [*Hesperia* 7 (1938) 284] line 21
(349/8)

436. A wreath, with which the *dēmos* of the Chersonesians

crowned the *boulē* in the archonship of Euboulos [345/4]; weight: --- dr. 5 ob.

στέφανος ᾧ ὁ δῆμος ὁ Χερρονησιτῶν ἐστεφάνωσεν
τὴν βουλὴν τὴν ἐπ' Εὐβούλου ἄρχοντος σταθμὸν
---ΙΙΙΙΙ

IG II², 1443 lines 119–21 (344/3)

437.    A wreath, with which the *dēmos* of the Chersonesians from Agora crowned the *dēmos* of the Athenians; weight: ---

στέφανος ᾧ ὁ δῆμος ὁ Χερρονησιτῶν ἀπ' Ἀγορᾶς
ἐστεφάνωσεν τὸν δῆμον τὸν Ἀθηναίων σταθμὸν ---

IG II², 1443 lines 117–19 (344/3)

438.    A wreath, with which the Chersonesians and Alopekonnesians and --- and the Madytians and --- benefactors crowned the *dēmos* of the Athenians in the archonship of Archias [346/5]; weight: --- 20+ dr.

ἐπὶ Ἀρχίου ἄρχοντος στέφανος ᾧ ἐστεφάνωσεν τὸν
δῆμον τὸν Ἀθηναίων ὁ δῆμος ὁ ἐν Χερρονήσῳ καὶ
Ἀλωπεκοννήσιοι καὶ --- καὶ Μαδύτιοι καὶ ---
εὐεργέται σταθμὸν . Ι ΔΔ---

IG II², 1443 lines 95–9 (344/3)

439.    A wreath, with which the *dēmos* of the Elaiousians crowned the *dēmos* of the Athenians in the archonship of Archias [346/5]; weight: 70 dr.

ἐπὶ Ἀρχίου ἄρχοντος στέφανος ᾧ ὁ δῆμος ὁ
Ἐλαιουσίων ἐστεφάνωσεν τὸν δῆμον τὸν Ἀθηναίων
σταθμὸν ⅎΔΔ

IG II², 1443 lines 93–5 (344/3)

440.    A gold wreath, which the Erythrians dedicated; weight: 20+ dr.

στέφανος χρυσοῦς ὃν Ἐρυθραῖοι ἀνέθεσαν σταθμὸν
τούτου---ΔΔ

IG II², 1437 lines 12–13 (after 350/49)
1438 line 18 [*Hesperia* 7 (1938) 284] line 19
(349/8)

441.    A gold wreath, which K[---], having been crowned with it by the Samothracians, dedicated to the [goddess; weight: ---]

στέφανος ᾧ στεφανωθεὶς Κ[--- ὑπὸ τῶν Σα]μοθρᾴκων

ἀνέθηκεν τῆ [θεῷ σταθμὸν ---]

*IG* II², 1443 lines 112–14 (344/3)

442. The wreath from the Karystians; weight: 70 dr.

στέφανος ὁ παρὰ Καρυστίων σταθμὸν ⊢ΔΔ

*IG* II², 1425 line 123 (368/7)

443. Another one from the Karystians; weight: 70 dr. 5 ob.

ἕτερος παρὰ Καρυστίων σταθμὸν ⊢ΔΔΙΙΙΙΙ

*IG* II², 1425 line 124 (368/7)

444. A wreath, with which the Knossians crowned the *dēmos* of the Athenians; weight: 50+ dr.

στέφανος ᾧ Κνώσιοι ἐστεφάνωσαν τὸν δῆμον τὸν Ἀθηναίων σταθμὸν ⊢---

*IG* II², 1443 lines 121–3 (344/3)

445. A wreath, a dedication of the Mytilenians; weight: 49 dr. 4½ ob.

στέφανος Μυτιληναίων ἀνάθημα σταθμὸν ΔΔΔΔΓⱵⱵⱵΙΙΙΙC

*IG* II², 1437 lines 14–15 (after 350/49)
1438 line 19 [*Hesperia* 7 (1938) 284] line 20 (349/8)

446. A wreath, with which the Naxians crowned the *dēmos* of the Athenians; weight: 110+ dr. 3+ ob.

στέφανος ᾧ ὁ δῆμος ὁ Ναξίων ἐστεφάνωσεν τὸν δῆμον τὸν Ἀθηναίων σταθμὸν ΗΔ---ΙΙΙ

*IG* II², 1441 lines 16–18 (347/6)

447. A wreath, with which the Naxians crowned the *dēmos* of the Athenians; weight: 77 dr. 1 ob.

στέφανος ᾧ Νάξιοι ἐστεφάνωσαν τὸν δῆμον τὸν Ἀθηναίων σταθμὸν ⊢ΔΔΓⱵⱵΙ

*IG* II², 1443 lines 114–15 (344/3)

448. A wreath, with which the Parians crowned the *boulē* of the Athenians; weight: ---

στέφανος ᾧ Πάριοι τὴν βουλὴν τὴν Ἀθηναίων ἐστεφάνωσαν σταθμὸν ---

*IG* II², 1441 lines 6–7 (347/6)

449. A gold wreath, which the *dēmos* in Samos dedicated; weight: 2+ dr.

στέφανος χρυσοῦς ὃν ὁ δῆμος ὁ ἐν Σάμῳ ἀνέθηκεν
σταθμὸν τούτου ---ΗΗ

IG II², 1437 lines 20–1 (after 350/49)

1438 lines 22–3 [*Hesperia* 7 (1938) 284] lines
23–4 (349/8)

450.    In the archonship of Archias [346/5] a wreath, with which
the *dēmos* in Samos crowned the *boulē* in the archonship of Themistokles [347/6]; weight: 49 dr. 2 + ob.

ἐπὶ Ἀρχίου ἄρχοντος στέφανος ᾧ ὁ δῆμος ὁ ἐν Σάμῳ
ἐστεφάνωσεν τὴν βουλὴν τὴν ἐπὶ Θεμιστοκλέους
ἄρχοντος σταθμὸν ΔΔΔΓΗΗΗΙΙ

IG II², 1443 lines 91–3 (344/3)

451.    In the archonship of Archias [346/5], a wreath, with
which the *dēmos* in Samos crowned the *dēmos* of the
Athenians ; weight: 77+ dr.

ἐπὶ Ἀρχίου ἄρχοντος στέφανος ᾧ ὁ δῆμος ὁ ἐν·Σάμῳ
τὸν δῆμον τὸν Ἀθηναίων ἐστεφάνωσεν σταθμὸν
ϜΔΔΓΗΗ

IG II², 1443 lines 89–90 (344/3)

452.    A wreath from the Samothracians, with which they
crowned the *boulē* in the archonship of Euboulos
[345/4]; weight: . . .

στέφανος παρὰ Σαμοθρᾴκων ᾧ ἐστεφάνωσαν τὴν
βουλὴν τὴν ἐπ' Εὐβούλου ἄρχοντος σταθμὸν ---

IG II², 1443 lines 110–12 (344/3)

453.    A wreath from the Samothracians, with which they
crowned the *dēmos* of the Athenians; weight: ---

στέφανος παρὰ Σαμοθρᾴκων ᾧ ἐστεφάνωσαν τὸν
δῆμον τὸν Ἀθηναίων σταθμὸν ---

IG II², 1443 lines 108–10 (344/3)

454.    Another wreath, the one from the Siphnians; weight: 66
dr. 5 ob.

ἕτερος ὁ παρὰ Σιφνίων στέφανος ϜΔΓΗΙΙΙΙΙ

IG II², 1425 line 125 (368/7)

455.    In the archonship of Diotimos [354/3] a gold wreath, a
dedication by the Thasians; weight: 86 dr. 5½ ob.

ἐπὶ Διοτίμου ἄρχοντος στέφανος χρυσοῦς Θασίων
ἀνάθημα σταθμὸν ϜΔΔΔΓΗΙΙΙΙC

IG II², 1436 lines 35–6 (350/49)

1437 lines 10–11 (after 350/49)
**1438 [*Hesperia* 7 (1938) 284] lines 15–16
(349/8)**
1441 lines 14–15 (347/6)

456. Another wreath, the one from the Troizenians to the
*boulē* in the archonship of Nausigenes [368/7]; weight:
82 dr. 2½ ob.

ἕτερος στέφανος ὁ παρὰ Τροζηνίων τῇ βουλῇ τῇ ἐπὶ
Ναυσιγένους ἄρχοντος σταθμὸν ⱶΔΔΔⱵⱵΙⲤ

*IG* II², 1425 lines 227–9 (368/7)

457. Another wreath from the Troizenians to the *dēmos*;
weight: 220 dr. 1½ ob.

ἕτερος στέφανος ὁ παρὰ Τροζηνίων τῷ δήμῳ
σταθμὸν ΗΗΔΔΙⲤ

*IG* II², 1425 lines 230–1 (368/7)

458. A wreath, which the *boulē* in the archonship of Diotimos
[354/3] dedicated; weight: 12+ dr. 1½ + ob.

στέφανος ὃν ἡ βουλὴ ἡ ἐπὶ Διοτίμου ἄρχοντος
ἀνέθηκεν σταθμὸν ---ΔⱵⱵ---ΙⲤ

*IG* II², 1437 lines 24–5 (after 350/49)
1438 [*Hesperia* 7 (1938) 284] line 25 (349/8)

459. Another gold wreath, which the *boulē* in the archonship
of Diotimos [354/3] dedicated; weight of this: 24+ dr.

ἕτερος στέφανος χρυσοῦς ὃν ἡ βουλὴ ἡ ἐπὶ Διοτίμου
ἄρχοντος ἀνέθηκεν σταθμὸν τούτου ---ΔΔⱵⱵⱵ

*IG* II², 1437 lines 26–7 (after 350/49)
**1438 [*Hesperia* 7 (1938) 284] lines 25–6
(349/8)**

460. Another wreath, the one from the *dēmon sullogeis* in the
archonship of Dysniketos [370/69]; weight: 37 dr. 2
1/4 ob.

ἕτερος στέφανος παρὰ δήμου συλλογέων τῶν ἐπὶ
Δυσνικήτου σταθμὸν ΔΔΔΓⱵⱵΙΙϽ

*IG* II², 1425 lines 126–7 (368/7)

461. Annual offerings in the year of Lysistratos [369/8]: the
wreath from the *dēmon sullogeis* in the archonship of
Lysistratos; weight: 26 dr. 1 ob.

ἐπέτειοι ἐπὶ Λυσιστράτου· στέφανος ὁ παρὰ δήμου
συλλογέων τῶν ἐπὶ Λυσιστράτου ἄρχοντος

σταθμὸν ΔΔΓΗ

IG II², 1425 lines 128–30 (368/7)
1436 line 15 (350/49) [36 dr.]

462.  Another wreath, the one from the *dēmon sullogeis* in the
      archonship of Nausigenes [368/7]; weight: 38 dr. 3½
      ob.

      ἕτερος στέφανος ὁ παρὰ δήμου συλλογέων τῶν ἐπὶ
      Ναυσιγένους ἄρχοντος σταθμὸν ΔΔΓΗΗΙΙC

      IG II², 1425 lines 224–6 (368/7)
      1436 line 16 (350/49) [39 dr. 3½ ob.]
      1438 lines 4–5 (349/8) [39 dr. 3½ ob.]
      1441 lines 12–13 (347/6)

463.  Another wreath from the year of Lysistratos [369/8],
      which the *dēmos* dedicated; weight: 70 dr.

      ἕτερος στέφανος ἐπὶ Λυσιστράτου ὃν ὁ δῆμος
      ἀνέθηκεν σταθμὸν ⊢ΔΔ

      IG II², 1425 lines 131–2 (368/7)

464.  A wreath, a prize-dedication, which the *dēmos* dedicated;
      weight: 140+ dr.

      στέφανος ἀριστεῖον ὃν ὁ δῆμος ἀνέθηκεν σταθμὸν
      ΗΔΔΔΔ---

      IG II², 1441 lines 10–11 (347/6)

465.  A gold wreath, with which the *dēmos* crowned the --- in
      the archonship of Apollodoros [319/8] ---; weight: 100
      dr.

      στέφανος χρυσοῦς ᾧ ἐστεφάνωσεν ὁ δῆμος --- τοὺς
      ἐπὶ Ἀπολλοδώρου ἄρχοντος --- σταθμὸν Η

      IG II², 1479 lines 4–6 (after 315/4)

466.  A wreath, on which are two Ys; the *dēmos* of the
      Athenians gave the Hipparchs in the archonship of
      Anaxicrates [307/6]; weight: --- dr. 2+ ob.

      στέφανος ἐφ᾽ ᾧ τὰ δύο ΥΥ· ὁ δῆμος ὁ Ἀθηναίων τοὺς
      ἱππάρχους τοὺς ἐπ᾽ Ἀναξικράτους ἄρχοντος
      σταθμὸν ---ΙΙ

      IG II², 1486 lines 3–5 (after 307/6)
      1485 lines 4–7 (304/3)

467.  Annual wreaths in the year of Euboulos [345/4]: a wreath,
      with which the generals in Skiathos crowned the *dēmos*
      of the Athenians; weight: 10+ dr.

ἐπ᾽ Εὐβούλου στέφανοι ἐπέτειοι· στέφανος ᾧ
ἐστεφάνωσαν οἱ στρατιῶται οἱ ἐν Σκιάθῳ τὸν
δῆμον τὸν Ἀθηναίων σταθμὸν Δ---

*IG* II², 1443 lines 106–8 (344/3)

468.    A wreath, a prize-dedication to Artemis Brauronia, which
the *hieropoioi* dedicated ---

στέφανος ἀριστεῖον Ἀρτέμιδος Βραυρωνίας ὃν
ἀνέθεσαν οἱ ἱεροποιοὶ οἱ ---

*IG* II², 1480 lines 15–16 (after 313/2)

469.    A wreath, a prize-dedication to Artemis Brauronia, which
the *hieropoioi* dedicated in the archonship of ---; the
weight is inscribed: 100+ dr.

στέφανος ἀριστεῖον Ἀρτέμιδος Βραυρωνίας ὃν
ἀνέθεσαν οἱ ἱεροποιοὶ ἐπὶ --- ἄρχοντος σταθμὸν
ἐπιγέγραπται ΗΙ---

*IG* II², 1480 lines 12–14 (after 313/2)

470.    A wreath, a prize-dedication to Athena Nike; weight: 45
dr.

στέφανος Ἀθηνᾶς Νίκης ἀριστεῖον σταθμὸν ΔΔΔΓ

*IG* II², 1437 line 34 (after 350/49)

471.    A wreath, a prize-dedication to Athena Nike; weight: 76+
dr.

στέφανος ἀριστεῖον Ἀθηνᾶς Νίκης σταθμὸν ϜΔΔΓⱵ---

*IG* II², 1441 lines 8–9 (347/6)

472.    A wreath, a prize-dedication to Athena Nike, which the
*dēmos* dedicated; weight: ---

στέφανος Ἀθηνᾶς Νίκης ἀριστεῖον ὃν ὁ δῆμος ἀνέθηκεν
σταθμὸν ---

*IG* II², 1443 lines 116–7 (344/3)

473.    A gold wreath, a prize-dedication to Athena Nike, which
[---]eus handed over to the treasurers; weight: 95+ dr.

στέφανος χρυσοῦς ἀριστεῖον Ἀθηνᾶς Νίκης ὃν
παρέδωκεν ταμίαις [---]ευς σταθμὸν ϜΔΔΔΔΓ---

*IG* II², 1479 lines 21–3 (315/4)

474.    A gold wreath, a prize-dedication to the goddess; weight
of this: 272 dr. 3½ ob.

στέφανος χρυσοῦς ἀριστεῖα τῆς θεοῦ σταθμὸν τούτου
ΗΗϜΔΔⱵΙΙⵦ

*IG* II², 1402 lines 1–2? (402/1)
1385 [*JHS* 58 (1938) 87] lines 17–18 (400/399)
**1388 lines 29–30 (398/7)**
1393 lines 14–15 (397/6)
1400 lines 32–3 (390/89)
1407 line 27 (385/4)

475.     A gold wreath, a prize-dedication to the goddess; weight:
245 dr. 1½ ob.

στέφανος χρυσοῦς ἀριστεῖα τῆς θεοῦ σταθμὸν
ΗΗΔΔΔΔΓΙϹ

*IG* II², **1388 lines 66–7 (398/7)**
1400 line 58 (390/89)
1407 lines 28–9 (385/4)

476.     In the year of Mystichides [386/5], a wreath, a prize-
dedication to the goddess; weight: 232 dr. 5 ob.

ἐπὶ Μυστιχίδου στέφανος ἀριστεῖα τῇ θεῷ σταθμὸν
ΗΗΔΔΔΙΗΙΙΙΙΙ

*IG* II², **1407 lines 28–9 (385/4)**

477.     A gold wreath, a prize-dedication to the goddess, from the
Panathenaia in the archonship of Sokratides [374/3];
weight: 182 dr. 2 ob.

στέφανος χρυσοῦς ἀριστεῖον τῆς θεοῦ ἐκ Παναθηναίων
τῶν ἐπὶ Σωκρατίδου ἄρχοντος σταθμὸν
ΗϜΔΔΔΙΗΙΙ

*IG* II², **1424a lines 64–6 (371/0)**
1425 lines 64–6 (368/7)

# PART VI

# *The Treasures of the Erechtheion*

The nomenclature of the Ionic temple north of the Parthenon still remains one of the thorniest issues in Greek archaeology. We call the temple 'the Erechtheion', while recognizing that only two ancient authors ever used that term: Pausanias and pseudo-Plutarch.[1] There is some considerable doubt whether the cult of Erechtheus was in fact housed inside this Ionic temple.[2]

The name for the temple used by classical Athenians seems to have been 'the temple of Athena Polias', or 'the temple in which is the ancient image', or simply 'the ancient temple'.[3] Strabo is clearest on this:

Τὸ δ' ἄστυ αὐτὸ πέτρα ἐστὶν ἐν πεδίῳ περιοικουμένη κύκλῳ· ἐπὶ δὲ τῇ πέτρᾳ τὸ τῆς Ἀθηνᾶς ἱερόν, ὅ τε ἀρχαῖος νεὼς ὁ τῆς Πολιάδος, ἐν ᾧ ὁ ἄσβεστος λύχνος, καὶ ὁ Παρθενών, ὃν ἐποίησεν Ἰκτῖνος, ἐν ᾧ τὸ τοῦ Φειδίου ἔργον ἐλεφάντινον, ἡ Ἀθηνᾶ.

The city itself is a rock situated in a plain and surrounded by dwellings. On the rock is the sacred precinct of Athena, comprising both the old temple of Athena Polias, in which is the lamp that is never quenched, and the Parthenon built by Ictinus, in which is the work in ivory by Pheidias, the Athena. (Trans. H. L. Jones.)[4]

Strabo is the last ancient author to refer to the temple as the Archaios Neos.

Even before the temple was built, an Athenian decree between 470 and 450 refers to the site as the Archaios Neos: ἐμ πόλει ὄπισθεν τοῦ νεὼ τοῦ ἀρχ[αίου] (to set up a stele 'on the Akropolis behind the Archaios Neos') appears in the regulations concerning the *praxiergidai* who washed and cleaned the ancient image.[5] The decree then mentions that the archon 'is to seal the temple for the month of Thargelion and hand the keys over to the *Praxiergidai*.'[6] What

---

[1] Paus. 1. 26. 4–5; [Plut.] *Vit. X orat.* 843 B–E.     [2] See Jeppesen (1979); (1983); (1987).
[3] Cf. Jahn and Michaelis (1901) 65–6 for ancient references; cf. App. V below.
[4] Strabo 9. 1. 16.
[5] *IG* I³, 7; cf. Lewis (1954) 17–21; Raubitschek, *DAA* 323.
[6] Lewis (1954) 20.

temple is being referred to at this date? The temple, while under construction, was called 'the temple on the Akropolis in which is the ancient image' in the building accounts.[7] These accounts include three long inscriptions comprising nearly thirty fragments of marble, dating from 409/8 to 406/5, which detail progress on the building and the contracts for the work to be done.[8] In the inventories the treasures of the building which we still call the Erechtheion, appeared under the heading, ἐν τῷ ἀρχαίῳ νεῷ, 'in the ancient temple'.

Yet we know that the temple was constructed decades later than the Parthenon. Why then was this new building called 'old'? The reasons are related to the history of the site. The first temple of Athena in the mid-sixth century stood immediately to the south of the Erechtheion, and the Porch of the Karyatids stands directly above the old foundations. The Erechtheion must be seen as a replacement of that temple, although not directly on top of the old foundations. The Persians burnt the old Temple of Athena, and at Plataia the Greeks vowed never to rebuild it, but to leave the ruins as a monument to the barbarity of the Persians.[9] It is generally thought that this explains why the temple was not built directly on the sacred site of the earlier temple.

The wooden image 'which fell from heaven' (Paus. 1. 26. 7) was housed in the temple we call the Erechtheion after its construction at the end of the fifth century. Where had this venerated object stood previously? It was undoubtedly housed in the old temple of Athena until the Persian invasion. Afterwards, when the temple had been destroyed, it was placed perhaps near the temple of Nike on the west entrance to the Akropolis. Raubitschek has suggested that coins and vase-paintings depict the cult statue on a base situated on the Nike *pyrgos*.[10] Yet the building accounts for the Erechtheion suggest that the cult statue was already in place, and that the construction had to accommodate the site of the statue by building around it.[11]

The Chandler stele, dating to 409/8–407/6, refers to unsmoothed areas in the part 'in front of the statue' (τοῦ πρὸς τοῦ ἀγάλματος).[12]

---

[7] *IG* I³, 474 line 1 (409/8).

[8] Cf. I. T. Hill (1969) 167.

[9] The ancient sources for the Oath of Plataia include: Lycurg. *In Leocr.* 81; Diod. Sic. 11. 29. 3; Aesch. 2. 115; Isoc. *Paneg.* 4. 156; Tod *GHI* ii. 204; although Theopompos (*FGrH* 115 F 153) says that the oath was a forgery.

[10] Raubitschek, *DAA* 359–64 no. 329; cf. Herington (1955) 41; I. T. Hill (1969) 145 and 239 n. 16.

[11] Dinsmoor (1932) 318–19; (1939) 155–6; (1947) 109 n. 4.

[12] *IG* I³, 474 line 75.

The inscriptions (*IG* I³, 474 and 475) show payments to workmen; one entry gives a payment of 4 drachmai to a painter for painting fourteen ceiling coffers on the ceiling 'above the beams which are over the statue' (ὑπὲρ τοῦ ἀγάλματος).[13] These references imply that a small *naiskos*, perhaps of mud-brick, housed the cult statue, constructed on or near the site of the Porch of the Karyatids. As the new temple was being built, the statue continued to stand there. This would account for the irregular orthostates and wall-joins that have been observed on the western part of the inner face of the south wall.[14]

A parallel for this practice may be seen in the fourth-century reconstruction of the temple at Delphi, where again a small mud-brick structure was built over the sacred *omphalos* while the new temple was constructed. The building accounts for the year 343 BC record payment to a workman named Deinon of Delphi 'to build with mud-bricks a shelter around the *omphalos*'.[15] At the site of the temple of Athena Polias, the temporary shelter served to house the cult statue and perhaps also the treasury when the Athenians returned from Salamis and Troizen in 480. When the Delian League funds were moved to the Akropolis in 454, it is likely that they were kept in this same shelter, with the cult statue of Athena to watch over and protect them. Thus, the temple referred to in the decree concerning the *Praxiergidai* is probably the temporary shelter on the site of the Dörpfeld foundations, in which was kept the ancient image even while the new temple which we call the Erechtheion was under construction.

The inventories of the Treasurers of Athena included the Archaios Neos only occasionally. There has been some controversy concerning which building on the Akropolis was called by this name in the fourth century BC. Travlos believed that the Athenians had rebuilt the western part of the sixth-century old temple of Athena on the Dörpfeld foundations after the Persian war, and that it continued to be used to house the tribute and treasures of the city and empire even after the Parthenon and Erechtheion were finished. According to this theory, when the inventories list treasures in the Archaios Neos, they are referring to that rebuilt portion of the old temple of Athena.[16] An alternative view is that the rebuilt old temple of Athena

---

[13] *IG* I³, 475 lines 262–5.
[14] Holland (1924*a*) 16–23, (1924*c*) 407–21; Paton (1927) 144–6; Dinsmoor (1947) 109 n. 4; I. T. Hill (1969) 176.
[15] Bourguet (1932) no. 32 lines 8–11.
[16] Travlos (1971*a*) 143.

was called the Opisthodomos in the inventory lists.[17] I place the
treasures of the 'Archaios Neos' inside the late fifth-century
Erechtheion, because among the inventoried items the ornaments
for the old wooden cult statue are listed. No. **VI.20** below lists as
treasures in the Archaios Neos: 'A wreath, which the goddess holds;
earrings, which the goddess has; the band which she has on her neck;
five necklaces; a gold owl; a gold aegis; a gold gorgoneion; a gold
phiale that she holds in her hand.' Since these items undoubtedly
adorned the cult statue, and the cult statue was housed in what we
call the Erechtheion, and these adornments are listed in the inventories under the heading 'In the Archaios Neos', then it follows that
all treasures listed under that heading were kept in that building; the
Archaios Neos was the name of the temple in the inventories. It is
still possible that the Opisthodomos was the formal name for the
temporary shelter rebuilt on the foundations of the old temple of
Athena, which Dinsmoor believed was in use until 353.[18]

   Pausanias mentions certain spoils from the Persian wars which he
saw in the temple of Athena Polias: 'a piece of Persian spoils—the
breastplate of Masistios, who commanded the cavalry at Plataia, and
a Persian sword (ἀκινάκης) they say belonged to Mardonios.'[19] Yet
Pausanias was sceptical that the Athenians could have taken
Mardonios' weapon: 'as Mardonios fought against Spartans and fell
to a Spartan, the Athenians could hardly have obtained the sword at
once and the Spartans would surely not have let them have it.'[20]
There are other reasons to doubt that these items were genuine: the
same dagger is involved in the alleged robbery which Demosthenes
accused Glauketes of perpetrating in the early fourth century.[21]
Demosthenes records that it weighed 300 darics. Unless
Demosthenes exaggerated the charges, it is difficult to explain the
dagger's reappearance by the time of Pausanias.[22]

   The cuirass of Masistios was a subject of curiosity and amazement
to the Greeks at Plataia, since it had gold over iron scales which gave
Masistios an aura of invincibility.[23] 'The reason why they could not
kill him at once was the armour he wore—a corslet of golden scales
under his scarlet tunic. No blow upon the corslet had any effect,
until at last a soldier saw how it was and struck him in the eye, and

[17] Cf. Dinsmoor (1947) 140.
[18] Dinsmoor (1947), esp. 109–10 n. 4 and 128 n. 93; cf. Ridgway (1992) 126 and n. 24.
[19] Paus. 1. 27. 1, trans. P. Levi. Cf. I. T. Hill (1969) 176.
[20] Paus. 1. 27. 1, trans. P. Levi.
[21] Dem. 24. 129.
[22] D. B. Thompson (1956) 286; cf. Morris (1992) 281–91, esp. 286.
[23] Hdt. 9. 22.

he fell dead.'[24] Yet the Spartans were said to have kept all treasures for themselves; it is unlikely that such prize spoils would have ended up on the Athenian Akropolis.

In conjunction with the Persian spoils allegedly stolen by Glauketes, Demosthenes mentions a silver-footed stool (δίφρος ἀργυρόπους) inside the temple, listed in the *Souda* as the seat of Xerxes from the battle of Salamis.[25] Plutarch's description, dependent on the philosopher and historian Phanias of Lesbos, records that 'A golden throne had been set up for him [Xerxes] and a crowd of secretaries were in attendance, whose duty it was to record the events of the battle.'[26] Was it a throne or a stool? Was it of gold or did it merely have silver feet? Again, there is some confusion or conflation in the sources about this.

After the victory at Plataia, the Greeks under the Spartan leadership of King Pausanias seized the tent of Xerxes, his throne, and gold and silver in abundance.[27] Likewise, after the naval battle near Salamis, Persian corpses were stripped of their gold decorations: 'On another occasion, when his [Themistokles'] eyes fell on a number of Persian corpses, which had been washed up along the sea-shore, and he saw that many of them were ornamented with gold bracelets and collars, he passed by them himself but pointed them out to a friend who was following him, with the words, "Help yourself! You are not Themistokles!"'[28] Many such spoils, from the Persian wars and the later Delian League campaigns, decorated the temples of Attica, not just on the Akropolis but in many demes, as Demosthenes takes for granted: 'The men who built the Propylaia and the Parthenon, and decked our other temples with the spoils of Asia, trophies in which we take a natural pride . . .'[29] Thucydides alludes to the Persian spoils in enumerating the wealth of Athens on the eve of the Peloponnesian war: 'In addition to this there was the uncoined gold and silver in offerings made either by individuals or by the state; there were the sacred vessels and furniture used in the processions and in the games; there were the *spoils taken from the Persians*, [my emphasis] and other resources of one kind or another, all of which would amount to no less than 500 talents.'[30]

There is no question that war booty did comprise a significant

[24] Hdt. 9. 22, trans. A. de Sélincourt.
[25] Dem. 24. 129.
[26] Plut. *Them.* 13. 1, trans. I. Scott-Kilvert.
[27] Hdt. 9. 80.
[28] Plut. *Them.* 18, trans. I. Scott-Kilvert.
[29] Dem. 22. 13, trans. J. H. Vince, cf. Harris (1990–1).
[30] Thuc. 2. 13. 4, trans. R. Warner.

portion of the treasures kept in Greek sanctuaries, and the Akropolis was no exception. Yet there are many inconsistencies which raise doubts about the famous relics alleged to have been housed in the temples. Are these spurious? The inventory lists provide some evidence, albeit not conclusive, suggesting that such items were kept on the Akropolis in the fifth and fourth centuries BC, but in the Parthenon and Chalkotheke, not in the temple of Athena Polias.

The catalogue below includes only items which were kept in the Erechtheion, or the 'Archaios Neos' as it was known to the Athenians, after 407/6 BC, when the building was completed.

Below are listed the inscriptions in which the objects kept in the Erechtheion were inventoried.

*Archaios Neos Inventories:*

1. 376/5: IG II², 1445 lines 43–7
2. 375/4: IG II², 1426 lines 1–9
3. 374/3: IG II², 1424 lines 1–30+1689 lines 1–5
4. 371/0: IG II², 1424a (add. pp. 800–3) lines 346–73
5. 368/7: IG II², 1425 lines 283–335
6. 367/6: IG II², 1428 (add. pp. 806–8) lines 164–196
7. (c.367/6): IG II², 1429 lines 35–59
8. (after 319/18): IG II², 1472 lines 1–22
9. (after 314/3): IG II², 1456 lines 1–37
10. 307/6: IG II², 1489 lines 1–42.
11. (after 306/5): IG II², 1487 lines 31–49

In addition it is conceivable that some or all of the items listed in inscriptions 18–31 of the Opisthodomos inventory list (see p. 42 above) moved to the Erechtheion, in which case many of the items listed in the catalogue of Part II would have to be appended to the following lists.

THE TREASURES

ARMS AND WEAPONS

1.     Two little silver shields, two silver miniature helmets, and a silver spear, unweighed

ἀσπιδίω δύο ἀργυρὼ καὶ κρανιδίω δύο καὶ δοράτιον ἀργυρᾶ ἄστατα

IG II², 1424 lines 5–6 (374/3)
1424a lines 357–8 (371/0)
1425 lines 300–1 (368/7)

1428 lines 169–70 (367/6)
1429 lines 35–6 (c.367/6)
1456 lines 9–11 (after 314/3)
1489 lines 27–30 (307/6)

2. 2 little silver shields
ἀσπίδια μικρὰ ἀργυρᾶ ΙΙ
    *IG* II², **1489 lines 25–6 (307/6)**

3. Against the cupboard, little silver shields
πρὸς τῇ φάτνῃ ἀσπίδες ἀργυραῖ μικραὶ
    *IG* II², **1489 lines 26–8 (307/6)**

4. Against the door-posts, 12 little gold shields
πρὸς τῇ παραστάδι ἀσπίδια χρυσᾶ ΔΙΙ
    *IG* II², **1489 lines 38–9 (307/6)**

5. A little gold shield, dedicated by Phylarche
χρυσοῦν ἀσπίδιον ὃ Φυλάρχη ἀνέθηκεν
    *IG* II², **1456 lines 6–7 (after 314/3)**

6. A gilt shield, which Iphikrates dedicated
ἀσπὶς ἐπίχρυσος ἣν Ἰφικράτης ἀνέθηκε
    *IG* II², **1489 lines 5–6 (307/6)**
    **1487 lines 39–40 (after 306/5)**

7. A little gold shield hanging from the door-post
ἀσπιδίσκιον χρυσοῦν ἀπηρτημένον ἀπὸ τῆς
    παραστάδος
    *IG* II², **1487 line 32–3 (after 306/5)**

8. Small silver spears --- cross-laced around the nail
δοράτια μικρὰ ἀργυρᾶ [---] περὶ τὸν ἧλον
    περιεπλιγμένα
    *IG* II², **1489 lines 29–31 (307/6)**

9. Small silver helmets
κρανίδια μικρὰ ἀργυρᾶ
    *IG* II², **1489 lines 28–9 (307/6)**

10. A small helmet from the base, having gold cheekpieces
and an ivory plume
κρανίδιον μικρὸν ἀπὸ τοῦ βάθρου παρειὰς χρυσᾶς
    ἔχον καὶ λόφον ἐλεφάντινον
    *IG* II², **1421 lines 123–5 (374/3)**

1424a lines 319–21 (371/0)
1425 lines 245–7 (368/7)
1428 line 160 (367/6)
1443 lines 208–9 (344/3)
1455 lines 10–11 (341/0)

11.     One gilt helmet, not in good condition

κυνῆ μία ἐπίχρυσος οὐχ ὑγιής
1460 lines 21–2 (after 330/29)

12.     A cavalry knife, ivory

μάχαιρα ἱππικὴ ἐλεφαντίνη
*IG* II², 1489 lines 37–8 (307/6)

13.     An ivory sacrificial knife, which [---]s dedicated, uninscribed

μάχαιρα ἐλεφαντίνη ἦν [---]ς ἀνέθηκεν ἀνεπίγραφος
*IG* II², 1456 lines 3–5 (after 314/3)

14.     A bronze sabre, against the door-post

ξιφομάχαιρα χαλκῆ πρὸς τῆ παραστάδι
*IG* II², 1424 line 20 (374/3)
**1424a lines 372–3 (371/0)**
1425 lines 324–5 (368/7)
1428 line 190 (367/6)
1429 line 56 (*c.*367/6)
1456 line 26 (after 314/3)

15.     Two swords, against the door-post

ξίφη δύο πρὸς τῆ παραστάδι
*IG* II², **1424a line 373 (371/0)**
1425 line 326 (368/7)
1428 line 191 (367/6)
1429 line 57 (*c.*367/6)

16.     3 bronze sabres

ξιφομάχαιραι χαλκαῖ ΙΙΙ
*IG* II², 1489 lines 36–7 (307/6)[31]

FIGURINES

17.     Silver figurine against the door-post, which B[---] dedicated.

τύπος ἀργυροῦς πρὸς τῆ παραστάδι ὃν B[---]

---

[31] Possibly incorporating VI.14.

ἀνέθηκεν

> *IG* II², 1489 lines 1–2 (307/6)
> 1487 lines 35–7 (after 306/5)

18a.    The Treasurers in the year of Nikomachos [341/0] made an additional contribution of the following objects, which were dedicated during their period of office. A silver owl on a small column; [an object] having 5 gold pieces which the Priestess Phanostrate, daughter of Anak[---], dedicated

τάδε προσπαρέδοσαν ταμίαι οἱ ἐπὶ Νικομάχου ἐπ᾽ αὐτῶν ἀνατεθέντα· γλαῦξ ἀργυρᾶ ἐπὶ κιονίσκου [---] χρυσοῦν ἔχον χρυσία Γ ὃ ἀνέθηκεν ἡ ἱέρεα Φανοστράτη Ἀνακ[---] θυγάτηρ

> *IG* II², 1456 lines 27–32 (after 314/3)

18b.    A little silver owl on a small boxwood column

γλαυκίδιον ἀργυροῦν ἐπὶ κιονίσκου πυξίνου μικρόν

> *IG* II², 1489 lines 33–5 (307/6)

19.    A little Palladion on a silver column, full of resin, not complete

παλλάδιον μικρὸν ἐπὶ κιονίσκου ἀργυροῦ κόμμιδος μεστὸν οὐκ ἐντελής

> *IG* II², 1489 lines 31–3 (307/6)

20.    A gold circlet, which the goddess has; earrings which the goddess has; a band which she has on her neck; five necklaces; a gold owl; a gold aegis; a gold gorgoneion; a gold phiale that she holds in her hand

στεφάνη ἣν ἡ θεὸς ἔχει· πλάστρα ἃ ἡ θεὸς ἔχει· ὄχθοιβος ὃν ἔχει ἐπὶ τῷ τραχήλῳ· ὅρμοι πέντε· γλαῦξ χρυσῆ· αἰγὶς χρυσῆ· γοργόνειον χρυσοῦν· φιάλη χρυσῆ ἣν ἐν τῇ χειρὶ ἔχει

> *IG* II², 1426 lines 4–7 (375/4)
> 1424 lines 11–16 (374/3)
> **1424a lines 362–6 (371/0)**
> 1425 lines 306–12 (368/7)
> 1428 lines 176–82 (367/6)
> 1429 lines 42–7 (*c*.367/6)
> 1456 lines 20–2 (after 314/3)

21.    A small snake

ὀφίδιον μικρόν

> *IG* II², 1472 line 17 (after 319/8)

22.　　　　　　[A statue] holds [---] in the right hand, and in the left
　　　　　　　hand it holds a bronze box

　　　　　　　--- ἐν τῇ δεξιᾷ χειρί· ἐν δὲ τῇ ἀριστερᾷ χειρὶ
　　　　　　　κιβώτιον χαλκοῦν ἔχει

　　　　　　　　　*IG* II², 1456 lines 34–5 (after 314/3)


JEWELLERY

23.　　　　　　A gold ring, unweighed, which Archedike dedicated

　　　　　　　δακτύλιος χρυσοῦς ἄστατος ὃν Ἀρχεδίκη ἀνέθηκεν

　　　　　　　　　*IG* II², 1424 lines 9–10 (374/3)
　　　　　　　　　**1424a lines 360–1 (371/0)**
　　　　　　　　　1425 lines 304–5 (368/7)
　　　　　　　　　1428 line 172 (367/6)
　　　　　　　　　1429 line 39 (*c.*367/6)


MISCELLANEOUS SILVER AND GOLD

24.　　　　　　A silver [object] against the door-post, which [---] dedi-
　　　　　　　cated

　　　　　　　ἀργυρᾶ πρὸς τῇ παραστάδι ἣν --- ἀνέθηκεν

　　　　　　　　　*IG* II², 1487 lines 33–5 (after 306/5)

25.　　　　　　A large silver [object] which the *diaitētai* in the archonship
　　　　　　　of Apollodoros [319/8] dedicated

　　　　　　　μεγάλη ἀργυρᾶ --- οἱ διαιτηταὶ οἱ ἐπὶ Ἀπολλοδώρου
　　　　　　　ἄρχοντος ἀνέθεσαν

　　　　　　　　　*IG* II², 1472 lines 20–2 (after 319/8)

26.　　　　　　A gold [object] against the [door-post ---

　　　　　　　---α χρυσῆ πρὸς τῇ [παραστάδι ---

　　　　　　　　　*IG* II², 1472 line 19 (after 319/8)

27.　　　　　　In the Archaios Neos, of the gold in a ceramic pot ---

　　　　　　　ἐν τῷ Ἀρχαίῳ νεῷ τοῦ χρυσοῦ ἐν χύτρᾳ---

　　　　　　　　　*IG* II², 1445 lines 43–4 (376/5)
　　　　　　　　　1447 line 6 (before 371/0)

28.　　　　　　An unfired gold nugget, which Philto dedicated,
　　　　　　　unweighed.

　　　　　　　χρυσίον ἄπυρον ὃ ἀνέθηκε Φιλτὼ ἄστατον

　　　　　　　　　*IG* II², 1426 lines 3–4 (375/4)
　　　　　　　　　1424, add. p. 799 lines 7–8 (374/3)

1424a lines 359–60 (371/0)
1425 lines 303–4 (368/7)
1428 line 171 (367/6)
1429, add. p. 809 line 38 (c.367/6)

VESSELS

29.  A gold lustral basin, unweighed, which the male statue holds

ἀπορραντήριον χρυσοῦν ἄστατον ὃ ἔχει ὁ ἀνδριὰς

IG II², 1424 lines 10–11 (374/3)
1424a lines 361–2 (371/0)
1425 lines 306–7 (368/7)
1428 lines 174–5 (367/6)
1429, add. p. 809 lines 40–1 (c.367/6)

30.  A silver brazier [and] --- on which is inscribed --- dedicated; Nikokrates of Kolonos made it; weight: 500+ dr.

ἐσχάρις ἀργυρᾶ --- ἐφ᾽ αἷς ἐπιγέγραπται [---]
ἀνέθηκεν· Νικοκράτης ἐκ Κολωνοῦ ἐποίησεν στα
Γ---

IG II², 1492 lines 70–3 (305/4)

31.  Against the lintel, a silver wine-cup

πρὸς τῷ ὑπερτοναίῳ κύλιξ ἀργυρᾶ

IG II², 1489 lines 39–40 (307/6)

32.  A silver wine-jug, marked ---, on which is inscribed 'Sacred to Athena'; weight --- dr. A silver wine-jug, on which is inscribed 'Sacred to Athena'; weight --- dr. 2 silver wine-jugs, on which is inscribed 'Sacred to Athena' ---

οἰνοχόη ἀργυρᾶ ἐφ᾽ ἧ τὸ [---] ἐφ᾽ ἧ ἐπιγέγραπται
ἱερα Ἀθηνᾶς στα--- οἰνοχόη ἀργυρᾶ ἐφ᾽ ἧ
ἐπιγέγραπται ἱερὰ Ἀθηνᾶς στα--- οἰνοχόαι
ἀργυραῖ ΙΙ ἐφ᾽ αἷς ἐπιγέγραπται ἱεραὶ Ἀθηνᾶς ---

IG II², 1492 lines 58–69 (305/4)

33.  A wooden phiale with gold

φιάλη ὑπόξυλος ἐπίχρυσος

IG II², 1426 lines 2–3 (375/4)
1424 line 7 (374/3)
**1424a line 359 (371/0)**
1425 line 302 (368/7)
1428 line 173 (367/6)

1429 line 37 (367/6)
1489 lines 35–6 (307/6)
1456 line 5? (after 314/13)

34.     A silver phiale, unweighed, which the wife of Glaukon
        dedicated

        φιάλη ἀργυρᾶ ἄστατος ἢν Γλαύκωνος γυνὴ ἀνέθηκεν

        *IG* II², 1424 lines 1–2 (374/3)
          **1424a lines 355–6 (371/0)**
          1425 lines 296–8 (368/7)
          1428 lines 166–7 (367/6)

35.     A silver phiale, unweighed, which Demo, wife of
        Akoumenos, dedicated

        φιάλη ἀργυρᾶ ἄστατος ἢν Δημὼ Ἀκουμενοῦ γυνὴ
        ἀνέθηκεν

        *IG* II², 1424 lines 3–4 (374/3)
          **1424a lines 356–7 (371/0)**
          1425 lines 298–9 (368/7)
          1428 line 168 (367/6)

36.     A silver phiale, unweighed, in a case, which Eukoline
        dedicated

        φιάλη ἀργυρᾶ ἄστατος ἐν καλιάδι ἢν Εὐκολίνη
        ἀνέθηκεν

        *IG* II², 1424, add. p. 799 line 1 (374/3)
          **1424a lines 354–5 (371/0)**
          1425 lines 295–6 (368/7)
          1428 lines 164–5 (367/6)

37.     A silver phiale, which Aristoboule dedicated

        φιάλη ἀργυρᾶ ἢν Ἀριστοβούλη ἀνέθηκεν

        *IG* II², 1424 lines 29–30 (374/3)
          **1424a lines 371–2 (371/0)**
          1425 lines 322–3 (368/7)
          1428 line 189 (367/6)
          1429 line 55 (*c.*367/6)
          1456 lines 13–14 (after 314/3)

38.     A silver embossed phiale, which Ionike dedicated

        φιάλη ἀργυρᾶ κονδυλωτὴ ἢν Ἰονίκη ἀνέθηκεν

        *IG* II², **1456 lines 14–16 (after 314/3)**

39.     A small silver phiale --- which Nikylla [wife of] Presbias
        dedicated

        φιάλιον ἀργυροῦν. --- ἀνέθηκεν Νίκυλλα Πρεσβίου ---

*IG* II², 1472 lines 7–10 (after 319/8)

40. The treasurers in the year of Chremes [326/5] made an additional contribution of these following things to treasurers in the year of Antikles [325/4]: A small silver phiale --- which Nikagora, wife of Philistides of Paiania, dedicated.

Τάδε προσπαρέδοσαν ταμίαι οἱ ἐπὶ Χρέμητος ταμίαις τοῖς ἐπὶ Ἀντικλέους· φιάλιον ἀργυροῦν --- ἀνέθηκεν Νικαγόρα Φιλιστίδου Παιανιέως γύνη

*IG* II², 1472 lines 10–15 (after 319/8)

41. A silver phiale

φιάλη ἀργυρᾶ

*IG* II², 1425 line 329 (368/7)
1456 lines 5–6 (after 314/3)

42. On the cupboard, 1+³² silver phialai; other silver phialai right opposite from the ---³³ sacred objects

ἐν τῇ φάτνῃ φιάλαι ---Ι ἀργυραῖ· ἕτεραι φιάλαι ἀπαντροκὺ τῶν ἱερῶν ἀργυραῖ ---Ι

*IG* II², 1489 lines 2–5 (307/6)
1487 lines 37–9 (after 306/5)
1490 lines 10–17? (304/3)

43. A small silver phiale against the lintel; another small phiale is against the door-post on the left as you enter. Against the door-post on the right as you enter is a silver phiale with gold overlay, which the judges dedicated

πρὸς τῷ ὑπερτοναίῳ φιάλιον μικρὸν ἀργυροῦν· πρὸς τῇ παραστάδι τῇ ἀριστερᾶς εἰσιόντι ἕτερον φιάλιον· πρὸς τῇ παραστάδι τῇ δεξιᾶς εἰσιόντι ἕτερον φιάλη ἀργυρᾶ ἐπίχρυσος ἦν οἱ διαιτηταὶ ἀνέθεσαν

*IG* II², 1489 lines 9–16 (307/6)
1487 lines 43–9 (after 306/5)

44. Phialai behind the door --- as you enter on the right.

φιάλαι ὄπισθεν τῆς θύρας --- δεξιᾶς εἰσιόντι

*IG* II², 1489 lines 7–8 (307/6)
1487 lines 40–2 (306/5)

45. A silver phiale in an oblong box

φιάλη ἀργυρᾶ ἐμ πλαισίῳ

---

³² Probably 4.      ³³ Probably 6.

IG II², 1489 lines 8–9 (307/6)
1487 lines 42–3 (after 306/5)

46.  A silver phiale, inscribed 'To Athena Polias'; Phryniskos of Thessaly dedicated it

φιάλη ἀργυρᾶ ἐφ' ᾗ ἐπιγέγραπται Ἀθηνᾶ Πολιάδι
Φρυνίσκος Θετταλὸς ἀνέθηκε
IG II², 1489 lines 17–19 (307/6)³⁴

47.  Another silver phiale, on which is inscribed 'Sacred to Athena Polias'; the priestess [---]strate --- dedicated it

ἑτέρα φιάλη ἀργυρᾶ ἐφ' ᾗ ἐπιγέγραπται ἱερὰ Ἀθηνᾶς
Πολιάδος ἀνέθηκε ἡ ἱέρεια [---]στράτη
IG II², 1489 lines 19–22 (307/6)

48.  A small silver phiale, on which are inscribed archaic letters.

φιάλιον ἀργυροῦν μικρὸν ἐφ' ᾧ ἐπιγέγραπται ἀρχαῖα
γράμματα
IG II², 1489 lines 22–4 (307/6)

49.  A smooth silver phiale

φιάλη ἀργυρᾶ λεία
IG II², 1456 line 7 (after 314/3)

50.  A smooth silver phiale

φιάλη ἀργυρᾶ λεία
IG II², 1456 line 27 (after 314/3)

51.  A small silver phiale, against the door-post

πρὸς τῇ παραστάδι φιάλιον μικρὸν ἀργυροῦν
IG II², 1456 lines 18–19 (after 314/3)

52.  A silver phiale, which --- dedicated

φιάλη ἀργυρᾶ ἣν --- ἀνέθηκεν
IG II², 1456 lines 8–9 (after 314/3)

53.  A silver phiale, which Nikophon of Themakos dedicated

φιάλη ἀργυρᾶ ἣν Νικοφῶν Θημακεῦς ἀνέθηκεν
IG II², 1425 lines 334–5 (368/7)
1428 lines 195–6 (367/6)
1456 lines 12–13 (after 314/3)

54.  A gold incense-burner has been fitted into the floor;

³⁴ cf. V.155.

inscribed with its weight: 19+ dr.

θυμιατήριον χρυσοῦν ἐν τῷ ἐδάφει ἐνήρμοσται·
σταθμὸν ἐπιγέγραπται ---ΔΓⱵⱵⱵ

IG II², 1456 lines 16–18 (after 314/3)

WREATHS

55. Two wreaths of overlaid wood

στεφάνω ὑποξύλω δύο

IG II², 1424a lines 353–4 (371/0)
1425 line 294 (368/7)

56. A gold wreath, which the treasurers dedicated in the
archonship of Euboulides [394/3]; unweighed.

στέφανος χρυσοῦς ὃν οἱ ταμίαι ἀνέθεσαν οἱ ἐπ'
Εὐβουλίδου ἄρχοντος ἄστατος

IG II², 1424a lines 348–9 (371/0)
1425 lines 285–7 (368/7)

57. A gold wreath, unweighed, which the treasurers dedicated
in the archonship of Demostratos [390/89]

στέφανος χρυσοῦς ἄστατος ὃν οἱ ταμίαι ἀνέθεσαν οἱ
ἐπὶ Δημοστράτου ἄρχοντος

IG II², 1424a lines 351–2 (371/0)
1425 lines 290–2 (368/7)

58. A gold wreath, unweighed, which the ambassadors dedicated, those who served with Dion L---

στέφανος χρυσοῦς ἄστατος ὃν οἱ πρέσβεις ἀνέθεσαν οἱ
μετὰ Δίωνος Λ---

IG II², 1424a lines 349–50 (371/0)
**1425 lines 288–9 (368/7)**

59. A gold wreath, which Konon dedicated; unweighed

στέφανος χρυσοῦς ὃν Κόνων ἀνέθηκε ἄστατος

IG II², 1424a line 347 (371/0)
1425 lines 284–5 (368/7)

60. A gold wreath, unweighed, which Timagoras dedicated

στέφανος χρυσοῦς ἄστατος ὃν Τιμαγόρας ἀνέθηκεν

IG II², 1424a lines 352–3 (371/0)
1425 lines 292–3 (368/7)

61. A gold wreath, unweighed, which the *boulē* in the

archonship of Kalleas [377/6] dedicated

στέφανος χρυσοῦς ἄστατος ὄν ἡ βουλὴ ἡ ἐπὶ
Καλλέου ἄρχοντος ἀνέθηκεν

> *IG* II², 1426 lines 7–8 (375/4)
> 1424 lines 16–17 (374/3)
> **1425 lines 327–8 (368/7)**

62. A gold wreath, which the *boulē* in the archonship of
Charisandros [376/5] dedicated

στέφανος χρυσοῦς ὄν ἡ βουλὴ ἡ ἐπὶ Χαρισάνδρου
ἄρχοντος ἀνέθηκεν

> *IG* II², 1426 lines 8–9 (375/4)
> 1424 lines 18–19 (374/3)
> 1424a lines 366–7 (371/0)
> **1425 lines 313–5 (368/7)**

63. A gold wreath, which the *boulē* in the archonship of
Hippodamas [375/4] dedicated

στέφανος χρυσοῦς ὄν ἡ βουλὴ ἡ ἐφ᾽ Ἱπποδάμαντος
ἀνέθηκεν

> *IG* II², 1424 lines 26–8 (374/3)
> **1424a lines 370–1 (371/0)**
> 1425 lines 320–2 (368/7)
> 1428 lines 187–8 (367/6)
> 1429 lines 52–3 (*c.*367/6)

64. In the archonship of Sokratides [374/3]: a gold wreath
which Timotheos dedicated

ἐπὶ Σωκρατίδου ἄρχοντος· στέφανος χρυσοῦς ὄν
Τιμόθεος ἀνέθηκεν

> *IG* II², **1424 lines 21–3 (374/3)**
> **1424a lines 367–8 (371/0)**
> 1425 lines 315–6 (368/7)
> 1428 line 183 (367/6)
> 1429 line 48 (*c.*367/6)

65. A gold wreath, which Philippos dedicated

στέφανος χρυσοῦς ὄν Φίλιππος ἀνέθηκε

> *IG* II², 1424 lines 23–4 (374/3)
> **1424a lines 368–9 (371/0)**
> 1425 lines 317–18 (368/7)
> 1428 line 184 (367/6)
> 1429 line 49 (*c.*367/6)

66. A gold wreath, which Kallikleia dedicated, the wife of
Thoukydides

στέφανος χρυσοῦς ὃν Καλλίκλεια ἀνέθηκεν
Θουκυδίδου γυνή

IG II², 1424 lines 24–5 (374/3)
**1424a lines 369–70 (371/0)**
1425 lines 318–9 (368/7)
1428 lines 185–6 (367/6)
**1429 lines 50–1 (*c*.367/6)**

OBSERVATIONS

From the year 434/3, when the treasurers made the first inventories, at least four stools were listed inside the room called 'the Parthenon' (**IV.27**). But none of them was singled out as the stool or throne of Dareios. These fifth-century lists are preserved in their entirety; if there were in the inventories a silver-footed δίφρος of such historical importance and value, surely it would have been specified. In the fourth-century inventories, such a stool does appear (**V.118**): 5 round-footed stools (δίφροι στρογγυλόποδες), one with silver feet (ἀργυρόπους)'.[35] These first appear in the inventories of the Hekatompedos Neos in 397/6. Where did they come from? And the one with silver feet—is this the throne of Xerxes? Were they of recent manufacture? Why else should they have been absent from the fifth-century lists?

The gold dagger of Mardonios may be the same as one of the golden daggers listed in the Parthenon (**IV.1–2**). Six are listed in one group; they appear in the first inventory (434) in the chamber called the Parthenon and continue to be listed together until 412. Another gold dagger, specifically identified as 'unweighed', was dedicated in 428/7. Could any of these be the gold dagger of Mardonios? Consider Demosthenes' testimony, that it weighed 300 darics. If it is the dagger of Mardonios, why is it unweighed? One such dagger in an inventory dated shortly after 385/4 (**V.2**) is described in greater detail: 'An iron [Persian] dagger (ἀκινάκης), having a gold grip, a sheath of ivory and gold, and a knob (πυγλίον) of gold.' Dorothy Thompson suggested that this is the dagger of Mardonios.[36] But if so, why did it not appear in the earlier lists? Again, one suspects that some spurious relics may have entered the temple.

There were a number of vases, mostly silver, in the Erechtheion. Of these, there were five wine-jugs, one kylix, one wooden phiale,

---

[35] IG II², 1394 lines 13–14 (397/6); 1414 lines 12–13 (385/4); 1412 lines 4, 9 (382/1).
[36] D. B. Thompson (1956) 285; cf. Morris (1992) 264–8.

one brazier, and at least twenty-three phialai. The phialai listed in **VI.42** are of an indeterminate number. A few of the vases are inventoried with their locations. The kylix (**VI.31**) was inventoried as being 'against the lintel', as was the small silver phiale (**VI.43**). Objects whose position is described in relation to the door include the phialai in **VI.43** and **VI.44**, and items 'against the door-post' were a sabre and two swords (**VI.14–15**).

Curiously, hardly any items kept in the Erechtheion were weighed by the treasurers in their annual inventories. Only three entries record weights, and all appear in the inventories after 314/3, towards the very end of the lists. A series of metal vases were recorded with their weights, but do not appear in the lists until 305/4 (**VI.32**). The vessel (**VI.54**) made by Nikokrates of Kolonos was also weighed, but this was a commissioned dedication, made from melted-down votive offerings, and also appears only in the inventory of 305/4 (**VI.30**).[37] And a 'gold incense-burner, fitted into the floor, weight inscribed on it: 19+dr.' had its weight recorded directly on to the vase; it could not be moved for weighing; a comparable item, a gold phiale, was stored in the Asklepieion, with its weight inscribed upon it; it was dedicated by the politician Aristophon of Azenia.[38]

Several types of knife were stored in the temple (**VI.14–16**), but one may have had special significance. The sabre listed as **VI.14** had a life of at least sixty years, since it appears in inventories from 374/3 to 314/3 BC. These were made of bronze with ivory, and may have been used for sacrifices on festival days.

The inventories record that the gold incense-burner (**VI.54**) was actually set into the floor. Unfortunately, no traces of floor-slabs are preserved inside the Erechtheion because of its repeated reuse in the post-classical period. It is difficult to ascertain to which part of the floor the treasurers might have been referring. The only clue is the relative proximity in the list, of this item to the ornaments of gold on the wooden image (**VI.20**), which follow with only one phiale intervening. If there is a correlation between the proximity of items within the lists and their placement inside the temple, we might deduce that the gold incense-burner was embedded in the floor near the cult statue of Athena, which is usually assumed to have been in the eastern cella of the Erechtheion.[39] Near the wooden image was

---

[37] Harris (1988).

[38] Aleshire (1992) 92.

[39] Jahn and Michaelis (1901) pl. 26; Paton (1927) 488–92; *contra* Travlos (1971*a*) 213–14, fig. 281, and (1971*b*).

another statue, called the *andrias*, which held a lustral basin of gold (**VI.29**). This might be associated with the statue of Hermes mentioned by Pausanias (1. 27. 1): 'In the temple of Athena Polias there is a wooden Herm, said to have been dedicated by Kekrops, now hidden from view by myrtle boughs'.[40] Myrtle was used for ritual sprinklings and might be appropriately found near the lustral basin which the statue held. Might we imagine that the statue held the lustral basin for the priests or worshippers? That the wooden male statue served as an attendant for the ritual cleansing? The physical interaction of worshippers with this statue before facing the ancient image may have heightened their suspension of disbelief upon confronting the cult statue and prepared them to accept it as a substitute for the goddess, just as the male statue took the place of a bathing attendant.

Compare this with the description of Alkinous' palace in book 7 of the *Odyssey*: 'Here the Phaeacian chieftains sat and enjoyed the food and wine which were always forthcoming, while youths of gold (χρύσειοι κοῦροι), fixed on stout pedestals, held flaming torches in their hands to light the banqueters in the hall by night.[41] These male statues of Homer may correspond to the ἀνδριάς holding a lustral basin mentioned in the inventories of the Erechtheion: 'Gold lustral basin, which the male statue holds.' Such ritual water-basins were placed in strategic areas of sanctuaries, at entrances or at boundaries between sacred and secular places. Before participation in a ceremony, water was used for purification.[42]

The description of the gold ornaments adorning the cult statue helps us to imagine what she looked like.[43] Contrary to the concept of a plain *xoanon* without features, this statue had enough ornament to cover the wood almost completely. If she were also draped in the Panathenaic robe, the effect would be to render the wood almost invisible.[44] The statue held a gold owl and a phiale, bore an aegis with gorgoneion, had a wreath on her head, and wore jewellery. That the image even had arms which could reach out and hold the phiale and owl is not expected, since we imagine the wooden image as a kind of roughly trimmed log, not something with fashioned arms. The phiale may have been on her lap, and the owl on her

---

[40] Trans. Palagia (1984) 517.

[41] *Od*. 7. 98–102, trans. E. V. Rieu.

[42] On the use of water-basins in Greek cults see Cole (1988).

[43] For bibliography on the cult statue of Athena see Mansfield (1985) 137–61. Kroll (1982) has used the evidence from the inventory lists to reconstruct the ancient image of Athena Polias.

[44] Romano (1988) has shown that the practice of dressing ξόανα in robes and jewellery was wide-spread in Greece.

shoulders, thus eliminating the need for restoring arms to her. Most probably she was carved as if of ivory, perhaps like the early ivory figurines from the Kerameikos cemetery. The arms may have been socketed in as was done for the marble korai. She had a mask for a face.[45]

Using the description of the adornments of the cult statue of Athena Polias, Jack Kroll was able to identify portrayals of it on coins dating to the end of the third century BC.[46] The literary sources suggest that the statue was standing, not seated, and that it held a phiale in the right hand and the gold owl in the left.[47] The coin representations depict naturalistic drapery, which reflected the use of real cloth for covering the wooden image.[48]

Very little jewellery appears in the inventories of the Erechtheion. Except for the jewellery that adored the cult statue (VI.20), only the private dedication of a single gold ring was inventoried (VI.23). This seems surprising. Likewise, no furniture is indicated, with the possible exception of some cupboards (VI.42). It is also curious that there is no mention at all of musical instruments in the Erechtheion. The Hekatompedon apparently had lyres and auloi, as did the Opisthodomos.

Twenty of the treasures kept in the Archaios Neos were private dedications. The votive offerings ought to reflect the social position of the donor, but in this case well-known individuals dedicated items that are equivalent in value to those dedicated by unknown individuals.[49] The dedicants were a mix of famous and important citizens such as Timotheos, Konon, and Iphikrates, and women without patronymics or husband's names (Aristoboule, Ionike), who may have been of the working class. Silver phialai were the most common individual dedication. One was given by a foreigner, Phryniskos of Thessaly (VI.46), who also dedicated in the Hekatompedon (V.155).

In the fourth century, wreaths, dedicated annually, were kept both in the Archaios Neos and in the Hekatompedon. Eleven gold wreaths (VI.56–66) appeared in the inventories of the Archaios Neos, and of these, eight were labelled with the name of an archon, providing a date for their dedication. A few of the wreaths were

[45] Kroll (1982) 74; cf. Wrede (1928).
[46] Kroll (1982), esp. 70 and pl. 11.
[47] Tertullian, Apol. 16. 3. 8; Σ Ar. Av. 516; Athenagoras, Legatio 17. 3; Strabo 12. 1. 41.
[48] Kroll (1982) 70–1.
[49] Kyrieleis (1988) noted that at the Heraion on Samos pinecones, coral, and other natural wonders were dedicated by the 'common man'.

dedicated by individuals, namely Konon (**VI.59**), Timotheos (**VI.64**), Philippos (**VI.65**), and Kallikleia, wife of Thoukydides (**VI.66**). Others were dedicated by the board of treasurers or the *boulē* (**VI.56–7, 61–3**).

Iphikrates, named as the dedicant of the gold shield (**VI.6**), was a soldier and general of the first half of the fourth century, responsible for advances in fighting tactics. During the years following the King's Peace, he served as a mercenary commander, with Chabrias and Timotheos, under Kallistratos of Aphidnai. In 376 BC, under their leadership, the Athenians regained naval supremacy. The next year brought a Panhellenic peace treaty. After Leuktra (371) Iphikrates played an important role in supporting the queen mother, Eurydike, in her bid for control over Macedon. A bronze honorific statue of him was erected in the Agora in 371 BC, and Pausanias mentions that a portrait of Iphikrates stood by the entrance to the Parthenon in his day.[50] His gold shield was probably a civic honour, which he then dedicated on the Akropolis. Yet it appears in the inventory lists only after 307/6, by which time he and many members of his family who could have made the dedication were dead. This may be an example of a dedication which had been inside the temple all along but for some reason was omitted from the annual inventories.

The armour in the Archaios Neos was votive in nature, either made of silver and gold or under-size, e.g. *aspidia* ('little shields'). There were at least five miniature shields made of silver in the Archaios Neos, and fourteen of gold or gilt. The shields, spears, and helmets listed as numbers **VI.3**, **VI.8**, and **VI.9** may be duplicates of the two miniature shields, two helmets, and one spear listed as **VI.1**. There were at least two miniature silver helmets and one gold. The gold helmet (**VI.10**) is said to be 'from the base'. It is not an item from the Parthenon, so the base in question is not the Chryselephantine statue base. What base might there have been in the Erechtheion? It is possible that the wooden image had an elaborate base with gold figures from which this helmet may have detached.

The range of items in the Erechtheion was neither so broad nor so multitudinous as in the Parthenon. It might be explained by the suggestion that the Erechtheion was the primary cult centre of the fourth-century Akropolis, and had to be functional. It could not have been crowded with as many items as filled the Hekatompedon,

[50] Paus. I. 24. 7.

since it was necessary to have room to worship and to take care of the wooden image. The sacrificial knife, incense-burner, phialai, and *aporranterion* were all functional objects which may have played important roles in the ceremonies. The description of such items in the inventories is a primary source of evidence for the use of the temple in the period of its prime.

# PART VII

# The Treasures and the Worshippers

## PRIVATE DEDICATIONS

Rarely in the fifth century and more frequently in the fourth, the treasurers included the name of the individual dedicant along with the description of the object kept in the temple. These names provide some information concerning the kind of dedicant who worshipped Athena on the Akropolis. The worshippers' names must have been inscribed on the item or attached with a tag; for how else could the treasurers identify these items in the inventories? Ceramic evidence for the use of writing to identify objects begins in the seventh century, with personal names and dedications painted on pottery.[1] Many metal scraps discovered on the Akropolis were found to have inscriptions.[2] These bronze objects with inscriptions from the Akropolis all date to the sixth century BC; they were presumably destroyed during the Persian wars. They include a pomegranate, shields, vases, and other metal dedications. Had they originated in the fifth or fourth century, it might have been possible to identify the bronzes exactly with treasures which appear in the inventories. But even without this possibility the bronze inscriptions from the Akropolis are models and parallels for how the treasury functioned in the classical period; the weight, the name of the dedicant, or other important identifying characteristics were inscribed on the inventoried objects in much the same manner as in the earlier period. The inscriptions on the votive offerings usually have a brief statement of who the dedicant is, and for which god the object was intended. Other circumstances, such as the dedicant's occupation or reason for prayer, are occasionally included.[3]

Seventy-two names of dedicants are preserved in the lists of the treasures kept in the Parthenon and Erechtheion. Some of the names are familiar from other historical sources, some are less familiar yet

[1] See *LSAG* for early examples; cf. Immerwahr (1990).
[2] See *IG* I², 401–2 for inscribed bronze private dedications; cf. Bather (1892–3).
[3] For example, *IG* II², 444 records 'Phrygia the bread-seller dedicated me to Athena' on the gorgoneion of a bronze shield-blazon.

known from relatively obscure sources, and others are not found
elsewhere. Twenty-one are included in Kirchner's *Prosopographia
Attica* or Davies's *Athenian Propertied Families*, indicating that they are
attested in literary or epigraphic sources as owning property or
performing civic liturgies or services. Several questions come
immediately to mind when one is confronted with a corpus of
ancient names. One would hope to learn about the status of these
individuals—were they citizens, courtesans, metics? Were they
official magistrates or private citizens when they dedicated their gift?
Did family members give dedications generation after generation?
Are there patterns to be seen in terms of relative value of gifts
according to class of dedicant? Did men and women contribute in
different quantities and types? What ritual or religious practices
might be observed in this list of names? All of these questions may
be addressed, but none definitively answered.

Eighteen of the dedicants in the Parthenon and Erechtheion were
male citizens. Eight are stated to be wives of citizens. Six were
daughters of citizens. Two were metics, ten were foreigners. Twelve
women were listed with only their first names. Fifty persons
gave items which were deposited in the Parthenon in their names,
twenty-three in the Erechtheion, and five in the Opisthodomos. A
pattern may be discerned in the placement of objects dedicated by
named individuals in the Parthenon and the Erechtheion. From 434
to 406 no votive offerings were associated with specific dedicants.
From 406/5 to 390 only offerings in the Parthenon were associated
with named individuals. After 389/8 the Erechtheion received more
new votive offerings associated with named individuals than did the
Parthenon. Whether this reflects a change in votive practice remains
to be explored. The Erechtheion was completed by the end of the
fifth century, but it may have taken a generation or so for it to
become the principal temple on the Akropolis .

The list below gives each named dedicant with the item dedicated. A rule (———) indicates that the dedicant is named in the
inventories but that the object cannot be restored, so that there is no
corresponding catalogue entry.

### DEDICANTS OF OBJECTS IN THE PARTHENON

*Male Citizens*

V.73. Andron of Elaious

V.273. Aristokritos of Anakaia

V.425. Aristophon

V.312. Eutrephes, son of Eumnemon

V.313. Kallias of Plotheia

V.314. Kallistratos, son of Kalliades, of Acharnai

V.315. Kleon

V.316. Leokrates, son of Aischron, of Phaleron

V.70. Meletades of Erchia

V.105, V.319. Stephanos, son of Thallos, of Lamptrai

V.54. Thrasyllos of Euonymon

*Mothers of Citizens*

V.317. Lysimache, mother of Telemachos

*Wives of Citizens*

V.148. Axiothea, wife of Sokles

V.138. Kallion, wife of Aristokles

V.318. Wife of Speuson

*Daughters of Citizens*

V.424. Aristomache, daughter of Aristokles

V.156. Glyke, daughter of Archestratos

V.274. Kleostrate, daughter of Nikerates

V.130. Polyippe, daughter of Meleteon of Acharnai

*Women Identified by First Name Only*

V.311. Aristola

V.421. Aspasia

V.151. Kleinomache

V.346. Paapis E[---]

V.101. Smikythe

——Sostrate. *IG* II², 1419 line 5:

    ---iai which Sostrate dedicated; number ---

    ---ιαι ἃς Σωστράτη ἀνέθηκεν ἀριθμός ---

*Metics*

V.97. Archias, (a metic) living in Peiraieus

V.149. Dorkas, (a metic) living in Peiraieus

*Foreigners*

**V.18.** Alexander, son of Polyperchon
**V.426.** Gelon of Pellana, son of Tlesonides
**V.427.** Hierokles of Phaselis
**V.428.** Lysander of Sparta, son of Aristokritos
**V.51.** Pharnab[azos]
**V.155.** Phryniskos of Thessaly
**V.152.** Platthis of Aegina
**V.358.** Roxane, wife of King Alexander
**V.383.** Spartokos of Pontos

*Males, Status Undetermined*

**V.79.** Aristarchos
**V.80.** Aristokles from [---]es
**V.173.** Demeas
**V.441.** K[---]
**V.277.** Kallimachos
—— Kephisodoros. *IG* II², 1400 lines 59–60:
    '--- which Kephisodoros dedicated'
    --- ὃ Κηφισόδωρος ἀνέθηκεν
—— -mos. *IG* II², 1417 line 6
    '---mos dedicated ---'
    ---μος ἀνέθηκεν ---
**V.131.** [---]os
—— Praxiteles. *IG* II², 1418 line 15:
    '--- which Praxiteles --- dedicated ---'
    ---ω ἃ Πραξιτέλης --- ἀνέθηκεν ---
—— Sosinomos. *IG* II², 1440 line 39:
    '--- Sosinomos dedicated ---'
    --- Σωσίνομος ἀνέθηκεν ---

*Proper Names Unable to be Classified*

**V.249.** An-
**V.150.** E[---]
    'Prokl[--- dedicated]'
    --- Προκλ --- [ἀνέθηκεν]
——Theo-. *IG* II², 1478 line 9:
    'Theo--- dedicated'
    --- ἀνέθηκεν Θεο---

## DEDICANTS OF OBJECTS IN THE ERECHTHEION

Twenty-three individuals are named in the inventories as having dedicated objects in the Erechtheion. There are a total of seven male citizens, five wives of citizens, two daughters of citizens (but they might be the same person; in both cases the individual is a priestess), six women listed only by their first name, one male foreigner, and two whose names are too fragmentary to determine their sex or classification.

*Male Citizens*

**VI.6.** Iphikrates
**VI.59.** Konon
**VI.53.** Nikophon of Themakos
—— Onesimos O[-. *IG* II², 1472 lines 5–6:
    '--- which Onesimos O[---] dedicated ---'
    --- ἀνέθηκεν Ὀνήσιμος Ὀ---
**VI.65.** Philippos
**VI.60.** Timagoras
**VI.64.** Timotheos

*Wives of Citizens*

**VI.35.** Demo, wife of Akoumenos
**VI.34.** Wife of Glaukon
**VI.66.** Kallikleia, wife of Thoukydides
**VI.40.** Nikagora, wife of Philistides of Paiania
**VI.39.** Nikylla, wife of Presbias

*Daughters of Citizens*

**VI.18.** Phanostrate, daughter of Anak---
**VI.47.** [---]strate

*Women Identified by First Name Only*

**VI.23.** Archedike
**VI.37.** Aristoboule
**VI.36.** Eukoline
**VI.38.** Ionike
**VI.28.** Philto
**VI.5.** Phylarche

*Foreigners*

**VI.46.** Phryniskos of Thessaly (also appears as a dedicant in the Parthenon
    **V.155**)

*Proper Names Unable to be Classified*

**VI.17.** B-

**VI.13.** [---]s


### DEDICANTS OF OBJECTS IN THE OPISTHODOMOS

*Male Citizens*

**II.66** Sophokles of Kolonos, son of Iophon

**II.31.** Xenotimos, son of Karkinos

*Wives of Citizens*

**II.37** (=**IV.32**; **V.164**) Kleito, wife of Aristokrates, son of Oulios, son of Kimon

**II.71** Thaumarete, wife of Timonides

*Woman Identified by First Name Only*

**II.37** (=**IV.32**; **V.164**) Dexilla


### FAMOUS DEDICANTS

Compared with the Asklepieion, where 908 names are listed in the inventories, very few dedicants were formally recognized in those of the Erechtheion.[4] The honour was rarely given. Of the 908 named individuals from the Asklepieion, only 132 are attested elsewhere as being Athenian citizens known from other sources. In the Erechtheion, of the twenty-three names only six are attested elsewhere. Such a low number is surprising: one might expect that only well-known personalities would be granted the honour of having their name included in the inventories. Apparently the distinction was not reserved for famous politicians or the wealthiest landowners in Athens, but was accorded to a variety of individuals, many of whom we would not have heard of save for these inscriptions. For the years 406/5 to 390/89 the names of thirty dedicants are associated with their gifts on the stelai; but between 389 and 300 only twenty-one more named dedicants are known. Conversely, between 406/5 and 390 no items were associated with the names of their dedicants in the Archaios Neos (Erechtheion), but between 389 and 300 eighteen items were added with named dedicants. It is interesting that in the early fourth century the practice seems

---

[4] Aleshire (1989) 53.

peculiar to the Parthenon, whereas later the Erechtheion was apparently the preferred repository.

Several foreigners are named in the inventories. They are Alexander, son of Polyperchon, of Macedon (**V.18.**); Gelon of Pellana, son of Tlesonides (**V.426**); Hierokles of Phaselis (**V.427**); Lysander of Sparta, son of Aristokritos (**V.428**); Pharnabazos (of Persia) (**V.51**); Phryniskos of Thessaly (**V.155;VI.46**); Platthis of Aigina (**V.152**); Spartokos from Pontos (**V.383**), and Roxane, wife of Alexander the Great, the only female foreigner recognized in the inventories (**V.358**). For some of these, it is possible to suggest the historical circumstances under which they may have made their dedications on the Athenian Akropolis.

Lysander, son of Aristokritos, of Sparta (**V.428**) was the Spartan leader at the end of the Peloponnesian war, outwitting the Athenians at the battle of Aegospotamoi (405).[5] After the surrender of Athens in the spring of 404, he was the undisputed yet unofficial ruler of Greece. Honours piled upon him from many city-states, and Plutarch records that 'he was the first Greek, so Douris tells us, in whose honour Greek cities erected altars and offered sacrifices as though he were a god, or for whom songs of triumph were sung'.[6] The city of Ephesos set up his portrait statue.[7] Samos authorized that a portrait statue of him be erected at Olympia, and its dedicatory inscription was recorded by Pausanias: 'In the amazing woods of Zeus king of the sky I stand by dedication of the people of Samos; Lysander has achieved everlasting glory for Aristokritos and for his country: is famous for courage.'[8] The Samians also instituted a new festival in his honour, known as the Lysandreia.[9] At home in Sparta, a painting recorded his success.[10] These were all honours given to him, but it is also recorded that he gave presents and dedications in return. At Delphi Lysander 'set up bronze statues of himself' and Kyros honored him with a chryselephantine ship which was set up in the Treasury of Brasidas and the Acanthians.[11] In Sparta Pausanias saw two sculpted eagles carrying two figures of Nike dedicated by Lysander in commemoration of his naval battles at Ephesos and Aigospotamoi.[12] In addition, Plutarch records that Lysander dedicated a talent of silver, fifty-two mina, and eleven staters at Delphi.[13]

---

[5] Cf. *RE* s.v. *Lysandros*; cf. Arist. *Ath. Pol.* 34. 3; *Pol.* 5. 1. 10, 5. 7. 2; Diod. Sic. 10. 9. 1, 13. 70–7, 14. 3–10, 14. 33. 5; Front. 2. 1. 18, Isoc. 8. 98, 16. 40, 18. 61, Justin 5. 5. 1, 6. 4. 6; Lys. 12. 71, 13. 34; Nep. *Lys.*; Paus. 3. 17. 4, 6. 3. 14, 9. 32. 9, 10. 9. 7; Plut. *Ages.* 3, 6–8; *Alc.* 35–8; *Lys.*; *De Pyth. orac.* 8; *De glor. Ath.* 7; Polyain. 1. 45. 2–4, 7. 19; Xen. *Hell.* 1. 5–2. 6, 2. 4. 28, 3. 2–6, 5. 13.

[6] Plut. *Lys.* 18.       [7] Paus. 6. 3. 15.       [8] Paus. 6. 3. 14, trans. P. Levi.

[9] Paus. 6. 3. 14; Plut. *Lys.* 18.       [10] Paus. 3. 17. 4.

[11] Paus. 10. 9. 7; Plut. *Lys.* 18; *Mor.* 394D.       [12] Paus. 3. 17 .4.       [13] Plut. *Lys.* 18.

Lysander supported the parties of Kritias and Theramenes and set up the oligarchy of the Thirty. He imposed a Spartan harmost in Athens, and set up decarchies in many of the other city-states which had been part of the Athenian alliance. Lysander reorganized the constitution of Athens in the middle of the summer of 404 BC, replacing the democracy with oligarchy. But by the end of the summer of 403 democracy had been restored, in part with the assistance of the Spartan king Pausanias, and Lysander's powers were diminished by the Spartans, who always feared any individual whose power approached that of the city-state. Sparta had begun to withdraw support and reverse his decisions by early 403, and Lysander found himself eclipsed by the growing power of Agesilaos.[14] It is likely that it was in 404, during the reign of terror under the Thirty, that the Athenians awarded him this wreath, which he then gave to Athena for safe keeping.[15] Lysander died in 395 at the battle of Haliartos against the Thebans and won posthumous honours from Sparta as a result.[16]

Pharnabazos (**V.51**) dedicated a robe which first appears in the inventories for 382/1 BC.[17] Anti-Spartan in disposition, he was a Persian satrap of Daskyleion (*c*.413–370 BC), who worked with the Greek generals serving with Alkibiades against Kalchedon (408 BC), gave the Athenians 20 talents, and secured for then an audience with the Great King.[18] Yet he colluded with Lysander to assassinate Alkibiades, who was in Phrygia in 404.[19] Pharnabazos later helped Konon to defeat the Spartans with Phoenician ships and Greek mercenaries between 397 and 394.[20] Artaxerxes II praised Konon, 'honoured him with immense gifts, and appointed an official to supply as much money as Konon might expend'.[21] Pharnabazos and Artaxerxes II gave Persian riches which made their way to Athens through Konon and his troops. By 382 Pharnabazos was involved in the Persian attempt to reconquer Egypt, and it is unlikely that the dedication was made in the year in which it is first preserved in the inventories (382/1 BC).

---

[14] Plut. *Lys.* 19–24.

[15] His wreaths first appear in the inventories in the year 401/0, but those for 405–401 are not well preserved.					[16] Plut. *Lys.* 29–30.

[17] For Pharnabazos' alliances with the Greeks see Bengtson (1975) 147–8 no. 206; 164–5 no. 219; 167–8 no. 222; Lewis and Stroud (1979) 191–3 esp. n. 16; Cargill (1981) 8.

[18] Xen. *Hell.* 1. 3. 8–4. 7; Plut. *Alc.* 31. 1.					[19] Plut. *Alc.* 39.

[20] Xen. *Hell.* 4. 3. 10–12, 4. 8. 6; Diod. Sic. 14. 79. 4–8, 14. 81. 4–6, 14. 83. 4–7, 14. 84. 3–5, 14. 85. 2–4; Paus. 6. 7. 6; Plut. *Artaxerxes* 21; Isoc. 4. 142; Nep. *Conon* 4; Photios 44^b20–38 (epitome of Ktesias, *Persica*), FGrH 688 F 30; Didymos, *Demosthenes* col. vii. 28–52 (Philochoros), FGrH 328 F 144–6; *Hell. Oxy.* 9. 2–3, 19. 1–3.

[21] Diod. Sic. 14. 81. 6; cf. Vickers (1984) 48.

Other individuals known from history also dedicated items to Athena. Three generations of one family made dedications on the Akropolis and a fourth was honoured with a portrait in the Agora: Konon II, Timotheos II, and Konon III.[22] Konon II's father (Timotheos I) was one of the first statesmen to receive the honour of having his portrait set up in Athens, probably to commemorate an athletic victory in his youth.[23] The marble monument was a column with a cylindrical capital, with the inscription running along the flutes: Τιμόθ[ε]ος [Κόνωνος] Ἀναφλύστιος. Later in Timotheos I's career he may have served as secretary of the board of overseers (*epistatai*) of the Parthenon in 443/2.

Konon II received a wreath for his military achievements in the early fourth century (**VI.59**).[24] Having escaped Lysander's assault at Aegospotamoi and received shelter and ships from Euagoras of Cyprus,[25] he was largely responsible for reversing the oligarchic movement fostered by Sparta after the Peloponnesian war and for restoring Athens' independence: 'Konon, son of Timotheos, and Epaminondas, son of Polymnis, restored injured Greece: Konon threw out the Lakonian colonists and put an end to governing boards of ten in the islands and coastal territories, and Epaminondas did the same in cities remote from the sea.'[26] After his victory in 394 near Carian Knidos, Konon II created a sanctuary of Aphrodite near Peiraieus, in honour of the Knidians' favourite goddess.[27] Statues of Konon II, Timotheos II, and Euagoras stood in the Athenian Agora not far from the Royal Stoa.[28] Konon was given the 'unique distinction of being thus mentioned in his inscription: "Whereas Conon freed the allies of Athens"' as if he were single-handedly responsible for the liberation.[29]

Konon II's wreath, dedicated on the Akropolis, appears in the inventories of the Erechtheion by 371 BC. Probably it was dedicated before his death in 389, although this could have been done posthumously. In his will of 389 BC, there was mention of 5000 gold

---

[22] The elder Konon is designated II in *APF* 506–12 no. 13700 and Table VI, as is Timotheos, with Konon III as the third generation whose name appears in the inventory lists: *PA* 8699, 13699, 13700; *APF* 506–12 no. 13700; cf. Strauss (1984); Seager (1967); Barbieri (1955).

[23] *APF* 507; *DAA* 49 no. 47; *IG* I², 651; *SIG* 50.

[24] Thuc. 7. 31. 4.

[25] Plut. *Lys.* 11.

[26] Paus. 8. 52. 4. For Euagoras see Bengtson (1975) 182 no. 234; Lewis and Stroud (1979); cf. Xen. *Hell.* 4. 8. 24; Lys. 19. 21; *IG* I³, 113.

[27] Paus. 1. 1. 3. On the victory at Knidos see Xen. *Hell.* 4. 3. 11–13, Seager (1967).

[28] Paus. 1. 3. 1–2; Dem. 20. 68–71; Isoc. 9. 57; Aeschin. 3. 243; Nep. *Timoth.* 2. 3; *Hell. Oxy.* 1. 1–3.

[29] Dem. 20. 68–70, trans. B. Strauss (1984) 38, after J. H. Vince.

staters set aside for dedications to Athena and to Apollo at Delphi.[30]
The wreath in the inventory lists may be the same one that the *dēmos*
awarded him after his victory at Knidos.[31]

Three Pentelic blocks forming a curved base were found on the
Akropolis, bearing the names Κόνων Τιμ[ο]θέου, Τιμόθεος
Κόνω[νος].[32] These belong to the statues which Pausanias described
as standing not far from the Parthenon in the second century AD:
'Konon's son Timotheos and Konon himself are there too.'[33]
I. T. Hill identified the site of the statues as 9 m. north of the
seventh column from the west on the north side of the Parthenon.[34]
Other city-states are also known to have honoured this family with
portrait statues: Ephesos and Samos, which had both honoured
Lysander with portraits, reversed their oligarchic support and set up
statues of Konon and Timotheos in their sanctuaries. Pausanias
records:

'Yet when the balance tipped again, and Konon won the sea battle off
Knidos [394 BC] and Mount Dorion, the Ionians changed sides, and you
can see a bronze Konon and Timotheos dedicated to Hera on Samos and
the same at Ephesos to the Ephesian goddess. Things go on in the same
way throughout the ages, and all mankind are like the Ionians: they pay
court to the strongest'.[35]

Erythrai also honoured Konon by name in an inscription which
records the gratitude of the community and their decision to set up
a bronze portrait, perhaps gilded, of Konon 'wherever Konon
decides'.[36] By 392 he was captured by the Persian satrap Tiribazos,
and was either executed or escaped to Cyprus, dying shortly thereafter.[37]

Konon II's son, Timotheos II (born *c.*411), gave a gift to Athena
in 374/3 which was inventoried in the Erechtheion (**VI.64**): This
wreath immediately joined the inventory lists of the Erechtheion. In
375 Timotheos led the Athenians to a sea victory over Sparta at
Alyzia, which turned the allies towards Athens again in the early days

---

[30] Lys. 19. 36.

[31] Dem. 22. 72, 24. 180.

[32] *IG* II², 3774; Tod *GHI* ii. 88–90 no. 128; cf. Jahn and Michaelis (1901), 52 n. 22 and pl. 38 no.
15; Milchhöfer (1891) LXI. 93–LXII. 11.

[33] Paus. 1. 24. 3. Cf. Nep. *Timoth.* 2; Dem. 20. 69–70; Σ Dem. 21. 62.

[34] I. T. Hill (1969) 187–8.

[35] Paus. 6. 3. 16.

[36] *SIG* 126; Tod *GHI* 21–2 no. 106. Lines 13–16 of the inscription read: ποήσασθαι δὲ [αὐτοῦ
ε]ἰκόνα χαλκῆν [ἐπίχρυσον] καὶ στῆσαι [ὅπου ἂν δόξει] Κόνωνι. '. . . and make a bronze statue of
him overlaid with gold, and set it up wherever Konon decides').

[37] Xen. *Hell.* 4. 8. 16; Diod. Sic. 14. 39. 41; Isocr. 4. 154.

of the second Athenian confederacy.[38] Aeschines records that because of this victory the Athenians set up a portrait of Timotheos.[39] Yet he was impeached as general the next year and tried at his *euthynai* in 373, but acquitted.[40] He was again tried at his *euthynai* in c.355 BC during the Social War, along with Iphikrates, for their refusal to begin battle during a storm in the Hellespont while acting as Athenian generals. Iphikrates was found innocent, but Timotheos was fined the sum of 100 talents, commuted to 10 talents at his death in 354, the burden of the debt falling to his son, Konon III.[41]

The latter dedicated a wreath which appears in the Parthenon (Hekatompedon) inventories after 315/4 (**V.420**). Little is known of him, except that he must have reached maturity by 356 BC, in order to have inherited his father's property and debts.[42]

Iphikrates I dedicated a gilt shield which first appears in the inventories at the very end of the fourth century (**VI.6**).[43] Iphikrates died before 325/4, and his son, Iphikrates II, cannot be the dedicant, since he died before 323. Iphikrates' daughter dedicated a necklace in the inventories of Artemis Brauronia in the middle of the fourth century, and it is possible that a member of her family made a dedication in Iphikrates' name later in the century.[44] Pausanias saw a statue of Iphikrates at the entrance to the Parthenon on the Akropolis, which was set up in 372/1. The cuttings in the bedrock to secure the base of his statue may have been discovered.[45]

Alexander, son of Polyperchon, was a Macedonian nobleman; his father was a taxiarch who competed with Kassander for control of Greece after King Alexander's death.[46] Alexander was born around 350 BC and died in 314. He dedicated a complete panoply, consisting of a ceremonial breast plate, a complete light shield, and bronze greaves with silver work (**V.18**). These items appear only in the inventories for 304/3. Since Alexander had died a decade earlier, we have to guess the year of dedication. He reached his majority and became a player in Macedonian politics after Alexander the Great's

[38] The primary sources for the peace of 375 are collected in Bengtson (1975) 223–4 no. 265; cf. Cargill (1981) 10 n. 11.

[39] Aeschin. 3. 243.

[40] Dem. 49. 6–24; Diod. Sic. 15. 47. 3.

[41] Dem. 49; Dion. Hal. *Dein.* 13. 667; Isocr. 15. 101, 15. 129–34; Nep. *Tim.* 3. 5; Plut. *De genio Socr.* 575E; *Reg. apop.*, Tim. 1; Plut. *Sulla* 6. 3–4; cf. Roberts (1982) 42–9; 202 n. 78; Tod *GHI* ii. 88–90 no. 128.

[42] *APF* 510–11.

[43] *PA* 7737; *APF* 248–9 no. 7737; Polyain. 3. 9. 29.

[44] See Linders (1972) 54 and *IG* II², 1524 lines 68–9.

[45] I. T. Hill (1969) 188, 247 n. 17; *Hesperia*, 15 (1946) 15–16 fig. 3 no. 26 or 27.

[46] Berve ii. 21 no. 39; cf. Berve ii. 325 no. 654.

death in 323. Diodoros describes the role he played, and in these years the most likely date for him to dedicate a panoply would be *c*.319/8 BC.[47]

The most famous female dedicant was Roxane, 'wife of king Alexander'(V.141, 358).[48] She dedicated a gold rhyton and necklaces, which appear in the inventories by 305/4. She died in 310, and certainly did not visit Athens before 323, the year of Alexander's death. Jahn and Michaelis suggest that the dedication must have been made between 327, the year of her marriage to Alexander, and 323, since it is unlikely that she would have been called 'wife of King Alexander' after his death.[49] Yet she had never been to Greece until after his death. Polyperchon took Roxane and her son with him, as pawns in the struggle for the succession, while he fought in the Peloponnese in 319, where he was defeated by Kassander. Polyperchon kept Roxane's son close by for the purpose of maintaining a strong political position among the successors.[50] When he became regent, he wrote letters and offered military assistance in the name of the 'kings' (the sons of Roxane and Barsine), making it clear that the boys would accompany him on campaign.[51] Since 319 is the likely date for the dedication by Polyperchon's son (V. 18), it is possible that Roxane dedicated her offering at the same time: that is, that they went to Athens together. After Polyperchon's defeat in the Peloponnese in 319, he went to Attika and Phokis, and had with him the young sons of Alexander.[52] It is highly probable that Roxane accompanied her son because of his youth. Mother and child were then taken to Pydna, and afterwards to Amphipolis, where Kassander kept her in captivity (316–310 BC).[53] There were historical ties between Amphipolis and Athens; however the distance between the two cities and the fact that Roxane was under guard would have necessitated a dedication by proxy if she were to have made her gifts during this period. Since Kassander was concerned with establishing personal power in Macedonia, it is not likely that he would have

---

[47] Diod. Sic. 18. 65 ff. and 19. 63 ff.

[48] Berve ii. 346 no. 688. Ancient sources on Roxane include Arr. *Anab* 4. 19. 5, 6. 15. 3, 7. 4. 4, 7. 27. 3; Diod. Sic. 18. 3. 3, 19. 105. 2; Strabo 11. 517; Curt. 8. 4. 21–7, 10. 6. 9; Plut. *Alex.* 47, 77; *De fortuna Alex.* 1. 11, 2. 6; Justin 13. 2. 5, 15. 2. 5; Paus. 9. 7. 2; Trogus, *Prol.* 15.

[49] Jahn and Michaelis (1901) 18 no. 188.

[50] Macurdy (1932*a*) 40; (1932*b*). Macurdy established that Roxane, after Antipater's death in 319, was not in Epiros with Olympias, as was generally believed, but was with Polyperchon as he advanced through the Peloponnese to wage war against Kassander.

[51] Diod. Sic. 18. 48. 4; Plut. *Phokion* 31.

[52] Diod. Sic. 18. 68. 1–2; Plut. *Phokion* 33 places Polyperchon in Attica, granting audience to the delegation from Athens.

[53] Diod. Sic. 19. 52. 1–4, 19. 61. 1; Justin 15. 1; cf. Macurdy (1932*b*) 260–1.

allowed Roxane to make such a visible dedication in Athens, which would have served as a reminder of her son's position as heir to the coveted throne of Macedonia.

Berve was inclined to believe that Roxane offered her dedication at the time of Alexander's death, around 323 BC.[54] For what purpose would the gift have been given after Alexander's death? Did Roxane hope to keep her position as Alexander's queen and save her life at his untimely death with this act? A dedication at Athens might have served to keep her visible and was perhaps made even as a wish—in the hope that Athena would protect her. More likely, her dedications were made at some time in the years 319–318 in an attempt to strengthen her son's position as heir apparent, in the midst of the conspiracies and wars which plagued Greece. By making a dedication to Athena, Roxane reminded all the successors that Alexander IV was the legitimate heir, and that their positions were held temporarily until he came of age. Indeed, when the council of successors decided that Alexander IV was approaching the age of kingship, Kassander had both him and Roxane secretly put to death.[55]

There are precedents within the Macedonian royal circle for sending votive offerings to Greek sanctuaries. Olympias, Alexander's mother, had dedicated offerings in Athens and elsewhere in Greece, and is known to have been fascinated with Greek religious cults;[56] she met Philip II while they were being initiated into the mysteries on Samothrace. Philip, of course, set up statues of his family at the Philippeion at Olympia, and often consulted the oracles at Delphi, especially after he seized control of the Amphictyonic Council. Alexander sent 300 shields to the Parthenon after his victory at the River Granikos in 334 BC.[57] Athena had a special significance for Alexander since in his day she was the patron goddess of Troy, and Alexander dedicated his own armour to her temple there and took from it ancient armour from the Trojan war, or so he believed.[58] After Alexander succeeded in taking Gaza in September and October of 332 BC, he sent his mother 'a great part of the spoils', from which Olympias dedicated gold wreaths at Delphi.[59] She argued with the Athenians over the rights to worship and dedicate offerings at the temple at Dodona.[60] And, more importantly, she

[54] Berve ii. 347 n. 2.
[55] Diod. Sic. 19. 105; Justin 15. 2; cf. Macurdy (1932*b*) 260–1; Macurdy (1932*a*) 53.
[56] e.g. Plut. *Alex.* 2. 1.        [57] Arr. *Anab.* 1. 17.        [58] Arr. *Anab.* 1. 11.
[59] Plut. *Alex.* 25. 2; *SIG* i. 252 nos. 5 ff.; cf. Macurdy (1932*a*) 34.
[60] Hyperides, *Euxen.* 24–6.

dedicated a gold phiale *c*.330 BC 'to the temple of Hygieia in Athens', which Hyperides records, complaining that it was an injustice: 'for I presume that when Olympias can furnish ornaments for shrines in Athens we may safely do so at Dodona, particularly when the god demands it.'[61] Her son, Alexander, may have sent new golden Nikai to Athens as well.[62]

### GENDER PATTERNS OF OFFERINGS

For most artefacts found through archaeological investigation, it is difficult to say which gender made or used them in antiquity.[63] The problem we face is how to 'find' women in ancient Greece and how to identify their participation within society. What we need are detailed and quantifiable means of examining the activities of males versus females in the ancient world. The inventory lists of dedications made in Greek temples provide just such data. Through them we can study the types of dedications (vases, wreaths, figurines, etc.) which different groups of people made. It is then possible to study gender-specific features of the dedications.

Sara Aleshire, in *The Athenian Asklepieion*, observed specific patterns in the dedication of objects to Asklepios. Men offered almost all of the wreaths, cult equipment, and medical dedications, and they gave coins somewhat more frequently than women. Jewellery and small vase-types were primarily women's dedications. But none of these categories is confined exclusively to male or female dedicants. The *typoi* ('anatomical votives') are dedicated almost equally by each gender.[64] In her study of gender patterns among stone votives, Aleshire found that men were far more likely to dedicate such valuable and visible items.[65] The inventories from the temples on the Akropolis do not provide much support for this distinction.

In the Erechtheion, of the ten silver phialai, eight were dedicated by women. Of the five gold wreaths, four were dedicated by men. Thus, phialai may be seen as primarily female dedications, and wreaths typically male. Of the four men who dedicated wreaths, three are known from other sources and were prominent individuals.

[61] Hyperides, *Euxen.* 26, trans J. O. Burtt.
[62] D. B. Thompson (1944) 177; H. A. Thompson (1940) 206–7.
[63] Gero and Conkey (1991) 5.
[64] Aleshire (1989) 46.
[65] Aleshire (1992) 91–2.

The social status of individuals was defined androcentrically: men were labelled with their patronymics, women with their father's or husband's names (or, in one case, the name of her son).[66] The way that women are identified in the inventories confirms the view that Athens was a male-orientated society. Men wrote the tablets recording dedications made by women; the treasurers usually classified women through their relationships to men, as someone's wife or daughter.

Yet twelve women in the inventories of the Parthenon and Erechtheion combined were listed by their first name only. They may have been relatively well-known women in their day, so the andronyms were omitted; or more likely they were working-class women. This is supported by the bronze fragments of sixth-century date discovered on the Akropolis, which name women by their first name and their occupation.[67]

Clearly any notion that women's names should not be spoken or used in public is inapplicable here. Here, the use of a woman's name does not bring shame, but honour. Thucydides (2. 46) has Perikles say that 'The greatest glory of a woman is to be least talked about by men', and there was an apparent taboo on the use of higher-class women's names in court cases.[68] But here we have public stelai inscribed with the names of women for all to view, perhaps read.

Most historians recognize a public–private dichotomy which governed gender relations in Greece. Yet it is clear that the Akropolis was open to women and should be considered one of their spheres. The sharp line between domestic and public is blurred in the sanctuaries, which are public spaces where women actively participated. As we have seen here in the inventories, both genders were present and were active in the same ritual.

Men and women, youths and adults, citizens and metics, all participated in the Panathenaic festival and a few are recorded on the inventories as dedicants. The Athenian festivals provided opportunities for all to serve in some position of honour. People who ordinarily might not have had the chance to fulfil a prestigious role in society were able to make meaningful contributions through the rites. Women and young girls, traditionally sheltered from public life, found social opportunities through religion. Metics, and the children of metics, were able to be *skaphēphoroi*.[69] All types of

---

[66] On androcentrism see Conkey and Spector (1984) 3–14; cf. Schaps (1977).

[67] See *IG* II², 401–62.

[68] Schaps (1977) 329.

[69] Parke (1977) 33–50 on the religious roles open to participants in the Panathenaic festival.

people from all walks of life had the opportunity to dedicate objects
of value to Athena, and had the potential for immortality through
the inscription of their name on stone.

STATE DEDICATIONS

The most common form of state dedication was the gold wreath.
These were presented to Athena by many city-states, most of which
were allies in the second Athenian confederacy. When the Athenians
labelled the wreaths, they tended to specify that it was from the
people rather than the city—e.g. 'from the Samians' rather than
'from Samos'. The localities represented include Abdera,
Alopekonnesos, Andros, Arethousa, the Boiotian League,
Kalkhedon, Chersonesos, Elaious, Ephesos, Erythrai, Karystos,
Knossos, the Mesogeion, Miletos, Lemnian Myrrina, Mytilene,
Naxos, Samos, Paros, Peparethos, the Pontos, Samothrace, Siphnos,
Skiathos, Tenedos, Thasos, and Troizen (**V.379–86, 430, 432–57,
467**).[70] The recipient of the wreath was sometimes Athena herself,
and sometimes the Athenian *boulē* or *dēmos*. That the wreaths ended
up in the Parthenon may indicate the degree to which state and religion blended together in this temple.

The wreaths which were labelled with the name of the archon for
the year in which they were dedicated provide some insight into
relations between Athens and her allies in the second confederacy
(378–338 BC). In 368/7 the following cities gave wreaths which were
inventoried in the Parthenon: Andros, Karystos, Siphnos, and
Troizen. Between 349/8 and 344/3 Athena received wreaths from
the Chersonese, Elaious, Erythrai, Khalkhedon, Knossos, Mytilene,
Naxos, Paros, Samos, Samothrace, and Skiathos. Likewise, several
Athenian generals dedicated wreaths which had been awarded to
them, and a few of these men were closely associated with the
league: Konon III, Iphikrates, and Timotheos II.

An indication that there were many more wreaths in the storerooms than were inventoried is given in *IG* II², 1474 (after 318/7)
lines 4–5 (**V.378**), where the total number of wreaths in the year in
question is given as 84. Wreaths were labelled with the name of the
archon in the year of the dedication or with the name of the dedicant. When neither piece of information was available, the treasurers made note of this and assigned a letter to each wreath
(**V.387–8**).[71]

[70] See App. II below.     [71] On letter-labels see Tod (1954).

The Athenian *boulē* gave the following items to Athena to be kept in the Parthenon: an iron sacrificial knife dedicated in 407/6 (**V.207**); a silver chest dedicated in 318/7 (**V.44**), and at least two gold wreaths, attested in 354/3 but possibly a regular type of dedication (**V.458–9**). In addition, many wreaths given by foreign cities were gifts to the *boulē* which were kept in the temple (**V.429, 433, 436, 448, 450, 452, 456**). The *boulē* of the Areopagos gave one item, a writing-tablet, in the year 382/1 (**V.168**).

The Athenian *dēmos* also gave public gifts to Athena. These included seven wreaths awarded by it to individuals and then handed over to the temple (**V.385, 413, 414, 420, 466**), thirteen given to the *dēmos* by other city-states (**V.382, 384, 386, 430–1, 436, 439, 444, 446–7, 451, 453, 457**), and three given by the *dēmos* directly to Athena (**463–5**).[72] The Athenians gave a silver drinking-cup and a protome of Pegasus, weighing 118 dr., in the year 405/4 (**V.241**), but the Athenians as a body never appear again as a donor. The committee of thirty *bouleutai* known as the *sullogeis tou dēmou* may have made their dedications of wreaths (**V.460–1**) from some surplus of funds left over after their payments to citizens for attending the assemblies.[73] These wreaths must have been tagged with the inscription recording their offering.

Very few foreign objects can be identified on the basis of the information given in the inscriptions. There were some foreign coins, including Persian shekels (**V.60**), Corinthian staters (**V.56**), Phokaian staters and *hektai* (**V.61–4**), Kyzikene gold staters (**V.59**), and gold Darics (**V.57**). The adjectives βαρβαρική and Μηδική were used once each for a gold phiale (**V.315**) and flute-case (**V.190**) respectively. The ἀκινάκης (**IV.2,V.2**) can also be assumed to have a foreign origin since it is specifically a foreign shape. Apart from these cases, there is little indication that any item has a foreign origin.

The Illyrian helmet stands out for its origin (**V.10**); Achaian helmets were also specified (**V.8–9**). Many of the other helmets may have been captured from foreign enemies as war booty, but there is no firm evidence. Some of the furniture is said to have been manu-factured by foreigners, e.g. the Thessalian throne (**V.122**) or the Chian and Milesian couches (**IV.25–6, V.114**). These thrones were identified with their places of origin because their workmanship had a reputation for quality, as we hear from Athenaios: 'The throne is

[72] See App. II.
[73] See Hansen (1991) 105, 129, 149, 368; Lewis (1968) 109.

Thessalian, a most comfortable seat for the limbs. But the glory of
the couch whereon we sleep belongs to Miletos and to Chios,
Oinopion's city of the sea.'[74] It is unlikely that these were gifts from
inhabitants of these regions; rather, the Athenians purchased the
furniture from these cities to give Athena furniture of the best
quality, and the treasurers included this information in the inventories in order to advertise the fact.

Virtually no items kept in the Parthenon or Erechtheion were
peculiarly suited to Athena's iconography. An owl or two, a
gorgoneion, a Palladion—these are the only items out of the hun-
dreds listed. This contrasts greatly with the Asklepieion, where the
predominant types are body parts, coins, and *typoi*.[75] In the inventories of Artemis Brauronia the gifts are feminine in nature, mainly
garments, mirrors, and jewellery, along with the necessary ritual
vessels and equipment, apparently reflecting the function of her cult
and its appeal for her worshippers.[76]

The cult equipment of the Parthenon is in some ways difficult to
distinguish from the dedications. The gold and silver vases may have
been used in rituals, or may have been dedications. Certainly, some
items were carried in the Panathenaic festival, but were they made
for that specific purpose? The table made of ivory may have been a
cult table in the cella, or just an ordinary functional table.[77] Likewise,
the couches may or may not have been for use at ritual meals and
the musical instruments may have accompanied rites. The evidence
of the inventories alone is not sufficient to enable a decision.

Recent studies in votive practice have shown that we should
rarely expect offerings to reflect the cult of the deity. Aside from a
few Palladia and *gorgoneia*, the treasures of Athena do not seem to be
focused on any one epithet or aspect of her persona. Rather, they
reflect the greatness of her power over Athens: the tremendous
wealth of a healthy, thriving cult. The dedicants were probably
motivated to present gifts to Athena for the same reasons as obtain
at other sanctuaries: to give thanks for favours, to ask that favours be
granted, and to honour the goddess.[78] Transitions from one phase of
life to the next were usually accompanied by religious actions, and
presenting a gift to Athena was one.[79] The stress of living under

[74] Athen. 28 B.
[75] Aleshire (1989) 40–5.
[76] Linders (1972) 3, 28.
[77] On cult tables see Aleshire (1989) 308 for additional bibliography; Dow and Gill (1965);
D. H. Gill (1974) 117–37.
[78] Cf. Van Straten (1981) 74.
[79] Van Straten (1981) 89; Muir (1985) 195.

difficult circumstances could often be alleviated by some act of piety. A gift re-established the direct line of communication between individual and deity, relieving the sense of alienation experienced in times of duress. The most common practice was the offering of ἀναθήματα, personal items given over to the deity.[80] The dedication served as a tangible physical manifestation of the divine relationship.

The constant underlying tension of mortal life, the recognition of one's own mortality, could be conquered through worship at the sanctuary. The deity was eternal, offerings made at the temple remained there permanently, and one might even be immortalized on stone as the donor of the object, as Burkert explains:

To give something to a god means renunciation of the thing given; but as the gift is 'set up' in a sanctuary, especially in durable forms like ceramics or metalwork, renunciation becomes demonstration of what is to stay. Through the invention of writing, even an individual's name can be preserved. In a way, sanctuaries are primarily public places designed for the display and preservation of *anathemata*'.[81]

The treasures which filled the Parthenon were permanent gifts, testimony of the enduring relationship between the Athenians and Athena. Yet time passes, and what seemed at one time permanent becomes ephemeral. The treasures were dispersed to the four corners of the earth, and virtually no trace of any object from the Parthenon has survived. Only the inscribed inventories on stone preserve the memory of these gifts to Athena from her worshippers.

### THE AKROPOLIS: PANHELLENIC, INTERNATIONAL, OR LOCAL SANCTUARY?

In view of the paucity of evidence for foreign dedicants on the Akropolis, and because the Greater Panathenaia occurred only once every four years, it seems legitimate to reopen the question of whether or not the Akropolis functioned as a local, panhellenic, or international sanctuary. The dedications were principally made by Athenian citizens and those dwelling in the area. Very few objects were dedicated by named foreigners. Items of foreign manufacture were also relatively rare, and may have been dedicated by Athenians.[82] The one exception is the catalogue of wreaths dedicated

[80] Cf. Burkert (1985) 69; Kyrieleis (1988) 215.　　　　[81] Burkert (1988) 43.

[82] I refer to items which are labelled in the inventories as having foreign origins, such as the Chian and Milesian couches, the Illyrian helmet, the Phokaian, Aeginetan, and Corinthian coins, the Persian swords (ἀκινάκαι), and the few items labelled βαρβαρική or Μηδική. For an alternative view see Vickers (1989) 101–11; (1990).

by Athenian allies. Thus, the contrast between local Attic sanctuaries and the Akropolis is not as great as one might expect. The description Aleshire gives of the Asklepieion is just as appropriate to the Parthenon: 'A few foreigners visited the shrine (probably while resident in Athens) and left behind evidence in the form of inscriptions recording their foreign ethnics, but the overwhelming majority of those who participated in the cult of Asklepios seem to have been Athenians or residents of Athens.'[83]

The festivals of Athens, and particularly the Panathenaia, served the local community in many ways. Feasts provided meat for the ordinary population, who would not normally eat such food. The bonds of kinship were strengthened through common tribal identifications and veneration of eponymous heroes. Festivals also united the allies of Athens with Attica. When faced with a common opponent in the Persian war, the ties of common worship united the Greeks: 'and then there is our common Greekness: we are one in blood and one in language; those shrines of the gods belong to us in common, and the sacrifices in common, and there are our habits, bred of a common upbringing.'[84] Likewise, the ties binding those who participated in the Panathenaia strengthened the alliance when it faced the Spartans and their allies in the Peloponnesian war.

Athens had more festivals than any other Greek city-state, with between 120 and 144 festival-days per year in the fifth and fourth centuries, roughly a third of the year.[85] Perikles praised Athens for this practice in the funeral oration: 'When our work is over, we are in a position to enjoy all kinds of recreation for our spirits. There are various kinds of contests and sacrifices regularly throughout the year.'[86] The common festivities, contests, dramatic presentations, rituals, and displays of shared communal wealth in the form of ritual vessels elevated the lives of the poor and provided roles for all to play in the community.

## PIETY AND THE PARTHENON

Ehrenberg argued that the worship of Athena was not a true religious experience, but rather an expression of city patriotism. 'Here religion had become the expression of that cultural patriotism which Pericles above all tried to teach the Athenians. True religious

[83] Aleshire (1989) 71.
[84] Hdt. 8. 144. 2, trans. D. Grene. Cf. Cartledge (1985) 99.
[85] Cartledge (1985) 99.
[86] Thuc. 2. 38, trans. R. Warner. Cf. Cartledge (1985) 116.

worship of Athena of course continued to exist—but not in the Parthenon.'[87] Patriotism cannot explain the numerous private dedications, given in times of plenty and times of stress. Nor can patriotism explain the paradox that in a culture where the conditions were poor, homes modest, and food rationed, the temple was lavishly decorated with sculptures, and talents of gold adorned the cult statue.[88] Athenians complained of the weight of the liturgies on their backs—the state-imposed burdens of financing triremes or sponsoring plays. But there are no references to state-imposed dedications by individuals. Rich and poor gave freely to Athena, of their own will, without constraint.

The Parthenon stood on the most prominent topographical feature of the city of Athens. An elaborate path extended from the Propylaia, down the steep slope, through the heart of the Agora, and on through the gates to the deme of Eleusis, along the road which today still bears the ancient name, the Sacred Way. The Propylaia, built between 438 and 432 BC in conjunction with the completion of the Parthenon, separated the secular from the sacred. The use of blue Eleusinian marble shows a conscious recognition of the importance of boundaries and processions through levels. The Propylaia served as a fortified barrier for the *temenos*. A series of walls prevented any intrusion through the north and south wings, and the five central passageways were locked and grilled. An elaborate political system ensured that the keys would not fall into the wrong hands. The *Ath. Pol.* records that:

the Prytanes have a chairman (*epistatēs*) who is chosen by lot. He holds the chairmanship for one day and one night, and he cannot hold it for a longer time; nor can the same man hold it twice. This chairman keeps the keys to the sanctuaries where the treasure and the public records are kept. He also holds the public seal. He is obliged to stay in the Tholos.[89]

The key to the Hekatompedon, where all of the Treasures were stored in the fourth century, was kept in the Chalkotheke.[90] The grills on the east and west porches of the temple served as additional barriers. These are all ritual as well as practical aspects of Greek religion: 'access to the divine is not free and simple, but regulated through steps and boundaries; it can be barred and reopened again.'[91]

[87] Ehrenberg (1969) 76.   [88] Burkert (1988) 27.
[89] Arist. *Ath. Pol.* 44. 1, trans. K. von Fritz.
[90] For the references to keys in the Akropolis inventories see App. IX.
[91] Burkert (1988) 35.

Three acts have been considered essential for a Greek cult to exist: prayer, sacrifice, and setting up votives.[92] There is no doubt that the worship of Athena contained all three elements, as surely as they existed at Brauron, at the Asklepieion, at Eleusis, or in any other Attic sanctuary. Ehrenberg's denial of true religious experience in the Parthenon denies the goddess a cult which is better attested than most others. The Panathenaia was the central religious festival of the Athenians. The Erechtheion may have been the house for the wooden image, and technically the more sacred of the two, but the Parthenon was certainly the most impressive house for Athena. As one entered through the Propylaia, it was the Parthenon, not the Erechtheion, which was seen in all its glory, with the three-quarter view showing it off at its best. At the end of the procession, the participants surely restored to the Parthenon what had been borrowed for the festivities. This represents an annual rededication of the items dispensed for the parade. Worshippers had the chance to physically touch, hold, and handle Athena's treasures; they returned these items to her, and then borrowed them once more the following year, when another group of worshippers shared the experience. The treasures of Athena used in the Panathenaic procession served as a tangible link between the worshippers and the goddess.

[92] Burkert (1988) 36.

# APPENDIX I

# Personal Names Associated with Objects in the Inventories

Note that the names of treasurers mentioned in the prescripts of the inventories are omitted.

THE PARTHENON

1. Alexander, son of Polyperchon (V.18).
   Berve ii. 21 no. 39 and ii. 325 no. 654.
   Polyperchon commanded a brigade after Issos (333) and in the Lamian war (321). The dedication may have been made in 319.
2. An- (V.249)
3. Andron of Elaious (V.73)
   *PA* 922
4. Archias, (a metic) living in Peiraieus (V.97)
5. Aristarchos (V.79)
6. Aristokles from [---]es (V.80)
7. Aristokritos of Anakaia (V.273)
   *PA* 1932; 7443. His family is known down to the Roman period.
8. Aristola (V.311)
   *PA* 1858; *APF* 55 no. 1848. She might be the daughter of Aristokles of Hamaxanteia, the Treasurer of Athena for 398/7 (*IG* II², 1388 line 6; 1391 line 9; 1392 line 6). Cf. Develin (1989) 205.
9. Aristomache, daughter of Aristokles (V.424)
10. Aristophon (V.425)
    *PA* 2107. Archon 330/29? Cf. Develin (1989) 391–2.
11. Aspasia (V.421)
    *APF* 458. This might be Perikles' lover and mother of Perikles II, who served as Hellenotamias in 411/10. The first occurrence in the inventories of her dedication is 395/4.
12. Axiothea, wife of Sokles (V.148)
13. Demeas (V.173)
14. Dorkas, (a metic) living in Peiraieus (V.149)
15. E[---] (V.150)
16. Eutrephes, son of Eumnemon (V.312)

17. Gelon of Pellana, son of Tlesonides (**V.426**)
18. Glyke, daughter of Archestratos (**V.156**)
    This may be the daughter of Archestratos, the Treasurer of Athena for 429/8 (*PA* 2398), or of the proposer of a decree in the *boule* in 405/4 (*PA* 2402); cf. Develin (1989) 442.
19. Hierokles of Phaselis (**V.427**)
20. K[---] (**V.441**)
21. Kallias of Plotheia (**V.313**)
22. Kallimachos (**V.277**)
23. Kallion, wife of Aristokles (**V.138**)
24. Kallistratos, son of Kalliades, of Acharnai (**V.314**)
    *PA* 8149.
25. Kephisodoros.
    *IG* II$^2$,1400 lines 59–60.
26. Kleinomache (**V.151**)
27. Kleon (**V.315**)
    *PA* 8669. Probably the Treasurer of Athena for 377/6 (*APF* 229 no. 7252). Cf. Develin (1989) 237.
28. Kleostrate, daughter of Nikeratos (**V.274**)
    *PA* 10741; *APF* 405.
    The daughter of Nikeratos (II), trierarch in Samos in 409, killed by the Thirty.
29. Leokrates, son of Aischron, of Phaleron (**V.316**)
    *PA* 9095.
30. Lysander of Sparta, son of Aristokritos (**V.428**)
    Cf. Pauly-Wissowa s.v. Lysandros. Spartan general, commander at Aigospotamoi.
31. Lysimache, mother of Telemachos (**V.317**)
    *PA* 4549, 9432; *APF* 170–1 no. 4549B.
    Possibly the sister of Lysikles, Treasurer of Athena for 416/15. Cf. Develin (1989) 148. If this is the same Lysimache, she was priestess of Athena for 64 years.
32. Meletades of Erchia (**V.70**)
33. Paapis E[---] (**V.346**)
34. Pharnab[azos] (**V.51**)
    Berve ii. 379 no. 766.
    Pharnabazos was the Persian satrap who assisted Konon in defeating the Peloponnesians at Knidos (394) and rebuilding the long walls. His dedication first enters the inventory lists in 382/1.
35. Phryniskos of Thessaly (**V.155; VI.46**)
36. Platthis of Aegina (**V.152**)
37. Polyippe, daughter of Meleteon of Acharnai (**V.130**)
    *PA* 9799 and11968; *APF* 204–5 no. 5976.
    The daughter of the victorious choregos in second half of the 5th cent.

($IG$ $I^2$, 769).
38. Praxiteles
    $IG$ $II^2$, 1418 line 15
39. Prokl[-
    $IG$ $II^2$, 1382 line 25=$IG$ $I^3$, 342 line 26.
40. Roxane, wife of King Alexander (**V.358**)
    Berve ii. 346 no. 688.
41. Smikythe (**V.101**)
    This may be the daughter of Epainetos son of Antiphilos of Kephisia
    (*PA* 4753).
42. Sosinomos
    $IG$ $II^2$, 1440 line 39
43. Sostrate
    $IG$ $II^2$, 1419 line 5
44. Spartokos of Pontos (**V.383**)
45. Stephanos, son of Thallos, of Lamptrai (**V.105, V.319**)
    *PA* 12883; *APF* 491 no. 12883.
    Lys. 19. 46 cites him as an example of a wealthy property owner of
    the fifth cent. He died by 389.
46. Theo-
    $IG$ $II^2$, 1478 line 9.
47. Thrasyllos of Euonymon (**V.54**)
    *PA* 7343
    Known only from the inventories, although the grave stele of his son
    is known (Thrasymedes of Euonymon, son of Thrasyllos, $IG$ $II^2$,
    6176).

*Anonymous:*

48. Wife of Speuson (**V.318**)
49. [---]mos
    $IG$ $II^2$, 1417 line 6
50. [---]os (**V.131**)


THE ERECHTHEION

51. Archedike (**VI.23**)
52. Aristoboule (**VI.37**)
53. B- (**VI.17**)
54. Demo, wife of Akoumenos (**VI.35**)
55. Eukoline (**VI.36**)
56. Ionike (**VI.38**)
57. Iphikrates (**VI.6**)
    *PA* 7737; *APF* 248–9 no. 7737
    There is a problem in that his dedication of a golden shield is

recorded only at the end of the 4th cent., while the famous Iphikrates died before 325/4. Iphikrates' son, Iphikrates II, cannot be the dedicant, since he died before 323. Iphikrates' daughter dedicated a necklace in the inventories of Artemis Brauronia (*IG* II², 1524 lines 65–9, and 72–3 in 352/1 and 350/49); see Linders (1972) 54.

58. Kallikleia, wife of Thoukydides (**VI.66**)
59. Konon (**VI.59**)
    *PA* 8707; *APF* 506–12.
    A political figure, he held his first generalship in 414/3.
60. Nikagora, wife of Philistides of Paiania (**VI.40**)
    *PA* 14448
61. Nikophon of Themakos (**VI.53**)
62. Nikylla, wife of Presbias (**VI.39**)
63. Onesimos O[-
    *IG* II², 1472 lines 5–6
64. Phanostrate, daughter of Anak--- (**VI.18**)
65. Philippos (**VI.65**)
    *PA* 14375; *APF* 537 no. 14375
    Possibly *PA* 14375. In Dem. 29. 23–4 Philippos is an example of a man who had performed many liturgies.
66. Philto (**VI.28**)
67. Phryniskos of Thessaly (**VI.46**; **V.155**)
68. Phylarche (**VI.5**)
69. Timagoras (**VI.60**)
70. Timotheos (**VI.64**)
    *PA* 13700; *APF* 510 no. 13700
    This dedication was made after his victory at Alyzeia.

*Anonymous:*

71. Wife of Glaukon (**VI.34**)
72. [---]s (**VI.13**)
73. [---]strate (**VI.47**)

THE OPISTHODOMOS

74. Dexilla (**II.37**; **IV.32**; **V.164**)
75. Kleito, daughter of Aristokrates, wife of Oulios, son of Kimon (**II.37**; **IV.32**; **V.164**)
76. Sophokles of Kolonos, son of Iophon (**II.66**)
    *PA* 12833; 12834
    Treasurer of Athena in 400/399: Develin (1989) 203. Cf. *IG* II², 1374 line 3; 1375 line 4. This is the grandson of Sophokles of Kolonos, son of Sophilos, the tragedian. The present Sophokles was a teacher of drama and is said to have won twelve contests.

77. Thaumarete, wife of Timonides (**II.71**)
78. Xenotimos, son of Karkinos (**II.31**)
    *PA* 8254; *APF* 283–4 no. 8254.
    The family had four generations of tragic poets. The father dedicated on the Akropolis in mid 5th cent. Cf. *DAA* 135 no. 127. Xenotimos is mentioned in Ar. *Wasps* 1501 ff.

# APPENDIX II

# Civic Dedications in the Inventories

Below are listed the official Athenian state dedications, followed by civic offerings in alphabetical order by city.

THE PARTHENON

*Athenian Dedications*

1. The Athenians (**V.241**)
2. The *boulē* in the archonship of Antigenes [407/6] (**V.207**)
3. The *boulē* in the archonship of Archippos of Rhamnous [318/7] (**V.44**)
4. The *boulē* in the archonship of Diotimos [354/3] (**V.458**)
5. The *boulē* in the archonship of Diotimos [354/3] (**V.459**)
6. The *boulē* of the Areopagus (**V.168**)
7. The *dēmos* [318/7] (**V.420**)
8. The *dēmos* (**V.464**)
9. The *dēmos* of the Athenians (**V.385**)
10. The *dēmos* of the Athenians in the archonship of Anaxicrates [307/6] (**V.466**)
11. The *dēmos* in the archonship of Apollodoros [319/8] (**V.465**)
12. The *dēmos* in the archonship of Archippos [318/7] (**V.414**)
13. The *dēmos* in the archonship of Lysistratos [369/8] (**V.463**)
14. The *dēmos* of the Athenians in the archonship of Philokles [322/1] (**V.413**)
15. The *hieropoioi* (**V.468**)
16. The *hieropoioi* in the archonship of [---] (**V.469**)
17. The committee of 30 members of the *boulē* in the archonship of Dysniketos [370/69] (**V.460**)
18. The committee of 30 members of the *boulē* in the archonship of Lysistratos [369/8] (**V.461**)
19. The committee of 30 members of the *boulē* in the archonship of Nausigenes [368/7] (**V.462**)
20. The treasurers in the archonship of Archippos [321/0] (**V.253**)
21. The treasurers in the archonship of Euxenippos [305/4] (**V.388**)
22. The treasurers in the archonship of Kephisodoros [366/5] (**V.162**)
23. The treasurers in the archonship of Neaichmos [320/19] (**V.258**)

24. The treasurers in the archonship of Neaichmos (320/19] (**V.**320)
25. The treasurers in the archonship of Nikodoros [314/3] (**V.**296)
26. The treasurer of the Stratiotic Fund (**V.**67)

*Dedications from other city-states*

27. The Abderans (**V.**432)
28. The Andrians in the archonship of Nausigenes [368/7] (**V.**433)
29. The Arethousians (**V.**434)
30. The Boiotian League in the archonship of Anaxikrates [307/6] (**V.**415)
31. The *dēmos* of the Chersonesians from Agora archonship of Euboulos [345/4] (**V.**436)
32. The *dēmos* of the Chersonnesians from Agora (**V.**437)
33. The Chersonesians, Alopekonesians, ---, and Madytians (**V.**438)
34. The Elaiousians (**V.**439)
35. The Ephesians (**V.**379)
36. The Erythrians (**V.**440)
37. The Kalchedonians (**V.**435)
38. The Karystians (**V.**442)
39. The Karystians (**V.**443)
40. The Knossians (**V.**444)
41. The *dēmos* of the Milesians (**V.**384)
42. The *dēmos* of [Lemnian] Myrrina (**V.**382)
43. The Mytilenians (**V.**445)
44. The *dēmos* of the Naxians (**V.**446)
45. The Naxians (**V.**447)
46. The Parians (**V.**448)
47. The *dēmos* of the Peparethians (**V.**381)
48. The *dēmos* in Samos (**V.**449)
49. The *dēmos* in Samos (**V.**450)
50. The *dēmos* in Samos (**V.**451)
51. The Samothracians (**V.**452)
52. The Samothracians (**V.**453)
53. The Siphnians (**V.**454)
54. The Generals in Skiathos (**V.**467)
55. The *dēmos* of the Tenedians (**V.**380)
56. The Thasians (**V.**455)
57. The Troizenians (**V.**456)
58. The Troizenians (**V.**457)
59. The *dēmos* of the inland --- (**V.**386)

THE ERECHTHEION

*Athenian dedications*

60. The *boulē* in the archonship of Kalleas [377/6] (**VI.61**)
61. The *boulē* in the archonship of Charisandros [376/5] (**VI.62**)
62. The *boule* in the archonship of Hippodamas [375/4] (**VI.63**)
63. The ambassadors (πρέσβεις) (**VI.58**)
64. The *diaitētai* in the archonship of Apollodoros [319/8] (**VI.25**)
65. The treasurers in the archonship of Demostratos [390/89] (**VI.57**)
66. The treasurers in the archonship of Euboulides [394/3] (**VI.56**)
67. The treasurers in the archonship of Nikomachos [341/0] (**VI.18**)

There are no dedications from other city-states in the Erechtheion.

# APPENDIX III

# The Inventories in Chronological Order

## PRONEOS

1. 434/3–431/0: *IG* I³, 292–5 [EM 6772+5397+5165+12796]
2. 430/29–427/6: *IG* I³, 296–9 [EM 6788]
3. 426/5–423/2: *IG* I³, 300–3 [EM xxv–xxvi+EM 6746+5411+6773]
4. 419/8: *IG* I³, 304 [Ag. I 5390]
5. 418/7–415/4: *IG* I³, 305–8 [EM 6788]
6. 414/3–411/0: *IG* I³, 309–13 [BM xxv–xxvi+EM 6746+5411+6773]
7. 409/8–407/6 (?): *IG* I³, 314–16 [EM 6774]

## HEKATOMPEDON

8. 434/3–427/6: *IG* I³, 317–24 [EM 6762+635+12720+636+6775+4486]
9. 422/1–419/8: *IG* I³, 325–8 [BM xxvii+Paris Cabinet des Médailles]
10. 418/7–415/4: *IG* I³, 329–32 [BM xxvii+Paris Cabinet des Médailles]
11. 414/3–411/0: *IG* I³, 333–7 [EM 6778+6791+6792+6762A]
12. 410/9–407/6: *IG* I³, 338–40 [EM 6778+6791+6792+6762A]
13. 406/5 (?): *IG* I³, 341=*IG* II², 1383 [EM 7796]
14. 405/4 (?): *IG* I³, 342=*IG* II², 1383 [EM 7797–9]

## PARTHENON

15. 434/3–431/0: *IG* I³, 343–6 [EM 6793]
16. 430/29–427/6: *IG* I³, 347–50 [EM 6779+6780+13411+6780A]
17. 422/1–419/8: *IG* I³, 351–4 [EM 6779+6780+13411+6780A]
18. 414/3–412/1: *IG* I³, 355–7 [EM 6793]
19. 411 or 411/0: *IG* I³, 358 [EM 5307]
20. 410/9 or 409/8: *IG* I³, 359 [EM 6708A]
21. 408/7 (?): *IG* I³, 360 [EM 6708B]
22. 407/6 (?): *IG* I³, 361 [EM 6686]
23. 406/5–405/4: *IG* I³, 362 [EM 6747]

UNDIFFERENTIATED

24. 407/6–403/2: *IG* II², 1502
25. 404/3 (?): EM 12915+12976 [*Hesperia*, 41 (1972) 425–6]
26. 403/2: *IG* II², 1370+1371+1384 (delete 1503) [EM 7790+7789A+ 7800] [*SEG* 23. 81; *IG* II², add. p. 797; *JHS* 58 (1938) 84; *ÉAC* 3 (1965) 67]
27. 403/2: *IG* II², 1373 [EM 2646]
28. 403/2: *IG* II², 1399 [EM 7866]
29. 402/1: *IG* II², 1372+1402+EM 13409 [EM 8183+12397+13409] [*Eph.* 1953–4, ii. 107–12; *ÉAC* 1 (1963) 45]
30. 402/1 or 401/0: EM 12932 [*Hesperia*, 7 (1938) 272 no. 7]
31. 402/1 or 401/0: *IG* II², 1376 [BM 1 33+EM 7806]
32. 402/1 or 401/0: *IG* II², 1379 [EM 7795]
33. 401/0: *IG* II², 1381+1386+*Hesperia*, 9 (1940) 310 no. 28 [EM 7861+ 6158+Ag. I 4508] [*JHS* 58 (1938) 73; *Hesperia*, 9 (1940) 310–11 no. 28; *IG* II², add. p. 798]
34. *c.*400: *IG* II², 1503+EM 5201 [*JHS* 58 (1938) 81; *ÉAC* 3 (1965) 67–8]
35. 400/399: *IG* II², 1374 [EM 7862]
36. 400/399: *IG* II², 1375+EM 13410 (*Hesperia*, 41 (1972) 422–3 no. 54)+EM 12951 (*BSA* 70 (1975) 183–9 [EM 7791+7814+13410+ 12951]
37. 400/399: *IG* II², 1385 (lost)
38. 400/399: EM 12916 (*Hesperia*, 7 (1938) 277 no. 11; *BSA* 70 (1975) 184)
39. 399/8: *IG* II², 1390 [EM 5237]
40. 399/8: *IG* II², 1377 [EM 7793]
41. 399/8: *IG* II², 1378+1398 [EM 7792+7819] [*IG* II², add. pp. 797–8; *JHS* 51 (1931) 71]
42. 398/7: *IG* II², 1391 [EM 78]
43. 398/7: *IG* II², 1392 [NM GL 1479+EM 7801]
44. 398/7: *IG* II², 1388+1403+1408+EM 6790 [BM 1 29+EM 7811+ 7815+6790] [*SEG* 17. 39; 23. 83; *ÉAC* 3 (1965) 75]
45. 397/6 (?): *IG* II², 1394 [EM 7794A]
46. 397/6: *IG* II², 1393+1406+1448+1449+EM 12963+EM 12961 [*Hesperia*, 41 (1972) 423 no. 55+426 no. 58] [EM 7802–4+7838+ 7812+7813+12963+12961] [*JHS* 51 (1931) 156, 162; *BSA* 75 (1970) 188; *Hesperia*, 41 (1972) 423–4, 426–7; *ÉAC* 3 (1965) 71]
47. 396/5: *IG* II², 1417 [BM 1 31]
48. 395/4: *IG* II², 1395 [EM 6270+7805+2629]+Ag. I 1182 [*Hesperia*, 5 (1936) 389 no. 8; Hondius (1925) 52]
49. 395/4: *IG* II², 1409 [EM 7817]
50. 394/3: *IG* II², 1401 [EM 7807–10]+EM 2512 [*GRB Mon.* 10 (1984) 55–6]
51. 393/2 (?): *IG* II², 1404 [EM 7836]

52. Date uncertain, beg. 4th cent.: *IG* II$^2$, 1396 [EM 7818]
53. Date uncertain, beg. 4th cent.: *IG* II$^2$, 1397 [EM 7920]
54. Date uncertain, beg. 4th cent.: *IG* II$^2$, 1405 [EM 7837]
55. 391/0: *IG* II$^2$, 1389 [EM 5538]
56. 390/89: *IG* II$^2$, 1400 [EM 7839]
57. After 390: *IG* II$^2$, 1380 [EM 7794]
58. Before 385/4: Ag. I 5363 [*Hesperia*, 32 (1963) 165]
59. 385/4: *IG* II$^2$, 1407 (lost+1414 [BM I 32] [Woodward (1940) 377–94]
60. After 385/4?: *IG* II$^2$, 1416 [?]
61. After 385/4? *IG* II$^2$, 1418+1419 [EM 5603+6868]
62. After 385/4?: *IG* II$^2$, 1420 [EM 5430+5607]
63. Before 350: *IG* II$^2$, 1452 [EM 7834]
64. Between 384/3 and 378/7: *IG* II$^2$, 1433 [EM 7883]
65. Between 384/3 and 376/5: Ag. I 4996 [*Hesperia*, 32 (1963) 168]
66. Between 384/3 and 378/7: *IG* II$^2$, 1413 [EM 7826+7827]
67. 382/1: *IG* II$^2$, 1412 [EM 7824+7825]
68. 377/6: *IG* II$^2$, 1410 [EM 7859]
69. 376/5: *IG* II$^2$, 1411 [EM 7820]
70. 376/5: *IG* II$^2$, 1445 [EM 7821]
71. *c.*375/4: *IG* II$^2$, 1415 [EM 7835]
72. 375/4: *IG* II$^2$, 1446 [EM 7822]+Ag. I 5895 [*Hesperia*, 30 (1961) 241 no. 37]
73. 375/4: *IG* II$^2$, 1426 [EM 5301]
74. 374/3: *IG* II$^2$, 1421+1423+1424+1689 (del. Ag. I 4527 [Hesperia, 9 (1940) 320 no. 32 *AM* 66 (1941) 237 no. 7] [EM 481+6789+7921+ 7828+7828A+2691+2738+5297] Ferguson (1932) 114. Schweigert, (1940) joined an Agora fragment to the rest which Lewis has now withdrawn from the group; *AM* 66 (1941) 237 no. 7; cf. Lewis (1988) 299 n. 9
75. Before 371/0: *IG* II$^2$, 1447 [EM 7823]
76. 371/0: *IG* II$^2$, 1424A [EM 13293] *IG* II$^2$, add. pp. 800–5 [*Delt.* (1927/8) 127]
77. 368/7: *IG* II$^2$, 1425 [EM 7856–7857]
78. Near 368/7: *IG* II$^2$, 1427 [EM 5284]
79. 367/6: *IG* II$^2$, 1428 [EM 7853] *IG* II$^2$, add. 806–808 [*Delt.* (1927/8) 125]
80. *c.*367/6: Ag. I 4527 [*Hesperia*, 9 (1940) 320 no. 32]
81. *c.*367/6 or 366/5: *IG* II$^2$, 1429 [EM 7829]
82. *c.*367/6: *IG* II$^2$, 1430 [EM 7830]
83. *c.*367/6: *IG* II$^2$, 1431 [EM 7881]
84. *c.*367/6: *IG* II$^2$, 1434 (lost)
85. After 366/5: *IG* II$^2$, 1450 [EM 7833]
86. Between 366/5 and 353/2: *IG* II$^2$, 1439 [EM 7865]
87. After 365/4: *IG* II$^2$, 1451 [EM 7832]

88. After 360/59: South Slope fragment Akr. 18/5/89, to be published by Angelos Matthaiou

89. 354/3: *IG* II², 1442 [EM 7868] [Develin (1989) 286]

90. Before 353/2: Ag. I 5325 [*Hesperia*, 9 (1940) 324–5 no. 34]

91. Before 353/2: Ag. I 2104 (unpubl.)

92. Before 353/2: Ag. I 6430 (unpubl.)

93. After 352/1: D. M. Robinson Collection, Mississippi, *AJP* 58 (1937) 38–44

94. Before 350: *IG* II², 1435 (lost)

95. Before 350: *IG* II², 1453 [EM 7867]

96. 350/49: *IG* II², 1436 [EM 7864]

97. 349/8: *IG* II², 1440+1438+1507+1508+1463+1692+EM 12931 [*SEG* 19. 129; *SEG* 14. 83, *AJA* 36 (1932) 164 n. 3; *Hesperia,* 7 (1938) 281 no. 16; *ÉAC* 1 (1955–6) 135–46]

98. Shortly after 350: *IG* II², 1437+1432 [EM 7869+7882]

99. 347/6: *IG* II², 1441 [EM 7870]

100. Between 346/5 and 336/5: I 2260 [*Hesperia*, 25 (1956) 101–9]

101. 344/3: *IG* II², 1443 [EM 426]+Pesaro frag. [Lazzarini (1985) 34–5]

102. 341/0: *IG* II², 1455+1444 [EM 7873+7874+7877+7831] [*HSCP* suppl. 1 (1940) 395–400; *Hesperia,* 25 (1956) 101–9]

103. Shortly after 340/39: *IG* II², 1459 [EM 7880]

104. After 330/29: *IG* II², 1460+1461 [EM 7884+7885] [*HSCP* suppl. 1 (1940) 403]

105. After 330?: *IG* II², 1501B [EM 7919]

106. 321/0: *IG* II², 1466+1468+1470 [EM 7887A+7889+5254A]

107. After 320/19: *IG* II², 1469 [EM 7890]

108. After 319/8: *IG* II², 1472 [EM 7892]

109. Not before 318/7: *IG* II², 1471+1462 [EM 7891+7886]

110. After 318/7: *IG* II², 1474 [EM 7894]

111. Shortly after 318/17: *IG* II², 1475 [EM 7895]

112. After 316/5: *IG* II², 1457+1458+1464+1478 [EM 7879+5287+7887+12403] [Rhodes (1981) 550]

113. After 315/4: *IG* II², 1479A [EM 7896]

114. After 313/2: *IG* II², 1456+1483 [EM 7875+7876+5312] [Lewis (1988) 298 n. 6]

115. After 313/2: *IG* II², 1480+1509 (?) [EM 7897+394] [Rhodes (1981) 607–8]

116. 307/6: *IG* II², 1484+1476 (?)+1489 [EM 7898+lost+7903] [Lewis (1988) 300]

117. 305/4 (?): *IG* II², 1491+1492+1486 (?) [EM 7905+7906+7900] [Lewis (1988) 298]

118. 304/3: *IG* II², 1477+1467 (?)+1485+1473 (?)+1490 [Roman Ag. 1065+EM 2945+7899+7893+7904] [Lewis (1988) 299–300]

119. End of 4th cent.: *IG* II², 1481 [Vienna]

120. End 4th cent.: *IG* II², 1482 [EM 2715]
121. End 4th cent., after 306/5: *IG* II², 1487 [EM 7901+7902] [Lewis (1988) 303 n. 23]
122. End 4th cent.: *IG* II², 1488 [EM 7902A]

# APPENDIX IV

# Primary Sources for the Opisthodomos

IG I³, 52 lines 15–18
IG I³, 52 lines 52–6
IG I³, 207 line 17
IG I³, 369 line 20
IG I³, 378 line 13
IG II², 1388
IG II², 1396
IG II², 1400
IG II², 1401
IG II², 1403
IG II², 1469
IG II², 1471
Aristides i. 548. 14 Dindorf
Ar. *Plut.* 1191–2 and Σ
Dem. 13. 14 and Σ
Dem. 24. 136 and Σ
Harp. s.v. ὀπισθόδομος
Hesych. s.v. ὀπισθόδομος
Lucian, *Timon* 53
Phot. s.v. ὀπισθόδομος
Plut. *Demetr.* 23

# APPENDIX V

# Primary Sources for the Erechtheion

This list includes references to the statue of Athena Polias, the altar, the sea-shrine, Kekrops, the temple of Athena Polias, the old temple, 'the temple in which is the old statue', and the lamp of Kallimachos.

IG I³, 4 lines 9–10
IG I³, 7 line 6
IG I³, 64a lines 20–1
IG I³, 341 lines 1–5
IG I³, 474
IG I³, 475
IG II², 334 lines 9–10
IG II², 687 line 144
IG II², 983 lines 5–6
IG II², 1055

IG II², 1076 lines 21–2, ed. Oliver (1940) 528
IG II², 1357
IG II², 1424 lines 1–30
IG II², 1424a lines 346–73
IG II², 1425 lines 283–335
IG II², 1428 lines 164–96
IG II², 1487 line 31
IG II², 1504 line 6
IG XII. 1. 977 lines 9–11

Aesch. *Eum.* 855
*Anthol. Pal.* 6. 2
Antiph. 6. 39
Apollod. 3. 178, 190–6, 204
Aristid. i. 193. 13 Dindorf
Σ Ar. *Lys.* 273, 759
Σ Ar. *Plut.* 1193
Athenagoras *Leg.* 1; 17
Cic. *Nat. D.* 3. 49
Clem. Alex. *Protr.* 3. 45
Σ Dem. 22. 13
Dem. 36. 15
Dio Cass. 54. 7
Dion. Hal. 14. 2
Harp. s.vv. Βούτης, Ἐτεοβουτάδαι
Hdt. 5. 72, 77, 82, 90; 8. 41, 51–5
Hesych. s.v. Πραξιεργίδαι
Himerios. *Ecl.* 5. 211
Homer *Il.* 2. 546–9

Homer *Od.* 7. 80–1
Isoc. 17. 17
Paus. 1. 26. 4–5; 1. 27; 8. 2. 3; 8.10. 4
Philochoros *FGrH* IIIb 328 F 67
Σ Pindar *Nem.* 10. 64
Plut. *Alc.* 34
Plut. *Cim.* 5
Plut. *Numa* 9. 6
Plut. *Sol.* 12
Plut. *Them.* 10. 6
Plut. *Sympot. quaestt.* 9. 6
[Plut.] *Vit. X. orat.* 843 B–E
Soph. *Aj.* 202
Strabo 9. 1. 16
Tert. *Apol.* 16. 3. 8
Thuc. 1. 126
Xen. *Hell.* 1. 4. 12; 1. 6. 1; 2. 3. 20
Vitr. 4. 8. 4

# APPENDIX VI

# Primary Sources for the Parthenon

This list includes references to the Hekatompedon

*IG* I³, 32
*IG* I³, 436–50
*IG* II², 91–2
*IG* II², 212 line 35 (347/6)
*IG* II², 1688 line 7

Ael. *NA* 6. 49
Anonymus Argentinensis Gr. 84 (Strasburg Papyrus)
Aristid. i. 548. 15 Dindorf
Arist. *Hist. An.* 6. 24
Arr. *Anab.* 1. 16. 7
Dem. 22. 13. 76 and Σ
Dem. 24. 136
Harp. s.v. ἀργυρόπους δίφρος
Heraclid. Pont. 1. 1
Hdt. 8. 53
Hesych. s.v. ἑκατόμπεδος
Himerios, *Orat.* 31. 57, 47. 14
Paus. 1. 1. 2; 1. 24. 5–7; 1. 37. 1; 8. 41. 9
Philoch. Σ Ar. *Pax* 605
Plut. *Cato* 5. 3
Plut. *De glor. Ath.* 5, 7, 8
Plut. *Demetr.* 23
Plut. *De soll. an.* 13
Plut. *Per.* 12–13, 17
Strabo 9. 1. 12
Xen. *Hell.* 1. 6. 1; 2. 3. 20

# APPENDIX VII

# Primary Sources for the Panathenaic Festival

*IG* I³, 82
*IG* I², 395
*IG* II², 344 + *Hesperia,* 28 (1959)
239–47

*IG* II², 657
*IG* II², 1034
*IG* II², 2311–17
*IG* II², 3025–6

Ael. *VH* 6. 1
Σ Ael. Arist. 13. 189. 4–5 (iii. 323
   Dindorf)
Apollod. 3. 14. 6; 3. 15. 7
Aristides, ii. 48. 8–, Dindorf
Aristides, i. 239. 15–20, 308. 5,
   320. 12. Dindorf
Ar. *Av.* 827 and Σ, 1550 ff.
Ar. *Eccl.* 728 ff.
Σ. Ar. *Eq.* 566
Σ. Ar. *Nub.* 971
Ar. *Nub.* 988 and Σ
Σ. Ar. *Pax* 418
Ar. *Ran.* 1089 and Σ
Arist. *Ath. Pol.* 18. 2–5; 43. 1; 49.
   3; 54. 6–7; 57. 1; 60. 1–4; 62. 2
Athen. 167 F, 565 F
Dem. 4. 26, 21. 156, 22. 78
Diod. Sic. 4. 60. 4, 20. 46. 2
Diog. Laert. 1. 57
Dion. Hal. *Ant. Rom.* 7. 72
*Etym. Mag.* 149. 18, 805. 43
Euseb. *Chron. Ol.* 53. 3
Σ Eur. *Hec.* 466–71
Eur. *Her.* 777–80
Harp. s.v. εὐανδρία, λαμπάς,
   Παναθήναια, τοπεῖον
Heliodor. *Aethiop.* 1. 10

Hdt. 5. 56, 82
Himerios, *Orat.* 47. 102
Homer. *Il.* 2. 550–1
Hesych. s.vv. ἐργαστῖναι, ἐν
   Ἐχελιδῶν
Isoc. 4. 159
Lycurg. *In Leoc.* 102
Lys. 21. 1–4
Marcellinus, *Vit. Thuc.* 3
Men. *Georgos* fr. 494 (*CAF* iii. 142)
Paus. 1. 23. 4, 1. 26. 5, 1. 29. 1, 1.
   30. 2, 8. 2. 1
Philostr. *VA* 8. 16
Philostr. *VS* 2. 550
Phot. 129. 18
Pl. *Euthyphro* 6 c
Pl. *Parm.* 127 A and Σ
Σ Pl. *Phdr.* 231 E
Plaut. *Merc.* 64 ff
Plut. *Alc.* 13
Plut. *Demetr.* 10. 12
Plut. *De glor. Ath.* 5
Plut. *Per.* 13
Plut. *Sol.* 1–4
Plut. *Them.* 5
Plut. *Thes.* 24
[Plut.] *Vit. X orat.* (Lycurgus)
Poll. 3. 55, 6. 163

Steph. Byz. s.v. Ἐχελίδαι

Thuc. 1. 20; 2, 13; 5. 47; 6. 56–8

Xen. *Mem.* 3. 3. 12

[Xen.] *Rep. Ath.* 3. 4

# References to the Chryselephantine Statue in the Inventories

1. *Base of statue*: **V.13, 80, 156**

2. *Nike in statue's hand*: **V.89, 94–5, 96, 239**

### TESTIMONIA FOR THE CHRYSELEPHANTINE STATUE BY PHIDIAS IN THE PARTHENON

IG I³, 453–60
Ar. *Pax* 605–18 and Σ
[Arist.] *De mundo* 399ᵇ
L. Ampelius, *Liber memorialis* 8. 10
Athen. 405
Cic. *Orat.* 73. 257
Cic. *Tusc.* 1. 15. 34
Dio Chrys. *Olympian Discourse* 6
Diod. Sic. 12. 38–40
Himerius, *Orat.* 41. 19, 47. 128
Isoc. 18. 57
Lucian, *Gallus* 24
Marinus, *Vita Procli* 30
Paus. 1. 24. 5–7, 5. 11. 10, 10. 34. 8

Philo, *De ebrietate* 89
Philochoros, *FGrH* IIIв 328 F 121
 Jacoby
[Pl.] *Hippias major* 290в
Pliny *NH* 34. 34, 36. 18–19
Plut. *De Isid. et Osir.* 71, 75
Plut. *De vitando aere alieno* 2
Plut. *Per.* 13. 31
Pollux 7. 92
Σ Dom. 22, 13. 76
Strabo 9. 1. 12
Thuc. 2. 13. 5
Val. Max. *Memorabilia* 8. 14. 6
Zosimus 4. 18

Pliny and Pausanias are the two most thorough sources for the description of the statue. From Pausanias (1. 24. 5–7) we learn that it had a sphinx and two griffins on the helmet; that Athena was upright (not seated), wearing a robe that reached down to her feet; that she had a Medusa on her breast (i.e. on the aegis); that she held a Nike in one hand (see the second list at the start of the appendix) and in the other a spear; and that near the spear was a serpent. On the base was a relief depicting the birth of Pandora; for parts which had fallen off see **V.13, 80, 96**.

Pliny (*NH* 36. 18) provides the following testimony. The size of the statue was 26 cubits; it was made of gold and ivory; on the shield was a relief depicting the Amazonomachy on the convex surface (cf. Plut. *Per.*

31, which adds that on the shield Phidias put his self-portrait as an old man and a likeness of Perikles) and the battle of the gods and giants on the concave surface; on the sole of the goddess's shoes were depicted the Lapiths and Centaurs; on the relief of the base was the birth of Pandora with twenty gods present; the goddess held a Nike in her hand; there was a serpent; and under the point of the spear itself sat the high sphinx, indicating that the spear must have rested against the helmet.

SELECT BIBLIOGRAPHY

*LIMC* ii, s.v. Athena.

BROMMER, F. (1957), *Athena Parthenos* (Bremen).

CARPENTER, R. (1953–4), 'The Nike of Athena Parthenos', *Eph.*, (B'), 41–55.

DINSMOOR, W. B. (1934), 'The Repair of the Athena Parthenos: A Story of Five Dowels', *AJA* 38: 93–106.

—— (1937), 'The Final Account of the Athena Parthenos', *Eph.*: 507–11.

DONNAY, G. (1967), 'Les comptes de l'Athéna chryséléphantine du Parthénon', *BCH* 91: 50–86.

—— 'L'Athéna chryséléphantine dans les inventaires du Parthénon', *BCH* 92: 21–8.

——(1968*b*), 'La date du procès de Phidias', *L'Antiquité classique*, 37: 19–36.

EDDY, S. (1977), 'The Gold in the Athena Parthenos', *AJA* 81: 107–11.

GERKAN, A. VON (1955–6), 'Das Gold der Parthenon', *Wissenschaftliche Zeitschrift der Ernst Moritz Arndt-Universität Greifswald*, 5: 55–8.

HARRISON, E. B. (1966), 'The Composition of the Amazonomachy on the Shield of Athena Parthenos', *Hesperia*, 35: 107–33.

HERINGTON, C. J. (1955), *Athena Parthenos and Athena Polias* (Manchester).

HOOKER, G. T. W. (ed.) (1963), *Parthenos and Parthenon* (suppl. to *Greece and Rome*, 10).

LEIPEN, N. (1971), *Athena Parthenos: A Reconstruction* (Toronto).

MANSFIELD, J. (1985), 'The Robe of Athena and the Panathenaic "Peplos"' (Ph.D. diss, University of California at Berkeley).

MORGAN, C. H. (1952), 'Pheidias and Olympia', *Hesperia*, 21: 295–339.

PINNEY, G. (1988), 'Pallas and Panathenaea', in J. Christiansen and T. Melander (eds.), *Ancient Greek and Related Pottery* (Copenhagen), 467–77.

RIDGEWAY, B. S. (1992), 'Images of Athena on the Akropolis', in J. Niels (ed.), *Goddess and Polis* (Princeton), 119–42, 210–15.

SALIS, A. VON (1940), 'Die Giganten als Schilde der Athena Parthenos', *JDAI* 55: 90–169.

SCHLORB, B. (1963), 'Beiträge zur Schildamazonomachie der Athena Parthenos', *AM* 78: 156–72.

SCHUCHHARDT, W. (1963), 'Athena Parthenos', *Antike Plastik*, 2: 31–53.

STEVENS, G. P. (1955), 'Remarks on the Colossal Chryselephantine Statue of Athena in the Parthenon', *Hesperia*, 24: 240–76.

—— (1957), 'How the Parthenos was Made', *Hesperia*, 26: 350–61.

—— (1961), 'Concerning the Parthenos', *Hesperia*, 30: 1–7.

STROKA, V. M. (1967), *Piräusreliefs und Parthenosschild: Versuch einer Wiederherstellung der Amazonomachie des Phidias* (Bochum).

# The Door and Keys to the Temples on the Akropolis

The inventories provide the most detailed information we possess on the appearance of the doors of the Hekatompedos Neos (Parthenon): see **II.60=V.203** and **V.202**. There is also one mention of the 'doors of the Opisthodomos': **II.59**. Keys are mentioned in the inventories as well, and most were kept in the Chalkotheke:

1.      The key of the Hekatompedon
        κλεὶς τοῦ ἑκατομπέδου
            *IG* II², 1424a lines 386–7
                1425 line 389

2.      7 Lakonian keys
        κλεῖδες ΓΙΙ Λακωνικαί
            *IG* II², 1424a line 391

3.      A forged key
        κλεὶς ἀνάπαιστος
            *IG* II², 1424a line 393
                1425 line 399

4.      Another [key], broken
        ἑτέρα κατεαγῦα
            *IG* II², 1424a line 394
                1425 line 400

5.      Another [key], of the Stoa
        ἑτέρα τῆς στοᾶς
            *IG* II², 1424a line 394
                1425 line 400

6.      Another key ---
        κλεὶς ἑτέρα πα[---

*IG* II², 1414 line 47

7.     A forged [key] of the Chalkotheke

κλεὶς ἀνά]παιστος χαλκοθήκ[ης

*IG* II², 1472 line 35

# APPENDIX X

# *Broken or Damaged Items in the Hekatompedon and Opisthodomos*

| Type of Object | Hekatompedon | Opisthodomos |
|---|---|---|
| Doors | V.203 | II.60 |
| Gold [objects] | V.171c | |
| Silver-plated incense-burner | V.222 | |
| Lyre | V.194 | |
| Onyx | V.144 | |
| *Pentorobos* | | II.64 |
| Gold phialai | V.310, 324 | |
| Silver platter | V.355 | |
| Stool | V.116 | |
| Thrones | V.123, 124a, 124b | |
| Silver washbasin | V.231 | II.100 |
| Silver wine-jug | | II.81 |
| Gold wine-jug | V.292 | |
| Writing stick | V.167 | |

# APPENDIX XI

# The Standard Weight used in Making Gold and Silver Vases

In 1968 David Lewis presented evidence gleaned from the inventory lists (Lewis 1968b). A number of gold wreaths were purchased with silver, and these ratios may be used to determine the relative values of gold and silver over a century. Lewis tabulated a selection of the evidence, listing the date of dedication, the reference in *IG* or *SEG,* the gold weight of the wreath, its assumed cost in silver, and the resulting ratio. I present here a modified table, reflecting the new reference-numbers in *IG* I³, and including a concordance of these important dedications with their catalogue numbers in this book. The scatter chart presents another view of these data, plotting the date of the dedication with the ratio of gold to silver which the dedication indicates. Note the dip in the ratio at the end of the Peloponnesian war, and the subsequent recovery.

*Table for the ratio of the cost of gold in silver, modified from Lewis (1968b)*

| Date | Cat. Nr. | Reference (*IG*#) | Gold Weight in dr. | Assumed Cost | gold–silver ratio |
|------|----------|-------------------|--------------------|--------------|-------------------|
| 434/3 | V.96 | I³, 323 lines 50–2 | 60 | 1000 | 16.66 |
| 434/3 | V.335 | I³, 317 lines 7–8 | 1200 | 3 T. | 15 |
| 432/1 | V.375 | I³, 319 line 20 | 80 | 1200 | 15 |
| 429/8 | III.41 | I³, 297 lines 22–3 | 33½ | 500 | 14.92 |
| 428/7 | V.96 | I³, 323 lines 50–2 | 70 | 1000 | 16.66 |
| 427/2 | V.361 | I³, 325 line 9 | 62 | 1000 | 15 |
| 427/2 | V.374 | I³, 325 lines 9–10 | 33⅓ | 500 | 15.87 |
| 427/2 | V.377 | I³, 325 line 10 | 135½ | 2000 | 14.53 |
| 427/2 | IV.61 | I³, 351 line 22 | 33 | 500 | 15.15 |
| 427/2 | IV.62 | I³, 351 lines 22–3 | 33 | 500 | 15.15 |
| 422/1 | V.362 | I³, 325 line 11 | 135½ | 2000 | 13.51 |
| 420/19 | V.363 | I³, 328 line 48 | 326½ | 375 | 14.15 |
| 418/7 | V.366 | I³, 329 lines 13–14 | 1250 | 3 T. | 14.40 |
| 418/7 | V.365 | I³, 329 lines 14–15 | 35 | 500 | 14.28 |
| 417/6 | V.376 | I³, 330 lines 29–30 | 53 | 750 | 14.15 |
| 415/4 | | *SEG* X 199 line 181 | 72? | 1000 | 13.88? |
| 414/3 | V.333 | *SEG* X 199 line 182 | 72 | 10,000? | 13.12 |

| | | | | | |
|---|---|---|---|---|---|
| 402/1 | V.474 | II², 1388 lines 29-30 | 272 dr. 3½ ob. | 3000 | 11.01 |
| 402/1 | V.416 | II², 1388 lines 36-7 | 85 | 1000 | 11.76 |
| 398/7 | V.475 | II², 1388 line 67 | 245 dr. 1½ ob. | 3000 | 11.01 |
| 378/7 | V.419 | II², 1425 line 31 | 193⅔ | 2500? | 12.91? |
| 374/3 | V.477 | II², 1425 line 66 | 182⅓ | 2500? | 13.71? |
| 370/69 | V.418 | II², 1425 line 122 | 200 | 2500? | 12.50? |
| 370/69 | V.461 | II², 1425 line 127 | 37 dr. 2½ ob. | 500 | 13.36 |
| 369/8 | V.462 | II², 1425 line 130 | 36⅙? | 500 | 13.82 |
| 368/7 | V.434 | II², 1425 line 226 | 38 dr. 3½ ob. | 500 | 12.96 |
| 367/6 | V.393 | II², 1436 line 17 | 38 | 500 | 13.16 |
| 366/5 | V.394 | II², 1436 line 18 | 38 dr. 5½ ob. | 500 | 12.87 |
| 365/4 | V.395 | II², 1436 line 19 | 38 dr. 5 ob. | 500 | 12.87 |
| 364/3 | V.396 | II², 1436 line 20 | 39½ | 500 | 12.66 |
| 363/2 | V.398 | II², 1436 lines 21-2 | 250 | 3000 | 12.00 |
| 363/2 | V.397 | II², 1436 line 23 | 39½ | 500 | 12.66 |
| 362/1 | V.399 | II², 1436 line 24 | 39½ | 500 | 12.66 |
| 361/0 | V.400 | II², 1436 lines 25-6 | 250 | 3000 | 12.00 |
| 361/0 | V.401 | II², 1436 lines 10-11 | 40 | 500 | 12.50 |
| 360/59 | V.402 | II², 1436 line 27 | 40 dr. ¾ ob. | 500 | 12.46 |
| 359/8 | V.403 | II², 1436 line 28 | 40½ | 500 | 12.45 |
| 358/7 | V.404 | II², 1436 line 29 | 40½ | 500 | 12.35 |
| 357/6 | V.405 | II², 1436 line 30 | 41½ | 500 | 12.05 |
| 357/6 | V.406 | II², 1436 lines 31-2 | 243 | 3000 | 12.35 |
| 356/5 | V.407 | II², 1436 line 33 | 41½ | 500 | 12.05 |
| 355/4 | V.408 | II², 1436 line 34 | 41⅙ | 500 | 12.15 |
| 348/7 | V.464 | II², 1441 lines 10-11 | 140+ | 1500? | *c.*10.00? |

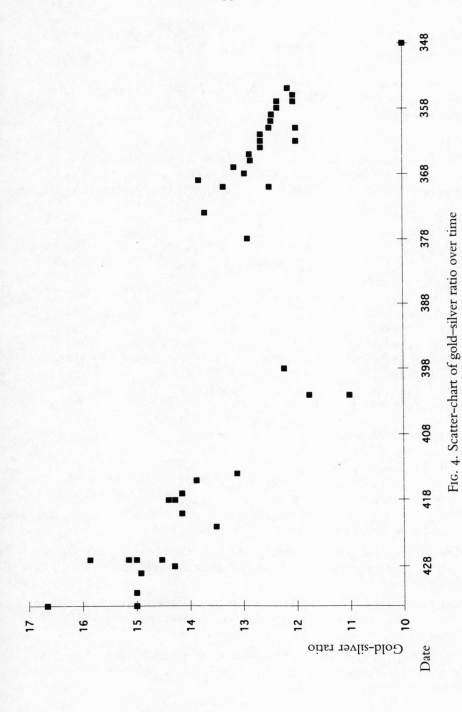

Fɪɢ. 4. Scatter-chart of gold–silver ratio over time

# The Golden Nikai Revisited

The following list includes all epigraphical references to the golden Nikai kept on the Akropolis as a form of gold bullion reserves. An asterisk (★) indicates a reference to supports for the statues in the Chalkotheke.

IG I³, 468
IG I³, 469
IG I³, 52 B
IG II², 1370+1371+1384, add. p. 797 lines 13–20
IG II², 1388 lines 16–24
IG II², 1393 (+1404+1448+1449) lines 6–11
IG II², 1400 lines 8–12
IG II², 1407 lines 8–11
IG II², 1409 line 19
IG II², 1421 lines 59–61+1423 lines 1–8+1424 lines 31–4+1689 line 6
IG II², 1424a, add. pp. 800–5 lines 5–21, 50–62, 106–11, 378★
IG II², 1425 lines 14–16, 45–62, 101–6, 382★
IG II², 1428 (add. pp. 806–8) lines 11–41, 125–7
IG II², 1431 lines 1–4
IG II², 1440 B, lines 40–5
IG II², 1493 lines 7–9
IG II², 1494 lines 4–5
IG II², 1502 lines 1–9
Hesperia, 9 (1940) 109–22 nos. 27–8

In addition, the following literary references are helpful.

Arist. Ath. Pol. 49. 3: καὶ τῆς ποιήσεως τῶν Νικῶν καὶ τῶν ἄθλων τῶν εἰς τὰ Παναθήναια (ἡ βουλή) συνεπιμελεῖται μετὰ τοῦ ταμίου τῶν στρατιωτικῶν.

The boulē, along with the Treasurer of the Stratiotic Funds, is also in charge of the production of the figures of Nike and the prizes at the Panathenaic festival.

Ath. Pol. 47. 1: (οἱ ταμίαι τῆς Ἀθηνᾶς) παραλαμβάνουσι δὲ τό τε ἄγαλμα τῆς Ἀθηνᾶς καὶ τὰς Νίκας καὶ τὸν ἄλλον κόσμον καὶ τὰ χρήματα ἐναντίον τῆς Βουλῆς.

Before the *boulē*, the Treasurers of Athena receive charge of the statue of Athena, the figures of Nike, the other adornments, and the money.

Dem. 24. 121: οἶμαι δέ, νὴ τὸν Δία τὸν Ὀλύμπιον, ὦ ἄνδρες δικασταί, οὐκ ἀπὸ ταὐτομάτου τὴν ὕβριν καὶ τὴν ὑπερηφανίαν ἐπελθεῖν Ἀνδροτίωνι, ἀλλ᾽ ὑπὸ τῆς θεοῦ ἐπιπεμφθεῖσαν, ἵν᾽, ὥσπερ οἱ τὰ ἀκρωτήρια τῆς Νίκης περικόψαντες ἀπώλοντ᾽ αὐτοὶ ὑφ᾽ αὑτῶν, οὕτω καὶ οὗτοι αὐτοὶ αὑτοῖς δικαζόμενοι ἀπόλοιντο, καὶ τὰ χρήματα καταθεῖεν δεκαπλάσια κατὰ τοὺς νόμους ἢ δεθεῖεν.

By Olympian Zeus, gentlemen of the jury, I believe that an outrageous arrogance came upon Androtion not by accident, but was inflicted upon him by the goddess, in order that, just as the mutilators of the figures of Nike perished by their own doing, thus should these men be ruined by litigating among themselves, and should either pay the tenfold penalty according to the laws, or be imprisoned.

Demetrios, *De Elocutione*, 281: Τάχα δὲ καὶ ὁ εὐφημισμὸς καλούμενος μετέξοι τῆς δεινότητος, καὶ ὁ τὰ δύσφημα εὔφημα ποιῶν, καὶ τὰ ἀσεβήματα εὐσεβήματα, οἷον ὡς ὁ τὰς Νίκας χρυσᾶς χωνεύειν κελεύων καὶ καταχρῆσθαι τοῖς χρήμασιν εἰς τὸν πόλεμον οὐχ οὕτως εἶπεν προχείρως, ὅτι κατακόψωμεν τὰς Νίκας εἰς τὸν πόλεμον· δύσφημον γὰρ ἂν οὕτως καὶ λοιδοροῦντι ἐοικὸς ἦν τὰς θεάς, ἀλλ᾽ εὐφημότερον, ὅτι συγχρησόμεθα ταῖς Νίκαις εἰς τὸν πόλεμον· οὐ γὰρ κατακόπτοντι τὰς Νίκας ἔοικεν οὕτως ῥηθέν, ἀλλὰ συμμάχους μεταποιοῦντι.

A so-called 'euphemism' may also contain a certain degree of shrewdness, and one observing this device makes the inauspicious auspicious, and the impious pious. For example, a speaker proposing to melt down the golden figures of Nike and to use the funds for the war, did not say out-right, 'Let us cut up the figures for the war', for this would have seemed blasphemous and insulting to the goddesses. He instead said more convincingly, 'We shall avail ourselves of the figures' assistance for the war', for spoken in this way, these words seemed not to imply destroying the figures of Nike, but enlisting them as allies.

Paus. 1. 29. 16: Λυκούργῳ δὲ ἐπορίσθη μὲν τάλαντα ἐς τὸ δημόσιον πεντακοσίοις πλείονα καὶ ἑξακισχιλίοις ἢ ὅσα Περικλῆς ὁ Ξανθίππου συνήγαγε, κατεσκεύασε δὲ πομπεῖα τῇ θεῷ καὶ Νίκας χρυσᾶς καὶ παρθένοις κόσμον ἑκατόν . . . ὅσα μὲν οὖν ἀργύρου πεποιημένα ἦν καὶ χρυσοῦ, Λαχάρης καὶ ταῦτα ἐσύλησε τυραννήσας· τὰ δὲ οἰκοδομήματα καῖ ἐς ἡμᾶς ἔτι ἦν.

Lykourgos added to the public treasury 6500 talents more than Xanthippos' son Perikles collected. He provided the processional accoutrements for the goddess, golden figures of Nike, and ornaments for 100 unwed girls . . . Everything made of silver or gold Lachares plundered upon becoming tyrant, but the buildings have survived to our own age.

[Plut.] *Vit. X orat.* 852 B: ἔτι δὲ αἱρεθεὶς ὑπὸ τοῦ δήμου χρήματα πολλὰ (Λυκοῦργος) συνήγαγεν εἰς τὴν ἀκρόπολιν, καὶ παρασκευάσας τῇ θεῷ κόσμον, νίκας τε ὁλοχρύσους πομπεῖά τε χρυσᾶ καὶ ἀργυρᾶ καὶ κόσμον χρυσοῦν εἰς ἑκατὸν κανηφόρους·

Moreover, when elected by the people, Lykourgos brought much money to the Akropolis, and provided adornments for the goddess, solid gold figures of Nike, processional accoutrements of gold and silver, and golden ornaments for 100 basket-carriers.

Ar. *Frogs*, 720: ἔς τε τἀρχαῖον νόμισμα καὶ τὸ καινὸν χρυσίον.

as is the case with the coinage of old and the new gold.

Philochoros and Hellanikos (*FGrH* 328F 141, 323a F 26) in a scholion on this verse: τῷ προτέρῳ ἔτει ἐπὶ Ἀντιγένους Ἑλλάνικός φησι χρυσοῦν νόμισμα κοπῆναι. καὶ Φιλόχορος ὁμοίως τὸ ἐκ τῶν χρυσῶν Νικῶν.

Hellanikos says that in the previous year, in Antigenes' archonship [407/6], gold coins were struck, and Philochoros adds that this was done from the golden figures of Nike.

BIBLIOGRAPHY

CARPENTER, R. (1953–4), 'The Nike of Athena Parthenos', *Eph.* B' 41–55.
FERGUSON, W. S. (1932), *The Treasurers of Athena* (Cambridge, Mass.), esp. 85–95, 122–3 n. 2.
FOUCART, P. (1888), 'Les victoires en or de l'acropole', *BCH* 12: 283–93.
KRENTZ, P. (1979), '*SEG* XXI, 80 and the Rule of the Thirty', *Hesperia*, 48: 54–63.
MARK, I. S. (1979), 'Nike and the Cult of Athena Nike on the Athenian Acropolis' Ph.D. thesis; (New York Institute of Fine Arts).
SCHWEIGERT, E. (1940), 'Greek Inscriptions: The Accounts of the Golden Nikai', *Hesperia*, 9: 309–57.
THOMPSON, D. B. (1944), 'The Golden Nikai Reconsidered', *Hesperia*, 13: 173–209.
THOMPSON, H. A. (1940), 'A Golden Nike from the Athenian Agora', in *Athenian Studies Presented to W. S. Ferguson (HSCP* suppl. 1), 183–210.
THOMPSON, W. E. (1964), 'Gold and Silver Ratios at Athens during the Fifth Century', *NC* 4: 103–23.
—— (1965), 'The Date of the Athenian Gold Coinage', *AJP* 86: 165–74, 170–3.
—— (1970), 'The Golden Nikai and the Coinage of Athens', *NC* 10: 1–6.

WOODWARD, A. M. (1937), 'The Golden Nikai of Athena', *Eph.* A' 159–70.

——(1940), 'Two Attic Treasure Records', in *Athenian Studies Presented to W. S. Ferguson* (*HSCP* suppl. 1), 377–407.

# Persian Objects in the Inventory Lists

The idea of Persian objects among the treasures of Athena kept in the Parthenon has long been fascinating to epigraphers and archaeologists alike, yet has only rarely been explored.[1] However, Vickers has recently used the inventories of the treasures kept in the Parthenon in the fifth and fourth centuries in a novel approach to the 'Persian Question'. He uses this evidence to argue that many of the silver and gold vases dedicated to Athena in the Parthenon were manufactured on a Persian or Thraco-Macedonian weight standard.[2]

The argument is that most gold and silver plate was made as a substitute for bullion bars, and as such ought to have round numbers, in denominations of 10 or 100.[3] Any objects kept in the Parthenon which are recorded with uneven weights (e.g. a phiale weighing 194 drachmai), when calculated on Vickers's Persian Daric standard, come out as having even weights (150 sigloi or shekels in this case) and therefore, according to his theory, may have been manufactured on the Persian standard. This hypothesis, while intriguing, is improbable, as the inventory lists themselves indicate.

The underlying assumptions are that gold and silver plate served as bullion and were kept in the temple as a monetary reserve; the weight of these items should be a round number because they were equivalent to gold bars, only in a fancier shape. The dedications in the Parthenon did indeed serve as bullion and were kept as a monetary reserve (cf. Thuc. 2. 13. 4); however, this does not mean that they had to weigh an even amount. Many of the vases were apparently made with a certain even weight in mind, but did not achieve it exactly. For example, in *IG* II², 1424a lines 192–219 (**V.260**), 27 silver hydriai made their way into the Parthenón in 402 and 401 BC. All 27 were intended to weigh about 1000 drachmai, but only one achieved this exact weight. Instead, the hydriai range between 982 dr. and 1009 dr. 4 ob. The actual weight of the vase could thus vary by as much as 18 drachmai more or less than the intended number. An uneven weight is no indication that a vase could not have been manufactured on the Athenian standard.

---

[1] D. B. Thompson (1956); M. C. Miller (1986) 74–157; Morris (1992) 267–8.
[2] Vickers (1990).
[3] Vickers (1990) 620.

Furthermore, even when the craftsmen began with a round weight of gold, much could be filed away or otherwise lost during the process of manufacture. One inscription sheds light on this phenomenon:

[The weight] of the gold from the Akropolis we received, minus the gold lost in refining, is 2 talents 1580 dr. 5¾ ob. [The weight] of gold which we purchased: 1 talent 1689 dr. ¼ ob. (*IG* II², 1496 B lines 200–4)

In this case, the Athenians were melting down old offerings to convert to new cult objects during the Lykourgan reforms. The craftsmen neither begin nor end their work with round weights, and much is lost during the process.

A further examination of the treasures in the Parthenon which are known to have been made by Athenian craftsmen provides additional evidence that they did not always make vessels which had even weights. Twelve different Athenian craftsmen, commissioned to manufacture new vases for the Parthenon in the fourth century BC, are mentioned by name in the inventories and accounts of the Treasurers of Athena. Few of the vases created by them have even weights. For example, *IG* II², 1492 lines 22–32 records the silver hydriai made by Nikokrates of the attic deme Kolonos.[4] His first three hydriai weighed 1004 dr. (**V.216**), 1000 dr. (**V.215**), and 1004 dr. 2 ob. (**V.218**) respectively. These seem to be aiming for a weight of 1000. But the next vase he made weighed 1437 dr. (**V.251**). Here is clear evidence for an Athenian creating a vase with an odd weight. It is unlikely that Nikokrates was utilizing a Persian standard during the manufacture of this particular hydria.

In converting 23 'objects whose weights are awkwardly rendered in Attic drachmae' to round Persian weight standards, Vickers assigns the Attic drachma a constant weight of 4.3 g.[5] However, at the same time he uses 17 different values for the *sigloi* in grams. An example of this is his use of the speech of pseudo-Demosthenes *Against Timotheos*.[6] Vickers converts the value of the two phialai mentioned as weighing 237 Attic drachmai into 180 *sigloi*, and the described loan of 1351 dr. 2 ob. into 1025 *sigloi*. However, he uses two different *siglos*/gram values in these conversions, even though the phialai and the loan occur together in a single speech—a manipulation of the data sufficiently excessive to cast doubt on both the premiss and the method. In sum, the intriguing hypothesis that all vessels with odd weights were manufactured on a Persian standard forces one to manipulate and to read too much into the available evidence. It is far simpler to assume that vessels with uneven weights were originally aiming for a round figure on the Athenian standard, but missed the mark.

There are, however, items in the inventory lists which may in fact have

---

[4] On Nikokrates of Kolonos see Harris (1988) 329–37.
[5] Vickers (1990) 620–1, and his first table, 'Silver Vessels and Other Objects in the Parthenon Inventories'.
[6] [Dem.] 39. See Vickers (1990) 620.

been Persian in manufacture. These are the items described with the adjectives Μηδικός or βαρβαρικός. They include the ten Persian shekels which were kept in the Parthenon between 405 and 389 BC (**V.60**) and some gold Darics dedicated to Demeter and Kore (**V.57**). In addition, one phiale made of gold is listed as βαρβαρική (**V.315**), while a flute-case is described as Μηδική (**V.190**). Other than these, the only other possible items are the ἀκινάκαι, a peculiarly Persian type of dagger recorded by its Persian name, of which two are listed in the Parthenon inventories (**IV.2 = V.1, V.2**). Finally, Thucydides states that there were many Persian valuables kept on the Akropolis on the eve of the Persian war (2. 13), as does Pausanias (1. 27. 1), but these appear not to have been recorded.[7]

Overall, foreign items dedicated in the Parthenon were few, but when such an item was given, its foreign origin was the primary feature by which the treasurers distinguished it; the mere fact that it was foreign would be specifically noted in the inventory lists. Items from Illyria, Corinth, Sparta, Phokaia, Cyzikos, Chios, and Miletos were all inventoried by their ethnic adjective, and we can assume that if additional items were of Persian origin or manufacture, they would have been so specified in the inventories.

Even fewer foreigners appear to have dedicated objects in the Parthenon. Of the 77 personal names inscribed on the stelai, only 8 are foreign: Gelon of Pellana, Lysander of Sparta, son of Aristokritos, Phryniskos of Thessaly, Hierokles of Phaselis, Pharnabazos of Persia, Platthis of Aigina, Roxane, wife of King Alexander, and Spartokos of Pontos.[8] The other 70 named dedicants were all local worshippers from the demes of Attica, who gave gifts to Athena ranging from personal trinkets to gold and silver vases, wreaths, musical instruments, weapons, utensils, and furniture.

In sum, very few of the objects in the Parthenon can be positively identified as Persian in manufacture. They are rather mainly of local character, dedicated by Athenians and by citizens from Attic demes. As such, the inventories challenge the interpretation of the Akropolis as a Panhellenic or international sanctuary. Contrary to what might be expected, the lists suggest that the sanctuary of Athena acted principally as a local shrine sacred to the patron deity Athena and filled with treasures made locally and dedicated by local worshippers.

---

[7] Cf. Morris (1992) 264–8.

[8] Gelon V.426; Hierokles V.427; Lysander V.428; Pharnabazos V.51; Phryniskos V.155, VI.46; Platthis V.152; Roxane V.358; Spartokos V.383.

# Glossary

Ἀθηνᾶ Ἀρχηγέτις epithet of Athena as founder and leader of the city of Athens.

Ἀθηνᾶ Ἐργάνη epithet of Athena as protector of the work force.

Ἀθηνᾶ Νίκη epithet of Athena as the victorious one. See also Νίκη.

Ἀθηνᾶ Πολιάς epithet of Athena as guardian of the city of Athens.

ἀθλοθέται, οἱ a board of commissioners in charge of awarding the prizes for the athletic competitions at the Panathenaic festival.

ἀκινάκης, ὁ a Persian dagger, a short straight sword.

ἀκρωτήριον, τό projecting ornament on the roof of a temple or other classical building; usually made from a terracotta mould in the shape of a palmette.

ἀλαβαστοθήκη, ἡ a case for alabaster ornaments. An alabastron is an unguent flask in a test-tube shape, with a globular end. It cannot stand upright without a stand. This may have been a small box or casket lined with supports to keep the alabastra upright.

ἀνδριάς, ὁ a male statue. As ἀγάλμα is used for a statue of a god, ἀνδριάς signifies that the statue is a representation of a mortal.

ἀνθέμιον, τό honeysuckle decoration or flowery ornament.

ἀντιγραφεύς, ὁ a public secretary or copy-clerk; one who keeps a check on accounts.

ἀποβάτης, ὁ a ceremonial race held in the Agora from the altar of the Twelve Gods to the Eleusinion. The details of the race are debated. The runner, dressed as an armed hoplite, leapt on and off a moving chariot.

ἀπορραντήριον, τό ritual wash basin, a large shallow bowl for sprinkling with sacred water.

ἄρρητα, τά the unspoken objects; the mysterious contents of a basket carried in the Panathenaic procession by the ἀρρηφόροι.

ἀρρηφόροι αἱ selected girls, eight to eleven years old, who lived on the Akropolis in the service of Athena. Their duties included initiating the making of the peplos for the Greater Panathenaia by setting up the loom nine months before the Greater Panathenaia was to begin. They delivered the finished robe to the Archon and the Priestess of Athena to receive and inspect if. The *arrhephoroi* carried the ἄρρητα in the Panathenaic procession.

ἄρχων, ὁ chief magistrate. The nine archons were the highest state officials in Athens, comprised of the eponymous archon, the *archon basileus*, the *polemarchos*, and the six *thesmothetai*.

Ἀρχαῖος νεώς, ὁ  The Old Athena of Athena; the name was transferred to the Erechtheion.

βάθρον, τό  a base, pedestal, bench, seat, or platform.

βουλή, ἡ  The Council of Five Hundred, open after Kleisthenes' reforms to citizens thirty years of age or older selected by lot, 50 representatives for each tribe. The magistrates were responsible directly to the *boulē*, who also supervised the administration of all finances. The *boulē* met daily in the *Bouleutērion* in the *agora*, save holidays.

γοργονεῖον, τό  a mask of a gorgon or Medusa; an apotropaic device.

δῆμος, ὁ  the word refers to the entire Athenian people, the Assembly of the Athenians, or more narrowly may refer only to the poor majority of Athenians.

διαιτητής, ὁ (plur. διαιτηταί, οἱ) an arbiter. The arbiters in Athens were selected from men on the military rosters in their sixtieth year, and worked on behalf of the People's Courts to bring private suits to resolution without a trial. If both parties were satisfied with the arbiter's decision, the case would be closed. If one side wished to appeal to the People's Court, the arbiter sealed the testimonies, challenges, and laws inside a jar, attached to which he wrote his verdict on a tablet. In the new trial no new evidence could be admitted; only the testimony inside the jar was admissible. For sums of less than 1000 drachmae, the case would go before a jury of 201 jurors; for greater sums, before 401 jurors.

δίφρος, ὁ  a folding camp-stool or seat.

διφροφόρος, ὁ  a female metic who carried a camp-stool in the Panathenaic procession.

δοκιμεῖον, τό  testing device for establishing weight and/or shape of a votive.

δραχμή, ἡ  the basic Greek monetary unit, divisible into 6 obols, weighing roughly 4.3 grams of silver.

εἰσφορά, ἡ  occasional tax levied by the assembly on the wealthy citizens and metics, based on a property census, not income. After 347/6 BC it became an annual tax of 10 talents a year. Originally it seems intended to fund military efforts; by extension the word was also used for the levies placed on the allies in the first Athenian confederacy.

Ἑκατόμπεδον, τό; Ἑκατόμπεδος νεώς  the one-hundred foot cella; a name for the Parthenon and its predecessors on the site of the Athenian Akropolis.

ἐκκλησία, ἡ  The assembly of the Athenians in the classical period was open to all citizens over the age of 18, and was considered the sovereign body of the state. Citizens voted by a show of hands, and anyone could speak in a debate or propose an amendment. When it passed resolutions or made decisions it was called ὁ δῆμος (the People) in inscriptions. The *boulē* prepared the agenda and drafted propositions for the assembly, but the assembly had ultimate responsibility for approval and could amend the *boulē*'s decrees.

Ἑλληνοταμίαι, οἱ the board of treasurers appointed for administration of the tribute from the allies of the Delian League after 477 BC.

ἐξετασμός, ὁ a type of inventory, taken to resolve an inquiry when the annual records reveal a discrepancy.

ἐπιμελητής, ὁ (Eng. epimelete) supervisor or manager.

ἐπιστάτης, ὁ overseer, administrator, superintendent.

εὐανδρία, ἡ beauty contest of physical fitness for males at the Panathenaic festival.

εὔθυνα, ἡ the rendering of accounts as part of the annual audit or review after a year's term of office. All public officials had to undergo this examination, which involved bringing the accounts to the *logistai* in front of part of the People's Court, after which any citizen could bring charges over an abuse of office, resulting in a trial.

θυμιατήριον, τό an incense-burner or censer.

ἱεροποιοί, οἱ sacred administrators of sanctuaries and/or temples.

καθαίρεσις, ἡ a type of inventory, taken when a group of precious metal objects are to be melted down and used to manufacture new vessels.

κανηφόροι, αἱ young women who carried baskets in the Panathenaic festival. Lycurgus in the fourth century ordered that the Akropolis be furnished with 'gold and silver processional vessels and ornaments for one hundred κανηφόροι'. The baskets evidently held the smaller vases made of precious metals.

καρχήσιον, τό a type of cup or goblet narrower in the middle than at the lip or foot.

κιθάρα, ἡ a triangular shaped, stringed musical instrument.

κόρη, ἡ (pl. κόραι, αἱ) young women; statues of young women.

κύαθος, ὁ type of cup shape with a tall single handle, used as a cup or ladle.

κύλιξ, ἡ wine-cup, a shallow, wide-bowled vessel with two delicate horizontal handles and low stem.

κωλακρέται, οἱ financial administrators of the state treasury in Archaic Athens, abolished in 411.

λαφυροπώλης, ὁ a trader or seller of war spoils.

λογιστής, ὁ (pl. λογισταί, οἱ) board of ten magistrates, one from each tribe, serving as accountants or auditors who supervised the *euthynai* and inspected the financial accounts (λόγος).

μέτοικος, ὁ (Eng. metic) a resident alien in Athens. Many metics were merchants, intellectuals, or craftsmen, attracted to Athens by its international trade and relative openness to foreigners. To achieve the status of metic, one had to find a patron and with his assistance apply to register as a metic and pay the tax. A metic enjoyed legal protection but no political rights, and had to pay taxes and perform military services when called upon.

ναίσκος, ὁ little shrine, diminutive of ναός.

ναός, ὁ (νεώς in Attic) the dwelling of a god, a temple or shrine, or the main cella of a temple.

ναύκραροι, οἱ early financial administrators of Archaic Athens.

Νίκη, ἡ (pl. Νῖκαι αἱ) statues of Victory, a female personification of one of Athena's epithets, the Victorious one. Athena Nike was honoured on the Akropolis from at least the Geometric period, and had an altar and then a temple at the west end of the Akropolis in the area refered to as the Nike bastion.

νομοθέτης, ὁ (pl. νομοθέται) a committee of ten charged with the revision of the laws.

ξόανον, τό wooden aniconic statue worshipped in the early Archaic period in some Greek sanctuaries. The earliest statue of Athena on the Akropolis was of this form, according to Pausanias fashioned by Daidalos and brought from heaven. This venerated cult statue was later kept in the Old Athena temple and the Erechtheion.

οἴκημα, τό (pl. οἰκήματα, τά) structures on the Akropolis identified as shrines or treasuries, housing votives and articles for use in religious ceremonies or festivals.

οἶκος, ὁ a room or building, the house of a god or temple, the household.

οἰνοχόη, ἡ (pl. οἰνοχοαι, αἱ) wine-jugs, with rounded body and trefoil-shaped lip, for filling up from the κρατήρ to pour into a cup (κύλιξ).

ὀμφαλός, ὁ the knob or boss in the middle of a shield or bowl.

Παλλάδιον, τό a statue or figurine of Pallas Athena.

παράδοσις, ἡ the most common type of inventory, taken annually in order to pass down responsibility from one year's board of treasurers to the next. The paradosis was taken before the *boulē* as part of the annual scrutiny of service, see εὔθυνα.

πεντακοσιομέδιμνοι, οἱ the economic class of men who owned the equivalent of land which produced 26,200 litres (500 medimnoi) annually. Highest financial class of Athenian citizens.

πεντόροβος, ὁ an architectural ornament having five pointed branches or rays.

πέπλος, ὁ robe woven by the ἀρρηφόροι for the Panathenaic festival, presented to the goddess Athena.

περιρραντήριον, τό a lustral basin for sprinkling holy water in religious rites.

πίναξ, ὁ a platter or tablet.

πόλις, ἡ the city-state. Territory included city and countryside, usually less than 100 sq. km.

πομπεῖον, τό (pl. πομπεῖα, τά) ceremonial vessels used in religious processions.

πωληταί, οἱ the board of ten financial administrators in Athens responsible for letting out state contracts.

ῥύμβος, ὁ (=ῥόμβος) a magic wheel or bull-roarer; an instrument whirled around on a string used in the mysteries; also a boy's toy.

ῥυτόν, τό (Eng. rhyton) a drinking-horn, often in the form of an animal's head.

σίγλος, ὁ the Persian shekel was equivalent to roughly 7½ Attic obols.

σκάφη, ἡ a tray on which offerings were carried in the Panathenaic procession.

σκαφηφόρος, ὁ a metic who served as tray-bearer in the Panathenaic procession.

σκάφιον, τό a small tray or shallow bowl.

στέφανος, ὁ wreath, usually awarded to winners at athletic competitions or in reward for doing good service to a city-state.

στεφάνη, ἡ wreath or circlet; occurs in conjunction with στέφανος in the lists of parts of the silver Nikai, but little distinction seems possible to make by context.

στήλη, ἡ base for a statue, tablet for an inscription or grave marker.

συλλογεῖς τοῦ δήμου, οἱ committee of thirty selected from the *boulē*, three from each tribe, responsible for handing out the *symbola* which ensured that only citizens were admitted into the assembly. Control of entry into the Assembly was taken very seriously; impostors would be taken before the People's Court and could be condemned to death.

συνήγορος, ὁ (sing.) (pl συνήγοροι, οἱ) an advocate who speaks on behalf of an individual in court; an elected body of ten who assisted the *logistai* in auditing the accounts of magistrates during the *euthynai* after their year of office.

ταμίας, ὁ (pl. ταμίαι, οἱ) treasurer.

ταμίαι τῶν ἄλλων θεῶν, οἱ the board of treasurers of the Other Gods.

ταμίαι τῶν ἱερῶν χρημάτων τῶν τῆς Ἀθηναίας, οἱ (also called οἱ ταμίαι τῆς θεοῦ) the treasurers of Athena, an annual position open only to the *pentakosiomedimnoi*.

ταμίαι τῶν στρατιωτικῶν, οἱ treasurers of the Stratiotic Fund.

τέμενος, τό a piece of land designated as a sanctuary.

τύπος, ὁ a figurine or statue, usually used to refer to body parts given in the worship of Asklepios.

ὑδρία, ἡ a round-bodied vessel used as a water container, having two horizontal and one vertical handles.

φιάλη, ἡ a small shallow bowl without handles used for making liquid libations.

φόρος, ὁ the tribute or annual payments of the allies in the Athenian confederacy or Delian League.

χερνιβεῖον, τό a basin for water to wash the hands.

χιτών, ὁ a tunic-like garment worn next to the skin.

χιτωνίσκος, ὁ diminutive of χιτών, a shorter garment.

χορηγός, ὁ person discharging the *choregia*, the liturgy or obligation required of the wealthiest citizens of Athens to produce a dramatic or lyric performance at the Dionysia with their own expenses. Perikles served as choregos for Aeschylus' *The Persians* in 472 BC.

χοῦς, ὁ a bulbous oinochoe, a measure of grain or wine equivalent to about 12 κοτύλαι or 3.3 litres. Used in the Athenian festival of the Choes.

ψήφισμα, τό a proposition carried by vote in the Assembly; a decree of the People.

## ENGLISH

*agora* a market place, the business centre of a Greek city; specifically the administrative and commercial centre of ancient Athens, in the low lying area located just north of the Akropolis. The area was used for assembly meetings until the fourth century BC, and also contained meeting rooms, markets, the mint, exchange tables for foreign currencies, the lawcourts, rooms for dining, the state archives, the *bouleuterion*, the *tholos*, and several *stoai*, as well as many shrines to a variety of deities.

*akroterion* ornament on the roof of a temple or other classical building; usually made from a terracotta mould in the shape of a palmette.

*amphora* a two-handled jar used for storing and transporting goods.

*anta* (pl. *antae*) pilasters terminating the end of the lateral walls of a cella, often positioned so that the two wall ends face two columns, in which case it is said to be distyle in *antis*.

*cella* the enclosed chamber of a temple, also called a ναός or νεώς in Greek.

*cyma* (Gk. κῦμα, τό) architectural moulding of double curvature, occurring in the superstructure of classical buildings.

*dactyl* the shortest unit of length, equivalent to approximately a finger's length.

*daric* Persian monetary unit, made of gold, bearing the image of Darius I armed with bow and spear.

*deme* one of the 139 municipalities established in Kleisthenes' reforms, collected into thirty *trittyes*, grouped into the ten *phylai*.

*ephebe* youth in the Athenian military.

*epimelete* supervisor.

*epistyle* the architrave, or the horizontal architectural member above the columns in a Classical building.

*Erechtheion* the temple of Athena, or the Old Temple of Athena.

*harmost* governor of Athens under Sparta's supervision; any governor in the Spartan administrative system.

*Hekatompedon* or *Hekatompedos neos* the one-hundred-foot cella; a name for the Parthenon and its predecessors on the site of the Athenian

Akropolis.

*hexastyle* six columns across the front of a Classical temple.

*metic* see μέτοικος.

*Metroon* shrine of the Mother of the Gods located in the Athenian Agora; served as the primary archive for the Athenian state. The name 'Metroon' is not attested in fifth-century BC documents, but has been attributed to the building which also housed the Old Bouleuterion on the west side of the Agora.

*mina* 100 drachmae.

*obol* the smallest denomination of Athenian coins, six obols are equivalent to one drachma.

*Opisthodomos* the rear chamber of a temple; a building known as a treasury on the Akropolis.

*orthostate* the bottom course of stone blocks for the walls in a cella, usually of greater dimensions than the wall blocks above it.

*Panathenaia* the chief festival of Athena held in the summer month of Hekatombaion, including contests in poetry, music, beauty, and athletics. The ceremonies lasted eight days in the greater Panathenaia held once every four years (in the third year of each Olympiad), with the Lesser Panathenaia as substitute for the other three years, of only two days in length.

*Panathenaic procession* the parade of participants in the festival from the Dipylon gates of Athens to the Akropolis, carrying the treasures and sacred vessels for the ceremonies.

*peristyle* (1) the colonnade which surrounds a building; (2) the inner court of a room lined with a colonnade.

*proneos* (= *pronaos*) the porch in front of the cella in a temple, usually the main entrance into the temple in the East.

*stater* a monetary unit. 2 minas were equal to 1 stater, thiry staters made a talent, weighing roughly 860 grams of silver.

*stylobate* floor of a classical building, the upper step of the platform on which the columns rest.

*Synoikia* festival celebrating the unification of Attica by Theseus for the purpose of sharing the responsibilities of self-government. The phratries served as the basis for organizing the celebration, presided over by Zeus Phratrios and Athena Phratria, the common deities for all phratries.

*talent* a monetary unit equal to 6000 drachmai, or a weight equivelent to roughly 26 kg of silver.

# Bibliography

ALESHIRE, S. B. (1989), *The Athenian Asklepieion* (Amsterdam).

——(1992), 'The Economics of Dedication at the Athenian Asklepieion', in *Economics of Cult in the Ancient Greek World* (Boreas, 21; Uppsala), 85–99.

ALESSANDRI, S. (1982), 'Gli stateri falsi παρὰ Λάκωνος', *Annali della Scuola Normale Superiore di Pisa*[3], 12: 1239–54.

BADIAN, E. (1961), 'Harpalus', *JHS* 81: 16–43.

BANCROFT, S. (1979), 'Problems Concerning the Archaic Acropolis at Athens' (Ph.D. thesis; Princeton).

BANNIER, W. (1911), 'Zu den attischen Übergabeurkunden des 4. Jahrhunderts', *Rheinisches Museum für Philologie*, 66: 38–55.

BARBIERI, G. (1955), *Conone* (Rome).

BATHER, A. G. (1892–3), 'The Bronze Fragments of the Acropolis', *JHS* 13: 124–30.

BENGTSON, H. (1975), *Die Staatsverträge des Altertums*, ii[2] (Munich).

BERVE, H. (1926), *Das Alexanderreich auf prosopographischer Grundlage* (2 vols.; repr. New York, 1973).

BLOCH, H. (1940), 'Studies in Historical Literature of the Fourth Century B.C.', in *Athenian Studies Presented to W. S. Ferguson* (*HSCP* suppl. 1, 303–76.

BOARDMAN, J. (1967), 'Water in the Parthenon?', *Gymnasium*, 74: 508–9.

——(1970), *Greek Gems and Finger Rings* (London).

——(1980), *The Greeks Overseas*[2] (London).

——(1985), *The Parthenon and its Sculptures* (Austin, Tex.).

——(1988) 'Trade in Greek Decorated Pottery', *Oxford Journal of Archaeology*, 7: 27–33.

BÖCKH, A. (1828–77), *Corpus Inscriptionum Graecarum*, 4 vols. (Berlin).

BOEGEHOLD, A. (1972) 'The Establishment of a Central Archive in Athens', *AJA* 76: 23–30.

——(1990), 'Andokides and the Decree of Patrokleides', *Historia*, 39: 149–62.

BOTTERO, J. (1957), *Archives royales de Mari: Textes économiques et administratifs* (Paris).

BOURGUET, E. (1932), *Fouilles de Delphes*, iii/5. *Les Comptes du IVe siècle* (Paris).

BRONNER, O. (1935), 'Excavations on the North Slope of the Acropolis', *Hesperia*, 4: 109–88.

——(1938) 'Excavations on the North Slope of the Acropolis, 1937', *Hesperia*, 7: 161–263.

BRUNO, J. V. (ed.) (1974), *The Parthenon* (New York).

BURFORD, A. (1963), 'The Builders of the Parthenon', in Hooker (1963), 23–35.

——(1972), *Craftsmen in Greek and Roman Society* (London).

BURKE, E. (1985), 'Lycurgan Finances', *GRBS* 26: 251–64.

BURKERT, W. (1985), *Greek Religion* (Oxford).

——(1988), 'The Meaning and Function of the Temple in Classical Greece', in M. V. Fox (ed.) *Temple in Society* (Winona Lake, Ind.), 27–47.

BURSTEIN, S. M. (1978), 'I.G. II² 1485A and Athenian Relations with Lysimachus', *ZPE* 31: 181–5.

CAMP, J. McK. II (1978), 'A Spear-Butt from the Lesbians', *Hesperia,* 47: 192–5.

——(1986), *The Athenian Agora* (London).

CARGILL, J. (1981), *The Second Athenian League: Empire or Free Alliance?* (Berkeley and Los Angeles).

CARPENTER, R. (1953–4), 'The Nike of Athena Parthenos', *Eph.* (B'), 41–55.

CARTLEDGE, P. (1985), 'The Greek Religious Festivals', in Easterling and Muir (1985), 98–127.

CAVAIGNAC, E. (1908), *Études sur l'histoire financière d'Athènes au 5ᵉ siècle: Le Trésor d'Athènes* (Paris).

CAWKWELL, G. L. (1962), 'Notes on the Social War', *Classica et Mediaevalia,* 23: 34–49.

CLAY, D. (1977), 'A Gynasium Inventory from the Athenian Agora', *Hesperia,* 46: 259–67.

CLINTON, K. (1971), 'Inscriptions from Eleusis', *Eph.* 81–136.

——(1974), 'The Sacred Officials of the Eleusinian Mysteries', *Transactions of the American Philosophical Society,* 64/3.

——(1984), 'Eleusinian Treasures in the Late Fifth and Early Fourth Centuries', *Studies Presented to Sterling Dow* (GRB Mon. 10; Durham, NC), 51–60.

COLDSTREAM, J. N. (1977), *Geometric Greece* (New York).

——(1985), 'Greek Temples: Why and Where?', in Easterling and Muir (1985), 67–97.

COLE, S. G. (1988), 'The Uses of Water in Greek Sanctuaries', in Hägg, Marinatos, and Nordquist (1988), 161–5.

CONKEY, J. M., and SPECTOR, J. (1984), 'Archaeology and the Study of Gender', *Advances in Archaeological Method and Theory,* 7: 1–38.

CONNOR, W. R. (1987), 'Tribes, Festivals and Processions: Civic Ceremonial and Political Manipulation in Archaic Greece', *JHS* 107: 40–50.

——(1988), 'Sacred and Secular', *Ancient Society,* 19: 161–88.

CORBETT, P. E. (1970), 'Greek Temples and Greek Worshippers: The

Literary and Archaeological evidence', *BICS* 17: 149–58.

COUCH, H. N. (1929), *The Treasuries of the Greeks and Romans* (Menasha, Wis.).

CROSBY, M., and LANG, M. (1964), *Weights, Measures and Tokens* (The Athenian Agora, 10; Princeton).

DALLEY, S. (1984), *Mari and Karana: Two Old Babylonian Cities* (Harlow).

DAVIES, J. K. (1971), *Athenian Propertied Families, 600–300 B.C.* (Oxford).

DAVISON, J. A. (1955), 'Peisistratus and Homer', *TAPA* 86: 1–21.

——(1958), 'Notes on the Panathenaea', *JHS* 78: 23–42.

DEUBNER, L. (1966), *Attische Feste*[2] (Berlin).

DEVELIN, R. (1984), 'From Panathenaia to Panathenaia', *ZPE* 57: 133–8.

——(1989), *Athenian Officials 684–321 B.C.* (Cambridge).

DINSMOOR, W. B. (1913, 1921), 'Attic Building Accounts I–V', *AJA* 17 (1913), 53–80, 242–65, 371–98; ibid. 25 (1921), 118–29.

——(1931), *The Archons of Athens in the Hellenistic Age* (Cambridge, Mass.).

——(1932), 'The Burning of the Opisthodomus at Athens', *AJA* 36: 143–72, 307–26.

——(1934), 'The Repair of the Athena Parthenos: A Story of Five Dowels', *AJA* 38: 93–106.

——(1947), 'The Hekatompedon on the Athenian Acropolis', *AJA* 51: 109–51.

—— and FERGUSON, W. S. (1933), 'The Last Inventory of the Pronaos of the Parthenon', *AJA* 37: 52–7.

DINSMOOR, W. B. jun. (1973), 'New Parthenon Finds: An Early Destruction of the Building', *AJA* 77: 211.

DITTENBERGER, W. (1915–24), *Sylloge Inscriptionum Graecarum*[3] (4 vols., Leipzig).

DONNAY, G. (1968), 'L'Athéna chryséléphantine dans les inventaires du Parthénon', *BCH* 92: 21–8.

——(1967), 'Les Comptes de l'Athéna chryséléphantine du Parthénon, *BCH* 91: 50–86.

DÖRPFELD, W. (1881), 'Untersuchungen am Parthenon', *AM* 6: 283–302.

——(1886, 1887, 1890, 1897), 'Der alte Athena-Tempel auf der Akropolis, I–IV, *AM* 11 (1886), 337–51; ibid. 12 (1887), 25–61, 190–211; ibid. 15 (1890), 420–39; ibid. 22 (1897), 159–78.

——(1911), 'Zu den Bauwerken Athens', *AM* 36: 39–72.

——(1919), 'Das Hekatompedon in Athen', *JDAI* 34: 1–40.

DOW, S., and GILL, D. H. (1965), 'The Greek Cult Table', *AJA* 69: 103–14.

DYER, L. (1905), 'Olympian Treasuries and Treasuries in General', *JHS* 25: 301–19.

EASTERLING, P. E., and MUIR, J. (eds.) (1985), *Greek Religion and Society* (Cambridge).

EDDY, S. (1977), 'The Gold in the Athena Parthenos', *AJA* 81: 107–11.

EHRENBERG, V. (1969), *The Greek State*[2] (London).

EHRHARDT, C. (1966), 'The Fate of the Treasures of Delphi', *Phoenix* 20: 228–30.

FERGUSON, W. S. (1910), 'Egypt's Loss of Sea Power', *JHS* 30: 189–208.

——(1911), *Hellenistic Athens* (London).

——(1929) 'Lachares and Demetrius Poliorcetes', *Classical Philology*, 24: 1–31.

——(1930–2), 'Athenian War Finance', *Proceedings of the Massachusetts Historical Society*, 64: 347–63.

——(1932), *The Treasurers of Athena* (Cambridge, Mass.).

FORNARA, C. W. (1970), 'The Date of the Callias Decress', *GRBS* 11: 185–96.

FOUCART, P. (1878), 'Comptes des trésoriers des richesses sacrées', *BCH* 2: 37–40.

——(1888), 'Les victoires en or de l'Acropole', *BCH* 12: 283–93.

GAGARIN, M. (1981), *Drakon and Early Athenian Homicide* (New Haven).

GERO, J. M., and CONKEY, M. W. (1991), *Engendering Archaeology: Women and Prehistory* (Oxford).

GILL, D. H. (1974), 'Trapezomata: A Neglected Aspect of Greek Sacrifice', *Harvard Theological Review*, 67: 117–37.

GILL, D. W. J. (1988), 'Expressions of Wealth: Greek Art and Society', *Antiquity*, 62: 735–43.

GIOVANNINI, A. (1975), 'Athenian Currency in the Late Fifth and Early Fourth Century B.C.', *GRBS* 16: 185–195.

——(1990), 'Le Parthénon, le trésor d'Athéna et le tribut des alliés, *Historia*, 39: 129–48.

GOMME, A. W. (1953–4), 'Thucydides ii.13.3.', *Historia*, 2: 1–21.

HABICHT, C. (1979), *Untersuchungen zur politischen Geschichte Athens im 3. Jahrhundert v. Chr.* (Munich).

HÄGG, R., MARINATOS, N., and NORDQUIST, G. C. (eds.) (1988), *Early Greek Cult Practice: Proceedings of the Fifth International Symposium of the Swedish Institute at Athens* (Stockholm).

HAMILTON, R. (1992), *Choes and Anthesteria: Athenian Iconography and Ritual* (Ann Arbor, Mich.).

HANSEN, M. H. (1991), *The Athenian Democracy in the Age of Demosthenes* (Oxford).

HARRIS, D. (1988), 'Nikokrates of Kolonos, Metal-worker to the Parthenon Treasurers', *Hesperia*, 57: 329–37.

——(1990–1), 'Gold and Silver on the Athenian Acropolis: Thucydides 2.13.4 and the Inventory Lists", *Horos*, 8–9: 75–82.

——(1991), 'The Inventory Lists of the Parthenon Treasures' (Ph.D. thesis; Princeton).

——(1992), 'Bronze Statues on the Athenian Acropolis: The Evidence of a Lycurgan Inventory', *AJA* 96: 637–52.

—— (1993), 'Greek Sanctuaries, Forgotten Dedicants: Women, Children, and Foreigners in the Parthenon, Erechtheion, and Asklepieion', *AJA* 97: 337.

HERINGTON, C. J. (1955), *Athena Parthenos and Athena Polias* (Manchester).

—— (1963), 'Athena in Athenian Literature and Cult', in Hooker (1963), 61–75.

HESS, A. (1935), 'Der Opisthodomos als Tresor und die Akropolistopographie', *Klio*, 28: 21–84.

HICKS, E. L. (1874), *The Collection of Ancient Greek Inscriptions in the British Museum*: Attika, i (Oxford).

HIGNETT, C. (1952), *A History of the Athenian Constitution to the End of the Fifth Century B.C.* (Oxford).

HILL, B. H. (1966), 'Notes on Fifth-century Inventories', *Hesperia*, 35: 331–45.

HILL, I. T. (1969), *The Ancient City of Athens: Its Topography and Monuments*2 (Chicago).

HOFFMAN, H. (1961), 'The Persian Origin of Attic Rhyta', *Ant. K.* 4: 21–6.

—— (1967), 'Ein Wasserbecken im Parthenon?', *Gymnasium*, 74: 342–5.

HOLLAND, L. B. (1924*a*, *b*, *c*), 'The Erechtheum Papers, I, II, III', *AJA* 28: 1–23, 142–69, 402–25.

HOMOLLE, T. (1887), *Les Archives de l'intendance sacrée à Délos (315–166 av. J.-C.)* (Paris).

HONDIUS, J. J. (1925), *Novae Inscriptiones Atticae* (Lyons), 47–61.

HOOKER, G. T. W. (ed.) (1963), *Parthenos and Parthenon* (suppl. to Greece and Rome, 10).

IMMERWAHR, H. (1990), *Attic Script: A Survey* (Oxford).

JACOBY, F. (1923–62), *Die Fragmente der griechischen Historiker* (15 vols.; Leiden).

JAEGER, W. (1938), *Demosthenes: The Origin and Growth of his Policy* (Cambridge).

JAHN, O., and MICHAELIS, A. (1901), *Arx Athenarum a Pausania Descripta*2 (Bonn; repr. Chicago, 1976).

JEFFERY, L. H. (1990), *The Local Scripts of Archaic Greece: A Development from the Eighth to the Fifth Centuries*, rev. A. W. Johnsone (Oxford, 1st edn. 1961).

JEPPESON, K. (1979), 'Where was the So-called Erechtheion?', *AJA* 83: 381–94.

—— (1983), 'Further Inquiries on the Location of the Erechtheion and its Relationship to the Temple of the Polias', *AJA* 87: 325–33.

—— (1987), *The Theory of the Alternative Erechtheion* (Århus).

JOHNSON, A. C. (1914*a*), 'An Athenian Treasure List', *AJA* 18: 1–17.

—— (1914*b*), 'Notes on Attic Inscriptions', *Classical Philology*, 9: 417–41.

—— (1915), 'Studies in the Financial Administration of Athens', *AJP* 36: 424–52.

JOHNSON, J. (1935), 'A Revision of *IG* I² 310', *AJA* 35: 31–43.

JOHNSTON, A. W. (1987), '*IG* I², 2311 and the Number of Panathenaic Amphorae', *BSA* 82: 125–9.

JONES, D. M., and WILSON, N. G. (1969), *Scholia Vetera in Aristophanis Equites* (Amsterdam).

JORDAN, B. (1970), 'Herodotos 5. 71. 2 and the Naukraroi of Athens', *CSCA* 3: 153–75.

——(1979), *Servants of the Gods* (Göttingen).

KALLET-MARX, L. (1989*a*), 'The Kallias Decree, Thucydides, and the Outbreak of the Peloponnesian War', *CQ* 39: 94–113.

——(1989*b*), 'Did Tribute Fund the Parthenon?', *CSCA* 8: 252–66.

KIRCHNER, J. (1901–3), *Prosopographia Attica* (2 vols.; Berlin).

——(1935), *Imagines Inscriptionum Atticarum* (Berlin).

——(1940), *Inscriptiones Graecae*² (3 vols.; Berlin).

KLAFFENBACH, G. (1960), 'Bemerkungen zum griechischen Urkundenwesen', *Sitzungsberichte der Akademie der Wissenschaften zu Berlin*.

KNOEPFLER, D. (ed.) (1988), *Comptes et inventaires dans la cité grecque* (Neuchâtel and Geneva).

KORRES, M. (1989), Μελετὴ Ἀποκαταστάσεως Παρθενῶνος, ii (Athens).

——and BOURAS, Ch. (1983), Μελετὴ Ἀποκαταστάσεως Παρθενῶνος i, (Athens).

KOUMANOUDES, S. N., and MILLER, S. G. (1971), '*IG* II² 1477 and 3046 Rediscovered', *Hesperia*, 40: 448–58.

KRENTZ, P. (1979), '*SEG* XXI, 80 and the Rule of the Thirty', *Hesperia*, 48: 54–63.

KROLL, J. H. (1982), 'The Ancient Image of Athena Polias', *Hesperia*, suppl. 20: 65–76.

KYPARISSIS, N. (1927–8), Ἐπιγραφαὶ ἐκ τοῦ Παρθενῶος, *Delt.* 11: 123–34.

——and PEEK, W. (1941), 'Attische Urkunden', *AM* 66: 237.

KYRIELEIS, H. (1988), 'Offerings of the "Common Man" in the Heraion at Samos', in Hägg, Marinatos, and Nordquist (1988), 215–22.

LA FOLLETTE, L. (1986), 'The Chalkotheke on the Athenian Acropolis', *Hesperia*, 55: 75–87.

LALONDE, G. V. (1971), 'The Publication and Transmission of Greek Diplomatic Documents' (Ph.D. thesis; Washington).

LANG, M., and CROSBY, M. (1964), *Weights, Measures and Tokens* (The Athenian Agora, 10; Princeton).

LAZZARINI, M.-L. (1985), 'Una collezione epigrafica di Pesaro', *Rivista di filologia e di istruzione classica*, 113: 34–54.

LEEMANS, W. (1952), *Ishtar of Lagaba and her Dress* (Leiden).

LEHNER, H. (1870), *Über die athenischen Schatzverzeichnisse des vierten Jahrhunderts* (Ph.D. thesis; Strasburg).

LEIPEN, N. (1971), *Athena Parthenos: A Reconstruction* (Toronto).

LEWIS, D. M. (1954), 'Notes on Attic Inscriptions', *BSA* 49: 17–50.

——(1955), 'The Public Seals of Athens', *Phoenix* 9: 32–4.

——(1966), 'After the Profanation of the Mysteries', in E. Badian (ed.), *Ancient Society and Institutions: Presented to Victor Ehrenberg on his 75th Birthday* (Oxford), 177–91.

——(1968*a*), 'Dedications of Phialai at Athens', *Hesperia,* 37: 368–80.

——(1968*b*), 'New Evidence for the Gold–Silver Ratio', in C. M. Kraay and G. K. Jenkins (eds.), *Essays in Greek Coinage Presented to S. Robinson* (Oxford), 105–10.

——(1979–80), 'Athena's Robe', *Scripta Classica Israelica,* 5: 28–9.

——(1980), *Inscriptiones Graecae*[3], i (Berlin).

——(1988), 'The Last Inventories of the Treasurers of Athena', in Knoepfler (1988), 297–308.

——and STROUD, R. S. (1979), 'Athens Honors King Evagoras of Cyprus', *Hesperia,* 48: 180–93, pls. 60–1.

LINDERS, T. (1972), *Studies in the Treasure-Records of Artemis Brauronia found in Athens* (Stockholm).

——(1975), *The Treasurers of the Other Gods in Athens and their Functions* (Meisenheim am Glan).

——(1987), 'Gods, Gifts, Society', in Linders and Nordquist (1987), 115–22.

——(1988), 'The Purpose of Inventories: A Close Reading of the Delian Inventories of the Independence', in *Comptes et inventaires dans la cité grecque* (Neuchâtel), 37–47.

——and NORDQUIST, G. (eds.) (1987), *Gifts to the Gods: Proceedings of the Uppsala Symposium 1985* (Boreas 15; Uppsala).

LUSCHEY, H. (1939), *Die Phiale* (Bleicherode am Harz).

MACURDY, G. (1932*a*), *Hellenistic Queens* (Westport).

——(1932*b*), 'Roxane and Alexander IV in Epirus', *JHS* 52: 256–61.

MALLWITZ, A., and HERRMANN, H.-V. (1980), *Die Funde aus Olympia* (Athens).

MANSFIELD, J. (1985), 'The Robe of Athena and the Panathenaic Peplos' (Ph.D. thesis; Berkeley, Calif.).

MARK, I. S. (1979), 'Nike and the Cult of Athena Nike on the Athenian Acropolis' (Ph.D. thesis; New York Institute of Fine Arts).

MATTINGLY, H. B. (1974), 'Athens and Eleusis: Some New Ideas', in D. W. Bradeen and M. F. McGregor (eds.), Φόρος: *Tribute to Bejamin Dean Meritt* (Locust Valley, NY), 90–103.

MEIGGS, R. (1972), *The Athenian Empire* (Oxford).

——and LEWIS, D. M. (1988), *A Selection of Greek Historical Inscriptions to the End of the Fifth Century B.C.*[2] (Oxford).

MERITT, B. D. (1932), *Athenian Financial Documents of the Fifth Century B.C.* (Ann Arbor).

——(1936), 'Greek Inscriptions', *Hesperia,* 5: 389–90.

——(1942), 'Greek Inscriptions', *Hesperia,* 11: 275–303.

—— (1948), 'Greek Inscriptions', *Hesperia*, 17: 1–54.

—— (1974), 'The Choiseul Marble', in *Mélanges helléniques offerts à Georges Daux* (Paris), 255–67.

MICHAELIS, A. (1871), *Der Parthenon* (Leipzig).

MILCHHÖFER, A. (1891), *Schriftquellen zur Topographie von Athen* (Berlin; repr. Chicago, 1977).

—— (1894), 'Ὀπισθόδομος', *Philologus*, 53: 352–61.

MILLER, M. C. (1985), 'Perserie: The Arts of the East in Fifth-century Athens' (Ph.D. thesis; Harvard).

MILLS, H. (1984), 'Greek Clothing Regulations: Sacred and Profane?', *ZPE* 55: 255–65.

MITCHEL, F. W. (1962), 'Demades of Paeania and *IG* II² 1493, 1494, 1495', *TAPA* 93: 213–29.

—— (1966), '*IG* II² 1493: Corrigenda', *AJA* 70: 66.

—— (1970), *Lykourgan Athens, 338–322 B.C.* (Lectures in Memory of Louise Semple Taft, 2nd ser.).

MOMMSEN, A. (1864), *Heortologie: Antiquarische Untersuchungen über die städtischen Feste der Athener*² (Leipzig; repr. Amsterdam, 1968).

MORRIS, S. P. (1992), *Daidalos and the Origins of Greek Art* (Princeton).

MUHLY, J. D. (1973), *Copper and Tin* (New Haven).

—— (1985), 'Sources of Tin and the Beginnings of Bronze Metallurgy', *AJA* 89: 275–91.

MUIR, J. V. (1985), 'Religion and the New Education: The Challenge of the Sophists', in Easterling and Muir (1985), 191–218.

NEILS, J. (ed.) (1992), *Goddess and Polis: The Panathenaic Festival in Ancient Athens* (Princeton).

NOLAN, B. T. (1981), 'Inscribing Costs at Athens in the Fourth Century B.C.' (Ph.D. thesis; Ohio).

NORMAN, N. J. (1983), 'The Panathenaic Ship', *Archaeological News*, 12: 41–6.

NYLANDER, C. (1968), 'Assyria Grammata: Remarks on the 21st Letter of Themistokles', *Opuscula Atheniensia*, 8: 119–36.

OLIVER, J. H. (1940), 'Julia Domna as Athena Polias', *HSCP* suppl. 1: 521–30.

OPPENHEIM, A. (1949), 'The Golden Garments of the Gods', *Journal of Near Eastern Studies*, 7: 172–193.

ORLANDOS, A. K. (1977), Ἡ Ἀρχιτεκτονικὴ τοῦ Παρθεῶνος, Μέρος Β' (Athens).

OVERBECK, J. (1868), *Die antiken Schriftquellen zur Geschichte der bildenden Künste bei den Griechen* (Leipzig).

PALAGIA, O. (1984), 'A Niche for Kallimachos' Lamp?', *AJA* 88: 515–21.

PARKE, H. W. (1977), *Festivals of the Athenians* (London).

PATON, J. M. (ed.) (1927), *The Erechtheum* (Cambridge, Mass.).

POPE, H. (1935), *Non-Athenians in Attic Inscriptions* (New York).

—— (1947), *Foreigners in Attic Inscriptions* (Philadelphia).

POSNER, E. (1972), *Archives in the Ancient World* (Cambridge, Mass.).

PRITCHETT, W. K. (1971), *Ancient Greek Military Practices*, i (Berkeley, Calif.).

—— and AMYX, D. A. (1953), 'Attic Stelai', *Hesperia*, 22: 225–99.

—— —— (1956), 'Attic Stelai', *Hesperia*, 25: 178–328.

—— —— (1958), 'Attic Stelai', *Hesperia*, 27: 163–253, 255–310.

RANDALL, R. H., jun. (1953), 'The Erechtheum Workmen', *AJA* 57: 199–210.

RANGABÉ, A. R. (1855), *Antiquités helléniques* (Athens).

RANSOM, C. L. (1905), *Couches and Beds of the Greeks, Etruscans and Romans* (Chicago).

RAUBITSCHEK, A. E. with JEFFERY, L. H. (1949), *Dedications from the Athenian Akropolis: A Catalogue of the Inscriptions of the Sixth and Fifth Centuries B.C.* (Princeton).

RHODES, P. J. (1972), *The Athenian Boule* (Oxford).

—— (1981), *A Commentary on the Aristotelian* Athenaion Politeia (Oxford).

RICHTER, G. M. A. (1966), *The Furniture of the Greeks, Etruscans, and Romans* (London).

—— (1987), *A Handbook of Greek Art: A Survey of the Visual Arts of Ancient Greece* (New York).

—— and MILNE, M. J. (1935), *Shapes and Names of Athenian Vases* (New York).

RIDGWAY, B. S. (1977), *The Archaic Style in Greek Sculpture* (Princeton).

—— (1992), 'Images of Athena on the Akropolis', in O. Niels (ed.), *Goddess and Polis* (Princeton), 119–42, 210–15.

ROBERTS, J. (1982), *Accountability in Athenian Government* (Madison, Wis.).

ROBINSON, D. M. (1937), 'A New Fragment of an Attic Treasure-Record', *AJP* 58: 38–44.

ROBINSON, E. S. G. (1960), 'Some Problems in the Later Fifth Century Coinage of Athens', *American Numismatic Society Museum Notes*, 9: 1–15.

ROMANO, I. B. (1988), 'Early Greek Cult Images and Cult Practices', in Hägg, Marinatos, and Nordquist (1988), 127–33.

ROTROFF, S. I. (1977), 'The Parthenon Frieze and the Sacrifice to Athena', *AJA* 81: 379–82.

ROUSE, W. H. D. (1975), *Greek Votive Offerings*[2] (New York).

ROUX, G. (1984), 'Pourquoi le Parthénon?', *Comptes rendus des séances de l'Académie des inscriptions et belles-lettres*, 301–17.

SAMONS II, L. H. (1993), 'Athenian Finance and the Treasury of Athena', *Historia*, 42: 129–38.

SCHAPS, D. (1977), 'The Woman Least Mentioned: Etiquette and Women's Names', *CQ* 71: 323–30.

SCHEIBLER, I. (1983), *Griechische Töpferkunst* (Munich).

SCHROEDER, B. (1912), 'Thrakische Helme', *JDAI* 27: 317–44.

SCHUCHHARDT, W. (1963), 'Athena Parthenos', *Antike Plastik*, 2: 31–53.

SCHWEIGERT, E. (1938), 'Inscriptions from the North Slope of the Acropolis', *Hesperia*, 7: 264–310.

——(1940), 'Greek Inscriptions: The Accounts of the Golden Nikai', *Hesperia*, 9: 309–57.

SCHWENK, C. J. (1985), *Athens in the Age of Alexander: The Dated Laws and Decrees of the Lykourgan Era 338–322 BC* (Chicago).

SEAGER, R. (1967), 'Thrasybulus, Conon, and Athenian Imperialism, 396–386 B.C.', *JHS* 87: 95–115.

SEALEY, R. (1976), *A History of the Greek City-states 700–338 B.C.* (Berkeley, Los Angeles, and London).

SELTMAN, C. (1909), 'A Synopsis of the Coins of Antigonus I and Demetrius Poliorcetes', *NC*[4] 9: 264–73.

SHAPIRO, H. A. (1989), *Art and Cult under the Tyrants in Athens* (Mainz am Rhein).

SHEAR, T. L., jun. (1966), 'Studies in the Early Projects of the Periklean Building Program' (Ph.D. thesis; Princeton).

——(1978), *Kallias of Sphettos and the Revolt of Athens in 286 B.C.* (*Hesperia*, suppl. 17; Princeton).

SIMON, E. (1983), *Festivals of Attica* (Madison, Wis.).

SINCLAIR, R. K. (1988), *Democracy and Participation in Athens* (Cambridge).

SNODGRASS, A. (1967), *Arms and Armour of the Greeks*.

STEVENS, G. P. (1942), 'The Sills of the Grilles of the Pronaos and Opisthodomos of the Parthenon', *Hesperia*, 11: 354–64.

STRAUSS, B. S. (1984), 'Thrasybulus and Conon: A Rivalry in Athens in the 390s B.C.', *AJP* 105: 37–48.

STRONG, D. E. (1966), *Greek and Roman Gold and Silver Plate* (London).

STROUD, R. S. (1968), *Drakon's Law on Homicide* (California Publications in Classical Studies, 3; Berkeley and Los Angeles).

——(1972), 'Inscriptions from the North Slope of the Acropolis, II', *Hesperia*, 41: 422–50.

——(1974), 'An Athenian Law on Silver Coinage', *Hesperia*, 43: 171–4.

——(1982), 'Two False Readings in an Attic Treasury-inventory', *ZPE* 46: 267–70.

THOMAS, R. (1989), *Oral Tradition and Written Record in Classical Athens* (Cambridge).

THOMPSON, D. B. (1944), 'The Gold Nikai Reconsidered', *Hesperia*, 13: 173–209.

——(1956), 'The Persian Spoils at Athens', in S. S. Weinberg (ed.), *The Aegean and the Near East* (Locust Valley, NY., 1956), 281–91.

THOMPSON, H. A. (1940), 'A Golden Nike from the Athenian Agora', in *Athenian Studies Presented to W. S. Ferguson* (*HSCP* suppl. 1), 183–210.

THOMPSON, M., MØRKHOLM, O., and CRAAY, C. M. (1973), *An Inventory of Greek Coin Hoards* (New York).

THOMPSON, W. E. (1963), 'The Athenian Gold and Bronze Coinages of the Dekelian War' (Ph.D. diss., Princeton).

—— (1964*a*), 'Gold and Silver Ratios at Athens during the Fifth Century', *NC*⁶ 4: 103–23.

——(1964*b*), 'A Pronaos Inventory', *Hesperia*, 33: 86–7.

——(1965*a*), 'Prosopographical Notes on Athenian Treasurers', *Hesperia*, 34: 148–56.

——(1965*b*), 'The Early Parthenon Inventories', *AJA* 69: 223–30.

——(1965*c*), 'The Silver Cups in the Parthenon' *AJA* 69: 230–1.

——(1965*d*), 'The Date of the Athenian Gold Coinage', *AJP* 86: 159–74.

——(1965*e*), 'Agora I 1528', *Hesperia*, 34: 310–11.

——(1965*f*), 'The Hekatompedon Inventories 414/3–411/0', *Hesperia*, 34: 298–309.

——(1965*g*), 'A New Fragment of a Treasure Record from the North Slope of the Acropolis', *Hesperia*, 34: 25–8.

——(1965*h*), 'Two New Fragments of *I.G.* I² 233', *Hesperia*, 34: 29–33.

——(1966*a*), 'Conspectus Traditionum', *CQ*, NS 16: 286–90.

——(1966*b*), 'The Functions of Emergency Coinages of the Peloponnesian War', *Mnemosyne*, 19: 337–43.

——(1967), 'Notes on Athenian Finance', *Classica et Mediaevalia*, 28: 216–39.

——(1970*a*), 'The Golden Nikai and the Coinage of Athens', *NC* 10: 1–6.

——(1970*b*), 'The First Stele of the Hekatompedon Inventories', *CQ*, NS 20: 35–7.

——(1970*c*), 'Notes on the Treasurers of Athena', *Hesperia*, 39: 54–63.

——(1980), 'Phialai from Eleusis', *ZPE* 40: 211–12.

THREATTE, L., jun. (1980), *The Grammar of Greek Inscriptions*, i (Berlin and New York).

TOBIN, J. (1993), 'Some New Thoughts on Herodes Atticus's Tomb, his Stadium of 143/4, and Philostratus *VS* 2. 550', *AJA* 97: 81–9.

TOD, M. N. (1911–12), 'The Greek Numeral Notation', *BSA* 18: 98–132.

——(1926–7), 'Further Notes on the Greek Acrophonic Numerals', *BSA* 28: 141–57.

——(1936–7), 'The Greek Acrophonic Numerals', *BSA* 37: 236–58.

——(1938), 'Notes on Attic Inventories: Review of *IG* II²', *JHS* 58: 97–98.

—— (ed.) (1948), *A Selection of Greek Historical Inscriptions*, ii. *From 403 to 323 B.C.* (Oxford).

——(1950*a*), Epigraphical Notes on Freedmen's Occupations', *Epigraphica* 12: 3–26.

——(1950*b*), 'The Alphabetic Numeral System in Attica', *BSA* 45: 126–39.

——(1954), 'Letter-labels in Greek Inscriptions', *BSA* 49: 1–8.

TRAVLOS, J. (1971*a*), *Pictorial Dictionary of Ancient Athens* (London).

—— (1971*b*), 'The Interior Arrangement of the Erechtheion', *Athens Annals of Archaeology*, 4: 77–84.

TRÉHEUX, J. (1955–6), *L'Aménagement intérieur de la Chalkothèque d'Athènes* (Études d'Archéologie Classique, 1; Paris).

—— (1959), 'Études critiques sur les inventaires de l'indépendance délienne' (manuscript, Thèse lettres; Paris).

—— (1965), *Études sur les inventaires attiques* (Études d'Archéologie Classique, 3; Paris).

—— (1985), 'Pourquoi le Parthénon?', *RÉG* 98: 233–42.

VAN STRATEN, F. T. (1981), 'Gifts for the Gods', in H. S. Vetsnel *Faith, Hope and Worship* (Leiden), 65–151, 285–311.

VICKERS, M. (1984), 'Demus's Gold Phiale (Lysias 19. 25)', *AJAH* 9: 48–53.

—— (1989), 'Panagyurishte, Dalboki, Loukovit and Rogozen: Questions of Metrology and Status', in B. F. Cook (ed.), *The Rogozen Treasure*, (London, 1989), 101–11.

—— (1990) 'Golden Greece: Relative Values, Minae and Temple Inventories', *AJA* 94: 613–25.

VON FRITZ, K. (1950), *Aristotle's Constitution of the Athenians and Related Texts* (New York).

WADE-GERY, H. T. (1931), 'The Financial Decrees of Kallias', *JHS* 51: 57–85.

—— (1933), 'Review of W. S. Ferguson: *The Treasurers of Athena*', *JHS* 53: 134–7.

WALBANK, M. B. (1982), 'The Confiscation and Sale by the Poletai in 402/1 B.C. of the Property of the Thirty Tyrants', *Hesperia*, 51: 74–98.

WESENBERG, B. (1985), 'Parthenosgold für den Parthenonbau', *Archäologischer Anzeiger*, 49–53.

WEST, A. B. and WOODWARD, A. M. (1938), 'Studies in Attic Treasure-records, II', *JHS* 58: 69–89.

WHITE, J. W. (1895), 'The Opisthodomus on the Acropolis at Athens', *HSCP* 6: 1–53.

WILCKEN, U. (1932), *Alexander the Great*[2], trans. G. C. Richards (New York).

WILHELM, A. (1941), 'Zur Übergabe der ἱερὰ χρήματα der Athena', *Wiener Jahreshefte*, 33: 29–34.

WOODWARD, A. M. (1908), 'Some Unpublished Attic Inscriptions', *JHS* 28: 296–9.

—— (1909), 'Three New Fragments of Attic Treasure-records', *JHS* 29: 168–91.

—— (1910), 'Notes on Some Greek Inscriptions, Mainly in Athens', *JHS* 30: 260–6.

—— (1911), 'A Note on the First Issue of Gold Coins at Athens', *NC* 11: 351–6.

—— 1928), 'Some More Fragments of Attic Treasure-records of the Fifth Century', JHS 48: 159–77.

——(1931), 'Studies in Attic Treasure-records, I', *JHS* 51; 139–63.

——(1937), 'The Golden Nikai of Athena', *Eph.* A', 159–70.

——(1940), 'Two Attic Treasure Records', in *Athenian Studies Presented to W. S. Ferguson* (*HSCP* suppl. 1), 377–407.

——(1951), Ἀπουσία, *NC* 11: 109–11.

——(1953–4), 'An Attic Treasure-record: The Hekatompedon List for 402/1 BC', *Eph.* 2: 107–12.

——(1956), 'Treasure Records from the Athenian Agora', *Hesperia,* 25: 79–121, pls. 31–3.

——(1963), 'Financial Documents from the Athenian Agora', *Hesperia,* 32: 144–86.

——and LEWIS, D. M. (1975), 'A Transfer From Eleusis', *BSA* 70: 183–9.

WREDE W. (1928), 'Der Maskengott', *AM* 53: 81–92, figs. 1–3.

WYCHERLEY, R. E. (1957), *Literary and Epigraphical Testimonia* (The Athenian Agora, 3; Princeton).

# Index of Objects

## KEPT IN THE OPISTHODOMOS, PARTHENON, AND ERECHTHEION

aegis VI.20
Aigenetan staters V.54
Aithiopian phialai V.337
akroteria V.76–7, V.91, V.93
alabaster V.32–3
anvil II.74, V.34
apple II.36
arrowheads II.75
arrows V.3
aulos-case (συβήνη) II.68–70, IV.41, V.19,
    V.190

bars of silver V.67
base:
    (βάθρος) V.13, V.89, V.156, V.233, VI.10
    (στήλη) IV.20, V.90
basket II.1–4, II.7, II.38, IV.13, V.39, V.40–8,
    V.214
beads II.5, V.128
bellows II.36
belt (ζώνη) IV.38, V.92
blazons (on shields) IV.8, IV.10, V.20–1, V.27
boots (ὀπισθοκρηπῖδες) V.53
bosses (ὀμφαλοί) V.352
bow V.98
box:
    (καλιάς) III.1, VI.36
    (κιβωτίον, κιβωτός) II.7, II.31, II.36–7,
        II.71, II.75, IV.32, V.34, V.48, V.53, V.66,
        V.88, V.164, VI.22
    (κοίτη) II.33, IV.14, V.35, V.36
    oblong (πλαίσιον) VI.45
    painted II.37, V.164
box-wood VI.18
bracelet II.5, V.91–2, V.127–8, V.130
breast-plates IV.6, V.5, V.18
brazier (ἐσχάρα) V.242, VI.30
bricks V.84
bridle V.170
bronze II.38–9, II.76, IV.4–5, IV.12, V.10–12,
    V.14–16, V.18–19, V.24, V.26, V.36, V.39,
    V.46–7, V.86, V.99, V.147, V.169, V.171g,
    V.189, V.198–201, V.222, V.228–9, V.235,
    V.242–3, V.266, V.271–5, V.303, V.313,
    VI.16, VI.22

bronze-plated, brazen IV.7, V.25, V.28
bronze stele V.89
brooch V.91–2

campstool (ὀκλαδία) IV.29, V.119–20
ceramic pot (χύτρα) VI.27
chain:
    (ὁρμίσκος), II.36–7, IV.32, IV.34, V.164; see
        also necklace for ὅρμος
    (ἅλυσις) V.32, V.138
cheek-pieces VI.10
chestband V.91
chiton V.49
    small V.50
choker (χλιδών) II.37, IV.32, V.164
cicada V.84
city (πόλις) V.416
collars, wide (ὅρμοι πλατεῖς) IV.35, V.139
column V.182, VI.18–19
container:
    (ἔλυτρον) V.168
    (θήκη) II.32, II.34–5
    (κυλιχνίς) II.29–30, II.37, II.52–3, IV.32b,
        IV.52, V.37–8, V.147, V.164
Corinthian staters V.55
couch (κλίνη) IV.25–6, IV.28, V.112–15
counterfeit coins II.26, V.58, V.66
cow V.100–1
cup:
    (κότυλος) IV.56
    (κυμβίον) V.285–6
    see also drinking-cup; goblet; wine-cup
cupboard (φάτνη) VI.3, VI.42

dagger V.210
darics V.57
dedication (ἀνάθημα) V.372, V.445, V.455
diadem V.421
dies (for coins) II.74, V.34
door:
    of the Archaios Neos (Erechtheion) VI.44
    of the Hekatompedon II.60, V.202–3
    of the Opisthodomos II.59
door-post (παραστάς) VI.4, VI.7, VI.15, VI.17,
    VI.24, VI.26, VI.43, VI.51

drachma II.17
drapery V.91–2
drinking-cup:
(ἔκπωμα) V.240, V.241,
(ποτήριον) III.33–40, IV.55
drinking-horn (κέρας) III.2, IV.48b, V.240
duck V.226

earrings II.36, II.43, II.47–8, IV.36–7, V.91–2,
V.129, V.131–3, V.156, VI.20
equestrian head-gear II.31

feet V.91–2
figurine II.40, V.100–1, V.110–11, VI.17
first-fruit offering V.73
floor VI.54
flower (ἀνθέμιον) V.99
flowery wreath (ὅρμος ἀνθέμων) IV.22, V.103
foil V.202

garment (στολίς) V.91
gilt wood II.1–2, II.36, II.39, II.43, II.61, III.1,
IV.9, IV.11, IV.13–14, IV.54, V.21, V.27,
V.35, V.39–41, V.45, V.107, V.134,
V.171d, V.189, V.265, VI.33
glass II.36–7, IV.32, V.164, V.250, V.281
goat-stag V.145
goblet (καρχήσιον) III.1, IV.51, IV.53,
V.278–80, V.338
gold II.6–7, II.15–16, II.19, II.22–3, II.36–7,
II.47, II.52, II.55, II.72, II.82, II.99, III.6,
III.41, IV.15–19, IV.32, IV.34, IV.37,
IV.39, IV.40, IV.50, IV.53, IV.57–62, V.2,
V.13, V.34, V.48, V.54–5, V.57, V.59,
V.63, V.65, V.71–3, V.75, V.77, V.81–4,
V.87–9, V.92–7, V.105, V.129–33,
V.136–8, V.146, V.148–9, V.151–7, V.160,
V.163–6, V.171–3, V.188, V.202, V.211,
V.219–20, V.234, V.237–8, V.244–9,
V.261, V.277–8, V.284–6, V.289–93,
V.304, V.309–10, V.319–20, V.323–7,
V.329–30, V.333–6, V.339, V.342,
V.344–51, V.358, V.360–77, V.385, V.388,
V.394–5, V.397–8, V.400–1, V.403,
V.409–10, V.413–20, V.423–4, V.428,
V.432–3, V.435, V.440–1, V.449, V.455,
V.459, V.465, V.473–5, V.477, VI.4–5,
VI.7, VI.18, VI.20, VI.23, VI.26–9, VI.54,
VI.56–66
gold over bronze II.3–4, II.8–10, V.42–3,
V.171g, V.198–9, V.235, V.266, V.268–9,
V.271–2
gold overlay or gilt II.21, II.24, II.48, II.67–8,
II.76–7, IV.1–2, IV.20–4, IV.33, IV.41–2,
IV.47, V.1, V.12, V.22–3, V.30, V.69,
V.74, V.91, V.97–9, V.102–4, V.109,
V.135, V.150, V.170–1, V.182, V.186–7,
V.191–3, V.201, V.236, V.308, VI.6, VI.11,
VI.43

gold pieces (phialai?) (χρυσίδες) V.105
gold plate II.27, IV.3, IV.12b, V.29, V.76, V.78,
V.171k
gorgoneion IV.21, V.21–2, V.30–1, V.102,
V.317, VI.20
greaves V.6–7, V.18
griffin IV.22, IV.33, V.103, V.165

half-drachma II.18
half-obol V.54, V.65
hammer II.74
hand II.41, V.91–2, V.94–5, V.239, VI.20,
VI.22
head V.91–2, V.94
headband (χλιδώνιον) II.54–5
helmet:
(κράνος) IV.4–5, V.8–10, V.14–15; small
(κρανίδιον) V.13, VI.1, VI.9–10
(κυνῆ) IV.3, V.11–12, V.16, VI.11
horse IV.22, IV.52, V.103
hydria V.215, V.217–18, V.244–61

incense-burner (θυμιατήριον) II.9–12, IV.54,
V.88, V.222, V.226, V.232, V.262–77,
VI.54
cover for II.12, V.270
iron II.36, II.74, V.2, V.174, V.205, V.207
ivory II.1–2, II.7, II.30, II.40–1, II.68–71,
IV.30, IV.41, IV.43, V.2, V.13, V.17, V.38,
V.40–1, V.48, V.85, V.97–8, V.100–1,
V.106, V.110, V.120–1, V.123, V.125–6,
V.157, V.167, V.175–6, V.177–8, V.193,
V.194–5, V.206–7, V.209, V.301, VI.10,
VI.12

jasper II.37, II.46, IV.32, V.161, V.164, V.191
javelin V.17
jug (ἐπίχυσις) V.243

karchesion, see goblet
knife (μάχαιρα) V.205–7, VI.13
cavalry (μάχαιρα ἱππική) VI.12
surgical (μάχαιρα ἰατρική) V.209
kore IV.20, V.90
krater II.15, V.236–9
stand for V.235
kyathos V.282
kylix, see wine-cup
Kyzikene staters V.59

lamp III.4–5
leather II.39, IV.35, V.139, V.189, V.193
leg V.91–3
leopard V.98
linen II.63, V.49
lintel (ὑπερτόναιον) V.31, VI.31
lion's head IV.22, V.103
lustral basin (ἀπορραντήριον) V.204, VI.29
lyre II.71, IV.42–4, V.193–7, V.416

mask IV.24
meniskos V.172
monster-like figure (κάμπη) IV.21, V.102
muslin cloth (σινδόνη) V.52
muzzle II.72

nails II.60, II.76–7, IV.47, V.91, V.198–203,
　　V.271, VI.8
neckband (ὄχθοιβος) II.37, IV.32, V.91, V.164,
　　VI.20
necklace:
　　(περιτραχήλιον) V.141, VI.20
　　(στρεπτόν) V.135
　　(ὑποδερίς) II.36–7, IV.32, V.91–2, V.134,
　　　V.164
　　(ὅρμος) IV.39–40, V.91–2 V.136–7, V.140;
　　　see also chain (ὁρμίσκος), collar
Nike II.12, V.76, V.91–2, V.94–6, V.239, V.270

offering-tray V.228–9
olive, olive-branch (θαλλός) IV.34, V.416,
　　V.424, V.426–7
onyx II.37, IV.32, V.142–7, V.164
owl VI.18, VI.20

Palladion V.97, VI.19
panoply V.18
Pegasos V.241
pentorobos II.64
Persian daggers (ἀκινάκης) IV.1–2, V.1–2,
Persian shekels (σίγλοι Μηδικοί) V.60
petals II.9–10, V.95, V.268–9
phiale II.16, II.82–99, III.6–32, IV.48–52, V.88,
　　V.184, V.211–13, V.219–20, V.223–4,
　　V.227, V.253–4, V.258, V.296, V.300–52,
　　VI.20, VI.33–53
Phokaian coins II.20, V.61, V.62, V.63, V.64
platter V.151, V.225, V.353–7
plectrum II.71
plume VI.10
protome V.106, V.140, V.241

ram's head IV.40, V.106, V.137, V.140
reins II.31
resin VI.19
*rhumbos* V.107
rhyton V.358
ribbon V.91–2
ring II.6, II.36–7, II.44, II.49–53, II.56, II.58,
　　IV.32, V.146–50, V.152–7, V.159–60,
　　V.163, V.166, V.264, VI.23
robe (ξυστίς) V.51
rosette IV.39–40, V.136–7

sabre (ξιφομάχαιρα) IV.45, V.208, VI.14,
　　VI.16
sard II.49, II.56–7, V.158–9
seals II.6, II.36–7, II.44–6, II.49, II.53, II.56,
　　II.58, II.61, IV.33, V.157, V.159–63,

V.165–6, V.264
serpent II.42, V.108
　　see also snake
sheath (for daggers, knives) V.2, V.206–7, V.209
shelf II.84, V.67, V.91–2, V.325–6, V.328
shield (ἀσπίς) IV.7–11, V.20, V.22, V.24–31,
　　V.89, V.97, VI.6
shield, miniature (ἀσπιδίσκη) IV.21, V.23,
　　VI.1–5, VI.7
shield, light (πέλτη) IV.12, V.18, V.19
silver II.11–14, II.18–20, II.25–6, II.32, II.39,
　　II.42, II.45, II.48, II.51, II.56–8, II.78–81,
　　II.84, II.100, III.2–5, III.7–40, IV.24,
　　IV.47–53, IV.55–6, V.23, V.29–30, V.32,
　　V.37, V.44, V.58, V.60, V.67–9, V.74,
　　V.108, V.118, V.127, V.135, V.155, V.159,
　　V.161–3, V.171f, V.179, V.183–9, V.204,
　　V.212–5, V.218, V.221, V.223–7, V.230–2,
　　V.236, V.240–1, V.251–5, V.257–60,
　　V.262–4, V.270, V.273–4, V.276,
　　V.278–83, V.287–8, V.294, V.297–300,
　　V.305–8, V.311–12, V.314, V.316–18,
　　V.321–2, V.328, V.331–2, V.338, V.340,
　　V.343, V.353–7, V.359, VI.1–3, VI.8, VI.9,
　　VI.17–19, VI.24, VI.30–2, VI.34–53
silver overlay II.39, II.50, II.64, II.67, II.76–7,
　　IV.28, V.18, V.31, V.70, V.160, V.171e,
　　V.179, V.189, V.198–201, V.222, V.233,
　　V.267
silver piece (phiale? ἀργυρίς) III.25–8, III.30–2,
sling II.72
slivers (περιτμήματα) V.357
snake IV.22, V.103, VI.21
　　see also serpent
snood II.62
spear VI.1, VI.8
spear-points V.4
stand (ὑπόστατον) V.234–5
staters V.54, V.56, V.59, V.64, V.66
statue: (ἄγαλμα) V.89, V.94–5, VI.22
　　of man (ἀνδριάς) VI.29
　　of young man (νεανίσκος) V.98
stone II.5–6, II.29, II.45, II.65, IV.33, IV.35,
　　IV.37, IV.39–40, V.84, V.128, V.132–3,
　　V.136–7, V.139–40, V.156, V.163,
　　V.165–6, V.182, V.373
stool (δίφρος) IV.27, V.116, VI.118
supports (διερείσματα) V.39, V.222, V.273–5
sweet oil (μυρηρός) V.282
swords (ξίφη) IV.46, V.210, VI.15

table (τράπεζα) IV.30, V.121, V.276
test-pieces V.87–8
tetradrachm IV.15
throne II.40, IV.31, V.88, V.106, V.122–6
tin II.36, II.83, V.302
tokens V.85
torso V.91–2
trophy (τρόπαιον) V.98

washbasin (χερνιβεῖον) II.28, II.100, V.221,
V.230–3
weaving-blade (σπάθη) V.175
weighing-beam II.67
weights V.86, V.330
wheat stalks IV.23, V.109
wine-cup (κύλιξ) III.3, V.283–4, V.322, VI.31
wine-jug II.13–4, II.78–81, V.88, V.287–99,
VI.32

wood II.11–12, IV.44, V.25, V.33, V.106,
V.111, V.180–2, V.194, V.196–7, V.267,
V.270, V.421, VI.18, VI.55
*see also* gilt wood
wreath:
(στέφανος) III.41, IV.57–62, V.91–2, V.94–6,
V.359–477, VI.20, VI.55–66
(στεφάνη) V.91–2

# General Index

Achaia **V.8–9**, 239
Alexander the Great 38, 105–6, 229, 233–5
Alexander, son of Polyperchon 109, 226, 229, 233–4
allies of the Athenians 8, 32, 105, 238, 242
Androtion 32–3, 104
annual offerings 25, 77, 79, v.461, v.467
*apobatēs* 8
Archaios Neos 5, 32, 40, 201–3, 206, **VI.27**, 220–1, 227
    *see also* Erechtheion; temples, of Athena Polias
Areopagus **V.168**, 239
armour 1, 26–7, 108, 221
    *see also* war booty
*arrhēphoroi* 8
artists' signatures **V.215–18**, **V.221**, **V.225**, **V.251**, **V.253**, **V.258**, **V.261**, **V.296**, **V.320**, **vi.30**

*boulē* 2, 10, 16–17, 20, 79, **V.44**, **V.168**, **V.207**, **V.429**, **V.433**, **V.436**, **V.448**, **V.450**, **V.452**, **V.456**, **V.458–9**, **VI.61–3**, 221, 238–9

Chalkotheke 1–2, 8, 10, 18, 32, 37, 43, 108–10, 206, 243
Chandler stele 202
Chios **IV.25**, 111, **V.113**, 239–41
cloth 107, 230
    *see also* peplos
cult statues:
    Athena Parthenos, chryselephantine 2, 20–1, 31–3, 37–8, 62, 81, 112, 221
    wooden image of Athena 12, 202–4, 218–21

Dareios 217
dedications:
    by the Athenians **V.241**, **V.380–7**, **V.413–4**, **V.420**, **V.429–31**, **V.437–9**, **V.444**, **V.446–8**, **V.451**, **V.453**, **V.466–7**, 239
    by the demos 79, **V.380–7**, **V.413–4**, **V.420**, **V.429–31**, **V.436–9**, **V.444**, **V.446–7**, **V.449–51**, **V.453**, **V.457**, **V.463–7**, **V.472**, 238–9
    to specific gods:
        Ammon **V.321**; *see also* Zeus
        Aphrodite 113, **V.252**
        Apollo 2, **II.3**, **V.42**, **V.98**, 232
        Artemis Brauronia **II.44–6**, **II.64**, **II.82**, 113, **V.129**, **V.131**, **V.138**, **V.149**, **V.151**, **V.153–4**, **V.180f**, **V.211–3**, **V.223**,
        **V.259**, **V.261**, **V.322**, **V.351**, **V.468–9**, 233, 244
        Asklepios 24, **V.214–5**, **V.217–20**, **V.223**
        Athena 36, 113–14, **V.21**, **V.44**, **V.88**, **V.105**, **V.141**, **V.221**, **V.223**, **V.225**, **V.241**, **V.248**, **V.255**, **V.260**, **V.324**, **V.327**, **V.358**, **V.379**, **V.428**, **VI.32**, 232, 235, 238–41, 243
        Athena Nike **IV.60**, **IV.62**, 113, **V.222**, **V.256**, **V.323**, **V.410**, **V.470–3**, 229
        Athena Polias **v.141**, **V.221**, **V.225**, **V.241**, **V.255**, **V.260**, **V.358**, **VI.46–7**
        Demeter and Kore **II.65**, **II.79**, **V.257**, 113, **V.257**; *see also* under Two Goddesses; *and see* Eleusis
        Dionysus **V.98**, **V.110**
        Dioskouroi 113, **V.254**, **V.338**
        Goddess **II.16**, **V.325**, **V.441**, **V.474–7**, **VI.20**
        Herakles in Elaious **IV.53**
        Other Gods **V.329–30**
        Two Goddesses **II.23**, **II.28**, **II.65**, **V.57**, **V.88**, **V.104**, **V.226**, **V.328**
        Zeus 2, **ii.4**, **v.43**, **v.227**, **v.280**; *see also* Ammon
Delos 63, 78
Delphi 12, 19, 78, 203, 229, 232, 235
    *see also* Temple of Apollo
Demetrios Poliorketes 37–8
Dionysia **V.413–15**
*diphrophoroi* 27, 111
*dokimasia* 14–15, 35–6, 106–7
doors:
    of Erechtheion 1–2, 201, **VI.4**, **VI.17**, **VI.43**, **VI.44**, 218
    of Hekatompedon 5, 8, **II.60**, 243
    of the Opisthodomos **II.59**, 81
    of the Propylaia 243

Eleusis 41, 106, 243–4
Ephesos 12, **V.379**, 229, 232
Erechtheion 1–2, 10, 13, 32, 35, 40, 110, 114, 201–22, 223–4, 227–9, 231–2, 236, 244
*euthynai* 11, 15, 20, 35–6, 233

festivals:
    Athenian 35, 39
    calendar of 14, 16
    Chalkeia 14–15
    Dionysia **V.413–15**
    Lysandreia 229

Panathenaia 8, 10, 15, 19–20, 27–8, 61,
104–5, 112, 114, **V.24**, **V.413**, **V.417–20**,
**V.477**, 237, 240–2, 244
Synoikia 9
freedmen 35, 63, 114, **V.253**, **V.258**, **V.296**
furniture 1, 10, 26–7, 82, 110, 205, 217, 220,
239–41

goldsmiths, *see* smiths
griffin 26, 28

Hekatompedon 2, 4–5, 8, 10, 24–6, 30, 40,
42–4, 64, 78, 81, 105–200, 217, 220–1,
233, 243
decrees 17–18
*hellēnotamiai* 20, 22
*hieropoioi* **V.468–9**
hipparchs **V.414**, **V.466**
Homer 8–9, 107, 219

Illyrian objects 23, **IV.5**, 109, **V.10**, 239, 241
incense-burners 26, 63, 106, 114, 218, 221
inscribed dedications **IV.8G**, **V.34**, **V.44**, **V.88**,
**V.168**, **V.199**, **V.211–12**, **V.214–15**,
**V.218–19**, **V.221**, **V.223–4**, **V.227**,
**V.251**, **V.309–10**, **V.320**, **V.330**, **V.371**,
**V.387–8**, **V.415**, **V.422**, **V.425**, **V.469**,
**VI.13**, **VI.30**, **VI.32**, **VI.48**, **VI.54**
Iphikrates 220–1, 227, 233, 238

Kallias decrees 20–1, 40, 42
*kanēphoroi*, kanephoric ornament 35–6
Konon 105, 220, 227, 230–2, 238

Lachares 37–9
Lakedaimon, *see* Sparta
Lesbos 23, 78, 82, **IV.5**, **IV.10**, **IV.56**, 109, 113,
**V.10**, **V.20**
letter-labels 24, 34, 36, 108, **V.67**, **V.217–20**,
**V.251**, **V.253**, **V.258**, **V.271–2**, **V.320**,
**V.327**, **V.342**, **V.379–88**, **V.415**, **V.466**,
238
lustral basins, lustrations 13, 27, 218–19
Lykourgos 33–7, 39
Lysander 29, 229, 231–2

Mardonios 107, 204, 217
Masistios 107, 204
melting of metal dedications 28–9, 31–8, 65,
107, 114, 218
metal-smiths, *see* smiths
Methymna 78, **IV.41**, 113 , **V.191**
metics 29, 35, 114, 224–5, 237
Metroon 17, 22, **II.28**
Miletos 23, 26, 63, **IV.26**, 111, **V.114–15**,
**V.384**, 238–41
musical instruments 1, 9, 26–7, 62, 112–3, 220,
240
Myrrina **V.382**, 238

*naukraroi* 11–12, 14
Nikai, golden 10, 29, 32–6, 38, 108, 236, 272–4

Old Temple of Athena Polias, *see* Archaios Neos
olive oil 19
Olympia 64, 78, 108, 235–6
*see also* temples of Zeus
Olympias, mother of Alexander 235–236
Opisthodomos 1–2, 4–5, 10, 30–2, 40–63, 81,
109, 206, 224

Panathenaic festival, *see* festivals
Parthenon:
as name of whole temple 1–5, 9–10, 20, 25,
28, 40, 205, 221, 223–4, 225–6, 229, 231,
233, 235, 237–43
as specific room inside the temple 10, 26, 28,
30, 32, 81–103, **V.89**
Peisistratos, Peisistratids 14, 16
Peloponnesian war 22, 28–30, 104, 106, 114,
229–30
peplos 8, 219
Perikles 8, 20, 28, 81, 112, 237, 242
Persian:
objects 23, 109–10, 113, **V.190**, **V.315**,
204–5, 217, 230, 239, 241
sack of the Akropolis 18, 202ʲ
satraps 230, 232
war 18–19, 109, 203, 223, 242
war booty 19, 27, 107, 109–10, 204–6
Pharnabazos **V.51**, 229–30
Proneos 2, 10, 24–5, 27, 30, 64–80, 81
Propylaia 243–4
.public seal **II.28**, **II.39**, 62, **V.34**, **V.66**, **V.178**,
**V.189**, 243

reflecting pond 64, 112
robe 8, 230
*see also* cloth; peplos
Roxane, wife of Alexander 105, 229, 234–5

Samos **V.449–51**, 229, 232, 238
satrap, *see* Persian
sculpture *see* statues
shelves 1, 24, 30, 36, 41, 112
smiths 35–6, **V.81**
*see also* artists' signatures
Solon 13, 22
Sounion **V.74**
Sparta 29, 110, 204–5, 229–31, 242
statues, sculpture 18, 27, 32, 63–4, 82, 218–20,
221, 229, 231–3
*see also* cult statues
statue-bases 10, 112, 202, 221
Strasburg papyrus 81–2
*synoikismos* 9
taxes 11–12, 14, 37, **V.320**
temples:

of Apollo at Delphi 12, 203
of Artemis Brauronia II.31, 233, 244
of Artemis at Ephesos 12
of Asklepios 218, 228, 236, 242, 244
of Athena Polias 10, 12, 14–15, 17, 29, 41,
  203, 206; *see also* Archaios Neos;
  Erechtheion
of Athena Nike 13, V.76, 202
of the Dioskouroi V.338
of Hera at Samos 12
of Zeus at Olympia 64
*see also* Archaios Neos; Erechtheion;
  Hekatompedon; Parthenon
Themistokles 18, 205
Theseus 9
Thessaly V.122, V.155, 239–40
Timotheos 220–1, 227, 231–3, 238
tin 62
tragedies at the Dionysia V.413–15

treasurer of the military fund V.67
treasurers:
  of Athena:
    dedications by 113–14, V.258, V.320,
      V.388, V.415, V.473, VI.18, VI.40,
      VI.56–7, 221
    inventories of 10–11, 16, 22, 24–5, 28,
      30–2, 42, 108, 218, 221, 223, 238, 240
    responsibilities of, 9–11, 13–15, 18–20, 35,
      40–2, 105
  of the Other Gods 20–1, 24, 30, 40–2

war booty 28, 78, 107–9, 205–6, 239
women 8, 27, 29, 81, 106, 220, 224–8, 233–4,
  236–8
wreaths 1, 8, 26, 29, 32–3, 35, 61, 65, 104, 112,
  204, 220–1, 230–2, 236–9, 241

Xerxes 205

## DATE DUE

| | |
|---|---|
| FEB 03 1997 | |
| JAN 1 5 1998 | |
| OCT 0 9 2000 | |
| | |
| | |
| | |
| | |
| | |
| | |
| | |
| | |
| | |
| | |
| | |
| | |
| | |
| | |